The Anonymous Press
Study Edition
of
ALCOHOLICS ANONYMOUS

Second Edition

STATEMENT OF PURPOSE

The Anonymous Press is made up of a bunch of A.A. members staying sober by carrying the message of A.A. Our primary purpose is to carry the message of A.A. by making our basic text affordable to all. Where we can, we also try to make the text easier to study and understand.

We realize that A.A., The Fellowship that saved our lives, is held together by The Traditions so The Traditions are what guide us. All of our books are sold at cost and we are certainly not organized.

Our efforts have resulted in the distribution of our fellowship's basic text to hundreds of thousands of fellow alcoholics who otherwise may not have had a book of their own. Detoxes, rehabs, prisons and shelters can now afford to give away our text - offering countless alcoholics a chance to learn the unadulterated message of our program.

If you are a member of A.A. and would like to lend a hand to help in our work, volunteers and contributions are always welcome.

The Anonymous Press

Permission is granted to reproduce all or part of this book for use in the U.S.A. If it will help get the messsage to the still suffering alcoholic, please use whatever you want.

Our books are not available for sale outside The USA.

The Anonymous Press
PO Box 1212
Malo WA 99150-1212

(800) 800-4398
http://anonpress.org

Fax (509) 779-4339   e-mail: ap@anonpress.org

First Edition: Second Edition:
Five Printings 1994-1998   Fifth Printing 2006

The gray areas do not appear in the original text

ISBN 13 978-1-892959-03-4
ISBN 10 1-892959-03-8

Printed in The United States of America

FOREWORD

*W*E, OF Alcoholics Anonymous, are more than one hundred men and women who have recovered from a seemingly hopeless state of mind and body. To show other alcoholics *precisely how we have recovered* is the main purpose of this book. For them, we hope these pages will prove so convincing that no further authentication will be necessary. We think this account of our experiences will help everyone to better understand the alcoholic. Many do not comprehend that the alcoholic is a very sick person. And besides, we are sure that our way of living has its advantages for all.

It is important that we remain anonymous because we are too few, at present to handle the overwhelming number of personal appeals which may result from this publication. Being mostly business or professional folk, we could not well carry on our occupations in such an event. We would like it understood that our alcoholic work is an avocation.

When writing or speaking publicly about alcoholism, we urge each of our Fellowship to omit his personal name, designating himself instead as "a member of Alcoholics Anonymous."

Very earnestly we ask the press also, to observe this request, for otherwise we shall be greatly handicapped.

We are not an organization in the conventional

FOREWORD
to
THE ANONYMOUS PRESS STUDY EDITION
of
ALCOHOLICS ANONYMOUS

Second Edition

By making the Big Book easier to study, understand, and afford, we hope to be of some help to our fellow alcoholics, but we don't want to change the text in any way. So here is an explanation of what we have done and the precautions we have taken.

The more obscure references in the text are footnoted with explanations. These are shaded to differentiate them from the original text and are limited strictly to facts — no opinions. Also noted are the places where the modern text has been changed from the first printing of the first edition of *Alcoholics Anonymous*.

Next to the text is a numbering system to help make discussions on particular paragraphs or sections easier.

In the back are a word index and a subject index to the 1st 164 pages. Both are indexed by paragraph. Also included is a dictionary of the more uncommon words in the text. The definitions are reproduced from the unabridged Webster's dictionary available on store shelves at the time the text was written.

Shaded with a grey border to differentiate it from the modern text is the Original Manuscript of the Big Book. It is presented here in a retyped version to make it easier to read. It has been thoroughly proofread to be just like the original. Even the apparent mistakes are as they were.

The same paragraph numbers from the modern text are provided next to their corresponding paragraphs in the manuscript to make comparison easier.

If we made any mistakes, missed something or included anything we shouldn't have, we hope you will let us know.

The Anonymous Press

sense of the word. There are no fees or dues whatsoever. The only requirement for membership is an honest desire to stop drinking. We are not allied with any particular faith, sect or denomination, nor do we oppose anyone. We simply wish to be helpful to those who are afflicted.

We shall be interested to hear from those who are getting results from this book, particularly from those who have commenced work with other alcoholics. We should like to be helpful to such cases.

Inquiry by scientific, medical, and religious societies will be welcomed.

ALCOHOLICS ANONYMOUS.

THE DOCTOR'S OPINION

*W*E OF Alcoholics Anonymous believe that the reader will be interested in the medical estimate of the plan of recovery described in this book. Convincing testimony must surely come from medical men who have had experience with the sufferings of our members and have witnessed our return to health. A well-known doctor, chief physician at a nationally prominent hospital specializing in alcoholic and drug addiction, gave Alcoholics Anonymous this letter:

To Whom It May Concern:

I have specialized in the treatment of alcoholism for many years.

In late 1934 I attended a patient who, though he had been a competent businessman[1] of good earning capacity, was an alcoholic of a type I had come to regard as hopeless.

In the course of his third treatment he acquired certain ideas concerning a possible means of recovery. As part of his rehabilitation he commenced to present his conceptions to other alcoholics, impressing upon them that they must do likewise with still others. This has become the basis of a rapidly growing fellowship of these men and their families. This man and over one hundred others appear to have recovered.

I personally know scores of cases who were of the type with whom other methods had failed completely.

These facts appear to be of extreme medical importance; because of the extraordinary possibilities of rapid

[1] Bill Wilson

growth inherent in this group they may mark a new epoch in the annals of alcoholism. These men may well have a remedy for thousands of such situations.

You may rely absolutely on anything they say about themselves.

Very truly yours,
William D. Silkworth, M.D.

The physician who, at our request, gave us this letter, has been kind enough to enlarge upon his views in another statement which follows. In this statement he confirms what we who have suffered alcoholic torture must believe—that the body of the alcoholic is quite as abnormal as his mind. It did not satisfy us to be told that we could not control our drinking just because we were maladjusted to life, that we were in full flight from reality, or were outright mental defectives. These things were true to some extent, in fact, to a considerable extent with some of us. But we are sure that our bodies were sickened as well. In our belief, any picture of the alcoholic which leaves out this physical factor is incomplete.

The doctor's theory that we have an allergy to alcohol interests us. As laymen, our opinion as to its soundness may, of course, mean little. But as ex-problem drinkers, we can say that his explanation makes good sense. It explains many things for which we cannot otherwise account.

Though we work out our solution on the spiritual as well as an altruistic plane, we favor hospitalization for the alcoholic who is very jittery or befogged. More often than not, it is imperative that a man's brain be cleared before he is approached, as he has then a bet-

ter chance of understanding and accepting what we have to offer.

The doctor writes:

> The subject presented in this book seems to me to be of paramount importance to those afflicted with alcoholic addiction.
>
> I say this after many years' experience as Medical Director of one of the oldest hospitals in the country treating alcoholic and drug addiction.
>
> There was, therefore, a sense of real satisfaction when I was asked to contribute a few words on a subject which is covered in such masterly detail in these pages.
>
> We doctors have realized for a long time that some form of moral psychology was of urgent importance to alcoholics, but its application presented difficulties beyond our conception. What with our ultra-modern standards, our scientific approach to everything, we are perhaps not well equipped to apply the powers of good that lie outside our synthetic knowledge.
>
> Many years ago one of the leading contributors to this book came under our care in this hospital and while here he acquired some ideas which he put into practical application at once.
>
> Later, he requested the privilege of being allowed to tell his story to other patients here and with some misgiving, we consented. The cases we have followed through have been most interesting; in fact, many of them are amazing. The unselfishness of these men as we have come to know them, the entire absence of profit motive, and their community spirit, is indeed inspiring to one who has labored long and wearily in this alcoholic field. They believe in themselves, and still more in the Power which pulls chronic alcoholics back from the gates of death.
>
> Of course an alcoholic ought to be freed from his physical

craving for liquor, and this often requires a definite hospital procedure, before psychological measures can be of maximum benefit.

We believe, and so suggested a few years ago, that the action of alcohol on these chronic alcoholics is a manifestation of an allergy; that the phenomenon of craving is limited to this class and never occurs in the average temperate drinker. These allergic types can never safely use alcohol in any form at all; and once having formed the habit and found they cannot break it, once having lost their self-confidence, their reliance upon things human, their problems pile up on them and become astonishingly difficult to solve.

Frothy emotional appeal seldom suffices. The message which can interest and hold these alcoholic people must have depth and weight. In nearly all cases, their ideals must be grounded in a power greater than themselves, if they are to re-create their lives.

If any feel that as psychiatrists directing a hospital for alcoholics we appear somewhat sentimental, let them stand with us while on the firing line, see the tragedies, the despairing wives, the little children; let the solving of these problems become a part of their daily work, and even of their sleeping moments, and the most cynical will not wonder that we have accepted and encouraged this movement. We feel, after many years of experience, that we have found nothing which has contributed more to the rehabilitation of these men than the altruistic movement now growing up among them.

Men and women drink essentially because they like the effect produced by alcohol. The sensation is so elusive that, while they admit it is injurious, they cannot after a time differentiate the true from the false. To them, their alcoholic life seems the only normal one. They are restless, irritable and discontented, unless they can again experience

the sense of ease and comfort which comes at once by taking a few drinks—drinks which they see others taking with impunity. After they have succumbed to the desire again, as so many do, and the phenomenon of craving develops, they pass through the well-known stages of a spree, emerging remorseful, with a firm resolution not to drink again. This is repeated over and over, and unless this person can experience an entire psychic change there is very little hope of his recovery.

On the other hand—and strange as this may seem to those who do not understand—once a psychic change has occurred, the very same person who seemed doomed, who had so many problems he despaired of ever solving them, suddenly finds himself easily able to control his desire for alcohol, the only effort necessary being that required to follow a few simple rules.

Men have cried out to me in sincere and despairing appeal: "Doctor, I cannot go on like this! I have everything to live for! I must stop, but I cannot! You must help me!"

Faced with this problem, if a doctor is honest with himself, he must sometimes feel his own inadequacy. Although he gives all that is in him, it often is not enough. One feels that something more than human power is needed to produce the essential psychic change. Though the aggregate of recoveries resulting from psychiatric effort is considerable, we physicians must admit we have made little impression upon the problem as a whole. Many types do not respond to the ordinary psychological approach.

I do not hold with those who believe that alcoholism is entirely a problem of mental control. I have had many men who had, for example, worked a period of months on some problem or business deal which was to be settled on a certain date, favorably to them. They took a drink a day or so prior to the date, and then the phenomenon of craving at once became paramount to all other interests so that the

important appointment was not met. These men were not drinking to escape; they were drinking to overcome a craving beyond their mental control.

There are many situations which arise out of the phenomenon of craving which cause men to make the supreme sacrifice rather than continue to fight.

The classification of alcoholics seems most difficult, and in much detail is outside the scope of this book. There are, of course, the psychopaths who are emotionally unstable. We are all familiar with this type. They are always "going on the wagon for keeps." They are over-remorseful and make many resolutions, but never a decision.

There is the type of man who is unwilling to admit that he cannot take a drink. He plans various ways of drinking. He changes his brand or his environment. There is the type who always believes that after being entirely free from alcohol for a period of time he can take a drink without danger. There is the manic-depressive type, who is, perhaps, the least understood by his friends, and about whom a whole chapter could be written.

Then there are types entirely normal in every respect except in the effect alcohol has upon them. They are often able, intelligent, friendly people.

All these, and many others, have one symptom in common: they cannot start drinking without developing the phenomenon of craving. This phenomenon, as we have suggested, may be the manifestation of an allergy which differentiates these people, and sets them apart as a distinct entity. It has never been, by any treatment with which we are familiar, permanently eradicated. The only relief we have to suggest is entire abstinence.

This immediately precipitates us into a seething caldron of debate. Much has been written pro and con, but among physicians, the general opinion seems to be that most chronic alcoholics are doomed.

What is the solution? Perhaps I can best answer this by relating one of my experiences.

About one year prior to this experience a man was brought in to be treated for chronic alcoholism. He had but partially recovered from a gastric hemorrhage and seemed to be a case of pathological mental deterioration. He had lost everything worthwhile in life and was only living, one might say, to drink. He frankly admitted and believed that for him there was no hope. Following the elimination of alcohol, there was found to be no permanent brain injury. He accepted the plan outlined in this book. One year later he called to see me, and I experienced a very strange sensation. I knew the man by name, and partly recognized his features, but there all resemblance ended. From a trembling, despairing, nervous wreck, had emerged a man brimming over with self-reliance and contentment. I talked with him for some time, but was not able to bring myself to feel that I had known him before. To me he was a stranger, and so he left me. A long time has passed with no return to alcohol.

When I need a mental uplift, I often think of another case brought in by a physician prominent in New York. The patient had made his own diagnosis, and deciding his situation hopeless, had hidden in a deserted barn determined to die. He was rescued by a searching party, and, in desperate condition, brought to me. Following his physical rehabilitation, he had a talk with me in which he frankly stated he thought the treatment a waste of effort, unless I could assure him, which no one ever had, that in the future he would have the "will power" to resist the impulse to drink.

His alcoholic problem was so complex, and his depression so great, that we felt his only hope would be through what we then called "moral psychology," and we doubted if even that would have any effect.

However, he did become "sold" on the ideas contained in this book. He has not had a drink for a great many years. I see him now and then and he is as fine a specimen of manhood as one could wish to meet.

I earnestly advise every alcoholic to read this book through, and though perhaps he came to scoff, he may remain to pray.

William D. Silkworth, M.D.

Chapter 1

BILL'S STORY

1:1   *W*AR FEVER ran high in the New England town to which we new, young officers from Plattsburg were assigned, and we were flattered when the first citizens took us to their homes, making us feel heroic. Here was love, applause, war; moments sublime with intervals hilarious. I was part of life at last, and in the midst of the excitement I discovered liquor. I forgot the strong warnings and the prejudices of my people concerning drink. In time we sailed for "Over There." I was very lonely and again turned to alcohol.

1:2   We landed in England. I visited Winchester Cathedral. Much moved, I wandered outside. My attention was caught by a doggerel on an old tombstone:

"Here lies a Hampshire Grenadier
Who caught his death
Drinking cold small beer.
A good soldier is ne'er forgot
Whether he dieth by musket
Or by pot."

1:3   Ominous warning—which I failed to heed.

1:4   Twenty-two, and a veteran of foreign wars, I went home at last. I fancied myself a leader, for had not the men of my battery given me a special token of appreciation? My talent for leadership, I imagined, would place me at the head of vast enterprises which I would manage with the utmost assurance.

2:1   I took a night law course[1], and obtained employment
as investigator for a surety company. The drive for success was on. I'd prove to the world I was important.
My work took me about Wall Street and little by little I
became interested in the market. Many people lost
money—but some became very rich. Why not I? I studied economics and business as well as law. Potential alcoholic that I was, I nearly failed my law course. At one
of the finals I was too drunk to think or write. Though
my drinking was not yet continuous, it disturbed my wife.
We had long talks when I would still her forebodings by
telling her that men of genius conceived their best projects
when drunk; that the most majestic constructions of philosophic thought were so derived.

2:2   By the time I had completed the course, I knew the
law was not for me. The inviting maelstrom of Wall Street
had me in its grip. Business and financial leaders were
my heroes. Out of this alloy of drink and speculation, I
commenced to forge the weapon that one day would turn
in its flight like a boomerang and all but cut me to ribbons. Living modestly, my wife and I saved $1,000. It
went into certain securities, then cheap and rather un-
popular. I rightly imagined that they would some day have
a great rise. I failed to persuade my broker friends to
send me out looking over factories and managements, but
my wife and I decided to go anyway. I had developed a
theory that most people lost money in stocks through ignorance of markets. I discovered many more reasons
later on.

2:3   We gave up our positions and off we roared on a
motorcycle, the sidecar stuffed with tent, blankets, a[2]
change of clothes, and three huge volumes of a finan-

---

[1] At Brooklyn Law School.

[2] The word "a" did not appear in the first edition.

3:0   cial reference service. Our friends thought a lunacy commission should be appointed. Perhaps they were right. I had had some success at speculation, so we had a little money, but we once worked on a farm for a month to avoid drawing on our small capital. That was the last honest manual labor on my part for many a day. We covered the whole eastern United States in a year. At the end of it, my reports to Wall Street procured me a position there and the use of a large expense account. The exercise of an option brought in more money, leaving us with a profit of several thousand dollars for that year.

3:1   For the next few years fortune threw money and applause my way. I had arrived. My judgment and ideas were followed by many to the tune of paper millions. The great boom of the late twenties was seething and swelling. Drink was taking an important and exhilarating part in my life. There was loud talk in the jazz places uptown. Everyone spent in thousands and chattered in millions. Scoffers could scoff and be damned. I made a host of fair-weather friends.

3:2   My drinking assumed more serious proportions, continuing all day and almost every night. The remonstrances of my friends terminated in a row and I became a lone wolf. There were many unhappy scenes in our sumptuous apartment. There had been no real infidelity, for loyalty to my wife, helped at times by extreme drunkenness, kept me out of those scrapes.

3:3   In 1929 I contracted golf fever. We went at once to the country, my wife to applaud while I started out to overtake Walter Hagen[1]. Liquor caught up with me much faster than I came up behind Walter. I began to be jittery in the morning. Golf permitted drinking

---

[1] A golf champion from 1914 to 1929.

4:0   every day and every night. It was fun to carom around the exclusive course which had inspired such awe in me as a lad. I acquired the impeccable coat of tan one sees upon the well-to-do. The local banker watched me whirl fat checks in and out of his till with amused skepticism.

4:1   Abruptly in October 1929 hell broke loose on the New York stock exchange. After one of those days of inferno, I wobbled from a hotel bar to a brokerage office. It was eight o'clock—five hours after the market closed. The ticker still clattered. I was staring at an inch of the tape which bore the inscription XYZ-32[1]. It had been 52 that morning. I was finished and so were many friends. The papers reported men jumping to death from the towers of High Finance. That disgusted me. I would not jump. I went back to the bar. My friends had dropped several million since ten o'clock—so what? Tomorrow was another day. As I drank, the old fierce determination to win came back.

4:2   Next morning I telephoned a friend in Montreal. He had plenty of money left and thought I had better go to Canada. By the following spring we were living in our accustomed style. I felt like Napoleon[2] returning from Elba[3]. No St. Helena[4] for me! But drinking caught up with me again and my generous friend had to let me go. This time we stayed broke.

4:3   We went to live with my wife's parents. I found a job; then lost it as the result of a brawl with a taxi driver. Mercifully, no one could guess that I was to have no real employment for five years, or hardly draw a sober breath. My wife began to work in a department store, coming home exhausted to find me drunk.

---

[1] Actual symbol was PKF for Penick and Ford, now known as Penford Products.

[2] Napoleon Bonaparte, Emperor of France between 1804 and 1814.

[3] Italian island which Napoleon was exiled to and escaped from in 1815.

[4] British island off the West Coast of Africa. Napoleon was imprisoned there after a brief reign as emperor in 1815. He died there from cancer in 1821.

5:0   I became an unwelcome hanger-on at brokerage places.

5:1   Liquor ceased to be a luxury; it became a necessity. "Bathtub" gin[1], two bottles a day, and often three, got to be routine. Sometimes a small deal would net a few hundred dollars, and I would pay my bills at the bars and delicatessens. This went on endlessly, and I began to waken very early in the morning shaking violently. A tumbler full of gin followed by half a dozen bottles of beer would be required if I were to eat any breakfast. Nevertheless, I still thought I could control the situation, and there were periods of sobriety which renewed my wife's hope.

5:2   Gradually things got worse. The house was taken over by the mortgage holder, my mother-in-law died, my wife and father-in-law became ill.

5:3   Then I got a promising business opportunity. Stocks were at the low point of 1932, and I had somehow formed a group to buy. I was to share generously in the profits. Then I went on a prodigious bender, and that chance vanished.

5:4   I woke up. This had to be stopped. I saw I could not take so much as one drink. I was through forever. Before then, I had written lots of sweet promises, but my wife happily observed that this time I meant business. And so I did.

5:5   Shortly afterward I came home drunk. There had been no fight. Where had been my high resolve? I simply didn't know. It hadn't even come to mind. Someone had pushed a drink my way, and I had taken it. Was I crazy? I began to wonder, for such an appalling lack of perspective seemed near being just that.

5:6   Renewing my resolve, I tried again. Some time

---

[1] A slang term for a homemade liquor popular during Prohibition. Commonly made by flavoring a bath tub full of industrial alcohol by temporarily mixing in juniper leaves.

6:0   passed, and confidence began to be replaced by cock-sureness. I could laugh at the gin mills. Now I had what it takes! One day I walked into a cafe to telephone. In no time I was beating on the bar asking myself how it happened. As the whisky[1] rose to my head I told myself I would manage better next time, but I might as well get good and drunk then. And I did.

6:1   The remorse, horror and hopelessness of the next morning are unforgettable. The courage to do battle was not there. My brain raced uncontrollably and there was a terrible sense of impending calamity. I hardly dared cross the street, lest I collapse and be run down by an early morning truck, for it was scarcely daylight. An all night place supplied me with a dozen glasses of ale. My writhing nerves were stilled at last. A morning paper told me the market had gone to hell again. Well, so had I. The market would recover, but I wouldn't. That was a hard thought. Should I kill myself? No—not now. Then a mental fog settled down. Gin would fix that. So two bottles, and—oblivion.

6:2   The mind and body are marvelous mechanisms, for mine endured this agony two more years. Sometimes I stole from my wife's slender purse when the morning terror and madness were on me. Again I swayed dizzily before an open window, or the medicine cabinet where there was poison, cursing myself for a weakling. There were flights from city to country and back, as my wife and I sought escape. Then came the night when the physical and mental torture was so hellish I feared I would burst through my window, sash and all. Somehow I managed to drag my mattress to a lower floor, lest I suddenly leap. A doctor came with

---

[1] In the first edition this read: "whiskey."

7:0   a heavy sedative. Next day found me drinking both gin and sedative. This combination soon landed me on the rocks. People feared for my sanity. So did I. I could eat little or nothing when drinking, and I was forty pounds under weight.

7:1   My brother-in-law is a physician, and through his kindness and that of my mother I was placed in a nationally-known hospital[1] for the mental and physical rehabilitation of alcoholics. Under the so-called belladonna treatment[2] my brain cleared. Hydrotherapy and mild exercise helped much. Best of all, I met a kind doctor[3] who explained that though certainly selfish and foolish, I had been seriously ill, bodily and mentally.

7:2   It relieved me somewhat to learn that in alcoholics the will is amazingly weakened when it comes to combating liquor, though it often remains strong in other respects. My incredible behavior in the face of a desperate desire to stop was explained. Understanding myself now, I fared forth in high hope. For three or four months the goose hung high. I went to town regularly and even made a little money. Surely this was the answer—self-knowledge.

7:3   But it was not, for the frightful day came when I drank once more. The curve of my declining moral and bodily health fell off like a ski-jump. After a time I returned to the hospital. This was the finish, the curtain, it seemed to me. My weary and despairing wife was informed that it would all end with heart failure during delirium tremens, or I would develop a wet brain, perhaps within a year. She would soon have to give me over to the undertaker or the asylum.

7:4   They did not need to tell me. I knew, and almost welcomed the idea. It was a devastating blow to my

---

[1] The Charles B. Towns Hospital, New York, NY.

[2] Refers to the sedative and antispasmodic drug belladonna. Formerly used to relieve some of the effects of alcohol withdrawal.

[3] William Duncan Silkworth, M.D., Medical Director of Towns Hospital.

8:0   pride. I, who had thought so well of myself and my abilities, of my capacity to surmount obstacles, was cornered
at last. Now I was to plunge into the dark, joining that
endless procession of sots who had gone on before. I
thought of my poor wife. There had been much happiness after all. What would I not give to make amends.
But that was over now.

8:1   No words can tell of the loneliness and despair I found
in that bitter morass of self-pity. Quicksand stretched
around me in all directions. I had met my match. I had
been overwhelmed. Alcohol was my master.

8:2   Trembling, I stepped from the hospital a broken man.
Fear sobered me for a bit. Then came the insidious insanity of that first drink, and on Armistice Day[1] 1934, I
was off again. Everyone became resigned to the certainty that I would have to be shut up somewhere, or
would stumble along to a miserable end. How dark it is
before the dawn! In reality that was the beginning of my
last debauch. I was soon to be catapulted into what I
like to call the fourth dimension of existence. I was to
know happiness, peace, and usefulness, in a way of life
that is incredibly more wonderful as time passes.

8:3   Near the end of that bleak November, I sat drinking
in my kitchen. With a certain satisfaction I reflected
there was enough gin concealed about the house to carry
me through that night and the next day. My wife was at
work. I wondered whether I dared hide a full bottle of
gin near the head of our bed. I would need it before
daylight.

8:4   My musing was interrupted by the telephone. The
cheery voice of an old school friend asked if he might

---

[1] Now known as Veterans Day.

9:0　come over. *He was sober.* It was years since I could remember his coming to New York in that condition. I was amazed. Rumor had it that he had been committed for alcoholic insanity. I wondered how he had escaped. Of course he would have dinner, and then I could drink openly with him. Unmindful of his welfare, I thought only of recapturing the spirit of other days. There was that time we had chartered an airplane to complete a jag! His coming was an oasis in this dreary desert of futility. The very thing—an oasis! Drinkers are like that.

9:1　The door opened and he stood there, fresh-skinned and glowing. There was something about his eyes. He was inexplicably different. What had happened?

9:2　I pushed a drink across the table. He refused it. Disappointed but curious, I wondered what had got into the fellow. He wasn't himself.

9:3　"Come, what's this all about?" I queried.

9:4　He looked straight at me. Simply, but smilingly, he said, "I've got religion."

9:5　I was aghast. So that was it—last summer an alcoholic crackpot; now, I suspected, a little cracked about religion. He had that starry-eyed look. Yes, the old boy was on fire all right. But bless his heart, let him rant! Besides, my gin would last longer than his preaching.

9:6　But he did no ranting. In a matter of fact way he told how two men had appeared in court, persuading the judge to suspend his commitment. They had told of a simple religious idea and a practical program of action. That was two months ago and the result was self-evident. It worked!

9:7　He had come to pass his experience along to me—if

10:0   I cared to have it. I was shocked, but interested. Certainly I was interested. I had to be, for I was hopeless.

10:1   He talked for hours. Childhood memories rose before me. I could almost hear the sound of the preacher's voice as I sat, on still Sundays, way over there on the hillside; there was that proffered temperance pledge I never signed; my grandfather's good natured contempt of some church folk and their doings; his insistence that the spheres really had their music[1]; but his denial of the preacher's right to tell him how he must listen; his fearlessness as he spoke of these things just before he died; these recollections welled up from the past. They made me swallow hard.

10:2   That war-time day in old Winchester Cathedral came back again.

10:3   I had always believed in a Power greater than myself. I had often pondered these things. I was not an atheist. Few people really are, for that means blind faith in the strange proposition that this universe originated in a cipher and aimlessly rushes nowhere. My intellectual heroes, the chemists, the astronomers, even the evolutionists, suggested vast laws and forces at work. Despite contrary indications, I had little doubt that a mighty purpose and rhythm underlay all. How could there be so much of precise and immutable law, and no intelligence? I simply had to believe in a Spirit of the Universe, who knew neither time nor limitation. But that was as far as I had gone.

10:4   With ministers, and the world's religions, I parted right there. When they talked of a God personal to me, who was love, superhuman strength and direction, I became irritated and my mind snapped shut against such a theory.

---

[1] *Music of the spheres:* in mythology, the harmony produced by the movements of the heavenly bodies and heard only to the gods.

11:1   To Christ I conceded the certainty of a great man, not too closely followed by those who claimed Him. His moral teaching—most excellent. For myself, I had adopted those parts which seemed convenient and not too difficult; the rest I disregarded.

11:2   The wars which had been fought, the burnings and chicanery that religious dispute had facilitated, made me sick. I honestly doubted whether, on balance, the religions of mankind had done any good. Judging from what I had seen in Europe and since, the power of God in human affairs was negligible, the Brotherhood of Man a grim jest. If there was a Devil, he seemed the Boss Universal, and he certainly had me.

11:3   But my friend sat before me, and he made the point-blank declaration that God had done for him what he could not do for himself. His human will had failed. Doctors had pronounced him incurable. Society was about to lock him up. Like myself, he had admitted complete defeat. Then he had, in effect, been raised from the dead, suddenly taken from the scrap heap to a level of life better than the best he had ever known!

11:4   Had this power originated in him? Obviously it had not. There had been no more power in him than there was in me at the minute; and this was none at all.

11:5   That floored me. It began to look as though religious people were right after all. Here was something at work in a human heart which had done the impossible. My ideas about miracles were drastically revised right then. Never mind the musty past; here sat a miracle directly across the kitchen table. He shouted great tidings.

11:6   I saw that my friend was much more than inwardly

12:0 reorganized. He was on a different footing. His roots grasped a new soil.

12:1 Despite the living example of my friend there remained in me the vestiges of my old prejudice. The word God still aroused a certain antipathy. When the thought was expressed that there might be a God personal to me this feeling was intensified. I didn't like the idea. I could go for such conceptions as Creative Intelligence, Universal Mind or Spirit of Nature but I resisted the thought of a Czar[1] of the Heavens, however loving His sway might be. I have since talked with scores of men who felt the same way.

12:2 My friend suggested what then seemed a novel idea. He said, *"Why don't you choose your own conception of God?"*

12:3 That statement hit me hard. It melted the icy intellectual mountain in whose shadow I had lived and shivered many years. I stood in the sunlight at last.

12:4 *It was only a matter of being willing to believe in a Power greater than myself. Nothing more was required of me to make my beginning.* I saw that growth could start from that point. Upon a foundation of complete willingness I might build what I saw in my friend. Would I have it? Of course I would!

12:5 Thus was I convinced that God is concerned with us humans when we want Him enough. At long last I saw, I felt, I believed. Scales of pride and prejudice fell from my eyes. A new world came into view.

12:6 The real significance of my experience in the Cathedral burst upon me. For a brief moment, I had needed and wanted God. There had been a humble willingness to have Him with me—and He came. But soon the sense of His presence had been blotted out by

---

[1] Former title of the ruler of Russia.

13:0 worldly clamors, mostly those within myself. And so it had been ever since. How blind I had been.

13:1 At the hospital I was separated from alcohol for the last time. Treatment seemed wise, for I showed signs of delirium tremens.

13:2 There I humbly offered myself to God, as I then understood Him, to do with me as He would. I placed myself unreservedly under His care and direction. I admitted for the first time that of myself I was nothing; that without Him I was lost. I ruthlessly faced my sins and became willing to have my new-found Friend take them away, root and branch. I have not had a drink since.[1]

13:3 My schoolmate visited me, and I fully acquainted him with my problems and deficiencies. We made a list of people I had hurt or toward whom I felt resentment. I expressed my entire willingness to approach these individuals, admitting my wrong. Never was I to be critical of them. I was to right all such matters to the utmost of my ability.

13:4 I was to test my thinking by the new God-consciousness within. Common sense would thus become uncommon sense. I was to sit quietly when in doubt, asking only for direction and strength to meet my problems as He would have me. Never was I to pray for myself, except as my requests bore on my usefulness to others. Then only might I expect to receive. But that would be in great measure.

13:5 My friend promised when these things were done I would enter upon a new relationship with my Creator; that I would have the elements of a way of living which answered all my problems. Belief in the power of God, plus enough willingness, honesty and humility

---

[1] December 11, 1934.

14:0 to establish and maintain the new order of things, were the essential requirements.

14:1 Simple, but not easy; a price had to be paid. It meant destruction of self-centeredness. I must turn in all things to the Father of Light who presides over us all.

14:2 These were revolutionary and drastic proposals, but the moment I fully accepted them, the effect was electric. There was a sense of victory, followed by such a peace and serenity as I had never known. There was utter confidence. I felt lifted up, as though the great clean wind of a mountain top blew through and through. God comes to most men gradually, but His impact on me was sudden and profound.

14:3 For a moment I was alarmed, and called my friend, the doctor, to ask if I were still sane. He listened in wonder as I talked.

14:4 Finally he shook his head saying, "Something has happened to you I don't understand. But you had better hang on to it. Anything is better than the way you were." The good doctor now sees many men who have such experiences. He knows that[1] they are real.

14:5 While I lay in the hospital the thought came that there were thousands of hopeless alcoholics who might be glad to have what had been so freely given me. Perhaps I could help some of them. They in turn might work with others.

14:6 My friend had emphasized the absolute necessity of demonstrating these principles in all my affairs. Particularly was it imperative to work with others as he had worked with me. Faith without works was dead, he said. And how appallingly true for the alcoholic! For if an alcoholic failed to perfect and enlarge his

---

[1] The word "that" did not appear in the first edition.

15:0 spiritual life through work and self-sacrifice for others, he could not survive the certain trials and low spots ahead. If he did not work, he would surely drink again, and if he drank, he would surely die. Then faith would be dead indeed. With us it is just like that.

15:1 My wife and I abandoned ourselves with enthusiasm to the idea of helping other alcoholics to a solution of their problems. It was fortunate, for my old business associates remained skeptical for a year and a half, during which I found little work. I was not too well at the time, and was plagued by waves of self-pity and resentment. This sometimes nearly drove me back to drink, but I soon found that when all other measures failed, work with another alcoholic would save the day. Many times I have gone to my old hospital in despair. On talking to a man there, I would be amazingly lifted up and set on my feet. It is a design for living that works in rough going.

15:2 We commenced to make many fast friends and a fellowship has grown up among us of which it is a wonderful thing to feel a part. The joy of living we really have, even under pressure and difficulty. I have seen hundreds[1] of families set their feet in the path that really goes somewhere; have seen the most impossible domestic situations righted; feuds and bitterness of all sorts wiped out. I have seen men come out of asylums and resume a vital place in the lives of their families and communities. Business and professional men have regained their standing. There is scarcely any form of trouble and misery which has not been overcome among us. In one western city[2] and its environs there are one thousand[3] of us and our families. We meet frequently so that newcomers may find the fellowship

---

[1] In the first edition this read: "one hundred."

[2] Cleveland, Ohio.

[3] In the first edition this read: "eighty."

16:0 they seek. At these informal gatherings one may often see from 50 to 200 persons[1]. We are growing in numbers and power.

16:1 An alcoholic in his cups is an unlovely creature. Our struggles with them are variously strenuous, comic, and tragic. One poor chap committed suicide in my home[2]. He could not, or would not, see our way of life.

16:2 There is, however a vast amount of fun about it all. I suppose some would be shocked at our seeming worldliness and levity. But just underneath there is deadly earnestness. Faith has to work twenty-four hours a day in and through us, or we perish.

16:3 Most of us feel we need look no further for Utopia. We have it with us right here and now. Each day my friend's simple talk in our kitchen multiplies itself in a widening circle of peace on earth and good will to men.

[1] In the first edition this read: "40 to 80 persons."

[2] 182 Clinton Street, Brooklyn Heights, Brooklyn, New York.

Chapter 2

THERE IS A SOLUTION

17:1   WE OF ALCOHOLICS ANONYMOUS, know thousands[1] of men and women who were once just as hopeless as Bill. Nearly all have recovered.[2] They have solved the drink problem.

17:2   We are average Americans. All sections of this country and many of its occupations are represented, as well as many political, economic, social, and religious backgrounds. We are people who normally would not mix. But there exists among us a fellowship, a friendliness, and an understanding which is indescribably wonderful. We are like the passengers of a great liner the moment after rescue from shipwreck when camaraderie, joyousness and democracy pervade the vessel from steerage to Captain's table. Unlike the feelings of the ship's passengers, however, our joy in escape from disaster does not subside as we go our individual ways. The feeling of having shared in a common peril is one element in the powerful cement which binds us. But that in itself would never have held us together as we are now joined.

17:3   The tremendous fact for every one of us is that we have discovered a common solution. We have a way out on which we can absolutely agree, and upon which we can join in brotherly and harmonious action. This is the great news this book carries to those who suffer from alcoholism.

---

[1] In the first edition this read: "one hundred."

[2] In the first edition this read: "All have recovered."

18:1   An illness of this sort—and we have come to believe it an illness—involves those about us in a way no
other human sickness can. If a person has cancer all
are sorry for him and no one is angry or hurt. But not
so with the alcoholic illness, for with it there goes annihilation of all the things worth while in life. It engulfs
all whose lives touch the sufferer's. It brings misunderstanding, fierce resentment, financial insecurity, disgusted friends and employers, warped lives of blameless children, sad wives and parents—anyone can increase the list.

18:2   We hope this volume will inform and comfort those
who are, or who may be affected. There are many.

18:3   Highly competent psychiatrists who have dealt with
us have found it sometimes impossible to persuade an
alcoholic to discuss his situation without reserve.
Strangely enough, wives, parents and intimate friends
usually find us even more unapproachable than do the
psychiatrist and the doctor.

18:4   *But the ex-problem drinker[1] who has found this solution, who is properly armed with facts about himself,
can generally win the entire confidence of another alcoholic in a few hours. Until such an understanding is
reached, little or nothing can be accomplished.*

18:5   That the man who is making the approach has had
the same difficulty, that he obviously knows what he
is talking about, that his whole deportment shouts at
the new prospect that he is a man with a real answer,
that he has no attitude of Holier Than Thou, nothing
whatever except the sincere desire to be helpful; that
there are no fees to pay, no axes to grind, no people to
please, no lectures to be endured—these are the condi-

---

[1] In the first edition this read: "ex-alcoholic."

19:0   tions we have found most effective. After such an approach many take up their beds and walk again.

19:1   None of us makes a sole vocation of this work, nor do we think its effectiveness would be increased if we did. We feel that elimination of our drinking is but a beginning. A much more important demonstration of our principles lies before us in our respective homes, occupations and affairs. All of us spend much of our spare time in the sort of effort which we are going to describe. A few are fortunate enough to be so situated that they can give nearly all their time to the work.

19:2   If we keep on the way we are going there is little doubt that much good will result, but the surface of the problem would hardly be scratched. Those of us who live in large cities are overcome by the reflection that close by hundreds are dropping into oblivion every day. Many could recover if they had the opportunity we have enjoyed. How then shall we present that which has been so freely given us?

19:3   We have concluded to publish an anonymous volume setting forth the problem as we see it. We shall bring to the task our combined experience and knowledge. This should suggest a useful program for anyone concerned with a drinking problem.

19:4   Of necessity there will have to be discussion of matters medical, psychiatric, social, and religious. We are aware that these matters are, from their very nature, controversial. Nothing would please us so much as to write a book which would contain no basis for contention or argument. We shall do our utmost to achieve that ideal. Most of us sense that real tolerance of other people's shortcomings and viewpoints and a respect for their opinions are attitudes which make us

20:0   more useful to others. Our very lives, as ex-problem drinkers[1], depend upon our constant thought of others and how
we may help meet their needs.

20:1   You may already have asked yourself why it is that all
of us became so very ill from drinking. Doubtless you are
curious to discover how and why, in the face of expert
opinion to the contrary, we have recovered from a hopeless condition of mind and body. If you are an alcoholic
who wants to get over it, you may already be asking—
"What do I have to do?"

20:2   It is the purpose of this book to answer such questions
specifically. We shall tell you what we have done. Before
going into a detailed discussion, it may be well to summarize some points as we see them.

20:3   How many times people have said to us:"I can take it
or leave it alone. Why can't he?" "Why don't you drink
like a gentleman or quit?" "That fellow can't handle his
liquor." "Why don't you try beer and wine?" "Lay off the
hard stuff." "His will power must be weak." "He could
stop if he wanted to." "She's such a sweet girl, I should
think he'd stop for her sake." "The doctor told him that if
he ever drank again it would kill him, but there he is all lit
up again."

20:4   Now these are commonplace observations on drinkers which we hear all the time. Back of them is a world of
ignorance and misunderstanding. We see that these expressions refer to people whose reactions are very different from ours.

20:5   Moderate drinkers have little trouble in giving up liquor entirely if they have good reason for it. They can
take it or leave it alone.

20:6   Then we have a certain type of hard drinker. He
may have the habit badly enough to gradually impair

---

[1] In the first edition this read: "ex-alcoholic."

21:0 him physically and mentally. It may cause him to die a few years before his time. If a sufficiently strong reason—ill health, falling in love, change of environment, or the warning of a doctor—becomes operative, this man can also stop or moderate, although he may find it difficult and troublesome and may even need medical attention.

21:1 But what about the real alcoholic? He may start off as a moderate drinker; he may or may not become a continuous hard drinker; but at some stage of his drinking career he begins to lose all control of his liquor consumption, once he starts to drink.

21:2 Here is the fellow who has been puzzling you, especially in his lack of control. He does absurd, incredible, tragic things while drinking. He is a real Dr. Jekyll and Mr. Hyde.[1] He is seldom mildly intoxicated. He is always more or less insanely drunk. His disposition while drinking resembles his normal nature but little. He may be one of the finest fellows in the world. Yet let him drink for a day, and he frequently becomes disgustingly, and even dangerously anti-social. He has a positive genius for getting tight at exactly the wrong moment, particularly when some important decision must be made or engagement kept. He is often perfectly sensible and well balanced concerning everything except liquor, but in that respect he is incredibly dishonest and selfish. He often possesses special abilities, skills, and aptitudes, and has a promising career ahead of him. He uses his gifts to build up a bright outlook for his family and himself, and then pulls the structure down on his head by a senseless series of sprees. He is the fellow who goes to bed so intoxicated he ought to sleep the clock around. Yet early next

---

[1] A literary reference to describe a person with a split personality—one good and the other bad.

22:0   morning he searches madly for the bottle he misplaced the night before. If he can afford it, he may have liquor concealed all over his house to be certain no one gets his entire supply away from him to throw down the wastepipe. As matters grow worse, he begins to use a combination of high-powered sedative and liquor to quiet his nerves so he can go to work. Then comes the day when he simply cannot make it and gets drunk all over again. Perhaps he goes to a doctor who gives him morphine or some sedative with which to taper off. Then he begins to appear at hospitals and sanitariums.

22:1   This is by no means a comprehensive picture of the true alcoholic, as our behavior patterns vary. But this description should identify him roughly.

22:2   Why does he behave like this? If hundreds of experiences have shown him that one drink means another debacle with all its attendant suffering and humiliation, why is it he takes that one drink? Why can't he stay on the water wagon? What has become of the common sense and will power that he still sometimes displays with respect to other matters?

22:3   Perhaps there never will be a full answer to these questions. Opinions vary considerably as to why the alcoholic reacts differently from normal people. We are not sure why, once a certain point is reached, little can be done for him. We cannot answer the riddle.

22:4   We know that while the alcoholic keeps away from drink, as he may do for months or years, he reacts much like other men. We are equally positive that once he takes any alcohol whatever into his system, something happens, both in the bodily and mental sense, which makes it virtually impossible for him to

23:0 stop. The experience of any alcoholic will abundantly confirm this.

23:1 These observations would be academic and pointless if our friend never took the first drink, thereby setting the terrible cycle in motion. Therefore, the main problem of the alcoholic centers in his mind, rather than in his body. If you ask him why he started on that last bender, the chances are he will offer you any one of a hundred alibis. Sometimes these excuses have a certain plausibility, but none of them really makes sense in the light of the havoc an alcoholic's drinking bout creates. They sound like the philosophy of the man who, having a headache, beats himself on the head with a hammer so that he can't feel the ache. If you draw this fallacious reasoning to the attention of an alcoholic, he will laugh it off, or become irritated and refuse to talk.

23:2 Once in a while he may tell the truth. And the truth, strange to say, is usually that he has no more idea why he took that first drink than you have. Some drinkers have excuses with which they are satisfied part of the time. But in their hearts they really do not know why they do it. Once this malady has a real hold, they are a baffled lot. There is the obsession that somehow, someday, they will beat the game. But they often suspect they are down for the count.

23:3 How true this is, few realize. In a vague way their families and friends sense that these drinkers are abnormal, but everybody hopefully awaits the day when the sufferer will rouse himself from his lethargy and assert his power of will.

23:4 The tragic truth is that if the man be a real alcoholic, the happy day may not arrive. He has lost

24:0 control. At a certain point in the drinking of every alcoholic, he passes into a state where the most powerful desire to stop drinking is of absolutely no avail. This tragic situation has already arrived in practically every case long before it is suspected.

24:1 *The fact is that most alcoholics, for reasons yet obscure, have lost the power of choice in drink. Our so-called will power becomes practically nonexistent. We are unable, at certain times, to bring into our consciousness with sufficient force the memory of the suffering and humiliation of even a week or a month ago. We are without defense against the first drink.*

24:2 The almost certain consequences that follow taking even a glass of beer do not crowd into the mind to deter us. If these thoughts occur, they are hazy and readily supplanted with the old threadbare idea that this time we shall handle ourselves like other people. There is a complete failure of the kind of defense that keeps one from putting his hand on a hot stove.

24:3 The alcoholic may say to himself in the most casual way, "It won't burn me this time, so here's how!" Or perhaps he doesn't think at all. How often have some of us begun to drink in this nonchalant way, and after the third or fourth, pounded on the bar and said to ourselves, "For God's sake, how did I ever get started again?" Only to have that thought supplanted by "Well, I'll stop with the sixth drink." Or "What's the use anyhow?"

24:4 When this sort of thinking is fully established in an individual with alcoholic tendencies, he has probably placed himself beyond human aid, and unless locked up, may die or go permanently insane. These stark and ugly facts have been confirmed by legions of alco-

25:0   holics throughout history. But for the grace of God, there would have been thousands more convincing demonstrations. So many want to stop but cannot.

25:1   *There is a solution.* Almost none of us liked the self-searching, the leveling of our pride, the confession of shortcomings which the process requires for its successful consummation. But we saw that it really worked in others, and we had come to believe in the hopelessness and futility of life as we had been living it. When, therefore, we were approached by those in whom the problem had been solved, there was nothing left for us but to pick up the simple kit of spiritual tools laid at our feet. We have found much of heaven and we have been rocketed into a fourth dimension of existence of which we had not even dreamed.

25:2   The great fact is just this, and nothing less: That we have had deep and effective spiritual experiences* which have revolutionized our whole attitude toward life, toward our fellows and toward God's universe. The central fact of our lives today is the absolute certainty that our Creator has entered into our hearts and lives in a way which is indeed miraculous. He has commenced to accomplish those things for us which we could never do by ourselves.

25:3   If you are as seriously alcoholic as we were, we believe there is no middle-of-the-road solution. We were in a position where life was becoming impossible, and if we had passed into the region from which there is no return through human aid, we had but two alternatives: One was to go on to the bitter end, blotting out the consciousness of our intolerable situation as best we could; and the other, to accept spiritual help. This

* see "Spiritual Experience."

26:0   we did because we honestly wanted to, and were willing to make the effort.

26:1   A certain American business man had ability, good sense, and high character. For years he had floundered from one sanitarium to another. He had consulted the best known American psychiatrists. Then he had gone to Europe, placing himself in the care of a celebrated physician (the psychiatrist, Dr. Jung[1])[2] who prescribed for him. Though experience had made him skeptical, he finished his treatment with unusual confidence. His physical and mental condition were unusually good. Above all, he believed he had acquired such a profound knowledge of the inner workings of his mind and its hidden springs that relapse was unthinkable. Nevertheless, he was drunk in a short time. More baffling still, he could give himself no satisfactory explanation for his fall.

26:2   So he returned to this doctor, whom he admired, and asked him point-blank why he could not recover. He wished above all things to regain self-control. He seemed quite rational and well-balanced with respect to other problems. Yet he had no control whatever over alcohol. Why was this?

26:3   He begged the doctor to tell him the whole truth, and he got it. In the doctor's judgment he was utterly hopeless; he could never regain his position in society and he would have to place himself under lock and key or hire a bodyguard if he expected to live long. That was a great physician's opinion.

26:4   But this man still lives, and is a free man. He does not need a bodyguard nor is he confined. He can go anywhere on this earth where other free men may go

---

[1] Pronounced: Dr. Yung.

[2] "(the psychiatrist, Dr. Jung)" did not appear in the first edition.

27:0 without disaster, provided he remains willing to maintain a certain simple attitude.

27:1 Some of our alcoholic readers may think they can do without spiritual help. Let us tell you the rest of the conversation our friend had with his doctor.

27:2 The doctor said: "You have the mind of a chronic alcoholic. I have never seen one single case recover, where that state of mind existed to the extent that it does in you." Our friend felt as though the gates of hell had closed on him with a clang.

27:3 He said to the doctor, "Is there no exception?"

27:4 "Yes," replied the doctor, "there is. Exceptions to cases such as yours have been occurring since early times. Here and there, once in a while, alcoholics have had what are called vital spiritual experiences. To me these occurrences are phenomena. They appear to be in the nature of huge emotional displacements and rearrangements. Ideas, emotions, and attitudes which were once the guiding forces of the lives of these men are suddenly cast to one side, and a completely new set of conceptions and motives begin to dominate them. In fact, I have been trying to produce some such emotional rearrangement within you. With many individuals the methods which I employed are successful, but I have never been successful with an alcoholic of your description."*

27:5 Upon hearing this, our friend was somewhat relieved, for he reflected that, after all, he was a good church member. This hope, however, was destroyed by the doctor's telling him that while his religious convictions were very good, in his case they did not spell the necessary vital spiritual experience.

* see "Spiritual Experience."

28:1 Here was the terrible dilemma in which our friend found himself when he had the extraordinary experience, which as we have already told you, made him a free man.

28:2 We, in our turn, sought the same escape with all the desperation of drowning men. What seemed at first a flimsy reed, has proved to be the loving and powerful hand of God. A new life has been given us or, if you prefer, "a design for living" that really works.

28:3 The distinguished American psychologist, William James, in his book "Varieties of Religious Experience," indicates a multitude of ways in which men have discovered God. We have no desire to convince anyone that there is only one way by which faith can be acquired. If what we have learned and felt and seen means anything at all, it means that all of us, whatever our race, creed, or color are the children of a living Creator with whom we may form a relationship upon simple and understandable terms as soon as we are willing and honest enough to try. Those having religious affiliations will find here nothing disturbing to their beliefs or ceremonies. There is no friction among us over such matters.

28:4 We think it no concern of ours what religious bodies our members identify themselves with as individuals. This should be an entirely personal affair which each one decides for himself in the light of past associations, or his present choice. Not all of us join religious bodies, but most of us favor such memberships.

28:5 In the following chapter, there appears an explanation of alcoholism, as we understand it, then a chapter addressed to the agnostic. Many who once were in this class are now among our members. Surprisingly

29:0   enough, we find such convictions no great obstacle to a spiritual experience.

29:1   Further on, clear-cut directions are given showing how we recovered. These are followed by forty-three[1] personal experiences.

29:2   Each individual, in the personal stories, describes in his own language and from his own point of view the way he established his relationship with God. These give a fair cross section of our membership and a clear-cut idea of what has actually happened in their lives.

29:3   We hope no one will consider these self-revealing accounts in bad taste. Our hope is that many alcoholic men and women, desperately in need, will see these pages, and we believe that it is only by fully disclosing ourselves and our problems that they will be persuaded to say, "Yes, I am one of them too; I must have this thing."

---

[1] In the first edition, this read: "more than a score."

Chapter 3

MORE ABOUT ALCOHOLISM

30:1   *M*OST OF US have been unwilling to admit we were real alcoholics. No person likes to think he is bodily and mentally different from his fellows. Therefore, it is not surprising that our drinking careers have been characterized by countless vain attempts to prove we could drink like other people. The idea that somehow, someday he will control and enjoy his drinking[1] is the great obsession of every abnormal drinker. The persistence of this illusion is astonishing. Many pursue it into the gates of insanity or death.

30:2   We learned that we had to fully concede to our innermost selves that we were alcoholics. This is the first step in recovery. The delusion that we are like other people, or presently may be, has to be smashed.

30:3   We alcoholics are men and women who have lost the ability to control our drinking. We know that no real alcoholic *ever* recovers control. All of us felt at times that we were regaining control, but such intervals—usually brief—were inevitably followed by still less control, which led in time to pitiful and incomprehensible demoralization. We are convinced to a man that alcoholics of our type are in the grip of a progressive illness. Over any considerable period we get worse, never better.

30:4   We are like men who have lost their legs; they never grow new ones. Neither does there appear to be any kind of treatment which will make alcoholics of

---

[1] In the first edition this read: "liquor drinking."

31:0 our kind like other men. We have tried every imaginable remedy. In some instances there has been brief recovery, followed always by a still worse relapse. Physicians who are familiar with alcoholism agree there is no such thing as making a normal drinker out of an alcoholic. Science may one day accomplish this, but it hasn't done so yet.[1]

31:1 Despite all we can say, many who are real alcoholics are not going to believe they are in that class. By every form of self-deception and experimentation, they will try to prove themselves exceptions to the rule, therefore nonalcoholic. If anyone who is showing inability to control his drinking can do the right-about-face and drink like a gentleman, our hats are off to him. Heaven knows, we have tried hard enough and long enough to drink like other people!

31:2 Here are some of the methods we have tried: Drinking beer only, limiting the number of drinks, never drinking alone, never drinking in the morning, drinking only at home, never having it in the house, never drinking during business hours, drinking only at parties, switching from scotch to brandy, drinking only natural wines, agreeing to resign if ever drunk on the job, taking a trip, not taking a trip, swearing off forever (with and without a solemn oath), taking more physical exercise, reading inspirational books, going to health farms and sanitariums, accepting voluntary commitment to asylums—we could increase the list ad infinitum.

31:3 We do not like to pronounce any individual as alcoholic[2], but you can quickly diagnose yourself. Step over to the nearest barroom and try some controlled drinking. Try to drink and stop abruptly. Try it

[1] In the first edition this read: "...but it evidently hasn't done so yet."

[2] In the first edition this read: "We do not like to brand any individual as an alcoholic..."

32:0   more than once. It will not take long for you to decide,
if you are honest with yourself about it. It may be worth
a bad case of jitters if you get a full knowledge of your
condition.

32:1   Though there is no way of proving it, we believe that
early in our drinking careers most of us could have
stopped drinking. But the difficulty is that few alcoholics have enough desire to stop while there is yet time.
We have heard of a few instances where people, who
showed definite signs of alcoholism, were able to stop
for a long period because of an overpowering desire to
do so. Here is one.

32:2   A man of thirty was doing a great deal of spree drinking. He was very nervous in the morning after these
bouts and quieted himself with more liquor. He was ambitious to succeed in business, but saw that he would get
nowhere if he drank at all. Once he started, he had no
control whatever. He made up his mind that until he had
been successful in business and had retired, he would
not touch another drop. An exceptional man, he remained
bone dry for twenty-five years and retired at the age of
fifty-five, after a successful and happy business career.
Then he fell victim to a belief which practically every
alcoholic has—that his long period of sobriety and self-
discipline had qualified him to drink as other men. Out
came his carpet slippers and a bottle. In two months
he was in a hospital, puzzled and humiliated. He tried
to regulate his drinking for a while, making several trips
to the hospital meantime. Then, gathering all his forces,
he attempted to stop altogether and found he could
not. Every means of solving his problem which

33:0   money could buy was at his disposal. Every attempt failed. Though a robust man at retirement, he went to pieces quickly and was dead within four years.

33:1   This case contains a powerful lesson. Most of us have believed that if we remained sober for a long stretch, we could thereafter drink normally. But here is a man who at fifty-five years found he was just where he had left off at thirty. We have seen the truth demonstrated again and again: "Once an alcoholic, always an alcoholic." Commencing to drink after a period of sobriety, we are in a short time as bad as ever. If we are planning to stop drinking, there must be no reservation of any kind, nor any lurking notion that someday we will be immune to alcohol.

33:2   Young people may be encouraged by this man's experience to think that they can stop, as he did, on their own will power. We doubt if many of them can do it, because none will really want to stop, and hardly one of them, because of the peculiar mental twist already acquired, will find he can win out. Several of our crowd, men of thirty[1] or less, had been drinking only a few years, but they found themselves as helpless as those who had been drinking twenty years.

33:3   To be gravely affected, one does not necessarily have to drink a long time nor take the quantities some of us have. This is particularly true of women. Potential female[2] alcoholics often turn into the real thing and are gone beyond recall in a few years. Certain drinkers, who would be greatly insulted if called alcoholics, are astonished at their inability to stop. We, who are familiar with the symptoms, see large numbers of potential alcoholics among young

---

[1] In the first edition this read: "thirty-five."

[2] In the first edition this read: "feminine."

34:0   people everywhere. But try and get them to see it!*

34:1   As we look back, we feel we had gone on drinking many years beyond the point where we could quit on our will power. If anyone questions whether he has entered this dangerous area, let him try leaving liquor alone for one year. If he is a real alcoholic and very far advanced, there is scant chance of success. In the early days of our drinking we occasionally remained sober for a year or more, becoming serious drinkers again later. Though you may be able to stop for a considerable period, you may yet be a potential alcoholic. We think few, to whom this book will appeal, can stay dry anything like a year. Some will be drunk the day after making their resolutions; most of them within a few weeks.

34:2   For those who are unable to drink moderately the question is how to stop altogether. We are assuming, of course, that the reader desires to stop. Whether such a person can quit upon a nonspiritual basis depends upon the extent to which he has already lost the power to choose whether he will drink or not. Many of us felt that we had plenty of character. There was a tremendous urge to cease forever. Yet we found it impossible. This is the baffling feature of alcoholism as we know it—this utter inability to leave it alone, no matter how great the necessity or the wish.

34:3   How then shall we help our readers determine, to their own satisfaction, whether they are one of us? The experiment of quitting for a period of time will be helpful, but we think we can render an even greater service to alcoholic sufferers and perhaps to the med-

---

* True when this book was first published. In 1993 a membership survey showed that one-fifth of A.A.s were 30 years and under.

35:0   ical fraternity. So we shall describe some of the mental states that precede a relapse into drinking, for obviously this is the crux of the problem.

35:1   What sort of thinking dominates an alcoholic who repeats time after time the desperate experiment of the first drink? Friends who have reasoned with him after a spree which has brought him to the point of divorce or bankruptcy are mystified when he walks directly into a saloon. Why does he? Of what is he thinking?

35:2   Our first example is a friend we shall call Jim. This man has a charming wife and family. He inherited a lucrative automobile agency. He had a commendable World War record. He is a good salesman. Everybody likes him. He is an intelligent man, normal so far as we can see, except for a nervous disposition. He did no drinking until he was thirty-five. In a few years he became so violent when intoxicated that he had to be committed. On leaving the asylum he came into contact with us.

35:3   We told him what we knew of alcoholism and the answer we had found. He made a beginning. His family was re-assembled, and he began to work as a salesman for the business he had lost through drinking. All went well for a time, but he failed to enlarge his spiritual life. To his consternation, he found himself drunk half a dozen times in rapid succession. On each of these occasions we worked with him, reviewing carefully what had happened. He agreed he was a real alcoholic and in a serious condition. He knew he faced another trip to the asylum if he kept on. Moreover, he would lose his family for whom he had a deep affection.

36:1   Yet he got drunk again. We asked him to tell us exactly how it happened. This is his story: "I came to work on Tuesday morning. I remember I felt irritated that I had to be a salesman for a concern I once owned. I had a few words with the boss, but nothing serious. Then I decided to drive into the country and see one of my prospects for a car. On the way I felt hungry so I stopped at a roadside place where they have a bar. I had no intention of drinking. I just thought I would get a sandwich. I also had the notion that I might find a customer for a car at this place, which was familiar for I had been going to it for years. I had eaten there many times during the months I was sober. I sat down at a table and ordered a sandwich and a glass of milk. Still no thought of drinking. I ordered another sandwich and decided to have another glass of milk.

36:2   *"Suddenly the thought crossed my mind that if I were to put an ounce of whiskey in my milk it couldn't hurt me on a full stomach. I ordered a whiskey and poured it into the milk. I vaguely sensed I was not being any too smart, but felt reassured as I was taking the whiskey on a full stomach.* The experiment went so well that I ordered another whiskey and poured it into more milk. That didn't seem to bother me so I tried another."

36:3   Thus started one more journey to the asylum for Jim. Here was the threat of commitment, the loss of family and position, to say nothing of that intense mental and physical suffering which drinking always caused him. *He had much knowledge about himself as an alcoholic. Yet all reasons for not drinking were*

37:0 *easily pushed aside in favor of the foolish idea that he could take whiskey if only he mixed it with milk!*

37:1 Whatever the precise definition of the word may be, we call this plain insanity. How can such a lack of proportion, of the ability to think straight, be called anything else?

37:2 You may think this an extreme case. To us it is not far-fetched, for this kind of thinking has been characteristic of every single one of us. We have sometimes reflected more than Jim did upon the consequences. But there was always the curious mental phenomenon that parallel with our sound reasoning there inevitably ran some insanely trivial excuse for taking the first drink. Our sound reasoning failed to hold us in check. The insane idea won out. Next day we would ask ourselves, in all earnestness and sincerity, how it could have happened.

37:3 In some circumstances we have gone out deliberately to get drunk, feeling ourselves justified by nervousness, anger, worry, depression, jealousy or the like. But even in this type of beginning we are obliged to admit that our justification for a spree was insanely insufficient in the light of what always happened. We now see that when we began to drink deliberately, instead of casually, there was little serious or effective thought during the period of premeditation of what the terrific consequences might be.

37:4 Our behavior is as absurd and incomprehensible with respect to the first drink as that of an individual with a passion, say, for jay-walking. He gets a thrill out of skipping in front of fast-moving vehicles. He enjoys himself for a few years in spite of friendly warnings. Up to this point you would label him as a foolish

38:0 chap having queer ideas of fun. Luck then deserts him and he is slightly injured several times in succession. You would expect him, if he were normal, to cut it out. Presently he is hit again and this time has a fractured skull. Within a week after leaving the hospital a fast-moving trolley car breaks his arm. He tells you he has decided to stop jay-walking for good, but in a few weeks he breaks both legs.

38:1 On through the years this conduct continues, accompanied by his continual promises to be careful or to keep off the streets altogether. Finally, he can no longer work, his wife gets a divorce and he is held up to ridicule. He tries every known means to get the jay-walking idea out of his head. He shuts himself up in an asylum, hoping to mend his ways. But the day he comes out he races in front of a fire engine, which breaks his back. Such a man would be crazy, wouldn't he?

38:2 You may think our illustration is too ridiculous. But is it? We, who have been through the wringer, have to admit if we substituted alcoholism for jay-walking, the illustration would fit us exactly. However intelligent we may have been in other respects, where alcohol has been involved, we have been strangely insane. It's strong language—but isn't it true?

38:3 Some of you are thinking: "Yes, what you tell us is true, but it doesn't fully apply. We admit we have some of these symptoms, but we have not gone to the extremes you fellows did, nor are we likely to, for we understand ourselves so well after what you have told us that such things cannot happen again. We have not lost everything in life through drinking and we

39:0   certainly do not intend to. Thanks for the information."

39:1   That may be true of certain nonalcoholic people who, though drinking foolishly and heavily at the present time, are able to stop or moderate, because their brains and bodies have not been damaged as ours were. But the actual or potential alcoholic, with hardly an exception, will be *absolutely unable to stop drinking on the basis of self-knowledge.* This is a point we wish to emphasize and re-emphasize, to smash home upon our alcoholic readers as it has been revealed to us out of bitter experience. Let us take another illustration.

39:2   Fred is partner in a well known accounting firm. His income is good, he has a fine home, is happily married and the father of promising children of college age. He has so attractive a personality that he makes friends with everyone. If ever there was a successful business man, it is Fred. To all appearance he is a stable, well balanced individual. Yet, he is alcoholic. We first saw Fred about a year ago in a hospital where he had gone to recover from a bad case of jitters. It was his first experience of this kind, and he was much ashamed of it. Far from admitting he was an alcoholic, he told himself he came to the hospital to rest his nerves. The doctor intimated strongly that he might be worse than he realized. For a few days he was depressed about his condition. He made up his mind to quit drinking altogether. It never occurred to him that perhaps he could not do so, in spite of his character and standing. Fred would not believe himself an alcoholic, much less accept a spiritual remedy for his problem. We told him what

40:0   we knew about alcoholism. He was interested and conceded that he had some of the symptoms, but he was a long way from admitting that he could do nothing about it himself. He was positive that this humiliating experience, plus the knowledge he had acquired, would keep him sober the rest of his life. Self-knowledge would fix it.

40:1   We heard no more of Fred for a while. One day we were told that he was back in the hospital. This time he was quite shaky. He soon indicated he was anxious to see us. The story he told is most instructive, for here was a chap absolutely convinced he had to stop drinking, who had no excuse for drinking, who exhibited splendid judgment and determination in all his other concerns, yet was flat on his back nevertheless.

40:2   Let him tell you about it: "I was much impressed with what you fellows said about alcoholism, and[1] I frankly did not believe it would be possible for me to drink again. I rather[2] appreciated your ideas about the subtle insanity which precedes the first drink, but I was confident it could not happen to me after what I had learned. I reasoned I was not so far advanced as most of you fellows, that I had been usually successful in licking my other personal problems, and that I would therefore be successful where you men failed. I felt I had every right to be self-confident, that it would be only a matter of exercising my will power and keeping on guard.

40:3   "In this frame of mind, I went about my business and for a time all was well. I had no trouble refusing drinks, and began to wonder if I had not been making too hard work of a simple matter. One day I went to Washington to present some accounting evidence to

---

[1] In the first edition this read: "but."

[2] In the first edition this read: "somewhat."

41:0   a government bureau. I had been out of town before during this particular dry spell, so there was nothing new about that. Physically, I felt fine. Neither did I have any pressing problems or worries. My business came off well, I was pleased and knew my partners would be too. It was the end of a perfect day, not a cloud on the horizon.

41:1   "I went to my hotel and leisurely dressed for dinner. *As I crossed the threshold of the dining room, the thought came to mind that it would be nice to have a couple of cocktails with dinner. That was all. Nothing more.* I ordered a cocktail and my meal. Then I ordered another cocktail. After dinner I decided to take a walk. When I returned to the hotel it struck me a highball would be fine before going to bed, so I stepped into the bar and had one. I remember having several more that night and plenty next morning. I have a shadowy recollection of being in an airplane bound for New York and of finding a friendly taxicab driver at the landing field instead of my wife. The driver escorted me about for several days. I know little of where I went or what I said and did. Then came the hospital with unbearable mental and physical suffering.

41:2   "As soon as I regained my ability to think, I went carefully over that evening in Washington. *Not only had I been off guard, I had made no fight whatever against the first drink. This time I had not thought of the consequences at all.* I had commenced to drink as carelessly as though the cocktails were ginger ale. I now remembered what my alcoholic friends had told me, how they prophesied that if I had an alcoholic mind, the time and place would come—I would drink

42:0   again. They had said that though I did raise a defense, it would one day give way before some trivial reason for having a drink. Well, just that did happen and more, for what I had learned of alcoholism did not occur to me at all. I knew from that moment that I had an alcoholic mind. I saw that will power and self-knowledge would not help in those strange mental blank spots. I had never been able to understand people who said that a problem had them hopelessly defeated. I knew then. It was a crushing blow.

42:1   "Two of the members of Alcoholics Anonymous came to see me. They grinned, which I didn't like so much, and then asked me if I thought myself alcoholic and if I were really licked this time. I had to concede both propositions. They piled on me heaps of evidence to the effect that an alcoholic mentality, such as I had exhibited in Washington, was a hopeless condition. They cited cases out of their own experience by the dozen. This process snuffed out the last flicker of conviction that I could do the job myself.

42:2   "Then they outlined the spiritual answer and program of action which a hundred of them had followed successfully. Though I had been only a nominal churchman, their proposals were not, intellectually, hard to swallow. But the program of action, though entirely sensible, was pretty drastic. It meant I would have to throw several lifelong conceptions out of the window. That was not easy. But the moment I made up my mind to go through with the process, I had the curious feeling that my alcoholic condition was relieved, as in fact it proved to be.

42:3   "Quite as important was the discovery that spiritual principles would solve all my problems. I have since

43:0 been brought into a way of living infinitely more satisfy-ing and, I hope, more useful than the life I lived before. My old manner of life was by no means a bad one, but I would not exchange its best moments for the worst I have now. I would not go back to it even if I could."

43:1 Fred's story speaks for itself. We hope it strikes home to thousands like him. He had felt only the first nip of the wringer. Most alcoholics have to be pretty badly mangled before they really commence to solve their problems.

43:2 Many doctors and psychiatrists agree with our con-clusions. One of these men, staff member of a world-renowned hospital[1], recently made this statement to some of us: "What you say about the general hopelessness of the average alcoholic's plight is, in my opinion, correct. As to two of you men, whose stories I have heard, there is no doubt in my mind that you were 100% hopeless, apart from divine help. Had you offered yourselves as patients at this hospital, I would not have taken you, if I had been able to avoid it. People like you are too heart-breaking. Though not a religious person, I have pro-found respect for the spiritual approach in such cases as yours. For most cases, there is virtually no other solution."

43:3 Once more: The alcoholic at certain times has no effective mental defense against the first drink. Except in a few rare cases, neither he nor any other human being can provide such a defense. His defense must come from a Higher Power.

---

[1] Doctor Percy Polick, Bellevue Hospital, New York, NY.

Chapter 4

WE AGNOSTICS

44:1 *I*N THE PRECEDING chapters you have learned something of alcoholism. We hope we have made clear the distinction between the alcoholic and the non-alcoholic. If, when you honestly want to, you find you cannot quit entirely, or if when drinking, you have little control over the amount you take, you are probably alcoholic. If that be the case, you may be suffering from an illness which only a spiritual experience will conquer.

44:2 To one who feels he is an atheist or agnostic such an experience seems impossible, but to continue as he is means disaster, especially if he is an alcoholic of the hopeless variety. To be doomed to an alcoholic death or to live on a spiritual basis are not always easy alternatives to face.[1]

44:3 But it isn't so difficult. About half our original[2] fellowship were of exactly that type. At first some of us tried to avoid the issue, hoping against hope we were not true alcoholics. But after a while we had to face the fact that we must find a spiritual basis of life—or else. Perhaps it is going to be that way with you. But cheer up, something like half[3] of us thought we were atheists or agnostics. Our experience shows that you need not be disconcerted.

44:4 If a mere code of morals or a better philosophy of life were sufficient to overcome alcoholism, many of us

[1] In the first edition this read: "To be doomed to an alcoholic death or to live on a spiritual basis--not always easy alternatives to face."

[2] The word "original" did not appear in the first edition.

[3] In the first edition this read: "fifty."

45:0   would have recovered long ago. But we found that such codes and philosophies did not save us, no matter how much we tried. We could wish to be moral, we could wish to be philosophically comforted, in fact, we could will these things with all our might, but the needed power wasn't there. Our human resources, as marshalled by the will, were not sufficient; they failed utterly.

45:1   Lack of power, that was our dilemma. We had to find a power by which we could live, and it had to be a *Power greater than ourselves.* Obviously. But where and how were we to find this Power?

45:2   Well, that's exactly what this book is about. Its main object is to enable you to find a Power greater than yourself which will solve your problem. That means we have written a book which we believe to be spiritual as well as moral. And it means, of course, that we are going to talk about God. Here difficulty arises with agnostics. Many times we talk to a new man and watch his hope rise as we discuss his alcoholic problems and explain our fellowship. But his face falls when we speak of spiritual matters, especially when we mention God, for we have re-opened a subject which our man thought he had neatly evaded or entirely ignored.

45:3   We know how he feels. We have shared his honest doubt and prejudice. Some of us have been violently anti-religious. To others, the word "God" brought up a particular idea of Him with which someone had tried to impress them during childhood. Perhaps we rejected this particular conception because it seemed inadequate. With that rejection we imagined we had abandoned the God idea entirely. We were bothered

46:0 with the thought that faith and dependence upon a Power beyond ourselves was somewhat weak, even cowardly. We looked upon this world of warring individuals, warring theological systems, and inexplicable calamity, with deep skepticism. We looked askance at many individuals who claimed to be godly. How could a Supreme Being have anything to do with it all? And who could comprehend a Supreme Being anyhow? Yet, in other moments, we found ourselves thinking, when enchanted by a starlit night, "Who, then, made all this?" There was a feeling of awe and wonder, but it was fleeting and soon lost.

46:1 Yes, we of agnostic temperament have had these thoughts and experiences. Let us make haste to reassure you. We found that as soon as we were able to lay aside prejudice and express even a willingness to believe in a Power greater than ourselves, we commenced to get results, even though it was impossible for any of us to fully define or comprehend that Power, which is God.

46:2 Much to our relief, we discovered we did not need to consider another's conception of God. Our own conception, however inadequate, was sufficient to make the approach and to effect a contact with Him. As soon as we admitted the possible existence of a Creative Intelligence, a Spirit of the Universe underlying the totality of things, we began to be possessed of a new sense of power and direction, provided we took other simple steps. We found that God does not make too hard terms with those who seek Him. To us, the Realm of Spirit is broad, roomy, all inclusive; never exclusive or forbidding to those who earnestly seek. It is open, we believe, to all men.

47:1   When, therefore, we speak to you of God, we mean your own conception of God. This applies, too, to other spiritual expressions which you find in this book. Do not let any prejudice you may have against spiritual terms deter you from honestly asking yourself what they mean to you. At the start, this was[1] all we needed to commence spiritual growth, to effect our first conscious relation with God as we understood Him. Afterward, we found ourselves accepting many things which then seemed entirely out of reach. That was growth, but if we wished to grow we had to begin somewhere.[2] So we used our own conception, however limited it was.

47:2   We needed to ask ourselves but one short question. "Do I now believe, or am I even willing to believe, that there is a Power greater than myself?" As soon as a man can say that he does believe, or is willing to believe, we emphatically assure him that he is on his way. It has been repeatedly proven among us that upon this simple cornerstone a wonderfully effective spiritual structure can be built.*

47:3   That was great news to us, for we had assumed we could not make use of spiritual principles unless we accepted many things on faith which seemed difficult to believe. When people presented us with spiritual approaches, how frequently did we all say, "I wish I had what that man has. I'm sure it would work if I could only believe as he believes. But I cannot accept as surely true the many articles of faith which are so plain to him." So it was comforting to learn that we could commence at a simpler level.

47:4   Besides a seeming inability to accept much on faith,

---

* Please be sure to read "Spiritual Experience."

[1] In the first edition this read: "is."

[2] In the first edition this read: "That is growth, but if we wished to grow, we had to begin somewhere."

48:0   we often found ourselves handicapped by obstinacy, sensitiveness, and unreasoning prejudice. Many of us have been so touchy that even casual reference to spiritual things made us bristle with antagonism. This sort of thinking had to be abandoned. Though some of us resisted, we found no great difficulty in casting aside such feelings. Faced with alcoholic destruction, we soon became as open minded on spiritual matters as we had tried to be on other questions. In this respect alcohol was a great persuader. It finally beat us into a state of reasonableness. Sometimes this was a tedious process; we hope no one else will be prejudiced for as long as some of us were.

48:1   The reader may still ask why he should believe in a Power greater than himself. We think there are good reasons. Let us have a look at some of them.

48:2   The practical individual of today is a stickler for facts and results. Nevertheless, the twentieth century readily accepts theories of all kinds, provided they are firmly grounded in fact. We have numerous theories, for example, about electricity. Everybody believes them without a murmur of doubt. Why this ready acceptance? Simply because it is impossible to explain what we see, feel, direct, and use, without a reasonable assumption as a starting point.

48:3   Everybody nowadays, believes in scores of assumptions for which there is good evidence, but no perfect visual proof. And does not science demonstrate that visual proof is the weakest proof? It is being constantly revealed, as mankind studies the material world, that outward appearances are not inward reality at all. To illustrate:

48:4   The prosaic steel girder is a mass of electrons whirl-

49:0   ing around each other at incredible speed. These tiny
bodies are governed by precise laws, and these laws hold
true throughout the material world. Science tells us so.
We have no reason to doubt it. When, however, the perfectly logical assumption is suggested that underneath
the material world and life as we see it, there is an All
Powerful, Guiding, Creative Intelligence, right there our
perverse streak comes to the surface and we laboriously
set out to convince ourselves it isn't so. We read wordy
books and indulge in windy arguments, thinking we
believe this universe needs no God to explain it. Were
our contentions true, it would follow that life originated
out of nothing, means nothing, and proceeds nowhere.

49:1   Instead of regarding ourselves as intelligent agents,
spearheads of God's ever advancing Creation, we agnostics and atheists chose to believe that our human
intelligence was the last word, the alpha and the omega,
the beginning and end of all. Rather vain of us, wasn't
it?

49:2   We, who have traveled this dubious path, beg
you to lay aside prejudice, even against organized
religion. We have learned that whatever the human
frailties of various faiths may be, those faiths have
given purpose and direction to millions. People of
faith have a logical idea of what life is all about.
Actually, we used to have no reasonable conception
whatever. We used to amuse ourselves by cynically
dissecting spiritual beliefs and practices when we
might have observed that many spiritually-minded
persons of all races, colors, and creeds were demonstrating a degree of stability, happiness and usefulness which we should have sought ourselves.

50:1   Instead, we looked at the human defects of these people, and sometimes used their shortcomings as a basis of wholesale condemnation. We talked of intolerance, while we were intolerant ourselves. We missed the reality and the beauty of the forest because we were diverted by the ugliness of some of its trees. We never gave the spiritual side of life a fair hearing.

50:2   In our personal stories you will find a[1] wide variation in the way each teller approaches and conceives of the Power which is greater than himself. Whether we agree with a particular approach or conception seems to make little difference. Experience has taught us[2] that these are matters about which, for our purpose, we need not be worried. They are questions for each individual to settle for himself.

50:3   On one proposition, however, these men and women are strikingly agreed. Every one of them has gained access to, and believes in, a Power greater than himself. This Power has in each case accomplished the miraculous, the humanly impossible. As a celebrated American statesman[3] put it, "Let's look at the record."

50:4   Here are thousands[4] of men and women, worldly indeed. They flatly declare that since they have come to believe in a Power greater than themselves, to take a certain attitude toward that Power, and to do certain simple things, there has been a revolutionary change in their way of living and thinking. In the face of collapse and despair, in the face of the total failure of their human resources, they found that a new power, peace, happiness, and sense of direction flowed into them. This happened soon after they wholeheartedly met a few simple requirements. Once con-

---

[1] The word "a" did not appear in the first edition.

[2] The word "us" did not appear in the first edition.

[3] Alfred E. Smith, Governor of New York State.

[4] In the first edition this read: "one hundred."

51:0 fused and baffled by the seeming futility of existence, they show the underlying reasons why they were making heavy going of life.[1] Leaving aside the drink question, they tell why living was so unsatisfactory. They show how the change came over them.[2] When many hundreds of people are[3] able to say that the consciousness of the Presence of God is today the most important fact of their lives, they present a powerful reason why one should have faith.

51:1 This world of ours has made more material progress in the last century than in all the millenniums which went before. Almost everyone knows the reason. Students of ancient history tell us that the intellect of men in those days was equal to the best of today. Yet in ancient times material progress was painfully slow. The spirit of modern scientific inquiry, research and invention was almost unknown. In the realm of the material, men's minds were fettered by superstition, tradition, and all sorts of fixed ideas. Some of the contemporaries of Columbus[4] thought a round earth preposterous. Others came near putting Galileo[5] to death for his astronomical heresies.[6]

51:2 We asked ourselves this: Are not some of us just as biased and unreasonable about the realm of the spirit as were the ancients about the realm of the material? Even in the present century, American newspapers were afraid to print an account of the Wright brothers' first successful flight at Kitty Hawk.[7] Had not all efforts at flight failed before? Did not Professor Langley's flying machine go to the bottom of the Potomac River?[8] Was it not true that the best mathematical minds had proved man could never fly? Had not people said God had reserved this privilege to the

---

[1] In the first edition this read: "...they will show the underlying reasons why they were making heavy going of life. "

[2] In the first edition this read: "They will show how the change came over them."

[3] In the first edition this read: "When one hundred people, are..."

[4] Christopher Columbus. Italian explorer often credited with the discovery of North America.

[5] Galileo Galilei. Italian physicist and astronomer persecuted for his belief that the earth rotated around the sun. He died under house arrest in 1642.

[6] In the first edition this read: "Others like them came near putting Galileo to death for his astronomical heresies."

[7] Wilbur and Orville Wright flew the first piloted airplane, at Kitty Hawk, North Carolina in 1903.

[8] Samuel Langley. Launched the first successful nonpiloted airplane in 1896.   He later launched a larger plane that crashed and sank into the Potomac River near Washington D.C..

52:0 birds? Only thirty years later the conquest of the air was almost an old story and airplane travel was in full swing.

52:1 But in most fields our generation has witnessed complete liberation of our thinking. Show any longshoreman a Sunday supplement describing a proposal to explore the moon by means of a rocket and he will say "I bet they do it — maybe not so long either."[1] Is not our age characterized by the ease with which we discard old ideas for new, by the complete readiness with which we throw away the theory or gadget which does not work for something new which does?

52:2 We had to ask ourselves why we shouldn't apply to our human problems this same readiness to change our point of view.[2] We were having trouble with personal relationships, we couldn't control our emotional natures, we were a prey to misery and depression, we couldn't make a living, we had a feeling of uselessness, we were full of fear, we were unhappy, we couldn't seem to be of real help to other people — was not a basic solution of these bedevilments more important than whether we should see newsreels of lunar flight? Of course it was.

52:3 When we saw others solve their problems by a[3] simple reliance upon the Spirit of the Universe, we had to stop doubting the power of God. Our ideas did not work. But the God idea did.

52:4 The Wright brothers' almost childish faith that they could build a machine which would fly was the mainspring of their accomplishment. Without that, nothing could have happened. We agnostics and atheists were sticking to the idea that self-sufficiency would solve our problems. When others showed us that "God-suf-

---

[1] Not actually accomplished until 1969.

[2] In the first edition this read: "...this same readiness to change the point of view."

[3] The word "a" did not appear in the first edition.

53:0 ficiency" worked with them, we began to feel like those who had insisted the Wrights would never fly.

53:1 Logic is great stuff. We liked it. We still like it. It is not by chance we were given the power to reason, to examine the evidence of our senses, and to draw conclusions. That is one of man's magnificent attributes. We agnostically inclined would not feel satisfied with a proposal which does not lend itself to reasonable approach and interpretation. Hence we are at pains to tell why we think our present faith is reasonable, why we think it more sane and logical to believe than not to believe, why we say our former thinking was soft and mushy when we threw up our hands in doubt and said, "We don't know."

53:2 When we became alcoholics, crushed by a self-imposed crisis we could not postpone or evade, we had to fearlessly face the proposition that either God is everything or else He is nothing. God either is, or He isn't. What was our choice to be?

53:3 Arrived at this point, we were squarely confronted with the question of faith. We couldn't duck the issue. Some of us had already walked far over the Bridge of Reason toward the desired shore of faith. The outlines and the promise of the New Land had brought lustre to tired eyes and fresh courage to flagging spirits. Friendly hands had stretched out in welcome. We were grateful that Reason had brought us so far. But somehow, we couldn't quite step ashore. Perhaps we had been leaning too heavily on Reason that last mile and we did not like to lose our support.

53:4 That was natural, but let us think a little more closely. Without knowing it, had we not been brought to where we stood by a certain kind of faith? For did

54:0   we not believe in our own reasoning? Did we not have confidence in our ability to think? What was that but a sort of faith? Yes, we had been faithful, abjectly faithful to the God of Reason. So, in one way or another, we discovered that faith had been involved all the time!

54:1   We found, too, that we had been worshippers. What a state of mental goose-flesh that used to bring on! Had we not variously worshipped people, sentiment, things, money, and ourselves? And then, with a better motive, had we not worshipfully beheld the sunset, the sea, or a flower? Who of us had not loved something or somebody? How much did these feelings, these loves, these worships, have to do with pure reason? Little or nothing, we saw at last. Were not these things the tissue out of which our lives were constructed? Did not these feelings, after all, determine the course of our existence? It was impossible to say we had no capacity for faith, or love, or worship. In one form or another we had been living by faith and little else.

54:2   Imagine life without faith! Were nothing left but pure reason, it wouldn't be life. But we believed in life — of course we did. We could not prove life in the sense that you can prove a straight line is the shortest distance between two points, yet, there it was. Could we still say the whole thing was nothing but a mass of electrons, created out of nothing, meaning nothing, whirling on to a destiny of nothingness? Of course we couldn't. The electrons themselves seemed more intelligent than that. At least, so the chemist said.

54:3   Hence, we saw that reason isn't everything. Neither is reason, as most of us use it, entirely dependable,

55:0 though it emanate from our best minds. What about people who proved that man could never fly?

55:1 Yet we had been seeing another kind of flight, a spiritual liberation from this world, people who rose above their problems. They said God made these things possible, and we only smiled. We had seen spiritual release, but liked to tell ourselves it wasn't true.

55:2 Actually we were fooling ourselves, for deep down in every man, woman, and child, is the fundamental idea of God. It may be obscured by calamity, by pomp, by worship of other things, but in some form or other it is there. For faith in a Power greater than ourselves, and miraculous demonstrations of that power in human lives, are facts as old as man himself.

55:3 We finally saw that faith in some kind of God was a part of our make-up, just as much as the feeling we have for a friend. Sometimes we had to search fearlessly, but He was there. He was as much a fact as we were. We found the Great Reality deep down within us. In the last analysis it is only there that He may be found. It was so with us.

55:4 We can only clear the ground a bit. If our testimony helps sweep away prejudice, enables you to think honestly, encourages you to search diligently within yourself, then, if you wish, you can join us on the Broad Highway. With this attitude you cannot fail. The consciousness of your belief is sure to come to you.

55:5 In this book you will read the experience of a man who thought he was an atheist. His story is so interesting that some of it should be told now. His change of heart was dramatic, convincing, and moving.

56:1   Our friend was a minister's son. He attended church school, where he became rebellious at what he thought an overdose of religious education. For years thereafter he was dogged by trouble and frustration. Business failure, insanity, fatal illness, suicide — these calamities in his immediate family embittered and depressed him. Post-war disillusionment, ever more serious alcoholism, impending mental and physical collapse, brought him to the point of self-destruction.

56:2   One night, when confined in a hospital, he was approached by an alcoholic who had known a spiritual experience. Our friend's gorge rose as he bitterly cried out: "If there is a God, He certainly hasn't done anything for me!" But later, alone in his room, he asked himself this question: "Is it possible that all the religious people I have known are wrong?" While pondering the answer he felt as though he lived in hell. Then, like a thunderbolt, a great thought came. It crowded out all else:

56:3   *"Who are you to say there is no God?"*

56:4   This man recounts that he tumbled out of bed to his knees. In a few seconds he was overwhelmed by a conviction of the Presence of God. It poured over and through him with the certainty and majesty of a great tide at flood. The barriers he had built through the years were swept away. He stood in the Presence of Infinite Power and Love. He had stepped from bridge to shore. For the first time, he lived in conscious companionship with his Creator.

56:5   Thus was our friend's cornerstone fixed in place. No later vicissitude has shaken it. His alcoholic problem was taken away. That very night, years ago, it[1] dis-

---

[1] In the first edition this read: "That very night three years ago it..."

57:0 appeared. Save for a few brief moments of temptation the thought of drink has never returned; and at such times a great revulsion has risen up in him. Seemingly he could not drink even if he would. God had restored his sanity.

57:1 What is this but a miracle of healing? Yet its elements are simple. Circumstances made him willing to believe. He humbly offered himself to his Maker — then he knew.

57:2 Even so has God restored us all to our right minds. To this man, the revelation was sudden. Some of us grow into it more slowly. But He has come to all who have honestly sought Him.

57:3 When we drew near to Him He disclosed Himself to us!

Chapter 5

HOW IT WORKS

58:1 RARELY HAVE we seen a person fail who has thoroughly followed our path. Those who do not recover are people who cannot or will not completely give themselves to this simple program, usually men and women who are constitutionally incapable of being honest with themselves. There are such unfortunates. They are not at fault; they seem to have been born that way. They are naturally incapable of grasping and developing a manner of living which demands rigorous honesty. Their chances are less than average. There are those, too, who suffer from grave emotional and mental disorders, but many of them do recover if they have the capacity to be honest.

58:2 Our stories disclose in a general way what we used to be like, what happened, and what we are like now. If you have decided you want what we have and are willing to go to any length to get it-then you are ready to take certain steps.

58:3 At some of these we balked. We thought we could find an easier, softer way. But we could not. With all the earnestness at our command, we beg of you to be fearless and thorough from the very start. Some of us have tried to hold on to our old ideas and the result was nil until we let go absolutely.

58:4 Remember that we deal with alcohol-cunning, baf-

59:0 fling, powerful! Without help it is too much for us. But there is One who has all power-that One is God. May you find Him now!

59:1 Half measures availed us nothing. We stood at the turning point. We asked His protection and care with complete abandon.

59:2 Here are the steps we took, which are suggested as a program of recovery:

1. We admitted we were powerless over alcohol—that our lives had become unmanageable.
2. Came to believe that a Power greater than ourselves could restore us to sanity.
3. Made a decision to turn our will and our lives over to the care of God *as we understood Him.*
4. Made a searching and fearless moral inventory of ourselves.
5. Admitted to God, to ourselves, and to another human being the exact nature of our wrongs.
6. Were entirely ready to have God remove all these defects of character.
7. Humbly asked Him to remove our shortcomings.
8. Made a list of all persons we had harmed, and became willing to make amends to them all.
9. Made direct amends to such people wherever possible, except when to do so would injure them or others.
10. Continued to take personal inventory and when we were wrong promptly admitted it.
11. Sought through prayer and meditation to improve our conscious contact with God *as we understood Him,* praying only for knowledge of His will for us and the power to carry that out.

60:0   12. Having had a spiritual awakening[1] as the result of these steps, we tried to carry this message to alcoholics, and to practice these principles in all our affairs.

60:1   Many of us exclaimed, "What an order! I can't go through with it." Do not be discouraged. No one among us has been able to maintain anything like perfect adherence to these principles. We are not saints. The point is, that we are willing to grow along spiritual lines. The principles we have set down are guides to progress. We claim spiritual progress rather than spiritual perfection.

60:2   Our description of the alcoholic, the chapter to the agnostic, and our personal adventures before and after make clear three pertinent ideas:

    (a) That we were alcoholic and could not manage our own lives.

    (b) That probably no human power could have relieved our alcoholism.

    (c) That God could and would if He were sought.[2]

60:3   Being convinced, *we were at Step Three*, which is that we decided to turn our will and our life over to God as we understood Him. Just what do we mean by that, and just what do we do?

60:4   The first requirement is that we be convinced that any life run on self-will can hardly be a success. On that basis we are almost always in collision with something or somebody, even though our motives are good. Most people try to live by self-propulsion. Each person is like an actor who wants to run the whole show; is forever trying to arrange the lights, the ballet, the scenery and the rest of the players in his own way. If

---

[1] In the first edition, this read: "experience"

[2] In the first edition, this read: "That God could and would if sought."

61:0   his arrangements would only stay put, if only people would do as he wished, the show would be great. Everybody, including himself, would be pleased. Life would be wonderful. In trying to make these arrangements our actor may sometimes be quite virtuous. He may be kind, considerate, patient, generous; even modest and self-sacrificing. On the other hand, he may be mean, egotistical, selfish and dishonest. But, as with most humans, he is more likely to have varied traits.

61:1   What usually happens? The show doesn't come off very well. He begins to think life doesn't treat him right. He decides to exert himself more.[1] He becomes, on the next occasion, still more demanding or gracious, as the case may be. Still the play does not suit him. Admitting he may be somewhat at fault, he is sure that other people are more to blame. He becomes angry, indignant, self-pitying. What is his basic trouble? Is he not really a self-seeker even when trying to be kind? Is he not a victim of the delusion that he can wrest satisfaction and happiness out of this world if he only manages well? Is it not evident to all the rest of the players that these are the things he wants? And do not his actions make each of them wish to retaliate, snatching all they can get out of the show? Is he not, even in his best moments, a producer of confusion rather than harmony?

61:2   Our actor is self-centered—ego-centric, as people like to call it nowadays. He is like the retired business man who lolls in the Florida sunshine in the winter complaining of the sad state of the nation; the minister who sighs over the sins of the twentieth century; politicians and reformers who are sure all would be Utopia

[1] In the first edition this read: "He decides to exert himself some more."

62:0 if the rest of the world would only behave; the outlaw safe cracker who thinks society has wronged him; and the alcoholic who has lost all and is locked up. Whatever our protestations, are not most of us concerned with ourselves, our resentments, or our self-pity?

62:1   Selfishness—self-centeredness! That, we think, is the root of our troubles. Driven by a hundred forms of fear, self-delusion, self-seeking, and self-pity, we step on the toes of our fellows and they retaliate. Sometimes they hurt us, seemingly without provocation, but we invariably find that at some time in the past we have made decisions based on self which later placed us in a position to be hurt.

62:2   So our troubles, we think, are basically of our own making. They arise out of ourselves, and the alcoholic is an extreme example of self-will run riot, though he usually doesn't think so. Above everything, we alcoholics must be rid of this selfishness. We must, or it kills us! God makes that possible. And there often seems no way of entirely getting rid of self without His aid.[1] Many of us had moral and philosophical convictions galore, but we could not live up to them even though we would have liked to. Neither could we reduce our self-centeredness much by wishing or trying on our own power. We had to have God's help.

62:3   This is the how and why of it. First of all, we had to quit playing God. It didn't work. Next, we decided that hereafter in this drama of life, God was going to be our Director. He is the Principal; we are His agents. He is the Father, and we are His children. Most good ideas are simple, and this concept was the keystone of the new and triumphant arch through which we passed to freedom.

---

[1] In the first edition this read: "And there often seems no way of entirely getting rid of self without Him."

63:1 When we sincerely took such a position, all sorts of remarkable things followed. We had a new Employer. Being all powerful, He provided what we needed, if we kept close to Him and performed His work well. Established on such a footing we became less and less interested in ourselves, our little plans and designs. More and more we became interested in seeing what we could contribute to life. As we felt new power flow in, as we enjoyed peace of mind, as we discovered we could face life successfully, as we became conscious of His presence, we began to lose our fear of today, tomorrow or the hereafter. We were reborn.

63:2 We were now at Step Three. Many of us said to our Maker, *as we understood Him:* "God, I offer myself to Thee-to build with me and to do with me as Thou wilt. Relieve me of the bondage of self, that I may better do Thy will. Take away my difficulties, that victory over them may bear witness to those I would help of Thy Power, Thy Love, and Thy Way of life. May I do Thy will always!" We thought well before taking this step making sure we were ready; that we could at last abandon ourselves utterly to Him.

63:3 We found it very desirable to take this spiritual step with an understanding person, such as our wife, best friend or spiritual adviser. But it is better to meet God alone than with one who might misunderstand. The wording was, of course, quite optional so long as we expressed the idea, voicing it without reservation. This was only a beginning, though if honestly and humbly made, an effect, sometimes a very great one, was felt at once.

63:4 Next we launched out on a course of vigorous action, the first step of which is a personal housecleaning,

64:0   which many of us had never attempted. Though our decision was a vital and crucial step, it could have little permanent effect unless at once followed by a strenuous effort to face, and to be rid of, the things in ourselves which had been blocking us. Our liquor was but a symptom. So we had to get down to causes and conditions.

64:1   Therefore, we started upon a personal inventory. *This was Step Four.* A business which takes no regular inventory usually goes broke. Taking a commercial inventory is a fact-finding and a fact-facing process. It is an effort to discover the truth about the stock-in-trade. One object is to disclose damaged or unsalable goods, to get rid of them promptly and without regret. If the owner of the business is to be successful, he cannot fool himself about values.

64:2   We did exactly the same thing with our lives. We took stock honestly. First, we searched out the flaws in our make-up which caused our failure. Being convinced that self, manifested in various ways, was what had defeated us, we considered its common manifestations.

64:3   Resentment is the "number one" offender. It destroys more alcoholics than anything else. From it stem all forms of spiritual disease, for we have been not only mentally and physically ill, we have been spiritually sick. When the spiritual malady is overcome, we straighten out mentally and physically. In dealing with resentments, we set them on paper. We listed people, institutions or principles with whom we were angry. We asked ourselves why we were angry. In most cases it was found that our self-esteem, our pocketbooks, our ambitions, our personal relationships

65:0   (including sex) were hurt or threatened. So we were sore. We were "burned up."

65:1   On our grudge list we set opposite each name our injuries. Was it our self-esteem, our security, our ambitions, our personal, or sex relations, which had been interfered with?

65:2   We were usually as definite as this example:

I'm resentful at:	The Cause:	Affects My:
Mr. Brown	His attention to my wife.	Sex relations.
		Self-esteem (fear)
	Told my wife of my mistress.	Sex relations.
		Self-esteem (fear)
	Brown may get my job at the office.	Security.
		Self-esteem (fear)
Mrs. Jones	She's a nut—she snubbed me. She committed her husband for drinking. He's my friend. She's a gossip.	Personal relationship. Self esteem (fear)
My employer	Unreasonable—Unjust —Overbearing— Threatens to fire me for drinking and padding my expense account.	Self-esteem (fear) Security.
My wife	Misunderstands and nags. Likes Brown. Wants house put in her name.	Pride—Personal sex relations[1]— Security (fear)

65:3   We went back through our lives. Nothing counted but thoroughness and honesty. When we were finished we considered it carefully. The first thing ap-

---

[1] In the first edition this read: "Personal and sex relations."

66:0 parent was that this world and its people were often quite wrong. To conclude that others were wrong was as far as most of us ever got. The usual outcome was that people continued to wrong us and we stayed sore. Sometimes it was remorse and then we were sore at ourselves. But the more we fought and tried to have our own way, the worse matters got. As in war, the victor only *seemed* to win. Our moments of triumph were short-lived.

66:1 It is plain that a life which includes deep resentment leads only to futility and unhappiness. To the precise extent that we permit these, do we squander the hours that might have been worth while. But with the alcoholic, whose hope is the maintenance and growth of a spiritual experience, this business of resentment is infinitely grave. We found that it is fatal. For when harboring such feelings we shut ourselves off from the sunlight of the Spirit. The insanity of alcohol returns and we drink again. And with us, to drink is to die.

66:2 If we were to live, we had to be free of anger. The grouch and the brainstorm were not for us. They may be the dubious luxury of normal men, but for alcoholics these things are poison.

66:3 We turned back to the list, for it held the key to the future. We were prepared to look at it from an entirely different angle. We began to see that the world and its people really dominated us. In that state, the wrongdoing of others, fancied or real, had power to actually kill. How could we escape? We saw that these resentments must be mastered, but how? We could not wish them away any more than alcohol.

66:4 This was our course: We realized that the people who wronged us were perhaps spiritually sick.

67:0   Though we did not like their symptoms and the way these disturbed us, they, like ourselves, were sick too. We asked God to help us show them the same tolerance, pity, and patience that we would cheerfully grant a sick friend. When a person offended we said to ourselves, "This is a sick man. How can I be helpful to him? God save me from being angry. Thy will be done."

67:1   We avoid retaliation or argument. We wouldn't treat sick people that way. If we do, we destroy our chance of being helpful. We cannot be helpful to all people, but at least God will show us how to take a kindly and tolerant view of each and every one.

67:2   Referring to our list again. Putting out of our minds the wrongs others had done, we resolutely looked for our own mistakes. Where had we been selfish, dishonest, self-seeking and frightened? Though a situation had not been entirely our fault, we tried to disregard the other person involved entirely. Where were we to blame? The inventory was ours, not the other man's. When we saw our faults we listed them. We placed them before us in black and white. We admitted our wrongs honestly and were willing to set these matters straight.

67:3   Notice that the word "fear" is bracketed alongside the difficulties with Mr. Brown, Mrs. Jones, the employer, and the wife. This short word somehow touches about every aspect of our lives. It was an evil and corroding thread; the fabric of our existence was shot through with it. It set in motion trains of circumstances which brought us misfortune we felt we didn't deserve. But did not we, ourselves, set the ball rolling? Sometimes

68:0 we think fear ought to be classed with stealing. It seems to cause more trouble.

68:1 We reviewed our fears thoroughly. We put them on paper, even though we had no resentment in connection with them. We asked ourselves why we had them. Wasn't it because self-reliance failed us? Self-reliance was good as far as it went, but it didn't go far enough. Some of us once had great self-confidence, but it didn't fully solve the fear problem, or any other. When it made us cocky, it was worse.

68:2 Perhaps there is a better way—we think so. For we are now on a different basis; the basis of trusting and relying upon God. We trust infinite God rather than our finite selves. We are in the world to play the role He assigns. Just to the extent that we do as we think He would have us, and humbly rely on Him, does He enable us to match calamity with serenity.

68:3 We never apologize to anyone for depending upon our Creator. We can laugh at those who think spirituality the way of weakness. Paradoxically, it is the way of strength. The verdict of the ages is that faith means courage. All men of faith have courage. They trust their God. We never apologize for God. Instead we let Him demonstrate, through us, what He can do. We ask Him to remove our fear and direct our attention to what He would have us be. At once, we commence to outgrow fear.

68:4 Now about sex. Many of us needed an overhauling there. But above all, we tried to be sensible on this question. It's so easy to get way off the track. Here we find human opinions running to extremes—absurd extremes, perhaps. One set of voices cry that sex is a lust of our lower nature, a base necessity of procrea-

69:0 tion. Then we have the voices who cry for sex and more sex; who bewail the institution of marriage; who think that most of the troubles of the race are traceable to sex causes. They think we do not have enough of it, or that it isn't the right kind. They see its significance everywhere. One school would allow man no flavor for his fare and the other would have us all on a straight pepper diet. We want to stay out of this controversy. We do not want to be the arbiter of anyone's sex conduct. We all have sex problems. We'd hardly be human if we didn't. What can we do about them?

69:1 We reviewed our own conduct over the years past. Where had we been selfish, dishonest, or inconsiderate? Whom had we hurt? Did we unjustifiably arouse jealousy, suspicion or bitterness? Where were we at fault, what should we have done instead? We got this all down on paper and looked at it.

69:2 In this way we tried to shape a sane and sound ideal for our future sex life. We subjected each relation to this test—was it selfish or not? We asked God to mold our ideals and help us to live up to them. We remembered always that our sex powers were God-given and therefore good, neither to be used lightly or selfishly nor to be despised and loathed.

69:3 Whatever our ideal turns out to be, we must be willing to grow toward it. We must be willing to make amends where we have done harm, provided that we do not bring about still more harm in so doing. In other words, we treat sex as we would any other problem. In meditation, we ask God what we should do about each specific matter. The right answer will come, if we want it.

69:4 God alone can judge our sex situation. Counsel with

70:0 persons is often desirable, but we let God be the final judge. We realize that some people are as fanatical about sex as others are loose. We avoid hysterical thinking or advice.

70:1 Suppose we fall short of the chosen ideal and stumble? Does this mean we are going to get drunk? Some people tell us so. But this is only a half-truth. It depends on us and on our motives. If we are sorry for what we have done, and have the honest desire to let God take us to better things, we believe we will be forgiven and will have learned our lesson. If we are not sorry, and our conduct continues to harm others, we are quite sure to drink. We are not theorizing. These are facts out of our experience.

70:2 To sum up about sex: We earnestly pray for the right ideal, for guidance in each questionable situation, for sanity, and for the strength to do the right thing. If sex is very troublesome, we throw ourselves the harder into helping others. We think of their needs and work for them. This takes us out of ourselves. It quiets the imperious urge, when to yield would mean heartache.

70:3 If we have been thorough about our personal inventory, we have written down a lot. We have listed and analyzed our resentments. We have begun to comprehend their futility and their fatality. We have commenced to see their terrible destructiveness. We have begun to learn tolerance, patience and good will toward all men, even our enemies, for we look on them as sick people. We have listed the people we have hurt by our conduct, and are willing to straighten out the past if we can.

70:4 In this book you read again and again that faith did

71:0 for us what we could not do for ourselves. We hope you are convinced now that God can remove whatever self-will has blocked you off from Him. If you have already made a decision, and an inventory of your grosser handicaps, you have made a good beginning. That being so you have swallowed and digested some big chunks of truth about yourself.

Chapter 6

INTO ACTION

72:1 AVING MADE our personal inventory, what shall we do about it? We have been trying to get a new attitude, a new relationship with our Creator, and to discover the obstacles in our path. We have admitted certain defects; we have ascertained in a rough way what the trouble is; we have put our finger on the weak items in our personal inventory. Now these are about to be cast out. This requires action on our part, which, when completed, will mean that we have admitted to God, to ourselves, and to another human being, the exact nature of our defects. This brings us to *the Fifth Step* in the program of recovery mentioned in the preceding chapter.

72:2 This is perhaps difficult—especially discussing our defects with another person. We think we have done well enough in admitting these things to ourselves. There is doubt about that. In actual practice, we usually find a solitary self-appraisal insufficient. Many of us thought it necessary to go much further. We will be more reconciled to discussing ourselves with another person when we see good reasons why we should do so. The best reason first: If we skip this vital step, we may not overcome drinking. Time after time newcomers have tried to keep to themselves certain facts about their lives. Trying to avoid this humbling experience, they have turned to easier methods. Almost

73:0   invariably they got drunk. Having persevered with the rest of the program, they wondered why they fell. We think the reason is that they never completed their house-cleaning. They took inventory all right, but hung on to some of the worst items in stock. They only *thought* they had lost their egoism and fear; they only *thought* they had humbled themselves. But they had not learned enough of humility, fearlessness and honesty, in the sense we find it necessary, until they told someone else *all* their life story.

73:1   More than most people, the alcoholic leads a double life. He is very much the actor. To the outer world he presents his stage character. This is the one he likes his fellows to see. He wants to enjoy a certain reputation, but knows in his heart he doesn't deserve it.

73:2   The inconsistency is made worse by the things he does on his sprees. Coming to his senses, he is revolted at certain episodes he vaguely remembers. These memories are a nightmare. He trembles to think someone might have observed him. As fast as he can, he pushes these memories far inside himself. He hopes they will never see the light of day. He is under constant fear and tension—that makes for more drinking.

73:3   Psychologists are inclined to agree with us. We have spent thousands of dollars for examinations. We know but few instances where we have given these doctors a fair break. We have seldom told them the whole truth nor have we followed their advice. Unwilling to be honest with these sympathetic men, we were honest with no one else. Small wonder many in the medical profession have a low opinion of alcoholics and their chance for recovery!

73:4   We must be entirely honest with somebody if we

74:0 expect to live long or happily in this world. Rightly and naturally, we think well before we choose the person or persons with whom to take this intimate and confidential step. Those of us belonging to a religious denomination which requires confession must, and of course, will want to go to the properly appointed authority whose duty it is to receive it. Though we have no religious connection, we may still do well to talk with someone ordained by an established religion. We often find such a person quick to see and understand our problem. Of course, we sometimes encounter people who do not understand alcoholics.

74:1 If we cannot or would rather not do this, we search our acquaintance for a close-mouthed, understanding friend. Perhaps our doctor or psychologist will be the person. It may be one of our own family, but we cannot disclose anything to our wives or our parents which will hurt them and make them unhappy. We have no right to save our own skin at another person's expense. Such parts of our story we tell to someone who will understand, yet be unaffected. The rule is we must be hard on ourself, but always considerate of others.

74:2 Notwithstanding the great necessity for discussing ourselves with someone, it may be one is so situated that there is no suitable person available. If that is so, this step may be postponed, only, however, if we hold ourselves in complete readiness to go through with it at the first opportunity. We say this because we are very anxious that we talk to the right person. It is important that he be able to keep a confidence; that he fully understand and approve what we are driving at;

75:0 that he will not try to change our plan. But we must not use this as a mere excuse to postpone.

75:1 When we decide who is to hear our story, we waste no time. We have a written inventory and we are prepared for a long talk. We explain to our partner what we are about to do and why we have to do it. He should realize that we are engaged upon a life-and-death errand. Most people approached in this way will be glad to help; they will be honored by our confidence.

75:2 We pocket our pride and go to it, illuminating every twist of character, every dark cranny of the past. Once we have taken this step, withholding nothing, we are delighted. We can look the world in the eye. We can be alone at perfect peace and ease. Our fears fall from us. We begin to feel the nearness of our Creator. We may have had certain spiritual beliefs, but now we begin to have a spiritual experience. The feeling that the drink problem has disappeared will often come strongly. We feel we are on the Broad Highway, walking hand in hand with the Spirit of the Universe.

75:3 Returning home we find a place where we can be quiet for an hour, carefully reviewing what we have done. We thank God from the bottom of our heart that we know Him better. Taking this book down from our shelf we turn to the page which contains the twelve steps. Carefully reading the first five proposals we ask if we have omitted anything, for we are building an arch through which we shall walk a free man at last. Is our work solid so far? Are the stones properly in place? Have we skimped on the cement put into the foundation? Have we tried to make mortar without sand?

76:1   If we can answer to our satisfaction, we then look at *Step Six.* We have emphasized willingness as being indispensable. Are we now ready to let God remove from us all the things which we have admitted are objectionable? Can He now take them all—every one? If we still cling to something we will not let go, we ask God to help us be willing.[1]

76:2   When ready, we say something like this: "My Creator, I am now willing that you should have all of me, good and bad. I pray that you now remove from me every single defect of character which stands in the way of my usefulness to you and my fellows. Grant me strength, as I go out from here, to do your bidding. Amen." We have then completed *Step Seven.*

76:3   Now we need more action, without which we find that "Faith without works is dead."[2] Let's look at *Steps Eight and Nine.* We have a list of all persons we have harmed and to whom we are willing to make amends. We made it when we took inventory. We subjected ourselves to a drastic self-appraisal. Now we go out to our fellows and repair the damage done in the past. We attempt to sweep away the debris which has accumulated out of our effort to live on self-will and run the show ourselves. If we haven't the will to do this, we ask until it comes. Remember it was agreed at the beginning *we would go to any lengths for victory over alcohol.*

76:4   Probably there are still some misgivings. As we look over the list of business acquaintances and friends we have hurt, we may feel diffident about going to some of them on a spiritual basis. Let us be reassured. To some people we need not, and probably should not emphasize the spiritual feature on our first approach.

---

[1] In the first edition this read: "Should we still cling to something we will not let go, we ask God to help us be willing."

[2] From the Bible: James 2:20 and 2:26.

77:0 We might prejudice them. At the moment we are trying to put our lives in order. But this is not an end in itself. Our real purpose is to fit ourselves to be of maximum service to God and the people about us. It is seldom wise to approach an individual, who still smarts from our injustice to him, and announce that we have gone religious. In the prize ring, this would be called leading with the chin. Why lay ourselves open to being branded fanatics or religious bores? We may kill a future opportunity to carry a beneficial message. But our man is sure to be impressed with a sincere desire to set right the wrong. He is going to be more interested in a demonstration of good will than in our talk of spiritual discoveries.

77:1 We don't use this as an excuse for shying away from the subject of God. When it will serve any good purpose, we are willing to announce our convictions with tact and common sense. The question of how to approach the man we hated will arise. It may be he has done us more harm than we have done him and, though we may have acquired a better attitude toward him, we are still not too keen about admitting our faults. Nevertheless, with a person we dislike, we take the bit in our teeth. It is harder to go to an enemy than to a friend, but we find it much more beneficial to us. We go to him in a helpful and forgiving spirit, confessing our former ill feeling and expressing our regret.

77:2 Under no condition do we criticize such a person or argue. Simply we tell him that we will never get over drinking until we have done our utmost to straighten out the past. We are there to sweep off our side of the street, realizing that nothing worth while

78:0 can be accomplished until we do so, never trying to tell him what he should do. His faults are not discussed. We stick to our own. If our manner is calm, frank, and open, we will be gratified with the result.

78:1 In nine cases out of ten the unexpected happens. Sometimes the man we are calling upon admits his own fault, so feuds of years' standing melt away in an hour. Rarely do we fail to make satisfactory progress. Our former enemies sometimes praise what we are doing and wish us well. Occasionally, they will offer assistance. It should not matter, however, if someone does throw us out of his office. We have made our demonstration, done our part. It's water over the dam.

78:2 Most alcoholics owe money. We do not dodge our creditors. Telling them what we are trying to do, we make no bones about our drinking; they usually know it anyway, whether we think so or not. Nor are we afraid of disclosing our alcoholism on the theory it may cause financial harm. Approached in this way, the most ruthless creditor will sometimes surprise us. Arranging the best deal we can we let these people know we are sorry. Our drinking has made us slow to pay. We must lose our fear of creditors no matter how far we have to go, for we are liable to drink if we are afraid to face them.

78:3 Perhaps we have committed a criminal offense which might land us in jail if it were known to the authorities. We may be short in our accounts and unable to make good. We have already admitted this in confidence to another person, but we are sure we would be imprisoned or lose our job if it were known. Maybe it's only a petty offense such as padding the expense account. Most of us have done that sort of thing.

79:0   Maybe we are divorced, and have remarried but haven't kept up the alimony to number one. She is indignant about it, and has a warrant out for our arrest. That's a common form of trouble too.

79:1   Although these reparations take innumerable forms, there are some general principles which we find guiding. Reminding ourselves that we have decided to go to any lengths to find a spiritual experience, we ask that we be given strength and direction to do the right thing, no matter what the personal consequences may be. We may lose our position or reputation or face jail, but we are willing. We have to be. We must not shrink at anything.

79:2   Usually, however, other people are involved. Therefore, we are not to be the hasty and foolish martyr who would needlessly sacrifice others to save himself from the alcoholic pit. A man we know had remarried. Because of resentment and drinking, he had not paid alimony to his first wife. She was furious. She went to court and got an order for his arrest. He had commenced our way of life, had secured a position, and was getting his head above water. It would have been impressive heroics if he had walked up to the Judge and said, "Here I am."

79:3   We thought he ought to be willing to do that if necessary, but if he were in jail he could provide nothing for either family. We suggested he write his first wife admitting his faults and asking forgiveness. He did, and also sent a small amount of money. He told her what he would try to do in the future. He said he was perfectly willing to go to jail if she insisted. Of course she did not, and the whole situation has long since been adjusted.

80:1 Before taking drastic action which might implicate other people we secure their consent. If we have obtained permission, have consulted with others, asked God to help and the drastic step is indicated we must not shrink.

80:2 This brings to mind a story about one of our friends. While drinking, he accepted a sum of money from a bitterly-hated business rival, giving him no receipt for it. He subsequently denied having received the money and used the incident as a basis for discrediting the man. He thus used his own wrong-doing as a means of destroying the reputation of another. In fact, his rival was ruined.

80:3 He felt that he had done a wrong he could not possibly make right. If he opened that old affair, he was afraid it would destroy the reputation of his partner, disgrace his family and take away his means of livelihood. What right had he to involve those dependent upon him? How could he possibly make a public statement exonerating his rival?

80:4 After consulting with his wife and partner he came to the conclusion that is was better to take those risks than to stand before his Creator guilty of such ruinous slander. He saw that he had to place the outcome in God's hands or he would soon start drinking again, and all would be lost anyhow. He attended church for the first time in many years. After the sermon, he quietly got up and made an explanation. His action met widespread approval, and today he is one of the most trusted citizens of his town. This all happened years ago.[1]

80:5 The chances are that we have domestic troubles. Perhaps we are mixed up with women in a fashion we

---

[1] In the first edition this read: "This all happened three years ago."

81:0 wouldn't care to have advertised. We doubt if, in this
respect, alcoholics are fundamentally much worse than
other people. But drinking does complicate sex relations in the home. After a few years with an alcoholic, a
wife gets worn out, resentful and uncommunicative. How
could she be anything else? The husband begins to feel
lonely, sorry for himself. He commences to look around
in the night clubs, or their equivalent, for something besides liquor. Perhaps he is having a secret and exciting
affair with "the girl who understands." In fairness we
must say that she may understand, but what are we going to do about a thing like that? A man so involved
often feels very remorseful at times, especially if he is
married to a loyal and courageous girl who has literally
gone through hell for him.

81:1   Whatever the situation, we usually have to do something about it. If we are sure our wife does not know,
should we tell her? Not always, we think. If she knows
in a general way that we have been wild, should we tell
her in detail? Undoubtedly we should admit our fault.
She may insist on knowing all the particulars. She will
want to know who the woman is and where she is. We
feel we ought to say to her that we have no right to involve another person. We are sorry for what we have
done and, God willing, it shall not be repeated. More
than that we cannot do; we have no right to go further.
Though there may be justifiable exceptions, and though
we wish to lay down no rule of any sort, we have often
found this the best course to take.

81:2   Our design for living is not a one-way street. It is
as good for the wife as for the husband. If we can

82:0 forget, so can she. It is better, however, that one does not needlessly name a person upon whom she can vent jealousy.

82:1 Perhaps there are some cases where the utmost frankness is demanded. No outsider can appraise such an intimate situation. It may be that both will decide that the way of good sense and loving kindness is to let by-gones be by-gones. Each might pray about it, having the other one's happiness uppermost in mind. Keep it always in sight that we are dealing with that most terrible human emotion-jealousy. Good generalship may decide that the problem be attacked on the flank rather than risk a face-to-face combat.

82:2 If[1] we have no such complication, there is plenty we should do at home. Sometimes we hear an alcoholic say that the only thing he needs to do is to keep sober. Certainly he must keep sober, for there will be no home if he doesn't. But he is yet a long way from making good to the wife or parents whom for years he has so shockingly treated. Passing all understanding is the patience mothers and wives have had with alcoholics. Had this not been so, many of us would have no homes today, would perhaps be dead.

82:3 The alcoholic is like a tornado roaring his way through the lives of others. Hearts are broken. Sweet relationships are dead. Affections have been uprooted. Selfish and inconsiderate habits have kept the home in turmoil. We feel a man is unthinking when he says that sobriety is enough. He is like the farmer who came up out of his cyclone cellar to find his home ruined. To his wife, he remarked, "Don't see anything the matter here, Ma. Ain't it grand the wind stopped blowin'?"

---

[1] In the first edition this read: "Should."

83:1 Yes, there is a long period of reconstruction ahead. We must take the lead. A remorseful mumbling that we are sorry won't fill the bill at all. We ought to sit down with the family and frankly analyze the past as we now see it, being very careful not to criticize them. Their defects may be glaring, but the chances are that our own actions are partly responsible. So we clean house with the family, asking each morning in meditation that our Creator show us the way of patience, tolerance, kindliness and love.

83:2 The spiritual life is not a theory. *We have to live it.* Unless one's family expresses a desire to live upon spiritual principles we think we ought not to urge them. We should not talk incessantly to them about spiritual matters. They will change in time. Our behavior will convince them more than our words. We must remember that ten or twenty years of drunkenness would make a skeptic out of anyone.

83:3 There may be some wrongs we can never fully right. We don't worry about them if we can honestly say to ourselves that we would right them if we could. Some people cannot be seen—we send them an honest letter. And there may be a valid reason for postponement in some cases. But we don't delay if it can be avoided. We should be sensible, tactful, considerate and humble without being servile or scraping. As God's people we stand on our feet; we don't crawl before anyone.

83:4 If we are painstaking about this phase of our development, we will be amazed before we are half way through. We are going to know a new freedom and a new happiness. We will not regret the past nor wish to shut the door on it. We will comprehend the

84:0 word serenity and we will know peace. No matter how far down the scale we have gone, we will see how our experience can benefit others. That feeling of uselessness and self-pity will disappear. We will lose interest in selfish things and gain interest in our fellows. Self-seeking will slip away. Our whole attitude and outlook upon life will change. Fear of people and of economic insecurity will leave us. We will intuitively know how to handle situations which used to baffle us. We will suddenly realize that God is doing for us what we could not do for ourselves.

84:1 Are these extravagant promises? We think not. They are being fulfilled among us—sometimes quickly, sometimes slowly. They will always materialize if we work for them.

84:2 This thought brings us to *Step Ten*, which suggests we continue to take personal inventory and continue to set right any new mistakes as we go along. We vigorously commenced this way of living as we cleaned up the past. We have entered the world of the Spirit. Our next function is to grow in understanding and effectiveness. This is not an overnight matter. It should continue for our lifetime. Continue to watch for selfishness, dishonesty, resentment, and fear. When these crop up, we ask God at once to remove them. We discuss them with someone immediately and make amends quickly if we have harmed anyone. Then we resolutely turn our thoughts to someone we can help. Love and tolerance of others is our code.

84:3 And we have ceased fighting anything or anyone—even alcohol. For by this time sanity will have returned. We will seldom be interested in liquor. If tempted, we recoil from it as from a hot flame. We

85:0 react sanely and normally, and we will find that this has happened automatically. We will see that our new attitude toward liquor has been given us without any thought or effort on our part. It just comes! That is the miracle of it. We are not fighting it, neither are we avoiding temptation. We feel as though we had been placed in a position of neutrality—safe and protected. We have not even sworn off. Instead, the problem has been removed. It does not exist for us. We are neither cocky nor are we afraid. That is our experience. That is how we react so long as we keep in fit spiritual condition.

85:1 It is easy to let up on the spiritual program of action and rest on our laurels. We are headed for trouble if we do, for alcohol is a subtle foe. We are not cured of alcoholism. What we really have is a daily reprieve contingent on the maintenance of our spiritual condition. Every day is a day when we must carry the vision of God's will into all of our activities. "How can I best serve Thee—Thy will (not mine) be done." These are thoughts which must go with us constantly. We can exercise our will power along this line all we wish. It is the proper use of the will.

85:2 Much has already been said about receiving strength, inspiration, and direction from Him who has all knowledge and power. If we have carefully followed directions, we have begun to sense the flow of His Spirit into us. To some extent we have become God-conscious. We have begun to develop this vital sixth sense. But we must go further and that means more action.

85:3 *Step Eleven* suggests prayer and meditation. We shouldn't be shy on this matter of prayer. Better men

86:0 than we are using it constantly. It works, if we have the proper attitude and work at it. It would be easy to be vague about this matter. Yet, we believe we can make some definite and valuable suggestions.

86:1 When we retire at night, we constructively review our day. Were we resentful, selfish, dishonest or afraid? Do we owe an apology? Have we kept something to ourselves which should be discussed with another person at once? Were we kind and loving toward all? What could we have done better? Were we thinking of ourselves most of the time? Or were we thinking of what we could do for others, of what we could pack into the stream of life? But we must be careful not to drift into worry, remorse or morbid reflection, for that would diminish our usefulness to others. After making our review we ask God's forgiveness and inquire what corrective measures should be taken.

86:2 On awakening let us think about the twenty-four hours ahead. We consider our plans for the day. Before we begin, we ask God to direct our thinking, especially asking that it be divorced from self-pity, dishonest or self-seeking motives. Under these conditions we can employ our mental faculties with assurance, for after all God gave us brains to use. Our thought-life will be placed on a much higher plane when our thinking is cleared of wrong motives.

86:3 In thinking about our day we may face indecision. We may not be able to determine which course to take. Here we ask God for inspiration, an intuitive thought or a decision. We relax and take it easy. We don't struggle. We are often surprised how the right answers come after we have tried this for a while.

87:0 What used to be the hunch or the occasional inspiration gradually becomes a working part of the mind. Being still inexperienced and having just made conscious contact with God, it is not probable that we are going to be inspired at all times. We might pay for this presumption in all sorts of absurd actions and ideas. Nevertheless, we find that our thinking will, as time passes, be more and more on the plane of inspiration. We come to rely upon it.

87:1 We usually conclude the period of meditation with a prayer that we be shown all through the day what our next step is to be, that we be given whatever we need to take care of such problems. We ask especially for freedom from self-will, and are careful to make no request for ourselves only. We may ask for ourselves, however, if others will be helped. We are careful never to pray for our own selfish ends. Many of us have wasted a lot of time doing that and it doesn't work. You can easily see why.

87:2 If circumstances warrant, we ask our wives or friends to join us in morning meditation. If we belong to a religious denomination which requires a definite morning devotion, we attend to that also. If not members of religious bodies, we sometimes select and memorize a few set prayers which emphasize the principles we have been discussing. There are many helpful books also. Suggestions about these may be obtained from one's priest, minister, or rabbi. Be quick to see where religious people are right. Make use of what they offer.

87:3 As we go through the day we pause, when agitated or doubtful, and ask for the right thought or action. We constantly remind ourselves we are no longer

88:0 running the show, humbly saying to ourselves many times each day "Thy will be done." We are then in much less danger of excitement, fear, anger, worry, self-pity, or foolish decisions. We become much more efficient. We do not tire so easily, for we are not burning up energy foolishly as we did when we were trying to arrange life to suit ourselves.

88:1 It works—it really does.

88:2 We alcoholics are undisciplined. So we let God discipline us in the simple way we have just outlined.

88:3 But this is not all. There is action and more action. "Faith without works is dead." The next chapter is entirely devoted to *Step Twelve*.

Chapter 7

WORKING WITH OTHERS

89:1 PRACTICAL EXPERIENCE shows that nothing will so much insure immunity from drinking as intensive work with other alcoholics. It works when other activities fail. This is our *twelfth suggestion*: Carry this message to other alcoholics! You can help when no one else can. You can secure their confidence when others fail. Remember they are very ill.

89:2 Life will take on new meaning. To watch people recover, to see them help others, to watch loneliness vanish, to see a fellowship grow up about you, to have a host of friends—this is an experience you must not miss. We know you will not want to miss it. Frequent contact with newcomers and with each other is the bright spot of our lives.

89:3 Perhaps you are not acquainted with any drinkers who want to recover. You can easily find some by asking a few doctors, ministers, priests or hospitals. They will be only too glad to assist you. Don't start out as an evangelist or reformer. Unfortunately a lot of prejudice exists. You will be handicapped if you arouse it. Ministers and doctors are competent and you can learn much from them if you wish, but it happens that because of your own drinking experience you can be uniquely useful to other alcoholics. So cooperate; never criticize. To be helpful is our only aim.

90:1 When you discover a prospect for Alcoholics Anonymous, find out all you can about him. If he does not want to stop drinking, don't waste time trying to persuade him. You may spoil a later opportunity. This advice is given for his family also. They should be patient, realizing they are dealing with a sick person.

90:2 If there is any indication that he wants to stop, have a good talk with the person most interested in him— usually his wife. Get an idea of his behavior, his problems, his background, the seriousness of his condition, and his religious leanings. You need this information to put yourself in his place, to see how you would like him to approach you if the tables were turned.

90:3 Sometimes[1] it is wise to wait till he goes on a binge. The family may object to this, but unless he is in a dangerous physical condition, it is better to risk it. Don't deal with him when he is very drunk, unless he is ugly and the family needs your help. Wait for the end of the spree, or at least for a lucid interval. Then let his family or a friend ask him if he wants to quit for good and if he would go to any extreme to do so. If he says yes, then his attention should be drawn to you as a person who has recovered. You should be described to him as one of a fellowship who, as part of their own recovery, try to help others and who will be glad to talk to him if he cares to see you.

90:4 If he does not want to see you, never force yourself upon him. Neither should the family hysterically plead with him to do anything, nor should they tell him much about you. They should wait for the end of his next drinking bout. You might place this book where he can see it in the interval. Here no specific rule can be given. The family must decide these

---

[1] In the first edition this read: "Usually."

91:0 things. But urge them not to be over-anxious, for that might spoil matters.

91:1 Usually the family should not try to tell your story. When possible, avoid meeting a man through his family. Approach through a doctor or an institution is a better bet. If your man needs hospitalization, he should have it, but not forcibly unless he is violent. Let the doctor, if he will, tell him he has something in the way of a solution.

91:2 When your man is better, the doctor might suggest a visit from you. Though you have talked with the family, leave them out of the first discussion. Under these conditions your prospect will see he is under no pressure. He will feel he can deal with you without being nagged by his family. Call on him while he is still jittery. He may be more receptive when depressed.

91:3 See your man alone, if possible. At first engage in general conversation. After a while, turn the talk to some phase of drinking. Tell him enough about your drinking habits, symptoms, and experiences to encourage him to speak of himself. If he wishes to talk, let him do so. You will thus get a better idea of how you ought to proceed. If he is not communicative, give him a sketch of your drinking career up to the time you quit. But say nothing, for the moment, of how that was accomplished. If he is in a serious mood dwell on the troubles liquor has caused you, being careful not to moralize or lecture. If his mood is light, tell him humorous stories of your escapades. Get him to tell some of his.

91:4 When he sees you know all about the drinking game, commence to describe yourself as an alcoholic.

92:0   Tell him how baffled you were, how you finally learned that you were sick. Give him an account of the struggles you made to stop. Show him the mental twist which leads to the first drink of a spree. We suggest you do this as we have done it in the chapter on alcoholism. If he is alcoholic, he will understand you at once. He will match your mental inconsistencies with some of his own.

92:1   If you are satisfied that he is a real alcoholic, begin to dwell on the hopeless feature of the malady. Show him, from your own experience, how the queer mental condition surrounding that first drink prevents normal functioning of the will power. Don't, at this stage, refer to this book, unless he has seen it and wishes to discuss it. And be careful not to brand him as[1] an alcoholic. Let him draw his own conclusion. If he sticks to the idea that he can still control his drinking, tell him that possibly he can—if he is not too alcoholic. But insist that if he is severely afflicted, there may be little chance he can recover by himself.

92:2   Continue to speak of alcoholism as an illness, a fatal malady.[2] Talk about the conditions of body and mind which accompany it. Keep his attention focused mainly on your personal experience. Explain that many are doomed who never realize their predicament. Doctors are rightly loath to tell alcoholic patients the whole story unless it will serve some good purpose. But you may talk to him about the hopelessness of alcoholism because you offer a solution. You will soon have your friend admitting he has many, if not all, of the traits of the alcoholic. If his own doctor is willing to tell him that he is alcoholic, so much the better. Even though your protégé may not have en-

---

[1] The word "as" did not appear in the first edition.

[2] In the first edition this read: "Continue to speak of alcoholism as a sickness, a fatal malady."

93:0   tirely admitted his condition, he has become very curious to know how you got well. Let him ask you that
question, if he will. *Tell him exactly what happened
to you.*[1] Stress the spiritual feature freely. If the man
be agnostic or atheist, make it emphatic that *he does
not have to agree with your conception of God.* He
can choose any conception he likes, provided it makes
sense to him. *The main thing is that he be willing to
believe in a Power greater than himself and that he
live by spiritual principles.*

93:1   When dealing with such a person, you had better
use everyday language to describe spiritual principles.
There is no use arousing any prejudice he may have
against certain theological terms and conceptions about
which he may already be confused. Don't raise such
issues, no matter what your own convictions are.

93:2   Your prospect may belong to a religious denomination. His religious education and training may be far superior to yours. In that case he is going to wonder how you
can add anything to what he already knows. But he will be
curious to learn why his own convictions have not worked
and why[2] yours seem to work so well. He may be an
example of the truth that faith alone is insufficient. To be
vital, faith must be accompanied by self sacrifice and unselfish, constructive action. Let him see that you are not
there to instruct him in religion. Admit that he probably
knows more about it than you do, but call to his attention
the fact that however deep his faith and knowledge, he
could not have applied it or he would not drink. Perhaps
your story will help him see where he has failed to practice
the very precepts he knows so well. We represent no

---

[1] In the first edition this read: "Let him ask you that question, if he will. If he
does not ask, proceed with the rest of your story. *Tell him exactly what
happened to you.*"

[2] The word "why" did not appear in the first edition.

94:0 particular faith or denomination. We are dealing only with general principles common to most denominations.

94:1 Outline the program of action, explaining how you made a self-appraisal, how you straightened out your past and why you are now endeavoring to be helpful to him. It is important for him to realize that your attempt to pass this on to him plays a vital part in your own recovery. Actually, he may be helping you more than you are helping him. Make it plain he is under no obligation to you, that you hope only that he will try to help other alcoholics when he escapes his own difficulties. Suggest how important it is that he place the welfare of other people ahead of his own. Make it clear that he is not under pressure, that he needn't see you again if he doesn't want to. You should not be offended if he wants to call it off, for he has helped you more than you have helped him. If your talk has been sane, quiet and full of human understanding, you have perhaps made a friend. Maybe you have disturbed him about the question of alcoholism. This is all to the good. The more hopeless he feels, the better. He will be more likely to follow your suggestions.

94:2 Your candidate may give reasons why he need not follow all of the program. He may rebel at the thought of a drastic housecleaning which requires discussion with other people. Do not contradict such views. Tell him you once felt as he does, but you doubt whether you would have made much progress had you not taken action. On your first visit tell him about the Fellowship of Alcoholics Anonymous. If he shows interest, lend him your copy of this book.

95:1   Unless your friend wants to talk further about himself, do not wear out your welcome. Give him a chance to think it over. If you do stay, let him steer the conversation in any direction he likes. Sometimes a new man is anxious to proceed at once. And you may be tempted to let him do so. This is sometimes a mistake. If he has trouble later, he is likely to say you rushed him. You will be most successful with alcoholics if you do not exhibit any passion for crusade or reform. Never talk down to an alcoholic from any moral or spiritual hilltop; simply lay out the kit of spiritual tools for his inspection. Show him how they worked with you. Offer him friendship and fellowship. Tell him that if he wants to get well you will do anything to help.

95:2   If he is not interested in your solution, if he expects you to act only as a banker for his financial difficulties or a nurse for his sprees, you may have to drop him until he changes his mind. This he may do after he gets hurt some more.

95:3   If he is sincerely interested and wants to see you again, ask him to read this book in the interval. After doing that, he must decide for himself whether he wants to go on. He should not be pushed or prodded by you, his wife, or his friends. If he is to find God, the desire must come from within.

95:4   If he thinks he can do the job in some other way, or prefers some other spiritual approach, encourage him to follow his own conscience. We have no monopoly on God; we merely have an approach that worked with us. But point out that we alcoholics have much in common and that you would like, in any case, to be friendly. Let it go at that.

96:1   Do not be discouraged if your prospect does not respond at once. Search out another alcoholic and try again. You are sure to find someone desperate enough to accept with eagerness what you offer. We find it a waste of time to keep chasing a man who cannot or will not work with you. If you leave such a person alone, he may soon become convinced that he cannot recover by himself. To spend too much time on any one situation is to deny some other alcoholic an opportunity to live and be happy. One of our Fellowship[1] failed entirely with his first half dozen prospects. He often says that if he had continued to work on them, he might have deprived many others, who have since recovered, of their chance.

96:2   Suppose now you are making your second visit to a man. He has read this volume and says he is prepared to go through with the Twelve Steps of the program of recovery. Having had the experience yourself, you can give him much practical advice. Let him know you are available if he wishes to make a decision and tell his story, but do not insist upon it if he prefers to consult someone else.

96:3   He may be broke and homeless. If he is, you might try to help him about getting a job, or give him a little financial assistance. But you should not deprive your family or creditors of money they should have. Perhaps you will want to take the man into your home for a few days. But be sure you use discretion. Be certain he will be welcomed by your family, and that he is not trying to impose upon you for money, connections, or shelter. Permit that and you only harm him. You will be making it possible for him to be insincere.

---

[1] Bill Wilson.

97:0 You may be aiding in his destruction rather than his recovery.

97:1 Never avoid these responsibilities, but be sure you are doing the right thing if you assume them. Helping others is the foundation stone of your recovery. A kindly act once in a while isn't enough. You have to act the Good Samaritan every day, if need be. It may mean the loss of many nights' sleep, great interference with your pleasures, interruptions to your business. It may mean sharing your money and your home, counseling frantic wives and relatives, innumerable trips to police courts, sanitariums, hospitals, jails and asylums. Your telephone may jangle at any time of the day or night. Your wife may sometimes say she is neglected. A drunk may smash the furniture in your home, or burn a mattress. You may have to fight with him if he is violent. Sometimes you will have to call a doctor and administer sedatives under his direction. Another time you may have to send for the police or an ambulance. Occasionally you will have to meet such conditions.

97:2 We seldom allow an alcoholic to live in our homes for long at a time. It is not good for him, and it sometimes creates serious complications in a family.

97:3 Though an alcoholic does not respond, there is no reason why you should neglect his family. You should continue to be friendly to them. The family should be offered your way of life. Should they accept and practice spiritual principles, there is a much better chance that the head of the family will recover. And even though he continues to drink, the family will find life more bearable.

97:4 For the type of alcoholic who is able and willing to

98:0 get well, little charity, in the ordinary sense of the word, is needed or wanted. The men who cry for money and shelter before conquering alcohol, are on the wrong track. Yet we do go to great extremes to provide each other with these very things, when such action is warranted. This may seem inconsistent, but we think it is not.

98:1 It is not the matter of giving that is in question, but when and how to give. That often makes the difference between failure and success. The minute we put our work on a service plane, the alcoholic commences to rely upon our assistance rather than upon God. He clamors for this or that, claiming he cannot master alcohol until his material needs are cared for. Nonsense. Some of us have taken very hard knocks to learn this truth: Job or no job— wife or no wife—we simply do not stop drinking so long as we place dependence upon other people ahead of dependence on God.

98:2 Burn the idea into the consciousness of every man that he can get well regardless of anyone. The only condition is that he trust in God and clean house.

98:3 Now, the domestic problem: There may be divorce, separation, or just strained relations. When your prospect has made such reparation as he can to his family, and has thoroughly explained to them the new principles by which he is living, he should proceed to put those principles into action at home. That is, if he is lucky enough to have a home. Though his family be at fault in many respects, he should not be concerned about that. He should concentrate on his own spiritual demonstration. Argument and fault-finding are to be avoided like the plague.[1] In many homes this is a

---

[1] In the first edition this read: "Argument and fault-finding are to be avoided like leprosy."

99:0 difficult thing to do, but it must be done if any results are to be expected. If persisted in for a few months, the effect on a man's family is sure to be great. The most incompatible people discover they have a basis upon which they can meet. Little by little the family may see their own defects and admit them. These can then be discussed in an atmosphere of helpfulness and friendliness.

99:1 After they have seen tangible results, the family will perhaps want to go along. These things will come to pass naturally and in good time provided, however, the alcoholic continues to demonstrate that he can be sober, considerate, and helpful, regardless of what anyone says or does. Of course, we all fall much below this standard many times. But we must try to repair the damage immediately lest we pay the penalty by a spree.

99:2 If there be divorce or separation, there should be no undue haste for the couple to get together. The man should be sure of his recovery. The wife should fully understand his new way of life. If their old relationship is to be resumed it must be on a better basis, since the former did not work. This means a new attitude and spirit all around. Sometimes it is to the best interest of all concerned that a couple remain apart. Obviously, no rule can be laid down. Let the alcoholic continue his program day by day. When the time for living together has come, it will be apparent to both parties.

99:3 Let no alcoholic say he cannot recover unless he has his family back. This just isn't so. In some cases the wife will never come back for one reason or another. Remind the prospect that his recovery is not depend-

100:0 ent upon people. It is dependent upon his relationship with God. We have seen men get well whose families have not returned at all. We have seen others slip when the family came back too soon.

100:1 Both you and the new man must walk day by day in the path of spiritual progress. If you persist, remarkable things will happen. When we look back, we realize that the things which came to us when we put ourselves in God's hands were better than anything we could have planned. Follow the dictates of a Higher Power and you will presently live in a new and wonderful world, no matter what your present circumstances!

100:2 When working with a man and his family, you should take care not to participate in their quarrels. You may spoil your chance of being helpful if you do. But urge upon a man's family that he has been a very sick person and should be treated accordingly. You should warn against arousing resentment or jealousy. You should point out that his defects of character are not going to disappear over night. Show them that he has entered upon a period of growth. Ask them to remember, when they are impatient, the blessed fact of his sobriety.

100:3 If you have been successful in solving your own domestic problems, tell the newcomer's family how that was accomplished. In this way you can set them on the right track without becoming critical of them. The story of how you and your wife settled your difficulties is worth any amount of criticism.

100:4 Assuming we are spiritually fit, we can do all sorts of things alcoholics are not supposed to do. People have said we must not go where liquor is served; we

101:0 must not have it in our homes; we must shun friends who drink; we must avoid moving pictures which show drinking scenes; we must not go into bars; our friends must hide their bottles if we go to their houses; we mustn't think or be reminded about alcohol at all. Our experience shows that this is not necessarily so.

101:1 We meet these conditions every day. An alcoholic who cannot meet them, still has an alcoholic mind; there is something the matter with his spiritual status. His only chance for sobriety would be some place like the Greenland Ice Cap, and even there an Eskimo might turn up with a bottle of scotch and ruin everything! Ask any woman who has sent her husband to distant places on the theory he would escape the alcohol problem.

101:2 In our belief any scheme of combating alcoholism which proposes to shield the sick man from temptation is doomed to failure. If the alcoholic tries to shield himself he may succeed for a time, but he usually winds up with a bigger explosion than ever. We have tried these methods. These attempts to do the impossible have always failed.

101:3 So our rule is not to avoid a place where there is drinking, *if we have a legitimate reason for being there.* That includes bars, nightclubs, dances, receptions, weddings, even plain ordinary whoopee parties. To a person who has had experience with an alcoholic, this may seem like tempting Providence, but it isn't.

101:4 You will note that we made an important qualification. Therefore, ask yourself on each occasion, "Have I any good social, business, or personal reason for going to this place? Or am I expecting to steal a little vicarious pleasure from the atmosphere of such

102:0 places?" If you answer these questions satisfactorily, you need have no apprehension. Go or stay away, whichever seems best. But be sure you are on solid spiritual ground before you start and that your motive in going is thoroughly good. Do not think of what you will get out of the occasion. Think of what you can bring to it. But if you are shaky, you had better work with another alcoholic instead!

102:1 Why sit with a long face in places where there is drinking, sighing about the good old days. If it is a happy occasion, try to increase the pleasure of those there; if a business occasion, go and attend to your business enthusiastically. If you are with a person who wants to eat in a bar, by all means go along. Let your friends know they are not to change their habits on your account. At a proper time and place explain to all your friends why alcohol disagrees with you. If you do this thoroughly, few people will ask you to drink. While you were drinking, you were withdrawing from life little by little. Now you are getting back into the social life of this world. Don't start to withdraw again just because your friends drink liquor.

102:2 Your job now is to be at the place where you may be of maximum helpfulness to others, so never hesitate to go anywhere if you can be helpful. You should not hesitate to visit the most sordid spot on earth on such an errand. Keep on the firing line of life with these motives and God will keep you unharmed.

102:3 Many of us keep liquor in our homes. We often need it to carry green recruits through a severe hangover Some of us still serve it to our friends provided they are not alcoholic. But some of us think we should not serve liquor to anyone. We never argue this ques-

103:0   tion. We feel that each family, in the light of their own circumstances, ought to decide for themselves.

103:1   We are careful never to show intolerance or hatred of drinking as an institution. Experience shows that such an attitude is not helpful to anyone. Every new alcoholic looks for this spirit among us and is immensely relieved when he finds we are not witch burners. A spirit of intolerance might repel alcoholics whose lives could have been saved, had it not been for such stupidity. We would not even do the cause of temperate drinking any good, for not one drinker in a thousand likes to be told anything about alcohol by one who hates it.

103:2   Some day we hope that Alcoholics Anonymous will help the public to a better realization of the gravity of the alcoholic problem, but we shall be of little use if our attitude is one of bitterness or hostility. Drinkers will not stand for it.

103:3   *After all, our problems were of our own making. Bottles were only a symbol. Besides, we have stopped fighting anybody or anything. We have to!*

Chapter 8

TO WIVES

104:1 *W*ITH FEW EXCEPTIONS, our book thus far has spoken of men. But what we have said applies quite as much to women. Our activities in behalf of women who drink are on the increase. There is every evidence that women regain their health as readily as men if they try our suggestions.

104:2 But for every man who drinks others are involved—the wife who trembles in fear of the next debauch; the mother and father who see their son wasting away.

104:3 Among us are wives, relatives and friends whose problem has been solved, as well as some who have not yet found a happy solution. We want the wives of Alcoholics Anonymous to address the wives of men who drink too much. What they say will apply to nearly everyone bound by ties of blood or affection to an alcoholic.

104:4 As wives of Alcoholics Anonymous, we would like you to feel that we understand as perhaps few can. We want to analyze mistakes we have made. We want to leave you with the feeling that no situation is too difficult and no unhappiness too great to be overcome.

104:5 We have traveled a rocky road, there is no mistake about that. We have had long rendezvous with hurt pride, frustration, self-pity, misunderstanding and fear. These are not pleasant companions. We have been

105:0 driven to maudlin sympathy, to bitter resentment. Some of us veered from extreme to extreme, ever hoping that one day our loved ones would be themselves once more.

105:1 Our loyalty and the desire that our husbands hold up their heads and be like other men have begotten all sorts of predicaments. We have been unselfish and self-sacrificing. We have told innumerable lies to protect our pride and our husbands' reputations. We have prayed, we have begged, we have been patient. We have struck out viciously. We have run away. We have been hysterical. We have been terror stricken. We have sought sympathy. We have had retaliatory love affairs with other men.

105:2 Our homes have been battle-grounds many an evening. In the morning we have kissed and made up. Our friends have counseled chucking the men and we have done so with finality, only to be back in a little while hoping, always hoping. Our men have sworn great solemn oaths that they were through drinking forever. We have believed them when no one else could or would. Then, in days, weeks, or months, a fresh outburst.

105:3 We seldom had friends at our homes, never knowing how or when the men of the house would appear. We could make few social engagements. We came to live almost alone. When we were invited out, our husbands sneaked so many drinks that they spoiled the occasion. If, on the other hand, they took nothing, their self-pity made them killjoys.

105:4 There was never financial security. Positions were always in jeopardy or gone. An armored car could

106:0 not have brought the pay envelopes home. The checking account melted like snow in June.

106:1 Sometimes there were other women. How heartbreaking was this discovery; how cruel to be told they understood our men as we did not!

106:2 The bill collectors, the sheriffs, the angry taxi drivers, the policemen, the bums, the pals, and even the ladies they sometimes brought home—our husbands thought we were so inhospitable. "Joykiller, nag, wet blanket"—that's what they said. Next day they would be themselves again and we would forgive and try to forget.

106:3 We have tried to hold the love of our children for their father. We have told small tots that father was sick, which was much nearer the truth than we realized. They struck the children, kicked out door panels, smashed treasured crockery, and ripped the keys out of pianos. In the midst of such pandemonium they may have rushed out threatening to live with the other woman forever. In desperation, we have even got tight ourselves—the drunk to end all drunks. The unexpected result was that our husbands seemed to like it.

106:4 Perhaps at this point we got a divorce and took the children home to father and mother. Then we were severely criticized by our husband's parents for desertion. Usually we did not leave. We stayed on and on. We finally sought employment ourselves as destitution faced us and our families.

106:5 We began to ask medical advice as the sprees got closer together. The alarming physical and mental symptoms, the deepening pall of remorse, depression and inferiority that settled down on our loved ones—

107:0 these things terrified and distracted us. As animals on a treadmill, we have patiently and wearily climbed, falling back in exhaustion after each futile effort to reach solid ground. Most of us have entered the final stage with its commitment to health resorts, sanitariums, hospitals, and jails. Sometimes there were screaming delirium and insanity. Death was often near.

107:1 Under these conditions we naturally made mistakes. Some of them rose out of ignorance of alcoholism. Sometimes we sensed dimly that we were dealing with sick men. Had we fully understood the nature of the alcoholic illness, we might have behaved differently.

107:2 How could men who loved their wives and children be so unthinking, so callous, so cruel? There could be no love in such persons, we thought. And just as we were being convinced of their heartlessness, they would surprise us with fresh resolves and new attentions. For a while they would be their old sweet selves, only to dash the new structure of affection to pieces once more. Asked why they commenced to drink again, they would reply with some silly excuse, or none. It was so baffling, so heartbreaking. Could we have been so mistaken in the men we married? When drinking, they were strangers. Sometimes they were so inaccessible that it seemed as though a great wall had been built around them.

107:3 And even if they did not love their families, how could they be so blind about themselves? What had become of their judgment, their common sense, their will power? Why could they not see that drink meant ruin to them? Why was it, when these dangers were

108:0 pointed out that they agreed, and then got drunk again immediately?

108:1 These are some of the questions which race through the mind of every woman[1] who has an alcoholic husband. We hope this book has answered some of them. Perhaps your husband has been living in that strange world of alcoholism where everything is distorted and exaggerated. You can see that he really does love you with his better self. Of course, there is such a thing as incompatibility, but in nearly every instance the alcoholic only seems to be unloving and inconsiderate; it is usually because he is warped and sickened that he says and does these appalling things. Today most of our men are better husbands and fathers than ever before.

108:2 Try not to condemn your alcoholic husband no matter what he says or does. He is just another very sick, unreasonable person. Treat him, when you can, as though he had pneumonia. When he angers you, remember that he is very ill.

108:3 There is an important exception to the foregoing. We realize some men are thoroughly bad-intentioned, that no amount of patience will make any difference. An alcoholic of this temperament may be quick to use this chapter as a club over your head. Don't let him get away with it. If you are positive he is one of this type you may feel you had better leave. Is it right to let him ruin your life and the lives of your children? Especially when he has before him a way to stop his drinking and abuse if he really wants to pay the price.

108:4 The problem with which you struggle usually falls within one of four categories:

108:5 *One:* Your husband may be only a heavy drinker.

---

[1] In the first edition this read: "girl."

109:0 His drinking may be constant or it may be heavy only on certain occasions. Perhaps he spends too much money for liquor. It may be slowing him up mentally and physically, but he does not see it. Sometimes he is a source of embarrassment to you and his friends. He is positive he can handle his liquor, that it does him no harm, that drinking is necessary in his business. He would probably be insulted if he were called an alcoholic. This world is full of people like him. Some will moderate or stop altogether, and some will not. Of those who keep on, a good number will become true alcoholics after a while.

109:1 *Two*: Your husband is showing lack of control, for he is unable to stay on the water wagon even when he wants to. He often gets entirely out of hand when drinking. He admits this is true, but is positive that he will do better. He has begun to try, with or without your cooperation, various means of moderating or staying dry. Maybe he is beginning to lose his friends. His business may suffer somewhat. He is worried at times, and is becoming aware that he cannot drink like other people. He sometimes drinks in the morning and through the day also, to hold his nervousness in check. He is remorseful after serious drinking bouts and tells you he wants to stop. But when he gets over the spree, he begins to think once more how he can drink moderately next time. We think this person is in danger. These are the earmarks of a real alcoholic. Perhaps he can still tend to business fairly well. He has by no means ruined everything. As we say among ourselves, *"He wants to want to stop."*

109:2 *Three:* This husband has gone much further than husband number two. Though once like number two

110:0 he became worse. His friends have slipped away, his home is a near-wreck and he cannot hold a position. Maybe the doctor has been called in, and the weary round of sanitariums and hospitals has begun. He admits he cannot drink like other people, but does not see why. He clings to the notion that he will yet find a way to do so. He may have come to the point where he desperately wants to stop but cannot. His case presents additional questions which we shall try to answer for you. You can be quite hopeful of a situation like this.

110:1 *Four:* You may have a husband of whom you completely despair. He has been placed in one institution after another. He is violent, or appears definitely insane when drunk. Sometimes he drinks on the way home from the hospital. Perhaps he has had delirium tremens. Doctors may shake their heads and advise you to have him committed. Maybe you have already been obliged to put him away. This picture may not be as dark as it looks. Many of our husbands were just as far gone. Yet they got well.

110:2 Let's now go back to husband number one. Oddly enough, he is often difficult to deal with. He enjoys drinking. It stirs his imagination. His friends feel closer over a highball. Perhaps you enjoy drinking with him yourself when he doesn't go too far. You have passed happy evenings together chatting and drinking before your fire. Perhaps you both like parties which would be dull without liquor. We have enjoyed such evenings ourselves; we had a good time. We know all about liquor as a social lubricant. Some, but not all of us, think it has its advantages when reasonably used.

111:1   The first principle of success is that you should never be angry. Even though your husband becomes unbearable and you have to leave him temporarily, you should, if you can, go without rancor. Patience and good temper are most necessary.

111:2   Our next thought is that you should never tell him what he must do about his drinking. If he gets the idea that you are a nag or killjoy, your chance of accomplishing anything useful may be zero. He will use that as an excuse to drink more.[1] He will tell you he is misunderstood. This may lead to lonely evenings for you. He may seek someone else[2] to console him—not always another man.

111:3   Be determined that your husband's drinking is not going to spoil your relations with your children or your friends. They need your companionship and your help. It is possible to have a full and useful life, though your husband continues to drink. We know women who are unafraid, even happy under these conditions. Do not set your heart on reforming your husband. You may be unable to do so, no matter how hard you try.

111:4   We know these suggestions are sometimes difficult to follow, but you will save many a heartbreak if you can succeed in observing them. Your husband may come to appreciate your reasonableness and patience. This may lay the groundwork for a friendly talk about his alcoholic problem. Try to have him bring up the subject himself. Be sure you are not critical during such a discussion. Attempt instead, to put yourself in his place. Let him see that you want to be helpful rather than critical.

111:5   When a discussion does arise, you might suggest he

---

[1] In the first edition this read: "He will use that as an excuse to drink some more."

[2] The word "else" did not appear in the first edition.

112:0 read this book or at least the chapter on alcoholism. Tell him you have been worried, though perhaps needlessly. You think he ought to know the subject better, as everyone should have a clear understanding of the risk he takes if he drinks too much. Show him you have confidence in his power to stop or moderate. Say you do not want to be a wet blanket; that you only want him to take care of his health. Thus you may succeed in interesting him in alcoholism.

112:1 He probably has several alcoholics among his own acquaintances. You might suggest that you both take an interest in them. Drinkers like to help other drinkers. Your husband may be willing to talk to one of them.

112:2 If this kind of approach does not catch your husband's interest, it may be best to drop the subject, but after a friendly talk your husband will usually revive the topic himself. This may take patient waiting, but it will be worth it. Meanwhile you might try to help the wife of another serious drinker. If you act upon these principles, your husband may stop or moderate.

112:3 Suppose, however, that your husband fits the description of number two. The same principles which apply to husband number one should be practiced. But after his next binge, ask him if he would really like to get over drinking for good. Do not ask that he do it for you or anyone else. Just would he *like* to?

112:4 The chances are he would. Show him your copy of this book and tell him what you have found out about alcoholism. Show him that as alcoholics, the writers of the book understand. Tell him some of the interesting stories you have read. If you think he will be shy of a spiritual remedy, ask him to look at the chapter on

113:0 alcoholism. Then perhaps he will be interested enough to continue.

113:1 If he is enthusiastic your cooperation will mean a great deal. If he is lukewarm or thinks he is not an alcoholic, we suggest you leave him alone. Avoid urging him to follow our program. The seed has been planted in his mind. He knows that thousands of men, much like himself, have recovered.[1] But don't remind him of this after he had been drinking, for he may be angry. Sooner or later, you are likely to find him reading the book once more. Wait until repeated stumbling convinces him he must act, for the more you hurry him the longer his recovery may be delayed.

113:2 If you have a number three husband, you may be in luck. Being certain he wants to stop, you can go to him with this volume as joyfully as though you had struck oil. He may not share your enthusiasm, but he is practically sure to read the book and he may go for the program at once. If he does not, you will probably not have long to wait. Again, you should not crowd him. Let him decide for himself. Cheerfully see him through more sprees. Talk about his condition or this book only when he raises the issue. In some cases it may be better to let someone outside the family present the book. They can urge action without arousing hostility. If your husband is otherwise a normal individual, your chances are good at this stage.

113:3 You would suppose that men in the fourth classification would be quite hopeless, but that is not so. Many of Alcoholics Anonymous were like that. Everybody had given them up. Defeat seemed certain. Yet often such men had spectacular and powerful recoveries.

[1] In the first edition this read: "He knows that over a hundred men, much like himself, have recovered."

114:1   There are exceptions. Some men have been so impaired by alcohol that they cannot stop. Sometimes there
are cases where alcoholism is complicated by other disorders. A good doctor or psychiatrist can tell you
whether these complications are serious. In any event,
try to have your husband read this book. His reaction
may be one of enthusiasm. If he is already committed to
an institution, but can convince you and your doctor that
he means business, give him a chance to try our method,
unless the doctor thinks his mental condition too abnormal or dangerous. We make this recommendation with
some confidence. For years we have been working with
alcoholics committed to institutions. Since this book was
first published, A.A. has released thousands of alcoholics from asylums and hospitals of every kind. The majority have never returned.[1] The power of God goes deep!

114:2   You may have the reverse situation on your hands.
Perhaps you have a husband who is at large, but who
should be committed. Some men cannot or will not get
over alcoholism. When they become too dangerous, we
think the kind thing is to lock them up, but of course a
good doctor should always be consulted. The wives and
children of such men suffer horribly, but not more[2] than
the men themselves.

114:3   But sometimes you must start life anew. We know
women who have done it. If such women adopt a spiritual way of life their road will be smoother.

114:4   If your husband is a drinker, you probably worry
over what other people are thinking and you hate to
meet your friends. You draw more and more into yourself and you think everyone is talking about conditions
at your home. You avoid the subject of drink-

---

[1] In the first edition this read: "About a year ago a certain state institution
released four chronic alcoholics. It was fully expected they would all be
back in a few weeks. Only one of them returned. The others had no
relapse at all."

[2] In the first edition this read: "less".

115:0 ing, even with your own parents. You do not know what to tell the children. When your husband is bad, you become a trembling recluse, wishing the telephone had never been invented.

115:1 We find that most of this embarrassment is unnecessary. While you need not discuss your husband at length, you can quietly let your friends know the nature of his illness. But you must be on guard not to embarrass or harm your husband.

115:2 When you have carefully explained to such people that he is a sick person, you will have created a new atmosphere. Barriers which have sprung up between you and your friends will disappear with the growth of sympathetic understanding. You will no longer be self-conscious or feel that you must apologize as though your husband were a weak character.[1] He may be anything but that. Your new courage, good nature and lack of self-consciousness will do wonders for you socially.

115:3 The same principle applies in dealing with the children. Unless they actually need protection from their father, it is best not to take sides in any argument he has with them while drinking. Use your energies to promote a better understanding all around. Then that terrible tension which grips the home of every problem drinker will be lessened.

115:4 Frequently, you have felt obliged to tell your husband's employer and his friends that he was sick, when as a matter of fact he was tight. Avoid answering these inquiries as much as you can. Whenever possible, let your husband explain. Your desire to protect him should not cause you to lie to people when they have a right to know where he is and what he is doing. Dis-

[1] In the first edition this read: "You will no longer be self-conscious, nor feel that you must apologize as though your husband were a weak character."

116:0 cuss this with him when he is sober and in good spirits. Ask him what you should do if he places you in such a position again. But be careful not to be resentful about the last time he did so.

116:1 There is another paralyzing fear. You may be afraid your husband will lose his position; you are thinking of the disgrace and hard times which will befall you and the children. This experience may come to you. Or you may already have had it several times. Should it happen again, regard it in a different light. Maybe it will prove a blessing! It may convince your husband he wants to stop drinking forever. And now you know that he can stop if he will! Time after time, this apparent calamity has been a boon to us, for it opened up a path which led to the discovery of God.

116:2 We have elsewhere remarked how much better life is when lived on a spiritual plane. If God can solve the age-old riddle of alcoholism, He can solve your problems too. We wives found that, like everybody else, we were afflicted with pride, self-pity, vanity and all the things which go to make up the self-centered person; and we were not above selfishness or dishonesty. As our husbands began to apply spiritual principles in their lives, we began to see the desirability of doing so too.

116:3 At first, some of us did not believe we needed this help. We thought, on the whole, we were pretty good women, capable of being nicer if our husbands stopped drinking. But it was a silly idea that we were too good to need God. Now we try to put spiritual principles to work in every department of our lives. When we do that, we find it solves our problems too; the ensuing lack of fear, worry and hurt feelings is a wonderful

117:0 thing. We urge you to try our program, for nothing will be so helpful to your husband as the radically changed attitude toward him which God will show you how to have. Go along with your husband if you possibly can.

117:1 If you and your husband find a solution for the pressing problem of drink you are, of course, going to be very happy. But all problems will not be solved at once. Seed has started to sprout in a new soil, but growth has only begun. In spite of your new-found happiness, there will be ups and downs. Many of the old problems will still be with you. This is as it should be.

117:2 The faith and sincerity of both you and your husband will be put to the test. These work-outs should be regarded as part of your education, for thus you will be learning to live. You will make mistakes, but if you are in earnest they will not drag you down. Instead, you will capitalize them. A better way of life will emerge when they are overcome.

117:3 Some of the snags you will encounter are irritation, hurt feelings and resentments. Your husband will sometimes be unreasonable and you will want to criticize. Starting from a speck on the domestic horizon, great thunderclouds of dispute may gather. These family dissensions are very dangerous, especially to your husband. Often you must carry the burden of avoiding them or keeping them under control. Never forget that resentment is a deadly hazard to an alcoholic. We do not mean that you have to agree with your husband whenever there is an honest difference of opinion. Just be careful not to disagree in a resentful or critical spirit.

118:1   You and your husband will find that you can dispose of serious problems easier than you can the trivial ones. Next time you and he have a heated discussion, no matter what the subject, it should be the privilege of either to smile and say, "This is getting serious. I'm sorry I got disturbed. Let's talk about it later." If your husband is trying to live on a spiritual basis, he will also be doing everything in his power to avoid disagreement or contention.

118:2   Your husband knows he owes you more than sobriety. He wants to make good. Yet you must not expect too much. His ways of thinking and doing are the habits of years. Patience, tolerance, understanding and love are the watchwords. Show him these things in yourself and they will be reflected back to you from him. Live and let live is the rule. If you both show a willingness to remedy your own defects, there will be little need to criticize each other.

118:3   We women carry with us a picture of the ideal man, the sort of chap we would like our husbands to be. It is the most natural thing in the world, once his liquor problem is solved, to feel that he will now measure up to that cherished vision. The chances are he will not for, like yourself, he is just beginning his development. Be patient.

118:4   Another feeling we are very likely to entertain is one of resentment that love and loyalty could not cure our husbands of alcoholism. We do not like the thought that the contents of a book or the work of another alcoholic has accomplished in a few weeks that for which we struggled for years. At such moments we forget that alcoholism is an illness over which we could not possibly have had any power. Your husband will

119:0 be the first to say it was your devotion and care which brought him to the point where he could have a spiritual experience. Without you he would have gone to pieces long ago. When resentful thoughts come, try to pause and count your blessings. After all, your family is reunited, alcohol is no longer a problem and you and your husband are working together toward an undreamed-of future.

119:1 Still another difficulty is that you may become jealous of the attention he bestows on other people, especially alcoholics. You have been starving for his companionship, yet he spends long hours helping other men and their families. You feel he should now be yours. The fact is that he should work with other people to maintain his own sobriety. Sometimes he will be so interested that he becomes really neglectful. Your house is filled with strangers. You may not like some of them. He gets stirred up about their troubles, but not at all about yours. It will do little good if you point that out and urge more attention for yourself. We find it a real mistake to dampen his enthusiasm for alcoholic work. You should join in his efforts as much as you possibly can. We suggest that you direct some of your thought to the wives of his new alcoholic friends. They need the counsel and love of a woman who has gone through what you have.

119:2 It is probably true that you and your husband have been living too much alone, for drinking many times isolates the wife of an alcoholic. Therefore, you probably need fresh interests and a great cause to live for as much as your husband. If you cooperate, rather than complain, you will find that his excess enthusiasm will tone down. Both of you will awaken to a new

120:0 sense of responsibility for others. You, as well as your husband, ought to think of what you can put into life instead of how much you can take out. Inevitably your lives will be fuller for doing so. You will lose the old life to find one much better.

120:1 Perhaps your husband will make a fair start on the new basis, but just as things are going beautifully he dismays you by coming home drunk. If you are satisfied he really wants to get over drinking, you need not be alarmed. Though it is infinitely better that he have no relapse at all, as has been true with many of our men, it is by no means a bad thing in some cases. Your husband will see at once that he must redouble his spiritual activities if he expects to survive. You need not remind him of his spiritual deficiency—he will know of it. Cheer him up and ask him how you can be still more helpful.

120:2 The slightest sign of fear or intolerance may lessen your husband's chance of recovery. In a weak moment he may take your dislike of his high-stepping friends as one of those insanely trivial excuses to drink.

120:3 We never, never try to arrange a man's life so as to shield him from temptation. The slightest disposition on your part to guide his appointments or his affairs so he will not be tempted will be noticed. Make him feel absolutely free to come and go as he likes. This is important. If he gets drunk, don't blame yourself. God has either removed your husband's liquor problem or He has not. If not, it had better be found out right away. Then you and your husband can get right down to fundamentals. If a repetition is to be prevented, place the problem, along with everything else, in God's hands.

121:1   We realize that we have been giving you much direction and advice. We may have seemed to lecture. If that is so we are sorry, for we ourselves don't always care for people who lecture us. But what we have related is based upon experience, some of it painful. We had to learn these things the hard way. That is why we are anxious that you understand, and that you avoid these unnecessary difficulties.

121:2   So to you out there who may soon be with us—we say "Good luck and God bless you!"

Chapter 9

THE FAMILY AFTERWARD

122:1   OUR WOMEN FOLK have suggested certain attitudes a wife may take with the husband who is recovering. Perhaps they created the impression that he is to be wrapped in cotton wool and placed on a pedestal. Successful readjustment means the opposite. All members of the family should meet upon the common ground of tolerance, understanding and love. This involves a process of deflation. The alcoholic, his wife, his children, his "in-laws," each one is likely to have fixed ideas about the family's attitude towards himself or herself. Each is interested in having his or her wishes respected. We find the more one member of the family demands that the others concede to him, the more resentful they become. This makes for discord and unhappiness.

122:2   And why? Is it not because each wants to play the lead? Is not each trying to arrange the family show to his liking? Is he not unconsciously trying to see what he can take from the family life rather than give?

122:3   Cessation of drinking is but the first step away from a highly strained, abnormal condition. A doctor said to us, "Years of living with an alcoholic is almost sure to make any wife or child neurotic. The entire family is, to some extent, ill." Let families realize, as they start their journey, that all will not be fair weather. Each in his turn may be footsore and may straggle.

123:0 There will be alluring shortcuts and by-paths down which they may wander and lose their way.

123:1 Suppose we tell you some of the obstacles a family will meet; suppose we suggest how they may be avoided—even converted to good use for others. The family of an alcoholic longs for the return of happiness and security. They remember when father was romantic, thoughtful and successful. Today's life is measured against that of other years and, when it falls short, the family may be unhappy.

123:2 Family confidence in dad is rising high. The good old days will soon be back, they think. Sometimes they demand that dad bring them back instantly! God, they believe, almost owes this recompense on a long overdue account. But the head of the house has spent years in pulling down the structures of business, romance, friendship, health—these things are now ruined or damaged. It will take time to clear away the wreck. Though old buildings will eventually be replaced by finer ones, the new structures will take years to complete.

123:3 Father knows he is to blame; it may take him many seasons of hard work to be restored financially, but he shouldn't be reproached. Perhaps he will never have much money again. But the wise family will admire him for what he is trying to be, rather than for what he is trying to get.

123:4 Now and then the family will be plagued by spectres from the past, for the drinking career of almost every alcoholic has been marked by escapades, funny, humiliating, shameful or tragic. The first impulse will be to bury these skeletons in a dark closet and padlock the door. The family may be possessed by the idea

124:0   that future happiness can be based only upon forgetfulness of the past. We think that such a view is self-centered and in direct conflict with the new way of living.

124:1   Henry Ford[1] once made a wise remark to the effect
that experience is the thing of supreme value in life. That
is true only if one is willing to turn the past to good
account. We grow by our willingness to face and rectify errors and convert them into assets. The alcoholic's
past thus becomes the principal asset of the family and
frequently it is almost the only one!

124:2   This painful past may be of infinite value to other
families still struggling with their problem. We think each
family which has been relieved owes something to those
who have not, and when the occasion requires, each
member of it should be only too willing to bring former
mistakes, no matter how grievous, out of their hiding
places.[2] Showing others who suffer how we were given
help is the very thing which makes life seem so worth
while to us now. Cling to the thought that, in God's
hands, the dark past is the greatest possession you
have—the key to life and happiness for others. With it
you can avert death and misery for them.

124:3   It is possible to dig up past misdeeds so they become a blight, a veritable plague. For example, we know
of situations in which the alcoholic or his wife have
had love affairs. In the first flush of spiritual experience
they forgave each other and drew closer together.
The miracle of reconciliation was at hand. Then, under
one provocation or another, the aggrieved one would
unearth the old affair and angrily cast its ashes about.
A few of us have had these growing pains and they

---

[1] A pioneer of automated production. Became widely known and very wealthy
from manufacturing automobiles.

[2] In the first edition this read: "We think each family which has been relieved
owes something to those which have not, and when the occasion requires,
each member of it, should be only too willing to bring former mistakes, no
matter how grievous, out of their hiding places."

125:0 hurt a great deal. Husbands and wives have sometimes been obliged to separate for a time until new perspective, new victory over hurt pride could be re-won. In most cases, the alcoholic survived this ordeal without relapse, but not always. So we think that unless some good and useful purpose is to be served, past occurrences should not be discussed.

125:1 We families of Alcoholics Anonymous keep few skeletons in the closet. Everyone knows about the others' alcoholic troubles. This is a condition which, in ordinary life, would produce untold grief; there might be scandalous gossip, laughter at the expense of other people, and a tendency to take advantage of intimate information. Among us, these are rare occurrences. We do talk about each other a great deal, but we almost invariably temper such talk by a spirit of love and tolerance.

125:2 Another principle we observe carefully is that we do not relate intimate experiences of another person unless we are sure he would approve. We find it better, when possible, to stick to our own stories. A man may criticize or laugh at himself and it will affect others favorably, but criticism or ridicule coming from another often produces the contrary effect.[1] Members of a family should watch such matters carefully, for one careless, inconsiderate remark has been known to raise the very devil. We alcoholics are sensitive people. It takes some of us a long time to outgrow that serious handicap.

125:3 Many alcoholics are enthusiasts. They run to extremes. At the beginning of recovery a man will take, as a rule, one of two directions. He may either plunge into a frantic attempt to get on his feet in business, or

---

[1] In the first edition this read: "...but criticism or ridicule of him coming from another often produces the contrary effect."

126:0   he may be so enthralled by his new life that he talks or thinks of little else. In either case certain family problems will arise. With these we have had[1] experience galore.

126:1   We think it dangerous if he rushes headlong at his economic problem. The family will be affected also, pleasantly at first, as they feel their money troubles are about to be solved, then not so pleasantly as they find themselves neglected. Dad may be tired at night and preoccupied by day. He may take small interest in the children and may show irritation when reproved for his delinquencies. If not irritable, he may seem dull and boring, not gay and affectionate as the family would like him to be. Mother may complain of inattention. They are all disappointed, and often let him feel it. Beginning with such complaints, a barrier arises. He is straining every nerve to make up for lost time. He is striving to recover fortune and reputation and feels he is doing very well.

126:2   Sometimes mother and children don't think so. Having been neglected and misused in the past, they think father owes them more than they are getting. They want him to make a fuss over them. They expect him to give them the nice times they used to have before he drank so much, and to show his contrition for what they suffered. But dad doesn't give freely of himself. Resentment grows. He becomes still less communicative. Sometimes he explodes over a trifle. The family is mystified. They criticize, pointing out how he is falling down on his spiritual program.

126:3   This sort of thing can be avoided. Both father and the family are mistaken, though each side may have some justification. It is of little use to argue and only

---

[1] The word "had" did not appear in the first edition.

127:0 makes the impasse worse. The family must realize that dad, though marvelously improved, is still convalescing. They should be thankful he is sober and able to be of this world once more. Let them praise his progress. Let them remember that his drinking wrought all kinds of damage that may take long to repair. If they sense these things, they will not take so seriously his periods of crankiness, depression, or apathy, which will disappear when there is tolerance, love, and spiritual understanding.

127:1 The head of the house ought to remember that he is mainly to blame for what befell his home. He can scarcely square the account in his lifetime. But he must see the danger of over-concentration on financial success. Although financial recovery is on the way for many of us, we found we could not place money first. For us, material well-being always followed spiritual progress; it never preceded.

127:2 Since the home has suffered more than anything else, it is well that a man exert himself there. He is not likely to get far in any direction if he fails to show unselfishness and love under his own roof. We know there are difficult wives and families, but the man who is getting over alcoholism must remember he did much to make them so.

127:3 As each member of a resentful family begins to see his shortcomings and admits them to the others, he lays a basis for helpful discussion. These family talks will be constructive if they can be carried on without heated argument, self-pity, self-justification or resentful criticism. Little by little, mother and children will see they ask too much, and father will see he gives too

128:0 little. Giving, rather than getting, will become the guiding principle.

128:1 Assume on the other hand that father has, at the outset, a stirring spiritual experience. Overnight, as it were, he is a different man. He becomes a religious enthusiast. He is unable to focus on anything else. As soon as his sobriety begins to be taken as a matter of course, the family may look at their strange new dad with apprehension, then with irritation. There is talk about spiritual matters morning, noon and night. He may demand that the family find God in a hurry, or exhibit amazing indifference to them and say he is above worldly considerations. He may tell mother, who has been religious all her life, that she doesn't know what it's all about, and that she had better get his brand of spirituality while there is yet time.

128:2 When father takes this tack, the family may react unfavorably. They may be jealous of a God who has stolen dad's affections. While grateful that he drinks no more, they may not like the idea that God has accomplished the miracle where they failed. They often forget father was beyond human aid. They may not see why their love and devotion did not straighten him out. Dad is not so spiritual after all, they say. If he means to right his past wrongs, why all this concern for everyone in the world but his family? What about his talk that God will take care of them? They suspect father is a bit balmy!

128:3 He is not so unbalanced as they might think. Many of us have experienced dad's elation. We have indulged in spiritual intoxication. Like a gaunt prospector, belt drawn in over the last ounce of food, our pick struck gold. Joy at our release from a lifetime of

129:0   frustration knew no bounds. Father feels he has struck something better than gold. For a time he may try to hug the new treasure to himself. He may not see at once that he has barely scratched a limitless lode which will pay dividends only if he mines it for the rest of his life and insists on giving away the entire product.

129:1   If the family cooperates, dad will soon see that he is suffering from a distortion of values. He will perceive that his spiritual growth is lopsided, that for an average man like himself, a spiritual life which does not include his family obligations may not be so perfect after all. If the family will appreciate that dad's current behavior is but a phase of his development, all will be well. In the midst of an understanding and sympathetic family, these vagaries of dad's spiritual infancy will quickly disappear.

129:2   The opposite may happen should the family condemn and criticize. Dad may feel that for years his drinking has placed him on the wrong side of every argument, but that now he has become a superior person with God on his side. If the family persists in criticism, this fallacy may take a still greater hold on father. Instead of treating the family as he should, he may retreat further into himself and feel he has spiritual justification for so doing.

129:3   Though the family does not fully agree with dad's spiritual activities, they should let him have his head. Even if he displays a certain amount of neglect and irresponsibility towards the family, it is well to let him go as far as he likes in helping other alcoholics. During those first days of convalescence, this will do more to insure his sobriety than anything else. Though

130:0 some of his manifestations are alarming and disagreeable, we think dad will be on a firmer foundation than the man who is placing business or professional success ahead of spiritual development. He will be less likely to drink again, and anything is preferable to that.

130:1 Those of us who have spent much time in the world of spiritual make-believe have eventually seen the childishness of it. This dream world has been replaced by a great sense of purpose, accompanied by a growing consciousness of the power of God in our lives. We have come to believe He would like us to keep our heads in the clouds with Him, but that our feet ought to be firmly planted on earth.[1] That is where our fellow travelers are, and that is where our work must be done. These are the realities for us. We have found nothing incompatible between a powerful spiritual experience and a life of sane and happy usefulness.

130:2 One more suggestion: Whether the family has spiritual convictions or not, they may do well to examine the principles by which the alcoholic member is trying to live. They can hardly fail to approve these simple principles, though the head of the house still fails somewhat in practicing them. Nothing will help the man who is off on a spiritual tangent so much as the wife who adopts a sane spiritual program, making a better practical use of it.

130:3 There will be other profound changes in the household. Liquor incapacitated father for so many years that mother became head of the house. She met these responsibilities gallantly. By force of circumstances, she was often obliged to treat father as a sick or wayward child. Even when he wanted to assert himself

---

[1] In the first edition this read: "...but that our feet ought to be firmly planted on earth, nevertheless."

131:0 he could not, for his drinking placed him constantly in the wrong. Mother made all the plans and gave the directions. When sober, father usually obeyed. Thus mother, through no fault of her own, became accustomed to wearing the family trousers. Father, coming suddenly to life again, often begins to assert himself. This means trouble, unless the family watches for these tendencies in each other and comes to a friendly agreement about them.

131:1 Drinking isolates most homes from the outside world. Father may have laid aside for years all normal activities—clubs, civic duties, sports. When he renews interest in such things, a feeling of jealousy may arise. The family may feel they hold a mortgage on dad, so big that no equity should be left for outsiders. Instead of developing new channels of activity for themselves, mother and children demand that he stay home and make up the deficiency.[1]

131:2 At the very beginning, the couple ought to frankly face the fact that each will have to yield here and there if the family is going to play an effective part in the new life. Father will necessarily spend much time with other alcoholics, but this activity should be balanced. New acquaintances who know nothing of alcoholism might be made and thoughtful consideration given their needs. The problems of the community might engage attention. Though the family has no religious connections, they may wish to make contact with or take membership in a religious body.

131:3 Alcoholics who have derided religious people will be helped by such contacts. Being possessed of a spiritual experience, the alcoholic will find he has much in common with these people, though he may

---

[1] In the first edition this read: "...mother and children may demand that he stay home and make up the deficiency."

132:0   differ with them on many matters. If he does not argue about religion, he will make new friends and is sure to find new avenues of usefulness and pleasure. He and his family can be a bright spot in such congregations. He may bring new hope and new courage to many a priest, minister, or rabbi, who gives his all to minister to our troubled world. We intend the foregoing as a helpful suggestion only. So far as we are concerned, there is nothing obligatory about it. As non-denominational people, we cannot make up others' minds for them. Each individual should consult his own conscience.

132:1   We have been speaking to you of serious, sometimes tragic things. We have been dealing with alcohol in its worst aspect. But we aren't a glum lot. If newcomers could see no joy or fun in our existence, they wouldn't want it. We absolutely insist on enjoying life. We try not to indulge in cynicism over the state of the nations, nor do we carry the world's troubles on our shoulders. When we see a man sinking into the mire that is alcoholism, we give him first aid and place what we have at his disposal. For his sake, we do recount and almost relive the horrors of our past. But those of us who have tried to shoulder the entire burden and trouble of others find we are soon overcome by them.

132:2   So we think cheerfulness and laughter make for usefulness. Outsiders are sometimes shocked when we burst into merriment over a seemingly tragic experience out of the past. But why shouldn't we laugh? We have recovered, and have been given the power to help others.

132:3   Everybody knows that those in bad health, and those who seldom play, do not laugh much. So let

133:0   each family play together or separately, as much as their circumstances warrant. We are sure God wants us to be happy, joyous, and free. We cannot subscribe to the belief that this life is a vale of tears, though it once was just that for many of us. But it is clear that we made our own misery. God didn't do it. Avoid then, the deliberate manufacture of misery, but if trouble comes, cheerfully capitalize it as an opportunity to demonstrate His omnipotence.

133:1   Now about health: A body badly burned by alcohol does not often recover overnight nor do twisted thinking and depression vanish in a twinkling. We are convinced that a spiritual mode of living is a most powerful health restorative. We, who have recovered from serious drinking, are miracles of mental health. But we have seen remarkable transformations in our bodies. Hardly one of our crowd now shows any mark of dissipation.

133:2   But this does not mean that we disregard human health measures. God has abundantly supplied this world with fine doctors, psychologists, and practitioners of various kinds. Do not hesitate to take your health problems to such persons. Most of them give freely of themselves, that their fellows may enjoy sound minds and bodies. Try to remember that though God has wrought miracles among us, we should never belittle a good doctor or psychiatrist. Their services are often indispensable in treating a newcomer and in following his case afterward.

133:3   One of the many doctors who had the opportunity of reading this book in manuscript form told us that the use of sweets was often helpful, of course depending upon a doctor's advice. He thought all alcoholics

134:0 should constantly have chocolate available for its quick energy value at times of fatigue. He added that occasionally in the night a vague craving arose which would be satisfied by candy. Many of us have noticed a tendency to eat sweets and have found this practice beneficial.

134:1 A word about sex relations. Alcohol is so sexually stimulating to some men that they have over-indulged. Couples are occasionally dismayed to find that when drinking is stopped the man tends to be impotent. Unless the reason is understood, there may be an emotional upset. Some of us had this experience, only to enjoy, in a few months, a finer intimacy than ever. There should be no hesitancy in consulting a doctor or psychologist if the condition persists. We do not know of many cases where this difficulty lasted long.

134:2 The alcoholic may find it hard to re-establish friendly relations with his children. Their young minds were impressionable while he was drinking. Without saying so, they may cordially hate him for what he has done to them and to their mother. The children are sometimes dominated by a pathetic hardness and cynicism. They cannot seem to forgive and forget. This may hang on for months, long after their mother has accepted dad's new way of living and thinking.

134:3 In time they will see that he is a new man and in their own way they will let him know it. When this happens, they can be invited to join in morning meditation and then they can take part in the daily discussion without rancor or bias. From that point on, progress will be rapid. Marvelous results often follow such a reunion.

135:1   Whether the family goes on a spiritual basis or not, the alcoholic member has to if he would recover. The others must be convinced of his new status beyond the shadow of a doubt. Seeing is believing to most families who have lived with a drinker.

135:2   Here is a case in point: One of our friends is a heavy smoker and coffee drinker. There was no doubt he over-indulged. Seeing this, and meaning to be helpful, his wife commenced to admonish him about it. He admitted he was overdoing these things, but frankly said that he was not ready to stop. His wife is one of those persons who really feels there is something rather sinful about these commodities, so she nagged, and her intolerance finally threw him into a fit of anger. He got drunk.

135:3   Of course our friend was wrong—dead wrong. He had to painfully admit that and mend his spiritual fences. Though he is now a most effective member of Alcoholics Anonymous, he still smokes and drinks coffee, but neither his wife nor anyone else stands in judgment. She sees she was wrong to make a burning issue out of such a matter when his more serious ailments were being rapidly cured.

135:4   We have three little mottoes which are apropos. Here they are:

First Things First
Live and Let Live
Easy Does It.

Chapter 10

TO EMPLOYERS

136:1 AMONG MANY employers nowadays, we think of one member who has spent much of his life in the world of big business.[1] He has hired and fired hundreds of men. He knows the alcoholic as the employer sees him. His present views ought to prove exceptionally useful to business men everywhere.

136:2 But let him tell you:

136:3 I was at one time assistant manager of a corporation department employing sixty-six hundred men. One day my secretary came in saying that Mr. B— insisted on speaking with me. I told her to say that I was not interested. I had warned him several times that he had but one more chance. Not long afterward he had called me from Hartford on two successive days, so drunk he could hardly speak. I told him he was through—finally and forever.

136:4 My secretary returned to say that it was not Mr. B— on the phone; it was Mr. B—'s brother, and he wished to give me a message. I still expected a plea for clemency, but these words came through the receiver: "I just wanted to tell you Paul jumped from a hotel window in Hartford last Saturday. He left us a note saying you were the best boss he ever had, and that you were not to blame in any way."

136:5 Another time, as I opened a letter which lay on my

---

[1] In the first edition this read: "ONE of our friends, whose gripping story you will read, has spent much of his life in the world of big business."

137:0 desk, a newspaper clipping fell out. It was the obituary of one of the best salesmen I ever had. After two weeks of drinking, he had placed his toe on the trigger of a loaded shotgun—the barrel was in his mouth. I had discharged him for drinking six weeks before.

137:1 Still another experience: A woman's voice came faintly over long distance from Virginia. She wanted to know if her husband's company insurance was still in force. Four days before he had hanged himself in his woodshed. I had been obliged to discharge him for drinking, though he was brilliant, alert, and one of the best organizers I have ever known.

137:2 Here were three exceptional men lost to this world because I did not understand alcoholism as I do now. What irony—I became an alcoholic myself! And but for the intervention of an understanding person, I might have followed in their footsteps. My downfall cost the business community unknown thousands of dollars, for it takes real money to train a man for an executive position. This kind of waste goes on unabated. We think the business fabric is shot through with a situation which might be helped by better understanding all around.

137:3 Nearly every modern employer feels a moral responsibility for the well-being of his help, and he tries to meet these responsibilities. That he has not always done so for the alcoholic is easily understood. To him the alcoholic has often seemed a fool of the first magnitude. Because of the employee's special ability, or of his own strong personal attachment to him, the employer has sometimes kept such a man at work long beyond a reasonable period. Some employers have tried every known remedy. In only a few instances

138:0   has there been a lack of patience and tolerance. And we, who have imposed on the best of employers, can scarcely blame them if they have been short with us.

138:1   Here, for instance, is a typical example: An officer of one of the largest banking institutions in America knows I no longer drink. One day he told me about an executive of the same bank who, from his description, was undoubtedly alcoholic. This seemed to me like an opportunity to be helpful, so I spent two hours talking about alcoholism, the malady, and described the symptoms and results as well as I could. His comment was, "Very interesting. But I'm sure this man is done drinking. He has just returned from a three-months leave of absence, has taken a cure, looks fine, and to clinch the matter, the board of directors told him this was his last chance."

138:2   The only answer I could make was that if the man followed the usual pattern, he would go on a bigger bust than ever. I felt this was inevitable and wondered if the bank was[1] doing the man an injustice. Why not bring him into contact with some of our alcoholic crowd? He might have a chance. I pointed out that I had had nothing to drink whatever for three years, and this in the face of difficulties that would have made nine out of ten men drink their heads off. Why not at least afford him an opportunity to hear my story? "Oh no," said my friend, "this chap is either through with liquor, or he is minus a job. If he has your will power and guts, he will make the grade."

138:3   I wanted to throw up my hands in discouragement, for I saw that I had failed to help my banker friend understand. He simply could not believe that his

---

[1] In the first edition this read: "were."

139:0   brother-executive suffered from a serious illness. There was nothing to do but wait.

139:1   Presently the man did slip and was fired. Following his discharge, we contacted him. Without much ado, he accepted the principles and procedure that had helped us. He is undoubtedly on the road to recovery. To me, this incident illustrates lack of understanding as to what really ails the alcoholic, and lack of knowledge as to what part employers might profitably take in salvaging their sick employees.

139:2   If you desire to help it might be well to disregard your own drinking, or lack of it. Whether you are a hard drinker, a moderate drinker or a teetotaler[1], you may have some pretty strong opinions, perhaps prejudices. Those who drink moderately may be more annoyed with an alcoholic than a total abstainer would be. Drinking occasionally, and understanding your own reactions, it is possible for you to become quite sure of many things which, so far as the alcoholic is concerned, are not always so. As a moderate drinker, you can take your liquor or leave it alone. Whenever you want to, you control your drinking. Of an evening, you can go on a mild bender, get up in the morning, shake your head and go to business. To you, liquor is no real problem. You cannot see why it should be to anyone else, save the spineless and stupid.

139:3   When dealing with an alcoholic, there may be a natural annoyance that a man could be so weak, stupid and irresponsible. Even when you understand the malady better, you may feel this feeling rising.[2]

139:4   A look at the alcoholic in your organization is many times illuminating. Is he not usually brilliant, fast-thinking, imaginative and likeable? When sober, does

---

[1] A person who does not drink alcohol.

[2] In the first edition this read: "Even when you understand the malady better, you may find this feeling rising."

140:0   he not work hard and have a knack of getting things done? If he had these qualities and did not drink would he be worth retaining? Should he have the same consideration as other ailing employees? Is he worth salvaging? If your decision is yes, whether the reason be humanitarian or business or both, then the following suggestions may be helpful.

140:1   Can you discard the feeling that you are dealing only with habit, with stubbornness, or a weak will? If this presents difficulty, re-reading chapters two and three, where the alcoholic sickness is discussed at length might be worth while. You, as a business man, want to know the necessities before considering the result. If you concede that your employee is ill, can he be forgiven for what he has done in the past? Can his past absurdities be forgotten? Can it be appreciated that he has been a victim of crooked thinking, directly caused by the action of alcohol on his brain?

140:2   I well remember the shock I received when a prominent doctor in Chicago told me of cases where pressure of the spinal fluid actually ruptured the brain. No wonder an alcoholic is strangely irrational. Who wouldn't be, with such a fevered brain? Normal drinkers are not so affected, nor can they understand the aberrations of the alcoholic.

140:3   Your man has probably been trying to conceal a number of scrapes, perhaps pretty messy ones. They may be disgusting. You may be at a loss to understand how such a seemingly above-board chap could be so involved. But these scrapes can generally be charged, no matter how bad, to the abnormal action of alcohol on his mind. When drinking, or getting over a bout, an alcoholic, sometimes the model of honesty when

141:0　normal, will do incredible things. Afterward, his revulsion will be terrible. Nearly always, these antics indicate nothing more than temporary conditions.

141:1　This is not to say that all alcoholics are honest and upright when not drinking. Of course that isn't so, and such people often may impose on you. Seeing your attempt to understand and help, some men will try to take advantage of your kindness. If you are sure your man does not want to stop, he may as well be discharged, the sooner the better. You are not doing him a favor by keeping him on. Firing such an individual may prove a blessing to him. It may be just the jolt he needs. I know, in my own particular case, that nothing my company could have done would have stopped me for, so long as I was able to hold my position, I could not possibly realize how serious my situation was. Had they fired me first, and had they then taken steps to see that I was presented with the solution contained in this book, I might have returned to them six months later, a well man.

141:2　But there are many men who want to stop, and with them you can go far. Your understanding treatment of their cases will pay dividends.

141:3　Perhaps you have such a man in mind. He wants to quit drinking and you want to help him, even if it be only a matter of good business. You now know more about alcoholism. You can see that he is mentally and physically sick. You are willing to overlook his past performances. Suppose an approach is made something like this:

141:4　State that you know about his drinking, and that it must stop. You might say you appreciate his abilities, would like to keep him, but cannot if he continues to

drink. A firm attitude at this point has helped many of us.

Next he can be assured that you do not intend to lecture, moralize, or condemn; that if this was done formerly, it was because of misunderstanding. If possible express a lack of hard feeling toward him. At this point, it might be well to explain alcoholism, the illness. Say that you believe he is a gravely ill person, with this qualification—being perhaps fatally ill, does he want to get well?[1] You ask, because many alcoholics, being warped and drugged, do not want to quit. But does he? Will he take every necessary step, submit to anything to get well, to stop drinking forever?

If he says yes, does he really mean it, or down inside does he think he is fooling you, and that after rest and treatment he will be able to get away with a few drinks now and then? We believe a man should be thoroughly probed on these points. Be satisfied he is not deceiving himself or you.

Whether you mention this book is a matter for your discretion. If he temporizes and still thinks he can ever drink again, even beer, he might as well be discharged after the next bender which, if an alcoholic, he is almost certain to have. He should understand that emphatically. Either you are dealing with a man who can and will get well or you are not. If not, why waste time with him? This may seem severe, but it is usually the best course.

After satisfying yourself that your man wants to recover and that he will go to any extreme to do so, you may suggest a definite course of action. For most alcoholics who are drinking, or who are just getting

---

[1] In the first edition this read: "At this point, it might be well to explain alcoholism, the sickness. Say that you believe he is a gravely-ill person, with this qualification—being perhaps fatally ill, does he want to get well immediately?"

143:0   over a spree, a certain amount of physical treatment is desirable, even imperative. The matter of physical treatment should, of course, be referred to your own doctor. Whatever the method, its object is to thoroughly clear mind and body of the effects of alcohol. In competent hands, this seldom takes long nor is it very expensive. Your man will fare better if placed in such physical condition that he can think straight and no longer craves liquor. If you propose such a procedure to him, it may be necessary to advance the cost of treatment, but we believe it should be made plain that any expense will later be deducted from his pay. It is better for him to feel fully responsible.

143:1   If your man accepts your offer, it should be pointed out that physical treatment is but a small part of the picture. Though you are providing him with the best possible medical attention, he should understand that he must undergo a change of heart. To get over drinking will require a transformation of thought and attitude. We all had to place recovery above everything, for without recovery we would have lost both home and business.

143:2   Can you have every confidence in his ability to recover? While on the subject of confidence, can you adopt the attitude that so far as you are concerned this will be a strictly personal matter, that his alcoholic derelictions, the treatment about to be undertaken, will never be discussed without his consent? It might be well to have a long chat with him on his return.

143:3   To return to the subject matter of this book: It contains full suggestions by which the employee may

144:0 solve his problem. To you, some of the ideas which it contains are novel. Perhaps you are not quite in sympathy with the approach we suggest. By no means do we offer it as the last word on this subject, but so far as we are concerned, it has worked with us. After all, are you not looking for results rather than methods? Whether your employee likes it or not, he will learn the grim truth about alcoholism. That won't hurt him a bit, even[1] though he does not go for this remedy.

144:1 We suggest you draw the book to the attention of the doctor who is to attend your patient during treatment. If the book is read the moment the patient is able, while acutely depressed, realization of his condition may come to him.

144:2 We hope the doctor will tell the patient the truth about his condition, whatever that happens to be. When the man is presented with this volume it is best that no one tell him he must abide by its suggestions. The man must decide for himself.

144:3 You are betting, of course, that your changed attitude plus[2] the contents of this book will turn the trick. In some cases it will, and in others it may not. But we think that if you persevere, the percentage of successes will gratify you. As[3] our work spreads and our numbers increase, we hope your employees may be put in personal contact with some of us. Meanwhile, we are sure a great deal can be accomplished by the use of the book alone.

144:4 On your employee's return, talk with him. Ask him if he thinks he has the answer. If he feels free to discuss his problems with you, if he knows you under-

---

[1] The word "even" did not appear in the first edition.

[2] In the first edition this read: "and."

[3] In the first edition this read: "When."

145:0 stand and will not be upset by anything he wishes to say, he will probably be off to a fast start.

145:1 In this connection, can you remain undisturbed if the man proceeds to tell you shocking things? He may, for example, reveal that he has padded his expense account or that he has planned to take your best customers away from you. In fact, he may say almost anything if he has accepted our solution which, as you know, demands rigorous honesty. Can you charge this off as you would a bad account and start fresh with him? If he owes you money you may wish to make terms.

145:2 If he speaks of his home situation, you can undoubtedly make helpful suggestions. Can he talk frankly with you so long as he does not bear business tales or criticize his associates? With this kind of employee such an attitude will command undying loyalty.

145:3 The greatest enemies of us[1] alcoholics are resentment, jealousy, envy, frustration, and fear. Wherever men are gathered together in business there will be rivalries and, arising out of these, a certain amount of office politics. Sometimes we alcoholics have an idea that people are trying to pull us down. Often this is not so at all. But sometimes our drinking will be used politically.

145:4 One instance comes to mind in which a malicious individual was always making friendly little jokes about an alcoholic's drinking exploits. In this way he was slyly carrying tales. In another case, an alcoholic was sent to a hospital for treatment. Only a few knew of it at first but, within a short time, it was billboarded throughout the entire company. Naturally this sort of thing decreased the man's chance of recovery. The

---

[1] In the first edition this read: "we."

146:0 employer can many times protect the victim from this kind of talk. The employer cannot play favorites, but he can always defend a man from needless provocation and unfair criticism.

146:1 As a class, alcoholics are energetic people. They work hard and they play hard. Your man should be on his mettle to make good. Being somewhat weakened, and faced with physical and mental readjustment to a life which knows no alcohol, he may overdo. You may have to curb his desire to work sixteen hours a day. You may need to encourage him to play once in a while. He may wish to do a lot for other alcoholics and something of the sort may come up during business hours. A reasonable amount of latitude will be helpful. This work is necessary to maintain his sobriety.

146:2 After your man has gone along without drinking for[1] a few months, you may be able to make use of his services with other employees who are giving you the alcoholic run-around—provided, of course, they are willing to have a third party in the picture. An alcoholic who has recovered, but holds a relatively unimportant job, can talk to a man with a better position. Being on a radically different basis of life, he will never take advantage of the situation.

146:3 Your man may be trusted. Long experience with alcoholic excuses naturally arouses suspicion. When his wife next calls saying he is sick, you might jump to the conclusion he is drunk. If he is, and is still trying to recover, he will tell you about it even if it means the loss of his job. For he knows he must be honest if he would live at all. He will appreciate knowing you are not bothering your head about him,

---

[1] The word "for" did not appear in the first edition.

147:0 that you are not suspicious nor are you trying to run his life so he will be shielded from temptation to drink. If he is conscientiously following the program of recovery he can go anywhere your business may call him.

147:1 In case he does stumble, even once, you will have to decide whether to let him go. If you are sure he doesn't mean business, there is no doubt you should discharge him. If, on the contrary, you are sure he is doing his utmost, you may wish to give him another chance. But you should feel under no obligation to keep him on, for your obligation has been well discharged already.

147:2 There is another thing you might wish to do. If your organization is a large one, your junior executives might be provided with this book. You might let them know you have no quarrel with the alcoholics of your organization. These juniors are often in a difficult position. Men under them are frequently their friends. So, for one reason or another, they cover these men, hoping matters will take a turn for the better. They often jeopardize their own positions by trying to help serious drinkers who should have been fired long ago, or else given an opportunity to get well.

147:3 After reading this book, a junior executive can go to such a man and say approximately this, "Look here, Ed. Do you want to stop drinking or not? You put me on the spot every time you get drunk. It isn't fair to me or the firm. I have been learning something about alcoholism. If you are an alcoholic, you are a mighty sick man. You act like one. The firm wants to help you get over it, and if you are interested, there is a way out. If you take it, your past will be forgotten

148:0 and the fact that you went away for treatment will not be mentioned.[1] But if you cannot or will not stop drinking, I think you ought to resign."

148:1 Your junior executive may not agree with the contents of our book. He need not, and often should not show it to his alcoholic prospect. But at least he will understand the problem and will no longer be misled by ordinary promises. He will be able to take a position with such a man which is eminently fair and square. He will have no further reason for covering up an alcoholic employee.

148:2 It boils right down to this: No man should be fired just because he is alcoholic. If he wants to stop, he should be afforded a real chance. If he cannot or does not want to stop, he should be discharged. The exceptions are few.

148:3 We think this method of approach will accomplish several things. It will permit the rehabilitation of good men. At the same time you will feel no reluctance to rid yourself of those who cannot or will not stop. Alcoholism may be causing your organization considerable damage in its waste of time, men and reputation. We hope our suggestions will help you plug up this sometimes serious leak. We think we are sensible when we urge that you stop this waste and give your worthwhile man a chance.

148:4 The other day an approach was made to the vice president of a large industrial concern. He remarked: "I'm mighty glad you fellows got over your drinking. But the policy of this company is not to interfere with the habits of our employees. If a man drinks so much that his job suffers, we fire him. I don't see how you can be of any help to us for, as you see, we don't have

---

[1] In the first edition this read: "If you do, your past will be forgotten and the fact that you went away for treatment will not be mentioned."

149:0 any alcoholic problem." This same company spends millions for research every year. Their cost of production is figured to a fine decimal point. They have recreational facilities. There is company insurance. There is a real interest, both humanitarian and business, in the well-being of employees. But alcoholism—well, they just don't believe they have it.

149:1 Perhaps this is a typical attitude. We, who have collectively seen a great deal of business life, at least from the alcoholic angle, had to smile at this gentleman's sincere opinion. He might be shocked if he knew how much alcoholism is costing his organization a year. That company may harbor many actual or potential alcoholics. We believe that managers of large enterprises often have little idea how prevalent this problem is. Even if you feel your organization has no alcoholic problem, it might pay to take another look down the line. You may make some interesting discoveries.

149:2 Of course, this chapter refers to alcoholics, sick people, deranged men. What our friend, the vice president, had in mind was the habitual or whoopee drinker. As to them, his policy is undoubtedly sound, but he did not distinguish between such people and the alcoholic.

149:3 It is not to be expected that an alcoholic employee will receive a disproportionate amount of time and attention. He should not be made a favorite. The right kind of man, the kind who recovers, will not want this sort of thing. He will not impose. Far from it. He will work like the devil and thank you to his dying day.

149:4 Today I own a little company. There are two

150:0   alcoholic employees, who produce as much as five
normal salesmen. But why not? They have a new
attitude, and they have been saved from a living death.
I have enjoyed every moment spent in getting them
straightened out.

Chapter 11

A VISION FOR YOU

151:1 OR MOST normal folks, drinking means conviviality, companionship and colorful imagination. It means release from care, boredom and worry. It is joyous intimacy with friends and a feeling that life is good. But not so with us in those last days of heavy drinking. The old pleasures were gone. They were but memories. Never could we recapture the great moments of the past. There was an insistent yearning to enjoy life as we once did and a heartbreaking obsession that some new miracle of control would enable us to do it. There was always one more attempt—and one more failure.

151:2 The less people tolerated us, the more we withdrew from society, from life itself. As we became subjects of King Alcohol[1], shivering denizens of his mad realm, the chilling vapor that is loneliness settled down. It thickened, ever becoming blacker. Some of us sought out sordid places, hoping to find understanding companionship and approval. Momentarily we did—then would come oblivion and the awful awakening to face the hideous Four Horsemen—Terror, Bewilderment, Frustration, Despair. Unhappy drinkers who read this page will understand!

151:3 Now and then a serious drinker, being dry at the moment says, "I don't miss it at all. Feel better. Work better. Having a better time." As ex-problem drink-

[1] A song from the 1800's. A parody about temperance sung to the tune of "King Andrew" a song about US President Andrew Jackson.

152:0   ers, we smile at such a sally.[1] We know our friend is like a boy whistling in the dark to keep up his spirits. He fools himself. Inwardly he would give anything to take half a dozen drinks and get away with them. He will presently try the old game again, for he isn't happy about his sobriety. He cannot picture life without alcohol. Some day he will be unable to imagine life either with alcohol or without it. Then he will know loneliness such as few do. He will be at the jumping-off place. He will wish for the end.

152:1   We have shown how we got out from under. You say, "Yes, I'm willing. But am I to be consigned to a life where I shall be stupid, boring and glum, like some righteous people I see? I know I must get along without liquor, but how can I? Have you a sufficient substitute?"

152:2   Yes, there is a substitute and it is vastly more than that. It is a fellowship in Alcoholics Anonymous. There you will find release from care, boredom and worry. Your imagination will be fired. Life will mean something at last. The most satisfactory years of your existence lie ahead. Thus we find the fellowship, and so will you.

152:3   "How is that to come about?" you ask. "Where am I to find these people?"

152:4   You are going to meet these new friends in your own community. Near you, alcoholics are dying helplessly like people in a sinking ship. If you live in a large place, there are hundreds. High and low, rich and poor, these are future fellows of Alcoholics Anonymous. Among them you will make lifelong friends. You will be bound to them with new and wonderful ties, for you will escape disaster together and you will

[1] In the first edition this read: "As ex-alcoholics, we smile at such a sally."

153:0   commence shoulder to shoulder your common journey. Then you will know what it means to give of yourself that others may survive and rediscover life. You will learn the full meaning of "Love thy neighbor as thyself."

153:1   It may seem incredible that these men are to become happy, respected, and useful once more. How can they rise out of such misery, bad repute and hopelessness? The practical answer is that since these things have happened among us, they can happen with you. Should you wish them above all else, and be willing to make use of our experience, we are sure they will come. The age of miracles is still with us. Our own recovery proves that!

153:2   Our hope is that when this chip of a book is launched on the world tide of alcoholism, defeated drinkers will seize upon it, to follow its suggestions. Many, we are sure, will rise to their feet and march on. They will approach still other sick ones and fellowships of Alcoholics Anonymous may spring up in each city and hamlet, havens for those who must find a way out.

153:3   In the chapter "Working With Others" you gathered an idea of how we approach and aid others to health. Suppose now that through you several families have adopted this way of life. You will want to know more of how to proceed from that point. Perhaps the best way of treating you to a glimpse of your future will be to describe the growth of the fellowship among us. Here is a brief account:

153:4   Years ago, in 1935, one of our number made a journey to a certain western city[1].[2] From a business standpoint, his trip came off badly. Had he been suc-

---

[1] Akron, Ohio.

[2] In the first edition this read: "Nearly four years ago, one of our number made a journey to a certain western city."

154:0 cessful in his enterprise, he would have been set on his feet financially which, at the time, seemed vitally important. But his venture wound up in a law suit and bogged down completely. The proceeding was shot through with much hard feeling and controversy.

154:1 Bitterly discouraged, he found himself in a strange place, discredited and almost broke. Still physically weak, and sober but a few months, he saw that his predicament was dangerous. He wanted so much to talk with someone, but whom?

154:2 One dismal afternoon he paced a hotel lobby[1] wondering how his bill was to be paid. At one end of the room stood a glass covered directory of local churches. Down the lobby a door opened into an attractive bar. He could see the gay crowd inside. In there he would find companionship and release. Unless he took some drinks, he might not have the courage to scrape an acquaintance and would have a lonely week-end.

154:3 Of course he couldn't drink, but why not sit hopefully at a table, a bottle of ginger ale before him? After all, had he not been sober six months now?[2] Perhaps he could handle, say, three drinks—no more! Fear gripped him. He was on thin ice. Again it was the old, insidious insanity—that first drink. With a shiver, he turned away and walked down the lobby to the church directory. Music and gay chatter still floated to him from the bar.

154:4 But what about his responsibilities—his family and the men who would die because they would not know how to get well, ah—yes, those other alcoholics? There must be many such in this town. He would phone a clergyman[3]. His sanity returned and he thanked

---

[1] The Mayflower Hotel, 263 South Main Street, Akron, Ohio.

[2] In the first edition this read: "Then after all, had he not been sober six months now?"

[3] Walter Tunks of St. Paul's Episcopal Church, Akron, Ohio.

155:0   God. Selecting a church at random[1] from the directory, he stepped into a booth and lifted the receiver.

155:1   His call to the clergyman led him presently to a certain resident of the town, who, though formerly able and respected, was then nearing the nadir of alcoholic despair. It was the usual situation: home in jeopardy, wife ill, children distracted, bills in arrears and standing damaged. He had a desperate desire to stop, but saw no way out, for he had earnestly tried many avenues of escape. Painfully aware of being somehow abnormal, the man did not fully realize what it meant to be alcoholic.*

155:2   When our friend related his experience, the man agreed that no amount of will power he might muster could stop his drinking for long. A spiritual experience, he conceded, was absolutely necessary, but the price seemed high upon the basis suggested. He told how he lived in constant worry about those who might find out about his alcoholism. He had, of course, the familiar alcoholic obsession that few knew of his drinking. Why, he argued, should he lose the remainder of his business, only to bring still more suffering to his family by foolishly admitting his plight to people from whom he made his livelihood? He would do anything, he said, but that.

155:3   Being intrigued, however, he invited our friend to his home. Some time later, and just as he thought he was getting control of his liquor situation, he went on a roaring bender. For him, this was the spree that ended all sprees. He saw that he would have to face

---

* This refers to Bill's first visit with Dr. Bob. These men later became co-founders of A.A. Bill's story opens the text of this book; Dr. Bob's heads the Story Section.

[1] St. Paul's Episcopal Church.

155

156:0   his problems squarely that God might give him mastery.

156:1   One morning he took the bull by the horns and set out to tell those he feared what his trouble had been. He found himself surprisingly well received, and learned that many knew of his drinking. Stepping into his car, he made the rounds of people he had hurt. He trembled as he went about, for this might mean ruin, particularly to a person in his line of business.

156:2   At midnight he came home exhausted, but very happy. He has not had a drink since.[1] As we shall see, he now means a great deal to his community, and the major liabilities of thirty years of hard drinking have been repaired in four.

156:3   But life was not easy for the two friends. Plenty of difficulties presented themselves. Both saw that they must keep spiritually active. One day they called up the head nurse of a local hospital. They explained their need and inquired if she had a first class alcoholic prospect.

156:4   She replied, "Yes, we've got a corker. He's just beaten up a couple of nurses. Goes off his head completely when he's drinking.[2] But he's a grand chap when he's sober, though he's been in here eight times in the last six months. Understand he was once a well-known lawyer in town, but just now we've got him strapped down tight." *

156:5   Here was a prospect all right but, by the description, none too promising. The use of spiritual principles in

---

* This refers to Bill's and Dr. Bob's first visit to A.A. Number Three.

[1] June 10, 1935.

[2] In the first edition this read: "Goes off his head completely when drinking."

157:0   such cases was not so well understood as it is now. But one of the friends said, "Put him in a private room. We'll be down."

157:1   Two days later, a future fellow of Alcoholics Anonymous stared glassily at the strangers beside his bed. "Who are you fellows, and why this private room? I was always in a ward before."

157:2   Said one of the visitors, "We're giving you a treatment for alcoholism."

157:3   Hopelessness was written large on the man's face as he replied, "Oh, but that's no use. Nothing would fix me. I'm a goner. The last three times, I got drunk on the way home from here. I'm afraid to go out the door. I can't understand it."

157:4   For an hour, the two friends told him about their drinking experiences. Over and over, he would say: "That's me. That's me. I drink like that."

157:5   The man in the bed was told of the acute poisoning from which he suffered, how it deteriorates the body of an alcoholic and warps his mind. There was much talk about the mental state preceding the first drink.

157:6   "Yes, that's me," said the sick man, "the very image. You fellows know your stuff all right, but I don't see what good it'll do. You fellows are somebody. I was once, but I'm a nobody now. From what you tell me, I know more than ever I can't stop." At this both the visitors burst into a laugh. Said the future Fellow Anonymous: "Damn little to laugh about that I can see."

157:7   The two friends spoke of their spiritual experience and told him about the course of action they carried out.

157:8   He interrupted: "I used to be strong for the church,

158:0   but that won't fix it. I've prayed to God on hangover mornings and sworn that I'd never touch another drop but by nine o'clock I'd be boiled as an owl."

158:1   Next day found the prospect more receptive. He had been thinking it over. "Maybe you're right," he said. "God ought to be able to do anything." Then he added, "He sure didn't do much for me when I was trying to fight this booze racket alone."

158:2   On the third day the lawyer gave his life to the care and direction of his Creator, and said he was perfectly willing to do anything necessary. His wife came, scarcely daring to be hopeful, though she thought she saw something different about her husband already. He had begun to have a spiritual experience.

158:3   That afternoon he put on his clothes and walked from the hospital a free man. He entered a political campaign, making speeches, frequenting men's gathering places of all sorts, often staying up all night. He lost the race by only a narrow margin. But he had found God—and in finding God had found himself.

158:4   That was in June, 1935. He never drank again. He too, has become a respected and useful member of his community. He has helped other men recover, and is a power in the church from which he was long absent.

158:5   So, you see, there were three alcoholics in that town, who now felt they had to give to others what they had found, or be sunk. After several failures to find others, a fourth turned up. He came through an acquaintance who had heard the good news. He proved to be a devil-may-care young fellow whose parents could not make out whether he wanted to stop drinking or not. They were deeply religious people, much shocked by their son's refusal to have anything to do with the

159:0 church. He suffered horribly from his sprees, but it seemed as if nothing could be done for him. He consented, however, to go to the hospital, where he occupied the very room recently vacated by the lawyer.

159:1 He had three visitors. After a bit, he said, "The way you fellows put this spiritual stuff makes sense. I'm ready to do business. I guess the old folks were right after all." So one more was added to the Fellowship.

159:2 All this time our friend of the hotel lobby incident remained in that town. He was there three months. He now returned home, leaving behind his first acquaintance, the lawyer and the devil-may-care chap. These men had found something brand new in life. Though they knew they must help other alcoholics if they would remain sober, that motive became secondary. It was transcended by the happiness they found in giving themselves for others. They shared their homes, their slender resources, and gladly devoted their spare hours to fellow-sufferers. They were willing, by day or night, to place a new man in the hospital and visit him afterward. They grew in numbers. They experienced a few distressing failures, but in those cases they made an effort to bring the man's family into a spiritual way of living, thus relieving much worry and suffering.

159:3 A year and six months later these three had succeeded with seven more. Seeing much of each other, scarce an evening passed that someone's home did not shelter a little gathering of men and women, happy in their release, and constantly thinking how they might present their discovery to some newcomer. In addition to these casual get-togethers, it became customary to set apart one night a week for a meeting to be at-

160:0 tended by anyone or everyone interested in a spiritual way of life. Aside from fellowship and sociability, the prime object was to provide a time and place where new people might bring their problems.

160:1   Outsiders became interested. One man and his wife placed their large home at the disposal of this strangely assorted crowd. This couple has since become so fascinated that they have dedicated their home to the work. Many a distracted wife has visited this house to find loving and understanding companionship among women who knew her problem, to hear from the lips of their husbands what had happened to them, to be advised how her own wayward mate might be hospitalized and approached when next he stumbled.

160:2   Many a man, yet dazed from his hospital experience, has stepped over the threshold of that home into freedom. Many an alcoholic who entered there came away with an answer. He succumbed to that gay crowd inside, who laughed at their own misfortunes and understood his.[1] Impressed by those who visited him at the hospital, he capitulated entirely when, later, in an upper room of this house, he heard the story of some man whose experience closely tallied with his own. The expression on the faces of the women, that indefinable something in the eyes of the men, the stimulating and electric atmosphere of the place, conspired to let him know that here was haven at last.

160:3   The very practical approach to his problems, the absence of intolerance of any kind, the informality, the genuine democracy, the uncanny understanding which these people had were irresistible. He and his

---

[1] In the first edition this read: "He succumbed to that gay crowd inside, who laughed at their misfortune and understood him."

161:0   wife would leave elated by the thought of what they could now do for some stricken acquaintance and his family. They knew they had a host of new friends; it seemed they had known these strangers always. They had seen miracles, and one was to come to them. They had visioned the Great Reality—their loving and All Powerful Creator.

161:1   Now, this house will hardly accommodate its weekly visitors, for they number sixty or eighty as a rule. Alcoholics are being attracted from far and near. From surrounding towns, families drive long distances to be present. A community thirty miles away[1] has fifteen fellows of Alcoholics Anonymous. Being a large place, we think that some day its Fellowship will number many hundreds.*

161:2   But life among Alcoholics Anonymous is more than attending gatherings and visiting hospitals. Cleaning up old scrapes, helping to settle family differences, explaining the disinherited son to his irate parents, lending money and securing jobs for each other, when justified—these are everyday occurrences. No one is too discredited or has sunk too low to be welcomed cordially—if he means business. Social distinctions, petty rivalries and jealousies—these are laughed out of countenance. Being wrecked in the same vessel, being restored and united under one God, with hearts and minds attuned to the welfare of others, the things which matter so much to some people no longer signify much to them. How could they?

161:3   Under only slightly different conditions, the same thing is taking place in many[2] eastern cities. In one of

* Written in 1939.

[1] Cleveland, Ohio.

[2] In the first edition this read: "several."

162:0   these there is a well-known hospital[1] for the treatment of
alcoholic and drug addiction. Six years ago one of our
number[2] was a patient there. Many of us have felt, for
the first time, the Presence and Power of God within its
walls. We are greatly indebted to the doctor in attendance there[3], for he, although it might prejudice his own
work, has told us of his belief in ours.[4]

162:1   Every few days this doctor suggests our approach to
one of his patients. Understanding our work, he can do
this with an eye to selecting those who are willing and
able to recover on a spiritual basis. Many of us, former
patients, go there to help. Then, in this eastern city[5], there
are informal meetings such as we have described to you,
where you may now see scores of members.[6] There are
the same fast friendships, there is the same helpfulness to
one another as you find among our western friends. There
is a good bit of travel between East and West and we
foresee a great increase in this helpful interchange.

162:2   Some day we hope that every alcoholic who journeys will find a Fellowship of Alcoholics Anonymous at
his destination. To some extent this is already true. Some
of us are salesmen and go about. Little clusters of twos
and threes and fives of us have sprung up in other communities, through contact with our two larger centers.
Those of us who travel drop in as often as we can. This
practice enables us to lend a hand, at the same time avoiding certain alluring distractions of the road, about which
any traveling man can inform you.*

162:3   Thus we grow. And so can you, though you be but

* Written in 1939. In 1995 there are over 89,000 groups. There is A.A.
  activity in 141 countries, with an estimated membership of two million.

[1] Charles B. Towns Hospital, New York, NY.

[2] Bill Wilson.

[3] William Duncan Silkworth, M.D.

[4] In the first edition this read: "...has told us his belief in our work."

[5] New York, NY.

[6] In the first edition this read: "Then, in this eastern city, there are informal meetings such as we have described to you, where you may see thirty or forty, there are the same fast friendships, there is the same helpfulness to one another as you find among our western friends."

163:0   one man with this book in your hand. We believe and hope it contains all you will need to begin.

163:1   We know what you are thinking. You are saying to yourself: "I'm jittery and alone. I couldn't do that." But you can. You forget that you have just now tapped a source of power much greater than yourself.[1] To duplicate, with such backing, what we have accomplished is only a matter of willingness, patience and labor.

163:2   We know of an A.A. member who was living in a large community[2].[3] He had lived there but a few weeks when he found that the place probably contained more alcoholics per square mile than any city in the country. This was only a few days ago at this writing. (1939) The authorities were much concerned. He got in touch with a prominent psychiatrist who had undertaken certain responsibilities for the mental health of the community. The doctor proved to be able and exceedingly anxious to adopt any workable method of handling the situation. So he inquired, what did our friend have on the ball?

163:3   Our friend proceeded to tell him. And with such good effect that the doctor agreed to a test among his patients and certain other alcoholics from a clinic which he attends. Arrangements were also made with the chief psychiatrist of a large public hospital[4] to select still others from the stream of misery which flows through that institution.

163:4   So our fellow worker will soon have friends galore. Some of them may sink and perhaps never get up, but if our experience is a criterion, more than half of those approached will become fellows of Alcoholics Anonymous. When a few men in this city have found them-

---

[1] In the first edition this read: "You forget that you have just now tapped a source of power so much greater than yourself."

[2] Montclair, N.J.

164:0 selves, and have discovered the joy of helping others to face life again, there will be no stopping until everyone in that town has had his opportunity to recover—if he can and will.

164:1 Still you may say: "But I will not have the benefit of contact with you who write this book." We cannot be sure. God will determine that, so you must remember that your real reliance is always upon Him. He will show you how to create the fellowship you crave.*

164:2 Our book is meant to be suggestive only. We realize we know only a little. God will constantly disclose more to you and to us. Ask Him in your morning meditation what you can do each day for the man who is still sick. The answers will come, if your own house is in order. But obviously you cannot transmit something you haven't got. See to it that your relationship with Him is right, and great events will come to pass for you and countless others. This is the Great Fact for us.

164:3 Abandon yourself to God as you understand God. Admit your faults to Him and to your fellows. Clear away the wreckage of your past. Give freely of what you find and join us. We shall be with you in the Fellowship of the Spirit, and you will surely meet some of us as you trudge the Road of Happy Destiny.

164:4 May God bless you and keep you—until then.

---

* Alcoholics Anonymous will be glad to hear from you. Address P.O. Box 459, Grand Central Station, New York, NY 10163.

THE DOCTOR'S NIGHTMARE

171:1   *A co-founder of Alcoholics Anonymous. The birth of our Society dates from his first day of permanent sobriety, June 10, 1935. To 1950, the year of his death, he carried the A.A. message to more than 5,000 alcoholic men and women, and to all these he gave his medical services without thought of charge. In this prodigy of service, he was well assisted by Sister Ignatia at St. Thomas Hospital in Akron, Ohio, one of the greatest friends our Fellowship will ever know.*

171:2   *I* WAS BORN in a small New England village[1] of about seven thousand souls. The general moral standard was, as I recall it, far above the average. No beer or liquor was sold in the neighborhood, except at the State liquor agency where perhaps one might procure a pint if he could convince the agent that he really needed it. Without this proof the expectant purchaser would be forced to depart empty handed with none of what I later came to believe was the great panacea for all human ills. Men who had liquor shipped in from Boston or New York by express were looked upon with great distrust and disfavor by most of the good townspeople. The town was well supplied with churches and schools in which I pursued my early educational activities.

171:3   My father was a professional man of recognized ability and both my father and mother were most

171

---

[1] St. Johnsbury, Vermont.

172:0 active in church affairs. Both father and mother were considerably above the average in intelligence.

172:1 Unfortunately for me, I was the only child, which perhaps engendered the selfishness which played such an important part in bringing on my alcoholism.

172:2 From childhood through high school I was more or less forced to go to church, Sunday School and evening service, Monday night Christian Endeavor and sometimes to Wednesday evening prayer meeting. This had the effect of making me resolve that when I was free from parental domination, I would never again darken the doors of a church. This resolution I kept steadfastly for the next forty years, except when circumstances made it seem unwise to absent myself.

172:3 After high school came four years in one of the best colleges in the country[1] where drinking seemed to be a major extra-curricular activity. Almost everyone seemed to do it. I did it more and more, and had lots of fun without much grief, either physical or financial. I seemed to be able to snap back the next morning better than most of my fellow drinkers, who were cursed (or perhaps blessed) with a great deal of morning-after nausea. Never once in my life have I had a headache, which fact leads me to believe that I was an alcoholic almost from the start. My whole life seemed to be centered around doing what I wanted to do, without regard for the rights, wishes, or privileges of anyone else; a state of mind which became more and more predominant as the years passed. I was graduated "summa cum laude" in the eyes of the drinking fraternity, but not in the eyes of the Dean.

172:4 The next three years I spent in Boston, Chicago, and Montreal in the employ of a large manufacturing con-

---

[1] Dartmouth College in New Hampshire.

173:0 cern, selling railway supplies, gas engines of all sorts, and many other items of heavy hardware. During these years, I drank as much as my purse permitted, still without paying too great a penalty, although I was beginning to have morning jitters at times. I lost only a half day's work during these three years.

173:1 My next move was to take up the study of medicine, entering one of the largest universities in the country[1]. There I took up the business of drinking with much greater earnestness than I had previously shown. On account of my enormous capacity for beer, I was elected to membership in one of the drinking societies, and soon became one of the leading spirits. Many mornings I have gone to classes, and even though fully prepared, would turn and walk back to the fraternity house because of my jitters, not daring to enter the classroom for fear of making a scene should I be called on for recitation.

173:2 This went from bad to worse until Sophomore spring when, after a prolonged period of drinking, I made up my mind that I could not complete my course, so I packed my grip and went South to spend a month on a large farm owned by a friend of mine. When I got the fog out of my brain, I decided that quitting school was very foolish and that I had better return and continue my work. When I reached school, I discovered the faculty had other ideas on the subject. After much argument they allowed me to return and take my exams, all of which I passed creditably. But they were much disgusted and told me they would attempt to struggle along without my presence. After many painful discussions, they finally gave me my credits and I

[1] The University of Michigan.

174:0   migrated to another of the leading universities of the country[1] and entered as a Junior that fall.

174:1   There my drinking became so much worse that the boys in the fraternity house where I lived felt forced to send for my father, who made a long journey in the vain endeavor to get me straightened around. This had little effect however for I kept on drinking and used a great deal more hard liquor than in former years.

174:2   Coming up to final exams I went on a particularly strenuous spree. When I went in to write the examinations, my hand trembled so I could not hold a pencil. I passed in at least three absolutely blank books. I was, of course, soon on the carpet and the upshot was that I had to go back for two more quarters and remain absolutely dry, if I wished to graduate. This I did, and proved myself satisfactory to the faculty, both in deportment and scholastically.

174:3   I conducted myself so creditably that I was able to secure a much coveted internship in a western city[2], where I spent two years. During these two years I was kept so busy that I hardly left the hospital at all. Consequently, I could not get into any trouble.

174:4   When those two years were up, I opened an office downtown. I had some money, all the time in the world, and considerable stomach trouble. I soon discovered that a couple of drinks would alleviate my gastric distress, at least for a few hours at a time, so it was not at all difficult for me to return to my former excessive indulgence.

174:5   By this time I was beginning to pay very dearly physically and, in hope of relief, voluntarily incarcerated myself at least a dozen times in one of the

[1] Rush University near Chicago, Illinois.

[2] Akron, Ohio.

175:0 local sanitariums. I was between Scylla and Charybdis[1] now, because if I did not drink my stomach tortured me, and if I did, my nerves did the same thing. After three years of this, I wound up in the local hospital where they attempted to help me, but I would get my friends to smuggle me a quart, or I would steal the alcohol about the building, so that I got rapidly worse.

175:1 Finally my father had to send a doctor out from my home town who managed to get me back there in some way, and I was in bed about two months before I could venture out of the house. I stayed about town a couple of months more and then returned to resume my practice. I think I must have been thoroughly scared by what had happened, or by the doctor, or probably both, so that I did not touch a drink again until the country went dry.

175:2 With the passing of the Eighteenth Amendment[2] I felt quite safe. I knew everyone would buy a few bottles, or cases, of liquor as their exchequers permitted, and that it would soon be gone. Therefore it would make no great difference, even if I should do some drinking. At that time I was not aware of the almost unlimited supply the government made it possible for us doctors to obtain, neither had I any knowledge of the bootlegger who soon appeared on the horizon. I drank with moderation at first, but it took me only a relatively short time to drift back into the old habits which had wound up so disastrously before.

175:3 During the next few years, I developed two distinct phobias. One was the fear of not sleeping, and the other was the fear of running out of liquor. Not being

---

[1] In ancient lore, Scylla referred to a rock between Sicily and Italy; Charybdis was a whirlpool adjacent to it. Mariners often hit one while trying to avoid the other.

[2] A 1920 amendment to The Constitution which outlawed alcohol until repealed in 1933.

176:0 a man of means, I knew that if I did not stay sober enough to earn money, I would run out of liquor. Most of the time, therefore, I did not take the morning drink which I craved so badly, but instead would fill up on large doses of sedatives to quiet the jitters, which distressed me terribly. Occasionally, I would yield to the morning craving, but if I did, it would be only a few hours before I would be quite unfit for work. This would lessen my chances of smuggling some home that evening, which in turn would mean a night of futile tossing around in bed followed by a morning of unbearable jitters. During the subsequent fifteen years I had sense enough never to go to the hospital if I had been drinking, and very seldom did I receive patients. I would sometimes hide out in one of the clubs of which I was a member, and had the habit at times of registering at a hotel under a fictitious name. But my friends usually found me and I would go home if they promised that I should not be scolded.

176:1 If my wife was planning to go out in the afternoon, I would get a large supply of liquor and smuggle it home and hide it in the coal bin, the clothes chute, over door jambs, over beams in the cellar and in cracks in the cellar tile. I also made use of old trunks and chests, the old can container, and even the ash container. The water tank on the toilet I never used, because that looked too easy. I found out later that my wife inspected it frequently. I used to put eight or twelve ounce bottles of alcohol in a fur lined glove and toss it onto the back airing porch when winter days got dark enough. My bootlegger had hidden alcohol at the back steps where I could get it at my convenience. Sometimes I would bring it in my

177:0 pockets, but they were inspected, and that became too risky. I used also to put it up in four ounce bottles and stick several in my stocking tops. This worked nicely until my wife and I went to see Wallace Beery in "Tugboat Annie," after which the pant-leg and stocking racket were out!

177:1 I will not take space to relate all my hospital or sanitarium experiences.

177:2 During all this time we became more or less ostracized by our friends. We could not be invited out because I would surely get tight and my wife dared not invite people in for the same reason. My phobia for sleeplessness demanded that I get drunk every night, but in order to get more liquor for the next night, I had to stay sober during the day, at least up to four o'clock. This routine went on with few interruptions for seventeen years. It was really a horrible nightmare, this earning money, getting liquor, smuggling it home,   getting drunk, morning jitters, taking large doses of sedatives to make it possible for me to earn more money, and so on ad nauseam. I used to promise my wife, my friends, and my children that I would drink no more— promises which seldom kept me sober even through the day, though I was very sincere when I made them.

177:3 For the benefit of those experimentally inclined, I should mention the so-called beer experiment. When beer first came back, I thought that I was safe. I could drink all I wanted of that. It was harmless; nobody ever got drunk on beer. So I filled the cellar full, with the permission of my good wife. It was not long before I was drinking at least a case and a half a day. I put on thirty pounds of weight in about two

178:0 months, looked like a pig, and was uncomfortable from shortness of breath. It then occurred to me that after one was all smelled up with beer nobody could tell what had been drunk, so I began to fortify my beer with straight alcohol. Of course, the result was very bad, and that ended the beer experiment.

178:1 About the time of the beer experiment I was thrown in with a crowd of people[1] who attracted me because of their seeming poise, health, and happiness. They spoke with great freedom from embarrassment, which I could never do, and they seemed very much at ease on all occasions and appeared very healthy. More than these attributes, they seemed to be happy. I was self conscious and ill at ease most of the time, my health was at the breaking point, and I was thoroughly miserable. I sensed they had something I did not have, from which I might readily profit. I learned that it was something of a spiritual nature, which did not appeal to me very much, but I thought it could do no harm. I gave the matter much time and study for the next two and a half years, but still got tight every night nevertheless. I read everything I could find, and talked to everyone who I thought knew anything about it.

178:2 My wife became deeply interested and it was her interest that sustained mine, though I at no time sensed that it might be an answer to my liquor problem. How my wife kept her faith and courage during all those years, I'll never know, but she did. If she had not, I know I would have been dead a long time ago. For some reason, we alcoholics seem to have the gift of picking out the world's finest women. Why they

_____
[1] The Oxford Group.

179:0   should be subjected to the tortures we inflict upon them, I cannot explain.

179:1   About this time a lady called up my wife[1] one Saturday afternoon, saying she wanted me to come over that evening to meet a friend of hers[2] who might help me. It was the day before Mother's Day and I had come home plastered, carrying a big potted plant which I set down on the table and forthwith went upstairs and passed out. The next day she called again. Wishing to be polite, though I felt very badly, I said, "Let's make the call," and extracted from my wife a promise that we would not stay over fifteen minutes.

179:2   We entered her house at exactly five o'clock and it was eleven fifteen when we left. I had a couple of shorter talks with this man afterward, and stopped drinking abruptly. This dry spell lasted for about three weeks; then I went to Atlantic City to attend several days' meeting of a national society[3] of which I was a member. I drank all the scotch they had on the train and bought several quarts on my way to the hotel. This was on Sunday. I got tight that night, stayed sober Monday till after the dinner and then proceeded to get tight again. I drank all I dared in the bar, and then went to my room to finish the job. Tuesday I started in the morning, getting well organized by noon. I did not want to disgrace myself so I then checked out. I bought some more liquor on the way to the depot. I had to wait some time for the train. I remember nothing from then on until I woke up at a friend's house, in a town near home[4]. These good people notified my wife, who sent my newly made friend over to get me. He came and got me home and to bed, gave

---

[1] Henrietta Seiberling.
[2] Bill Wilson.
[3] The American Medical Association.
[4] Cuyahoga Falls, Ohio.

180:0 me a few drinks that night, and one bottle of beer the
next morning.

180:1   That was June 10, 1935, and that was my last drink.
As I write nearly four years have passed.

180:2   The question which might naturally come into your
mind would be: "What did the man do or say that was
different from what others had done or said?" It must be
remembered that I had read a great deal and talked to
everyone who knew, or thought they knew anything about
the subject of alcoholism. But this was a man who had
experienced many years of frightful drinking, who had
had most all the drunkard's experiences known to man,
but who had been cured by the very means I had been
trying to employ, that is to say the spiritual approach. He
gave me information about the subject of alcoholism which
was undoubtedly helpful. *Of far more importance was
the fact that he was the first living human with whom
I had ever talked, who knew what he was talking
about in regard to alcoholism from actual experience.
In other words, he talked my language.* He knew all
the answers, and certainly not because he had picked
them up in his reading.

180:3   It is a most wonderful blessing to be relieved of the
terrible curse with which I was afflicted. My health is
good and I have regained my self-respect and the respect of my colleagues. My home life is ideal and my
business is as good as can be expected in these uncertain
times.

180:4   I spend a great deal of time passing on what I learned
to others who want and need it badly. I do it for four
reasons:

181:0
1. Sense of duty.
2. It is a pleasure.
3. Because in so doing I am paying my debt to the man who took time to pass it on to me.
4. Because every time I do it I take out a little more insurance for myself against a possible slip.

181:1   Unlike most of our crowd, I did not get over my craving for liquor much during the first two and one-half years of abstinence. It was almost always with me. But at no time have I been anywhere near yielding. I used to get terribly upset when I saw my friends drink and knew I could not, but I schooled myself to believe that though I once had the same privilege, I had abused it so frightfully that it was withdrawn. So it doesn't behoove me to squawk about it for, after all, nobody ever had to throw me down and pour liquor down my throat.

181:2   If you think you are an atheist, an agnostic, a skeptic, or have any other form of intellectual pride which keeps you from accepting what is in this book, I feel sorry for you. If you still think you are strong enough to beat the game alone, that is your affair. But if you really and truly want to quit drinking liquor for good and all, and sincerely feel that you must have some help, we know that we have an answer for you. It never fails, if you go about it with one half the zeal you have been in the habit of showing when you were getting another drink.

181:3   Your Heavenly Father will never let you down!

SPIRITUAL EXPERIENCE

The terms "spiritual experience" and "spiritual awakening" are used many times in this book which, upon careful reading, shows that the personality change sufficient to bring about recovery from alcoholism has manifested itself among us in many different forms.

Yet it is true that our first printing gave many readers the impression that these personality changes, or religious experiences, must be in the nature of sudden and spectacular upheavals. Happily for everyone, this conclusion is erroneous.

In the first few chapters a number of sudden revolutionary changes are described. Though it was not our intention to create such an impression, many alcoholics have nevertheless concluded that in order to recover they must acquire an immediate and overwhelming "God-consciousness" followed at once by a vast change in feeling and outlook.

Among our rapidly growing membership of thousands of alcoholics such transformations, though frequent, are by no means the rule. Most of our experiences are what the psychologist William James calls the "educational variety" because they develop slowly over a period of time. Quite often friends of the newcomer are aware of the difference long before he is himself. He finally realizes that he has undergone a profound alteration in his reaction to life; that such a change could hardly have been brought about by himself alone. What often takes place in a few months could seldom have been accomplished by years of self discipline. With few exceptions our members find that they have tapped an unsuspected

inner resource which they presently identify with their own conception of a Power greater than themselves.

Most of us think this awareness of a Power greater than ourselves is the essence of spiritual experience. Our more religious members call it "God-consciousness."

Most emphatically we wish to say that any alcoholic capable of honestly facing his problems in the light of our experience can recover, provided he does not close his mind to all spiritual concepts. He can only be defeated by an attitude of intolerance or belligerent denial.

We find that no one need have difficulty with the spirituality of the program. *Willingness, honesty and open mindedness are the essentials of recovery. But these are indispensable.*

"There is a principle which is a bar against all information, which is proof against all arguments and which cannot fail to keep a man in everlasting ignorance—that principle is contempt prior to investigation."

—HERBERT SPENCER

The following is a reproduction of the 1938 Original Manuscript of *Alcoholics Anonymous*. This was the version of The Big Book distributed to friends and colleagues of AA's founders before the First Edition was printed.

When we sat down to transcribe the copies we could find, we came across a good number of apparent mistakes. We are not interested in adding any changes or opinions about what it was "supposed" to say, so we have left the text just as it originally appeared. Following the places where we found apparent grammatical or spelling errors we have added a † to assure the reader that it is an intentionally reproduced "typo."

The paragraph numbers correspond to the equivalent modern paragraph numbers in the front of this book.

A L C O H O L I C S

A N O N Y M O U S

Published by:

Works Publishing Co.,
17 Williams St.,
Newark, N.J.

FOREWORD

We, of Alcoholics Anonymous, are more than one hundred men and women who have recovered from a seemingly hopeless state of mind and body. To show other alcoholics PRECISELY HOW THEY CAN RECOVER is the main purpose of this book. For them, we think these pages will prove so convincing that no further authentication will be necessary. We hope this account of our experiences will help everyone to better understand the alcoholic. Many do not yet comprehend that he is a very sick person. And besides, we are sure that our new way of living has its advantages for all.

It is important that we remain anonymous because we are too few, at present, to handle the overwhelming number of personal appeals which will result from this publication. Being mostly business or professional folk we could not well carry on our occupations in such an event. We would like it clearly understood that our alcoholic work is an avocation only, so that when writing or speaking publicly about alcoholism, we urge each of our Fellowship to omit his personal name, designating himself instead as "A Member of Alcoholics Anonymous."

Very earnestly we ask the press also, to observe this request, for otherwise we shall be greatly handicapped.

We are not an organization in the conventional sense of the word. There are no fees nor dues whatsoever. The only requirement for membership is an honest desire to stop drinking. We are not allied with any particular faith, sect or denomination, nor do we oppose anyone. We simply wish to be helpful to those who are afflicted.

We shall be interested to hear from those who are getting results from this book, particularly from those who have commenced work with other alcoholics. We shall try to contact such cases.

Inquiry by scientific, medical and religious societies will be welcomed.

(This multilith volume will be sent upon receipt of $3.50, and the printed book will be mailed, at no additional cost, as soon as published.)

ALCOHOLICS ANONYMOUS

THE DOCTOR'S OPINION

We of Alcoholics Anonymous believe that the reader will be interested in the medical estimate of the plan of recovery described in this book. Convincing testimony must surely come from medical men who have had experience with the sufferings of our members and have witnessed our return to health. A well known doctor, chief physician at a nationally prominent hospital specializing in alcoholic and drug addiction, gave Alcoholics Anonymous this letter:

To Whom It May Concern:
I have specialized in the treatment of alcoholism for many years.

About four years ago I attended a patient who, though he had been a competent business man of good earning capacity, was an alcoholic of a type I had come to regard as hopeless.

In the course of his third treatment he acquired certain ideas concerning a possible means of recovery. As part of his rehabilitation he commenced to present his conceptions to other alcoholics, impressing upon them that they must do likewise with still others. This has become the basis of a rapidly growing fellowship of these men and their families. This man and over one hundred others appear to have recovered.

I personally know thirty of these cases who were of the type with whom other methods had failed completely.

These facts appear to be of extreme medical importance; because of the extraordinary possibilities of rapid growth inherent in this group they mark a new epoch in the annals of alcoholism. These men may well have a remedy for thousands of such situations.

You may rely absolutely on anything they say about themselves.

Very truly yours,
(Signed)- - - - - M.D.

The physician who, at our request, gave us this letter, has been kind enough to enlarge upon his views in another statement which follows. In this statement he confirms what anyone who has suffered alcoholic torture must believe — that the body of the alcoholic is quite as abnormal as his mind. It does not satisfy us to be told that we cannot control our drinking just because we were maladjusted to life, that we were in full flight from reality, or were outright mental defectives. These things were true to some extent, in fact, to a considerable extent with some of us. But we are sure that our bodies were sickened as well. In our belief, any picture of the alcoholic which leaves out this physical factor is incomplete.

The doctor's theory that we have a kind of allergy to alcohol interests us. As laymen, our opinion as to its soundness may, of course, mean little. But as ex-alcoholics, we can say that his explanation makes good sense. It explains many things for which we cannot otherwise account.

Though we work out our solution on the spiritual plane, we favor hospitalization for the alcoholic who is very jittery or befogged. More often than not, it is imperative that a man's brain be cleared before he is approached, as he has then a better chance of understanding and accepting what we have to offer.

The doctor writes:

The subject presented in this book seems to me to be of paramount importance to those afflicted with alcoholic addiction.

I say this after many years' experience as Medical Director of one of the oldest hospitals in the country treating alcoholic and drug addiction.

There was, therefore, a sense of real satisfaction when I was asked to contribute a few words on a subject which is covered in such masterly detail in these pages.

We doctors have realized for a long time that some form of moral psychology was of urgent importance to alcoholics, but its application presented difficulties beyond our conception. What with our ultra-modern standards, our scientific approach to everything, we are perhaps not well equipped to apply the powers of good that lie outside our synthetic knowledge.

About four years ago one of the leading contributors to this book came under our care in this hospital and while here he acquired some ideas which he put into practical application at once.

Later, he requested the privilege of being allowed to tell his story to other patients here and perhaps with some misgiving, we consented. The cases we have followed through have been most interesting; in fact, many of them are amazing. The unselfishness of these men as we have come to know them, the entire absence of profit motive, and their community spirit, is indeed inspiring to one who has labored long and wearily in this alcoholic field. They believe in themselves, and still more in the Power which pulls chronic alcoholics back from the gates of death.

Of course an alcoholic ought to be freed from his physical craving for liquor, and this often requires a definite hospital procedure, before psychological measures can be of maximum benefit.

We believe, and so suggested a few years ago, that the action of alcohol on these chronic alcoholics is a manifestation of an allergy; that the phenomenon of craving is limited to this class and never occurs in the average temperate drinker. These allergic types can never safely use alcohol in any form at all; and once having formed the habit and found they cannot break it, once having lost their self-confidence, their reliance upon things human, their problems pile up on them and become astonishingly difficult to solve.

Frothy emotional appeal seldom suffices. The message which can interest and hold these alcoholic people must have depth and weight. In nearly all cases, their ideals must be grounded in a power greater than themselves, if they are to re-create their lives.

If any feel that as psychiatrists directing a hospital for alcoholics we appear somewhat sentimental, let them stand with us a while on the firing line, see the tragedies, the despairing wives, the little children; let the solving of these problems become a part of their daily work, and even of their sleeping moments, and the most cynical will not wonder that we have accepted and encouraged this movement. We feel, after many years of experience, that we have found nothing which has contributed more to the rehabilitation of these men than the community movement now growing up among them.

Men and women drink essentially because they like the effect produced by alcohol. The sensation is so elusive that, while they admit it is injurious, they cannot after a time differentiate the true from the false. To them, their alcoholic life seems the only normal one. They are restless, irritable and discontented, unless they can again experience the sense of ease and comfort which comes at once by taking a few drinks — drinks which they see others taking with impunity. After they have succumbed to the desire again, as so many do, and the phenomenon of craving develops, they pass through the well-known stages of a spree, emerging remorseful, with a firm resolution not to drink again. This is repeated over and over, and unless this person can experience an entire psychic change there is very little hope of his recovery.

On the other hand — and strange as this may seem to those who do not understand — once a psychic change has occurred, the very same person who seemed doomed, who had so many problems he despaired of ever solving them, suddenly finds himself easily able to control his desire for alcohol, the only effort necessary being that required to follow a few simple rules.

Men have cried out to me in sincere and despairing appeal: "Doctor, I cannot go on like this! I have everything to live for! I must stop, but I cannot! You must help me!"

Faced with this problem, if a doctor is honest with himself, he must sometimes feel his own inadequacy. Although he gives all that is in him, it often is not enough. One feels that something more than human power is needed to produce the essential psychic change. Though the aggregate of recoveries resulting from psychiatric effort is perhaps considerable, we physicians must admit we have made little impression upon the problem as a whole. Many types do not respond to the ordinary psychological approach.

I do not hold with those who believe that alcoholism is entirely a mental condition. I have had many men who had, for example, worked a period of months on some problem or business deal which was to be settled on a certain date, favorably to them. They took a drink a day or so prior to the date, and then the phenomenon of craving at once became paramount to all other interests so that the important appointment was not met. These men were not drinking to escape; they were drinking to overcome a craving beyond their mental control.

There are many situations which arise out of the phenomenon of craving which cause men to make the supreme sacrifice rather than continue to fight.

The classification of alcoholics seems most difficult, and in much detail is outside the scope of this book. There are, of course, the constitutional psychopaths who are emotionally unstable. We are all familiar with this type. They are always "going on the wagon for keeps." They are over-remorseful and make many resolutions, but never a decision.

Then there are those who are never properly adjusted to life, who are the so-called neurotics. The prognosis of this type is unfavorable.

There is the type of man who is unwilling to admit that he cannot take a drink. He plans various ways of drinking. He changes his brand or his environment. There is the type who always believes that after being entirely free from alcohol for a period of time he can take a drink without danger. There is the manic-depressive type, who is, perhaps, the least understood by his friends, and about whom a whole chapter could be written.

Then there are types entirely normal in every respect except in the effect alcohol has upon them. They are often able, intelligent, friendly people.

All these, and many others, have one symptom in common: they cannot start drinking without developing the phenomenon of craving. This phenomenon, as we have suggested, may be the manifestation of an allergy which differentiates these people, sets them apart as a distinct entity. It has never been, by any treatment with which we are familiar, permanently eradicated. The only relief we have to suggest is entire abstinence.

This immediately precipitates us into a seething caldron of debate. Much has been written pro and con, but among physicians, the general opinion seems to be that most chronic alcoholics are doomed.

What is the solution? Perhaps I can best answer this by relating an experience of two years ago.

About one year prior to this experience a man was brought in to be treated for chronic alcoholism. He had but partially recovered from a gastric hemorrage and seemed to be a case of pathological mental deterioration. He had lost everything worth while in life and was only living, one might say, to drink. He frankly admitted and believed that for him there was no hope. Following the elimination of alcohol, there was found to be no permanent brain injury. He accepted the plan outlined in this book. One year later he called to see me, and I experienced a very strange sensation. I knew the man by name, and partly recognized his features, but there all resemblance ended. From a trembling, despairing, nervous wreck, had emerged a man brimming over with self-reliance and contentment. I talked with him for some time, but was not able to bring myself to feel that I had known him before. To me he was a stranger, and so he left me. More than three years have now passed with no return to alcohol.

When I need a mental uplift, I often think of another case brought in by a physician prominent in New York City. The patient had made his own diagnosis, and deciding his situation hopeless, had hidden in a deserted barn determined to die. He was rescued by a searching party, and, in desperate condition, brought to me. Following his physical rehabilitation, he had a talk with me in which he frankly stated he thought the treatment a waste of effort, unless I could assure him, which no one ever had, that in the future he would have the "will power" to resist the impulse to drink.

His alcoholic problem was so complex, and his depression so great, that we felt his only hope would be through what we then called "moral psychology", and we doubted if even that would have any effect.

However, he did become "sold" on the ideas contained in this book. He has not had a drink for more than three years. I see him now and then and he is as fine a specimen of manhood as one could wish to meet.

I earnestly advise every alcoholic to read this book through, and though perhaps he came to scoff, he may remain to pray.

Chapter One

BILL'S STORY

War fever ran high in the New England town to which we new, young officers from Plattsburg were assigned, and we were flattered when the first citizens took us to their homes, making us feel heroic. Here was love, applause, war; moments sublime with hilarious intervals. I was part of life at last, and in the midst of the excitement I discovered liquor. I forgot the strong warnings and the prejudices of my people concerning drink. In time we sailed for "Over There". I was very lonely and again turned to alcohol. _{1:1}

We landed in England. I visited Winchester Cathedral. Much moved, I wandered outside. My attention was caught by a doggerel on an old tombstone: _{1:2}

> "Here lies a Hampshire Grenadier
> Who caught his death
> Drinking cold small beer
> A good soldier is ne'er forgot
> Whether he dieth by musket
> Or by pot."

Ominous warning — which I failed to heed. _{1:3}

Twenty-two, and a veteran of foreign wars, I went home at last. I fancied myself a leader, for had not the men of my battery given me a special token of appreciation? My talent for leadership, I imagined, would place me at the head of vast enterprises which I would manage with utmost assurance. _{1:4}

I took a night law course, and obtained employment as investigator for a surety company. The drive for success was on. I'd prove to the world I was important. My work took me about Wall Street and little by little I became interested in the market. Many people lost money — but some became very rich. Why not I? I studied economics and business as well as law. Potential alcoholic that I was, I nearly failed my law course. At one of the finals I was too drunk to think or write. Though my drinking was not yet continuous, it disturbed my wife. We had long talks when I would still her forebodings by telling her that men of genius conceived their best projects when drunk; that the most majestic constructions of philosophic thought were so derived. _{2:1}

By the time I had completed the course, I knew the law was not for me. The inviting maelstrom of Wall Street had me in its grip. Business and financial leaders were my heroes. Out of this alloy of drink and speculation, I commenced to forge the weapon that one day would turn in its flight like a boomerang and all but cut me to ribbons. Living modestly, my wife and I saved $1,000. It went into certain securities then cheap and rather unpopular. I rightly imagined that they would some day have a great rise. I failed to persuade my broker friends to send me out looking over factories and managements, but my wife and I decided to go anyway. I had developed a theory that most people lost money in stocks through ignorance of markets. I discovered many more reasons later on. _{2:2}

We gave up our positions and off we roared on a motorcycle, the sidecar stuffed with tent, blankets, change of clothes, and three huge volumes of a financial reference service. Our friends thought a lunacy commission should be appointed. Perhaps _{2:3}

they were right. I had had some success at speculation, so we had a little money, but we once worked on a farm for a month to avoid drawing on our small capital. That was the last honest manual labor on my part for many a day. We covered the the[†] whole eastern United States in a year. At the end of it, my reports to Wall Street procured me a position there and the use of a large expense account. The exercise of an option brought in more money, leaving us with a profit of several thousand dollars for that year.

3:1   For the next few years fortune threw money and applause my way. I had arrived. My judgment and ideas were followed by many to the tune of paper millions. The great boom of the late twenties was seething and swelling. Drink was taking an important and exhilarating part in my life. There was loud talk in the jazz places uptown. Everyone spent in thousands and chattered in millions. Scoffers could scoff and be damned. I made a host of fair-weather friends.

3:2   My drinking assumed more serious proportions, continuing all day and almost every night. The remonstrances of my friends terminated in a row and I become a lone wolf. There were many unhappy scenes in our sumptuous apartment. There had been no real infidelity, for loyalty to my wife, helped at times by extreme drunkenness, kept me out of those scrapes.

3:3   In 1929 I contracted golf fever. We went at once to the country, my wife to applaud while I started out to overtake Walter Hagen. Liquor caught up with me much faster than I came up behind Walter. I began to be jittery in the morning. Golf permitted drinking every day and every night. It was fun to carom around the exclusive course which had inspired such awe in me as a lad. I acquired the impeccable coat of tan one sees upon the well-to-do. The local banker watched me whirl fat checks in and our[†] of his till with amused skepticism.

4:1   Abruptly in October 1929 hell broke loose on the New York stock exchange. After one of those days of inferno, I wobbled from a hotel bar to a brokerage office. It was eight o'clock — five hours after the market closed. The ticker still clattered. I was staring at an inch of the tape which bore the inscription PKF-32. It had been 52 that morning. I was finished and so were many friends. The papers reported men jumping to death from the towers of High Finance. That disgusted me. I would not jump. I went back to the bar. My friends had dropped several million since ten oclock — so what? Tomorrow was another day. As I drank, the old fierce determination to win came back.

4:2   Next morning I telephoned a friend in Montreal. He had plenty of money left and thought I had better go to Canada. By the following spring we were living in our accustomed to style. I felt like Napoleon returning from Elba. No St. Helena for me! But drinking caught up with me again and my generous friend had to let me go. This time we stayed broke.

4:3   We went to live with my wife's parents. I found a job; then lost it as the result of a brawl with a taxi driver. Mercifully, no one could guess that I was to have no real employment for five years, or hardly draw a sober breath. My wife began to work in a department store, coming home exhausted to find me drunk. I became an unwelcome hanger-on at brokerage places.

5:1   Liquor ceased to be a luxury; it became a necessity. "Bathtub" gin, two bottles a day, and often three, got to be routine. Sometimes a small deal would net a few hundred dollars, and I would pay my bills at the bars and delicatessens. This went on endlessly, and I began to waken very early in the morning shaking violently. A tumbler full of gin followed by half a dozen bottles of beer would be required if I were to eat any breakfast. Nevertheless, I still thought I could control the situation, and there were periods of sobriety which renewed my wife's hope.

---

† This accurately reflects the language of the original.

Gradually things got worse. The house was taken over by the mortgage holder, my mother-in-law died, my wife and father-in-law became ill. 5:2

Then I got a promising business opportunity. Stocks were at the low point of 1932, and I had somehow formed a group to buy. I was to share generously in the profits. Then I went on a prodigious bender, and that chance vanished. 5:3

I woke up. This had to be stopped. I saw I could not take so much as one drink. I was through forever. Before then, I had written lots of sweet promises, but my wife happily observed that this time I meant business. And so I did. 5:4

Shortly afterward I came home drunk. There had been no fight. Where had been my high resolve? I simply didn't know. It hadn't even come to mind. Someone had pushed a drink my way, and I had taken it. Was I crazy? I began to wonder, for such an appalling lacks of perspective seemed near being just that. 5:5

Renewing my resolve, I tried again. Some time passed, and confidence began to be replaced by cocksureness. I could laugh at the gin mills. Now I had what it takes! One day I walked into a cafe to telephone. In no time I was beating on the bar asking myself how it happened. As the whiskey rose to my head I told myself I would manage better next time, but I might as well get good and drunk then. And I did. 5:6

The remorse, horror and hopelessness of the next morning are unforgettable. The courage to do battle was not there. My brain raced uncontrollably and there was a terrible sense of impending calamity. I hardly dared cross the street, lest I collapse and be run down by an early morning truck, for it was scarcely daylight. An all night place supplied me with a dozen glasses of ale. My writhing nerves were stilled at last. A morning paper told me the market had gone to hell again. Well, so had I. The market would recover, but I wouldn't. That was a hard thought. Should I kill myself? No — not now. Then a mental fog settled down. Gin would fix that. So two bottles, and — oblivion. 6:1

The mind and body are marvelous mechanisms, for mine endured this agony for two more years. Sometimes I stole from my wife's slender purse when the morning terror and madness were on me. Again I swayed dizzily before an open window, or the medicine cabinet, where there was poison, cursing myself for a weakling. There were flights from city to country and back, as my wife and I sought escape. Then came the night when the physical and mental torture was so hellish I feared I would burst through my window, sash and all. Somehow I managed to drag my mattress to a lower floor, lest I suddenly leap. A doctor came with a heavy sedative. Next day found me drinking both gin and sedative. This combination soon landed me on the rocks. People feared for my sanity. So did I. I could eat little or nothing when drinking, and I was forty pounds under weight. 6:2

My brother-in-law is a physician, and through his kindness I was placed in a nationally-known hospital for the mental and physical rehabilitation of alcoholics. Under the so-called belladonna treatment my brain cleared. Hydrotherapy and mild exercise helped much. Best of all, I met a kind doctor who explained that though certainly selfish and foolish, I had been seriously ill, bodily and mentally. 7:1

It relieved me somewhat to learn that in alcoholics the will is amazingly weakened when it comes to combatting liquor, though It[†] often remains strong in other respects. My incredible behavior in the face of a desparate desire to stop was explained. Understanding myself now, I fared forth in high hope. For three or four months the goose hung high. I went to town regularly and even made a little money. Surely this was the answer — self-knowledge. 7:2

---

† This accurately reflects the language of the original.

7:3   But it was not, for the frightful day came when I drank once more. The curve of my declining moral and bodily health fell off like a ski-jump. After a time I returned to the hospital. This was the finish, the curtain, it seemed to me. My weary and despairing wife was informed that it would all end with heart failure during delirium tremens, or I would develop a wet brain, perhaps within a year. She would soon have to give me over to the undertaker, or the asylum.

7:4   They did not need to tell me. I knew, and almost welcomed the idea. It was a devastating blow to my pride. I, who had thought so well of myself and my abilities, of my capacity to surmount obstacles, was cornered at last. Now I was to plunge into the dark, joining that endless procession of sots who had gone on before. I thought of my poor wife. There had been much happiness after all. What would I not give to make amends. But that was over now.

8:1   No words can tell of the loneliness and despair I found in that bitter morass of self-pity. Quicksand stretched around me in all directions. I had met my match. I had been overwhelmed. Alcohol was my master.

8:2   Trembling, I stepped from the hospital a broken man. Fear sobered me for a bit. Then came the insidious insanity of that first drink, and on Armistice Day 1934, I was off again. Everyone became resigned to the certainty that I would have to be shut up somewhere, or would stumble along to a miserable end. How dark it is before the dawn! In reality that was the beginning of my last debauch. I was soon to be catapulted into what I like to call the fourth dimension of existence. I was to know happiness, peace, and usefulness, in a way of life that is incredibly more wonderful as time passes.

8:3   Near the end of that bleak November, I sat drinking in my kitchen. With a certain satisfaction I reflected there was enough gin concealed about the house to carry me through that night and the next day. My wife was at work. I wondered whether I dared hide a full bottle of gin near the head of our bed. I would need it before daylight.

8:4   My musing was interrupted by the telephone. The cheery voice of an old school friend asked if he might come over. <u>He was sober.</u> It was years since I could remember his coming to New York in that condition. I was amazed. Rumor had it that he had been committed for alcoholic insanity. I wondered how he had escaped. Of course he would have dinner, and then I could drink openly with him. Unmindful of his welfare, I thought only of recapturing the spirit of other days. There was that time we had chartered an airplane to complete a jag! His coming was an oasis in this drear[†] desert of futility. The very thing — an oasis! Drinkers are like that.

9:1   The door opened and he stood there, fresh-skinned and glowing. There was something about his eyes. He was inexplicably different. What had happened?

9:2   I pushed a drink across the table. He refused it. Disappointed but curious, I wondered what had got into the fellow. He wasn't himself.

9:3   "Come, what's all this about?" I queried.

9:4   He looked straight at me. Simply, but smilingly, he said, "I've got religion."

9:5   I was aghast. So that was it — last summer an alcoholic crackpot; now, I suspected, a little cracked about religion. He had that starry-eyed look. Yes, the old boy was on fire all right. But bless his heart, let him rant! Besides, my gin would last longer than his preaching.

9:6   But he did no ranting. In a matter of fact way he told how two men had appeared

---

[†] This accurately reflects the language of the original.

in court, persuading the judge to suspend his commitment. They had told of a simple religious idea and a practical program of action. That was two months ago and the result was self evident. It worked!

He had come to pass his experience along to me — if I cared to have it. I was shocked, but interested. Certainly I was interested. I had to be, for I was hopeless. 9:7

He talked for hours. Childhood memories rose before me. I could almost hear the sound of the preacher's voice as I sat, on still Sundays, way over there on the hillside; there was that proffered temperance pledge I never signed; my grandfather good natured contempt of some church folk and their doings; his insistence that the spheres really had their music; but his denial of the preacher's right to tell him how he must listen; his fearlessness as he spoke of these things just before he died; these recollections welled up from the past. They made me swallow hard. 10:1

That war-time day in old Winchester Cathedral came back again. 10:2

I had always believed in a power greater than myself. I had often pondered these things. I was not an atheist. Few people really are, for that means blind faith in the strange proposition that this universe originated in a cipher, and aimlessly rushes nowhere. My intellectual heroes, the chemists, the astronomers, even the evolutionists, suggested vast laws and forces at work. Despite contrary indications, I had little doubt that a mighty purpose and rhythm underlay all. How could there be so much of precise and immutable law, and no intelligence? I simply had to believe in a Spirit of the Universe, who knew neither time nor limitation. But that was as far as I had gone. 10:3

With ministers, and the world's religions, I parted right there. When they talked of a God personal to me, who was love, superhuman strength and direction, I became irritated and my mind snapped shut against such a theory. 10:4

To Christ I conceded the certainty of a great man, not too closely followed by those who claimed Him. His moral teaching — most excellent. For myself, I had adopted those parts which seemed convenient and not too difficult; the rest I disregarded. 11:1

The wars which had been fought, the burnings and chicanery that religious dispute had facilitated, made me sick. I honestly doubted whether, on balance, the religions of mankind had done any good. Judging from what I had seen in Europe and since, the power of God in human affairs was negligible, the Brotherhood of Man a grim jest. If there was a Devil, he seemed the Boss Universal, and he certainly had me. 11:2

But my friend sat before me, and he made the point-blank declaration that God had done for him what he could not do for himself. His human will had failed. Doctors had pronounced him incurable. Society was about to lock him up. Like myself, he had admitted complete defeat. Then he had, in effect, been raised from the dead, suddenly taken from the scrap heap to a level of life better than the best he had ever known! 11:3

Had this power originated in him? Obviously it had not. There had been no more power in him than there was in me at that minute; and this was none at all. 11:4

That floored me. It began to look as though religious people were right after all. Here was something at work in a human heart which had done the impossible. My ideas about miracles were drastically revised right then. Never mind the musty past; here sat a miracle directly across the kitchen table. He shouted great tidings. 11:5

11:6   I saw that my friend was much more than inwardly reorganized. He was on a different footing. His roots grasped a new soil.

12:5   Thus was I convinced that God is concerned with us humans, when we want Him enough. At long last I saw, I felt, I believed. Scales of pride and prejudice fell from my eyes. A new world came into view.

12:6   The real significance of my experience in the Cathedral burst upon me. For a brief moment, I had needed and wanted God. There had been a humble willingness to have Him with me — and He came. But soon the sense of His presence had been blotted out by worldly clamors, mostly those within myself. And so it had been ever since. How blind I had been.

13:1   At the hospital I was separated from alcohol for the last time. Treatment seemed wise, for I showed signs of delirium tremens. I have not had a drink since.

13:2   There I humbly offered myself to God, as I then understood Him, to do with me as He would. I placed myself unreservedly under His care and direction. I admitted for the first time that of myself I was nothing; that without Him I was lost. I ruthlessly faced my sins and became willing to have my new-found Friend take them away, root and branch.

13:3   My school mate visited me, and I fully acquainted him with my problems and deficiencies. We made a list of people I had hurt or toward whom I felt resentment. I expressed my entire willingness to approach these individuals, admitting my wrong. Never was I to be critical of them. I was to right all such matters to the utmost of my ability.

13:4   I was to test my thinking by the new God-consciousness within. Common sense would thus become uncommon sense. I was to sit quietly when in doubt, asking only for direction and strength to meet my problems as He would have me. Never was I to pray for myself, except as my requests bore on my usefulness to others. Then only might I expect to receive. But that would be in great measure.

13:5   My friend promised when these things were done I would enter upon a new relationship with my Creator; that I would have the elements of a way of life which answered all my problems. Belief in the power of God, plus enough willingness, honesty and humility to establish and maintain the new order of things, were the essential requirements.

14:1   Simple, but not easy; a price had to be paid. It meant destruction of self-centeredness. I must turn in all things to the Father of Light who presides over us all.

14:2   These were revolutionary and drastic proposals, but the moment I fully accepted them, the effect was electric. There was a sense of victory, followed by such a peace and serenity as I had never known. There was utter confidence. I felt lifted up, as though the great clean wind of a mountain top blew through and through. God comes to most men gradually, but His impact on me was sudden and profound.

14:3   For a moment I was alarmed, and called my friend, the doctor, to ask if I were still sane. He listened in wonder as I talked.

14:4   Finally he shook his head saying, "Something has happened to you I don't understand. But you had better hang on to it. Anything is better than the way you were." The good doctor now sees many men who have such experiences. He knows they are real.

14:5   While I lay in the hospital the thought came that there were thousands of hopeless alcoholics who might be glad to have what had been so freely given me. Perhaps I could help some of them. They in turn might work with others.

My friend had emphasized the absolute necessity of my demonstrating these principles in all my affairs. Particularly was it imperative to work with others, as he had worked with me. Faith without works was dead, he said. And how appallingly true for the alcoholic! For if an alcoholic failed to perfect and enlarge his spiritual life through work and self sacrifice for others, he could not survive the certain trials and low spots ahead. If he did not work, he would surely drink again, and it he drank, he would surely die. Then faith would be dead indeed. With us it is just like that. 14:6

My wife and I abandoned ourselves with enthusiasm to the idea of helping other alcoholics to a solution of their problems. It was fortunate, for my old business associates remained skeptical for a year and a half, during which I found little work. I was not too well at the time, and was plagued by waves of self-pity and resentment. This sometimes nearly drove me back to drink. I soon found that when all other measures failed, work with another alcoholic would save the day. Many times I have gone to my old hospital in despair. On talking to a man there, I would be amazingly lifted up and set on my feet. It is a design for living that works in rough going. 15:1

We commenced to make many fast friends and a fellowship has grown up among us of which it is a wonderful thing to feel a part. The joy of living we really have, even under pressure and difficulty. I have seen one hundred families set their feet in the path that really goes somewhere; have seem[†] the most impossible domestic situations righted; feuds and bitterness of all sorts wiped out. I have seen men come out of asylums and resume a vital place in the lives of their families and communities. Business and professional men have regained their standing. There is scarcely any form of trouble and misery which has not been overcome among us. In one Western city and its environs there are eighty of us and our families. We meet frequently at our different homes, so that newcomers may find the fellowship they seek. At these informal gatherings one may often see from 40 to 80 persons. We are growing in numbers and power. 15:2

An alcoholic in his cups is an unlovely creature. Our struggles with them are variously strenuous, comic, and tragic. One poor chap committed suicide in my home. He could not, or would not, see our way of life. 16:1

There is, however, a vast amoung[†] of fun about it all. I suppose some would be shocked at our seeming worldliness and levity. But just underneath there is deadly earnestness. God has to work twenty-four hours a day in and through us, or we perish. 16:2

Most of us feel we need look no further for Utopia, nor even for Heaven. We have it with us right here and now. Each day that simple talk in my kitchen multiplies itself in a widening circle of peace on earth and good will to men. 16:3

[†] This accurately reflects the language of the original.

Chapter Two

THERE IS A SOLUTION

17:1   We, of ALCOHOLICS ANONYMOUS, know one hundred men who were once just as hopeless as Bill. All have recovered. They have solved the drink problem.

17:2   We are ordinary Americans. All sections of this country and many of its occupations are represented, as well as many political, economic, social and religious backgrounds. We are people who normally would not mix. But there exists among us a fellowship, a friendliness, and an understanding which is indescribably wonderful. We are like the passengers of a great liner the moment after rescue from shipwreck, when camaraderie, joyousness and democracy pervade the vessel from steerage to Captain's table. Unlike the feelings of the ship's passengers, however, our joy in escape from disaster does not subside as we go our individual ways. The feeling of having shared in a common peril is one element in the powerful cement which binds us. But that in itself would never have held us together as we are now joined.

17:3   The tremendous fact for every one of us that we have discovered a common solution.[†] We have a way out on which we can absolutely agree, and upon which we can join in brotherly and harmonious action. This is the great news this book carries to those who suffer alcoholism.

18:1   An illness of this sort — and we have come to believe it an illness — involves those about us in a way no other human sickness can. If a person has cancer all are sorry for him and no one is angry or hurt. But not so with the alcoholic illness, for with it there goes annihilation of all the things worth while in life. It engulfs all whose lives touch the sufferer's. It brings misunderstanding, fierce resentment, financial insecurity, disgusted friends and employers, warped lives of blameless children, sad wives and parents — anyone can increase the list.

18:2   This volume will inform, instruct and comfort those who are, or who may be affected. They are many.

18:3   Highly competent psychiatrists who have dealt with us (often fruitlessly, we are afraid) find it almost impossible to persuade an alcoholic to discuss his situation without reserve. Strangely enough, wives, parents and intimate friends usually find us even more unapproachable than do the psychiatrist and the doctor.

18:4   But the ex-alcoholic who has found this solution, who is properly armed with certain medical information, can generally win the entire confidence of another alcoholic in a few hours. Until such an understanding is reached, little or nothing can be accomplished.

18:5   That the man who is making the approach has had the same difficulty, that he obviously knows what he is talking about, that his whole deportment shouts at the new prospect that he is a man with a real answer, that he has no attitude of holier than thou, nothing whatever except the sincere desire to be helpful; that there are no fees to pay, no axes to grind, no people to please, no lectures to be endured — these are the conditions we have found necessary. After such an approach many take up their beds and walk again.

[†] This accurately reflects the language of the original.

None of us makes a vocation of this work, nor do we think its **19:1** effectiveness would be increased if we did. We feel that elimination of the liquor problem is but a beginning. A much more important demonstration of our principles lies before us in our respective homes, occupations, and affairs. All of us spend much of our spare time in the sort of effort which we are going to describe. A few are fortunate enough to be so situated that they can give nearly all of their time to the work.

If we keep on the way we are going there is little doubt that much **19:2** good will result, but the surface of the problem would hardly be scratched. Those of us who live in large cities are overcome by the reflection that close by hundreds are dropping into oblivion every day, Many could recover if they had the opportunity we have enjoyed. How then shall we present that which has been so freely given us?

We have concluded to publish an anonymous volume setting forth the **19:3** problem as we see it. We shall bring to the task our combined experience and knowledge. This ought to suggest a useful program for anyone concerned with a drinking problem.

Of necessity there will have to be discussion of matters medical, **19:4** psychiatric, social, and religious. We are aware that these matters are, from their very nature, controversial. Nothing would please us so much as to write a book which would contain no basis for contention or argument. We shall do our utmost to achieve that ideal. Most of us sense that real tolerance of other people's shortcomings and viewpoints and a respect for their opinions are attitudes which make us more useful to others. Our very lives, as ex-alcoholics, depend upon our constant thought of others and how we may help meet their needs.

You may already have asked yourself why it is that all of us became **20:1** so very ill from drinking. Doubtless you are curious to discover how and why, in the face of expert opinion to the contrary, we have recovered from a hopeless condition of mind and body. If you are an alcoholic who wants to get over it, you may already be asking — "What do I have to do?"

It is the purpose of this book to answer such questions specifi- **20:2** cally. We shall tell you what we have done. Before going into a detailed discussion, it may be well to summarize some points as we see them.

How many times people have said to us: "I can take it or leave it **20:3** alone. Why can't he?" "Why don't you drink like a gentleman or quit?" "That fellow can't handle his liquor." "Why don't you try beer and wine?" "Lay off the hard stuff." "His will power must be weak." "He could stop if he wanted to." "She's such a sweet girl, I should think he'd stop for her." "The doctor told him that if he ever drank again it would kill him, but there he is all lit up again."

Now, these are commonplace observations on drinkers which we hear **20:4** all the time. Back of them is a world of ignorance and misunderstanding. We see that these expressions refer to people whose reactions are very different from ours.

Moderate drinkers have little trouble in giving up liquor entirely **20:5** if they have good reason for it. They can take it or leave it alone.

Then we have a certain type of hard drinker. He may have the habit **20:6** bad enough to gradually impair him physically and mentally. It may cause him to die a few years before his time. If a sufficiently strong reason — ill health, falling in love, change of environment, or the warning of a doctor — becomes operative, this man can also stop or moderate, although he may find it difficult and troublesome and may ever need medical attention.

21:1   But what about the real alcoholic? He may start off as a moderate drinker; he may or may not become a continuous hard drinker; but at some stage of his drinking career he begins to lose all control of his liquor consumption, once he starts to drink.

21:2   Here is the Fellow who has been puzzling you, especially in his lack of control. He does absurd, incredible, tragic things while drinking. He is a real Dr. Jekyll and Mr. Hyde. He is seldom mildly intoxicated. He is always more or less insanely drunk. His disposition while drinking resembles his normal nature but little. He may be one of the finest fellows in the world. Yet let him drink for a day, and he frequently becomes disgustingly, and even dangerously anti-social. He has a positive genius for getting tight at exactly the wrong moment, particularly when some important decision must be made or engagement kept. He is often perfectly sensible and well balanced concerning everything except liquor, but in that respect is incredibly dishonest and selfish. He often possesses special abilities, skills, and aptitudes, and has a promising career ahead of him. He uses his gifts to build up a bright outlook for his family and himself, then pulls the structure down on his head by a senseless series of sprees. He is the fellow who goes to bed so intoxicated he ought to sleep the clock around. Yet early next morning he searches madly for the bottle he misplaced the night before. If he can afford it, he may have liquor concealed all over his house to be certain no one gets his entire supply away from him to throw down the wastepipe. As matters grow worse, he begins to use a combination of high-powered sedative and liquor to quiet his nerves so he can go to work. Then comes the days when he simply cannot make it and gets drunk all over again. Perhaps he goes to a doctor who gives him a dose of morphine or some high-voltage sedative with which to taper off. Then he begins to appear at hospitals and sanitariums.

22:1   This is by no means a comprehensive picture of the true alcoholic, as our behavior patterns vary. But this description should identify him roughly.

22:2   Why does he behave like this? If hundreds of experiences have shown him that one drink means another debacle with all its attendant suffering and humiliation, why is it he takes that one drink? Why can't he stay on the water wagon? What has become of the common sense and will power that he still sometimes displays with respect to other matters?

22:3   Perhaps there never will be a full answer to these questions. Psychiatrists and medical men vary considerably in their opinion as to why the alcoholic reacts differently from normal people. No one is sure why, once a certain point is reached, nothing can be done for him. We cannot answer the riddle.

22:4   We know that while the alcoholic keeps away from drink as he may do for months or years, he reacts much like other men. We are equally positive that once he takes any alcohol whatever into his system, something happens, both in the bodily and mental sense, which makes it virtually impossible for him to stop. The experience of any alcoholic will abundantly confirm that.

23:1   These observations would be academic and pointless if our friend never took the first drink thereby setting the terrible cycle in motion. Therefore, the real problem of the alcoholic centers in his mind, rather than in his body. If you ask him why he started on that last bender, the chances are he will offer you any one of a hundred alibis. Sometimes these excuses have a certain plausibility, but none of theme really make sense in the light of the havoc an alcoholic's drinking bout creates. They sound to you like the philosophy of the man who, having a headache, beat him self on the head with a hammer so that he couldn't feel the ache. If you draw this fallacious reasoning to the attention of an alcoholic, he will laugh it off, or become irritated and refuse to talk.

Once in a while he may tell you the truth. And the truth, strange to say, is usually that he has no more idea why he took that first drink than you have. Some drinkers have excuses with which they are satisfied part of the time. But in their hearts they really do not know why they do it. Once this malady has a real hold, they are a baffled lot. There is the obsession that somehow, some day, they will beat the game. But they often suspect they are down for the count. 23:2

How true this is, few realize. In a vague way their families and friends sense that these drinkers are abnormal, but everybody hopefully waits the day when the sufferer will rouse himself from his lethargy and assert his power of will. 23:3

The tragic truth is that if the man be a real alcoholic, the happy day will seldom arrive. He has lost control. At a certain point in the drinking of every alcoholic, he passes into a state where the most powerful desire to stop drinking is of absolutely no avail. This tragic situation has already arrived in practically every case long before it is suspected. 23:4

The fact is that most alcoholics, for reasons yet obscure, have lost the power of choice in drink. Our so-called will power becomes practically non-existent. We are unable at certain times, no matter how well we understand ourselves, to bring into our consciousness with sufficient force the memory of the suffering and humiliation of even a week or a month ago. We are without defense against the first drink. 24:1

The almost certain consequences that follow taking even a glass of beer do not crowd into the mind to deter us. If these thoughts occur, they are hazy, and readily supplanted with the old treadbare idea that this time we shall handle ourselves like other people. There is a complete failure of the kind of defense that keeps one from putting his hand on a hot stove. 24:2

The alcoholic may say to himself in the most casual way, "It won't burn me this time, so here's how!" Or perhaps he doesn't think at all. How often have some of us begun to drink in this nonchalent way, and after the third or fourth, pounded on the bar and said to ourselves, "For God's sake, how did I ever get started again?" Only to have that thought supplanted by "Well, I'll stop with the sixth drink." Or "What's the use anyhow?" 24:3

When this sort of thinking is fully established in an individual with alcoholic tendencies, he has probably placed himself beyond all human aid, and unless locked up, is certain to die, or go permanently insane. These stark and ugly facts have been confirmed by legions of alcoholics throughout history. But for the grace of God, there would have been one hundred more convincing demonstrations. So many want to stop, but cannot. 24:4

There is a solution. Almost none of us liked the self-searching, the levelling of our pride, the confession of shortcomings which the process requires for its successful consummation. But we saw that it really worked in others, and we had come to believe in the hopelessness and futility of life as we had been living it. When, therefore, we were approached by those in whom the problem had been solved, there was nothing left for us but to pick up the simple kit of spiritual tools laid at our feet. We have found much of heaven and we have been rocketed into a fourth dimension of existence, of which we had not even dreamed. 25:1

The great fact is just this, and nothing less: that we have had deep and effective spiritual experiences, which have revolutionized our whole attitude toward life, toward our fellows, and toward God's universe. The central fact of our lives today is the absolute certainty that our Creator has entered into our hearts and lives in a way which is indeed miraculous. He has commenced to accomplish those things for us which we could never do by ourselves. 25:2

25:3   If you are seriously alcoholic, we believe you have no middle-of-the-road solution. You are in a position where life is becoming impossible, and if you have passed into the region from which there is no return through human aid, you have but two alternatives: one is to go on to the bitter end, blotting out the consciousness of your intolerable situation as best you can; and the other, to find what we have found. This you can do if you honestly want to, and are willing to make the effort.

26:1   A certain American business man had ability, good sense, and high character. For years he had floundered from one sanitarium to another. He had consulted the best known American psychiatrists. Then he had gone to Europe, placing himself in the care of a celebrated physician who prescribed for him. Though bitter experience had made him skeptical, he finished his treatment with unusual confidence. His physical and mental condition were unusually good. Above all, he believed he had acquired such a profound knowledge of the inner workings of his mind and its hidden springs, that relapse was unthinkable. Nevertheless, he was drunk in a short time. More baffling still, he could give himself no satisfactory explanation for his fall.

26:2   So he returned to this doctor, whom he admired, and asked him point-blank why he could not recover. He wished above all things to regain self-control. He seemed quite rational and well-balanced with respect to other problems. Yet he had no control whatever over alcohol. Why was this?

26:3   He begged the doctor to tell him the whole truth, and he got it. In the doctor's judgement he was utterly hopeless; he could never regain his position in society and he would have to place himself under lock and key, or hire a bodyguard if he expected to live long. That was a great physician's opinion.

26:4   But this man still lives, and is a free man. He does not need a bodyguard, nor is he confined. He can go anywhere on this earth where other free men may go with out disaster, provided he remains willing to maintain a certain simple attitude.

27:1   Some of our alcoholic readers may think they can do without spiritual help. Let us tell you the rest of the conversation our friend had with his doctor.

27:2   The doctor said: "You have the mind of a chronic alcoholic. I have never seen one single case recover, where that state of mind existed to the extent that it does in you." Our friend felt as though the gates of hell had closed on him with a clang.

27:3   He said to the doctor, "Is there no exception?"

27:4   "Yes," replied the doctor, "there is. Exceptions to cases such as yours have been occurring since early times. Here and there, once in a while, alcoholics have had what are called vital spiritual experiences. To me these occurrences are phenomena. They appear to be in the nature of huge emotional displacements and rearrangements. Ideas, emotions, and attitudes which were once the guiding forces of the lives of these men are suddenly cast to one side, and a completely new set of conceptions and motives begin to dominate them. In fact, I have been trying to produce some such emotional rearrangement within you. With many individuals the methods which I employed are successful, but I have never been successful with an alcoholic of your description."

27:5   Upon hearing this, our friend was somewhat relieved, for he reflected that, after all, he was a good church member. This hope, however, was destroyed by the doctor's telling him that his religious convictions were very good, but that in his case they did not spell the necessary vital spiritual experience.

28:1   Here was the terrible dilemma in which our friend found himself when he had the extraordinary experience, which as we have already told you, made him a free man.

We, in our turn, sought the same escape, will all[†] the desperation of drowning men. What seemed at first a flimsy reed, has proved to be the loving and powerful hand of God. A new life has been given us or, if you prefer, "a design for living that really works.[†] 28:2

The distinguished American psychologist, William James, in his book, "Varieties of Religious Experience," indicates a multitude of ways in which men have found God. As a group, we have no desire to convince anyone that there is only one way by which God can be discovered. If what we have learned, and felt, and seen, means anything at all, it means that all of us, whatever our race, creed or color, are the children of a living Creator with whom we may form a relationship upon simple and understandable terms as soon as we are willing and honest enough to try. Those having religious affiliations will find here nothing disturbing to their beliefs or ceremonies. There is no friction among us over such matters. 28:3

We think it no concern of ours, as a group, what religious bodies our members identify themselves with as individuals. This should be an entirely personal affair which each one decides for himself in the light of past association, or his present choice. Not all of us have joined religious bodies, but most of us favor such memberships. 28:4

In the following chapter, there appears an explanation of alcoholism as we understand it, then a chapter addressed to the agnostic. Many who once were in this class are now among our members; surprisingly enough, we find such convictions no great obstacle to a spiritual experience. 28:5

There is a group of personal narratives. Then clear-cut directions are given showing how an alcoholic may recover. These are followed by more than a score of personal experiences. 29:1

Each individual, in the personal stories, describes in his own language, and from his own point of view the way he found or rediscovered God. These give a fair cross section of our membership and a clear-cut idea of what has actually happened in their lives. 29:2

We hope no one will consider these self-revealing accounts in bad taste. Our hope is that many alcoholic men and women, desperately in need, will see these pages, and we believe that it is only by fully disclosing ourselves and our problems that they will be persuaded to say, "Yes, I am one of them too; I must have this thing." 29:3

[†] This accurately reflects the language of the original.

Chapter Three

MORE ABOUT ALCOHOLISM

30:1   Most of us have been unwilling to admit we were real alcoholics. No person likes to think he is bodily and mentally different from his fellows. Therefore, it is not surprising that our drinking careers have been characterized by countless vain attempts to prove we could drink like other people. The idea that somehow, someday he will control and enjoy his liquor drinking is the great obsession of every abnormal drinker. The persistance of this illusion is astonishing. Many pursue it into the gates of insanity or death.

30:2   We learned that we had to fully concede to our innermost selves that we were alcoholics. This is the first step in recovery. The delusion that we are like other people, or presently may be, had to be smashed.

30:3   We alcoholics are men and women who had lost the ability to control our drinking. We know that no real alcoholic ever recovered this control. All of us felt at times that we were regaining control, but such intervals — usually brief — were inevitably followed by still less control, which led in time to pitiful and incomprehensible demoralization. We are convinced to a man that alcoholics of our type are in the grip of a progressive illness. Over any considerable period we get worse, never better.

30:4   We are like men who have lost their legs; they never grow new ones. Neither does there appear to be any kind of treatment which will make alcoholics of our kind like other men. We have tried every imaginable remedy. In some instances there has been brief recovery, followed always by still worse relapse. Physicians who are familiar with alcoholism agree there is no such thing as making a normal drinker out of an alcoholic. Science may one day accomplish this, but it evidently hasn't done so yet.

31:1   Despite all we can say, many who are real alcoholics are not going to believe they are in that class. By every form of self-deception and experimentation, they will try to prove themselves exceptions to the rule, therefore non-alcoholic. If anyone, who is showing inability to control his drinking, can do the right-about-face and drink like a gentleman, our hats are off to him. Heaven knows, we have tried hard enough and long enough to drink like other people!

31:2   Here are some of the methods we have tried: drinking beer only, limiting the number of drinks, never drinking alone, never drinking in the morning, drinking only at home, never having it in the house, never drinking during business hours, drinking only at parties, switching from scotch to brandy, drinking only natural wines, agreeing to resign if ever drunk on the job, taking a trip, not taking a trip, swearing off forever (with and without a solemn oath), taking more physical exercise, reading inspirational books, consulting psychologists, going to health farms and sanitariums, accepting voluntary commitment to asylums — we could increase the list ad infinitum.

31:3   We do not like to brand any individual as an alcoholic, but you can quickly diagnose yourself. Step over to the nearest barroom and try some controlled drinking. Try to drink and stop abruptly. Try it more than once. It will not take long for you to decide, if you are honest with yourself about it. It will be worth a bad case of jitters if you get thoroughly sold on the idea that you are a candidate for Alcoholics Anonymous!

Though there is no way of proving it, we believe that early in our drinking careers most of us could have stopped drinking. But the difficulty is that few alcoholics have enough desire to stop while there is yet time. We have heard of a few instances where people, who showed definite signs of alcoholism, were able to stop because of an overpowering desire to to[†] so. Here is one.

A man of thirty was doing a great deal of spree drinking. He was very nervous in the morning after these bouts and quieted himself with more liquor. He was ambitious to succeed in business, but saw that he would get nowhere if he drank at all. Once he started, he had no control whatever. He made up his mind that until he had been successful in business and had retired, he would not touch another drop. An exceptional man, he remained bone dry for twenty-five years, and retired at the age of fifty-five, after a successful and happy business career. Then he fell victim to a belief which practically every alcoholic has — that his long period of sobriety and self-discipline had qualified him to drink as other men. Out came his carpet slippers and a bottle. In two months he was in a hospital, puzzled and humiliated. He tried to regulate his drinking for a while, making several trips to the hospital meantime. Then, gathering all his forces, he attempted to stop, and found he could not. Every means of solving his problem which money could buy was at his disposal. Every attempt failed. Though a robust man at retirement, he went to pieces quickly, and was dead within four years.

This case contains a powerful lesson. Most of us have believed that if we remained sober for a long stretch, we could thereafter drink normally. But here is a man who at fifty-five years found he was just where he had left off at thirty. We have seen the truth demonstrated again and again; "once an alcoholic, always an alcoholic." Commencing to drink after a period of sobriety, we are in a short time as bad as ever. If you are planning to stop drinking, there must be no reservation of any kind, nor any lurking notion that someday you will be immune to alcohol.

Young people may be encouraged by this man's experience to think that they can stop as he did, on their own will power. We doubt if many of them can do it, because none will really want to stop, and hardly one of them, because of the peculiar mental twist already acquired, will find he can win out. Several of our crowd, men of thirty-five or less, had been drinking but a few years, but they found themselves as helpless as those who had been drinking twenty years.

To be gravely affected, one does not necessarily have to drink a long time, nor take the quantities some of us have. This is particularly true of women. Potential feminine alcoholics often turn into the real thing and are gone beyond recall in a few years. Certain drinkers, who would be greatly insulted if called alcoholic, are astonished at their inability to stop. We, who are familiar with the symptoms, see large numbers of potential alcoholics among young people everywhere. But try and get them to see it!

As we look back, we feel we had gone on drinking many years beyond the point where we could quit on our will power. If anyone questions whether he has entered this dangerous area, let him try leaving liquor alone for one year. If he is a real alcoholic and very far advanced, there is scant chance of success. In the early days of our drinking we occasionally remained sober for a year or more, becoming serious drinkers again later. Though you may be able to stop for a considerable period, you may yet be a potential alcoholic. We think few, to whom this book will appeal, can stay dry anything like a year. Some will be drunk the day after making their resolutions; most of them within a few weeks.

For those who are unable to drink moderately the question is how to stop altogether. We are assuming, of course, that the reader desires to stop. Whether such a person can quit upon a non-spiritual basis depends somewhat upon the strength of

[†] This accurately reflects the language of the original.

his character, and how much he really wants to be done with it. But even more will it depend upon the extent to which he has already lost the power to choose whether he will drink or not. Many of us felt that we had plenty of character. There was a tremendous urge to cease forever. Yet we found it impossible. This is the baffling feature of alcoholism as we know it — this utter inability to leave it alone, no matter how great the necessity or the wish.

34:3   How then shall we help our readers determine, to their own satisfaction, whether they are one of us? The experiment of quitting for a period of time will be helpful, but we think we can render an even greater service to alcoholic sufferers, and perhaps to the medical fraternity. So we shall describe some of the mental states that precede a relapse into drinking, for obviously this is the crux of the problem.

35:1   What sort of thinking dominates an alcoholic who repeats time after time the desperate experiment of the first drink? Friends, who have reasoned with him after a spree which has brought him to the point of divorce or bankruptcy, are mystified when he walks directly into a saloon. Why does he? Of what is he thinking?

35:2   Our first example is a friend we shall call Jim. This man has a charming wife and family. He inherited a lucrative automobile agency. He had a commendable world war record. He is a good salesman. Everybody likes him. He is an intelligent man, normal so far as we can see, except for a nervous disposition. He did no drinking until he was thirty-five. In a few years he became so violent when intoxicated that he had to be committed. On leaving the asylum, he came into contact with us.

35:3   We told him what we know of alcoholism and the answer we had found. He made a beginning. His family was re-assembled, and he began to work as a salesman for the business he had lost through drinking. All went well for a time, but he failed to enlarge his spiritual life. To his consternation, he found himself drunk half a dozen times in rapid succession. On each of these occasions we worked with him, reviewing carefully what had happened. He agreed he was a real alcoholic and in serious condition. He knew he faced another trip to the asylum if he kept on. Moreover, he would lose his family, for whom he had deep affection.

36:1   Yet he got drunk again. We asked him to tell us exactly how it happened. This is his story: "I came to work on Tuesday morning. I remember I felt irritated that I had to be a salesman for a concern I once owned. I had a few words with the boss, but nothing serious. Then I decided to drive into the country and see one of my prospects for a car. On the way I felt hungry so I stopped at a roadside place where they have a bar. I had no intention of drinking. I just thought I would get a sandwich. I also had the notion that I might find a customer for a car at this place, which was familiar, for I had been going to it for years. I had eaten there many times during the months I was sober. I sat down at a table and ordered a sandwich and a glass of milk. Still no thought of drinking. I ordered another sandwich and decided to have another glass of milk.

36:2   "Suddenly the thought crossed my mind that if I were to put an ounce of whiskey in my milk, it couldn't hurt me on a full stomach. I ordered a whiskey and poured it into the milk. I vaguely sensed I was not being any too smart, but felt reassured, as I was taking the whiskey on a full stomach. The experiment went so well that I ordered another whiskey and poured it into more milk. That didn't seem to bother me so I tried another."

36:3   Thus started on[†] more journey to the asylum for Jim. Here was the threat of commitment, the loss of family and position, to say nothing of that intense mental and physical suffering which drinking always caused him. He had much knowledge about himself as an alcoholic. Yet all reasons for not drinking were easily pushed aside in favor of the foolish idea he could take whiskey if only he mixed it with milk!

---

† This accurately reflects the language of the original.

Whatever the precise medical definition of the word may be, we call 37:1
this plain insanity. How can such a lack of proportion, of the ability
to think straight, be called anything else?

You may think this an extreme case. To us it is not-far[†] fetched. 37:2
for this kind of thinking has been characteristic of every single one
of our group. Some of us have sometimes reflected more than Jim did,
upon the consequences. But there was always the curious mental phenomenon, that parallel with our sound reasoning there inevitably ran some
insanely trivial excuse for taking the first drink. Our sound reasoning
failed to hold us in check. The insane idea won out. Next day we would
ask ourselves, in all earnestness and sincerity, how it could have
happened.

In some circumstances we have gone out deliberately to get drunk, 37:3
feeling ourselves justified by nervousness, anger, worry, depression,
jealousy or the like. But even in this type of beginning we are obliged
to admit that our justification for a spree was insanely insufficient
in the light of what always happened. We now see that when we began to
drink deliberately, instead of casually, there was little serious or
effective thought during the period of premeditation, of what the
terrific consequences might be.

Our behavior is as absurd and incomprehensible with respect to the 37:4
first drink as that of an individual with a passion, say, for jay-
walking. He gets a thrill out of skipping in front of fast-moving
vehicles. He enjoys himself a few years in spite of friendly warnings.
Up to this point you would label him as a foolish chap, having queer
ideas of fun. Luck then deserts him and he is slightly injured several
times in succession. You would expect him, if he were normal, to cut it
out. Presently he is hit again and this time has a fractured skull.
Within a week after leaving the hospital, a fast-moving trolley car
breaks his arm. He tells you he has decided to stop jay-walking for
good, but in a few weeks he breaks both legs.

On through the years this conduct continues, accompanied by his 38:1
continual promises to be careful or to keep off the streets altogether.
Finally, he can no longer work, his wife gets a divorce, he is held up
to ridicule. He tries every known means to get the jay-walking idea out
of his head. He shuts himself up in an asylum, hoping to mend his ways.
But the day he comes out he races in front of a fire engine, which
breaks his back. Such a man would be crazy, wouldn't he?

You may think our illustration is too ridiculous. But is it? We, who 38:2
have been through the wringer, have to admit if we substituted alcoholism for jay-walking, the illustration would fit us exactly. However
intelligent we may have been in other respects, where alcohol has been
involved, we have been strangely insane. It's strong language — but
isn't it true?

Some of you are thinking: "Yes, what you tell us is true, but it 38:3
doesn't fully apply. We admit we have some of these symptoms, but we
have not gone to the extremes you fellows did, nor are we likely to, for
we understand ourselves so well after what you have told us that such
things cannot happen again. We have not lost everything in life through
drinking and we certainly do not intend to. Thanks for the information."

That may be true of certain non-alcoholic people who, though drinking 39:1
foolishly and heavily at the present time, are able to stop or moderate,
because their brains and bodies have not been warped and degenerated as
ours were. But the actual or potential alcoholic, with hardly an exception, will be <u>absolutely unable to stop drinking on the basis of self-
knowledge.</u> This is a point we wish to emphasize and reemphasize, to smash
home upon our alcoholic readers as it has been revealed to us out of bitter
experience. Let us take another illustration.

[†] This accurately reflects the language of the original.

Page 18.

39:2   Fred is partner in a well known accounting firm. His income is good, he has a fine home, is happily married and the father of promising children of college age. He is so attractive a personality that he makes friends with everyone. If ever there was a successful business man, it is Fred. To all appearances he is a stable, well balanced individual. Yet, he is alcoholic. We first saw Fred about a year ago in a hospital where he had gone to recover from a bad case of jitters. It was his first experience of this kind, and he was much ashamed of it. Far from admitting he was an alcoholic, he told himself he came to the hospital to rest his nerves. The doctor intimated strongly that he might be worse than he realized. For a few days he was depressed about his condition. He made up his mind to quit drinking altogether. It never occurred to him that perhaps he could not do so, in spite of his character and standing. Fred would not believe himself an alcoholic, much less accept a spiritual remedy for his problem. We told him about alcoholism. He was interested and conceded that he had some of the symptoms, but he was a long way from admitting that he could do nothing about it himself. He was positive that this humiliating experience, plus the knowledge he had acquired, would keep him sober the rest of his life. Self-knowledge would fix it.

40:1   We heard no more of Fred for a while. One day we were told that he was back in the hospital. This time he was quite shaky. He soon indicated he was anxious to see us. The story he told is most instructive for here was a chap absolutely convinced he had to stop drinking, who had no excuse for drinking, who exhibited splendid judgment and determination in all his other concerns, yet was flat on his back nevertheless.

40:2   Let him tell you about it: "I was much impressed with what you fellows said about alcoholism, but I frankly did not believe it would be possible for me to drink again. I somewhat appreciated your ideas about the subtle insanity which precedes the first drink, but I was confident it could not happen to me after what I had learned. I reasoned I was not so far advanced as most of you fellows, that I had been usually successful in licking my other personal and[†] problems, that I would therefore be successful where you men failed. I felt I had every right to be self-confident, that it would be only a matter of exercising my will power and keeping on guard.

40:3   "In this frame of mind, I went about my business and for a time all was well. I had no trouble refusing drinks, and began to wonder if I had not been making too hard work of a simple matter. One day I went to Washington to present some accounting evidence to a government bureau. I had been out of town before during this particular dry spell, so there was nothing new about that. Physically, I felt fine. Neither did I have any pressing problems or worries. My business came off well, I was pleased and knew my partners would be too. It was the end of a perfect day, not a cloud on the horizon.

41:1   "I went to my hotel and leisurely dressed for dinner. <u>As I crossed the threshold of the dining room, the thought came to mind it would be nice to have a couple of cocktails with dinner.</u> <u>That was all.</u> <u>Nothing more.</u> I ordered a cocktail and my meal. Then I ordered another cocktail. After dinner I decided to take a walk. When I returned to the hotel it struck me a highball would be fine before going to bed, so I stepped into the bar and had one. I remember having several more that night and plenty next morning. I have a shadowy recollection of being in an airplane bound for New York, of finding a friendly taxicab driver at the landing field instead of my wife. The driver escorted me about for several days. I know little of where I went, or what I said and did. Then came the hospital with its unbearable mental and physical suffering.

41:2   "As soon as I regained my ability to think, I went carefully over that evening in Washington. <u>Not only had I been off guard, I had made no fight whatever against</u>

<hr>

† This accurately reflects the language of the original.

that first drink. This time I had not thought of the consequences at all. I had commenced to drink as carelessly as though the cocktails were ginger ale. I now remembered what my alcoholic friends had told me, how they phophesied† that if I had an alcoholic mind, the time and place would come — I would drink again. They had said that though I did raise a defense, it would one day give way before some trivial reason for having a drink. Well, just that did happen and more, for what I had learned of alcoholism did not occur to me at all. I knew from that moment that I had an alcoholic mind. I saw that will power and self-knowledge would not help in those strange mental blank spots. I had never been able to understand people who said that a problem had them hopelessly defeated. I knew then. It was a crushing blow.

"Two of the members of Alcoholics Anonymous came to see me. They 42:1 grinned, which I didn't like so much, and then asked me if I thought myself alcoholic and if I were really licked this time. I had to concede both propositions. They piled on me heaps of medical evidence to the effect that an alcoholic mentality, such as I had exhibited in Washington, was a hopeless condition. They cited cases out of their own experience by the dozen. This process snuffed out the last flicker of conviction that I could do the job myself.

"Then they outlined the spiritual answer and program of action 42:2 which a hundred of them had followed successfully. Though I had been only a nominal churchman, their proposals were not, intellectually, hard to swallow. But the program of action, though entirely sensible, was pretty drastic. It meant I would have to throw several lifelong conceptions out of the window. That was not easy. But the moment I made up my mind to go through with the process, I had the curious feeling that my alcoholic condition was relieved, as in fact it proved to be.

"Quite as important was the discovery that spiritual principles 42:3 would solve all my problems. I have since been brought into a way of living infinitely more satisfying and, I hope, more useful than the life I lived before. My old manner of life was by no means a bad one, but I would not exchange its best moments for the worst I have now. I would not go back to it even if I could."

Fred's story speaks for itself. We hope it strikes home to thou- 43:1 sands like him. He had felt only the first nip of the wringer. Most alcoholics have to be pretty badly mangled before they really commence to solve their problems.

Most doctors and psychiatrists agree with our conclusions. One of 43:2 these men, staff member of a world-renowned hospital, recently made this statement to some of us: "What you say about the general hopelessness of the average alcoholic's plight is, in my opinion, correct. As to two of you men, whose stories I have heard, there is no doubt in my mind that you were 100% hopeless, apart from Divine help. Had you offered yourselves as patients at this hospital, I would not have taken you, if I had been able to avoid it. People like you are too heartbreaking. Though not a religious person, I have profound respect for the spiritual approach in such cases as yours. For most cases, there is virtually no other solution."

Once more: the alcoholic at certain times has no effective mental 43:3 defense against the first drink. Except in a few rare cases, neither he nor any other human being can provide such a defense. His defense must come from a higher Power.

† This accurately reflects the language of the original.

Chapter Four

WE AGNOSTICS

44:1   In the preceding chapters, you have learned something of alcoholism. We hope we have made clear the distinction between the alcoholic
and the non-alcoholic. If, when you honestly want to, you find you
cannot quit entirely, or if, when drinking, you have little control
over the amount you take, you are probably alcoholic. If that be the
case, you may be suffering from an illness which only a spiritual
experience will conquer.

44:2   To one who feels he is an atheist or agnostic such an experience
seems impossible, but to continue as he is means disaster especially if
he is an alcoholic of the hopeless variety. To be doomed to an alcoholic
hell or be "saved" — not easy alternatives to face.

44:3   But it isn't so difficult. About half our fellowship were of exactly that type. At first some of us tried to avoid the issue, hoping
against hope we were not true alcoholics. But after a while we had to
face the fact that we must find a spiritual basis of life — or else.
Perhaps it is going to be that way with you. But cheer up, something
like fifty of us thought we were atheists or agnostics. Our experience
shows that you need not disconcerted.

44:4   If a mere code of morals, or a better philosophy of life were
sufficient to overcome alcoholism, many of us would have recovered long
ago. But we found that such codes and philosophies did not save us, no
matter how much we tried. We could wish to be moral, we could wish to
be philosophically comforted, in fact, we could will these things with
all our might, but the needed power wasn't there. Our human resources,
as marshalled by the will, were not sufficient; they failed utterly.

45:1   Lack of power, that was our dilemma. We had to find a power by which
we could live, and it had to be A Power Greater Than Ourselves.
Obviously. But where and how were we to find this Power?

45:2   Well, that's exactly what this book is about. Its main object is to
enable you to find a Power greater than yourself, which will solve your
problem. That means we have written a book which we believe to be
spiritual as well as moral. And it means, of course, that we are going
to talk about God. Here difficulty arises with agnostics. Many times we
talk to a new man and watch his hope rise as we discuss his alcoholic
problems and explain our fellowship. But his face falls when we speak
of spiritual matters, especially when we mention God, for we have re-
opened a subject which our man thought he had neatly evaded or entirely
ignored.

45:3   We know how he feels. We have shared his honest doubt and prejudice.
Some of us have been violently anti-religious. To others, the word
"God" brought up a particular idea of Him with which someone had tried
to impress us during childhood. Perhaps we rejected this particular
conception because it seemed inadequate. With that rejection we imagined we had abandoned the God idea entirely. We were bothered with the
thought that faith and dependence upon a Power beyond ourselves was
somewhat weak, even cowardly. We looked upon this world of warring
individuals, warring theological systems, inexplicable calamity, with
deep skepticism. We looked askance at many individuals who claimed to
be godly. How could a Supreme Being have anything to do with it all?
And who could comprehend a Supreme Being anyhow? Yet, in other moments,
we found ourselves thinking, when enchanted by the starlit night,

"Who, then, made all this?" There was a feeling of awe and wonder, but it was fleeting and soon lost.

Yes, we of agnostic temperament have had these thoughts and experiences. Let us make haste to reassure you. We found that as soon as we were able to lay aside prejudice and express even a willingness to believe in a Power greater that ourselves, we commenced to get results, even though it was impossible for any of us to fully define or comprehend that Power, which is God. 46:1

Much to our relief, we discovered we did not need to consider another's conception of God. Our own conception, however inadequate, was sufficient to make the approach and to effect a contact with Him. As soon as we admitted the possible existence of a Creative Intelligence, A Spirit of the Universe underlying the totality of things, we began to be possessed of a new sense of power and direction, provided we took other simple steps. We found that God does not make hard terms with those who seek Him. To us, the Realm of Spirit is broad, roomy, all inclusive; never exclusive or forbidding. It is open, we believe, to all men. 46:2

When, therefore, we speak to you of God, we mean your own conception of God. This applies, too, to other spiritual expressions which you find in this book. Do not let any prejudice you may have against spiritual terms deter you from honestly asking yourself what they mean to you. At the start, this is all you will need to commence spiritual growth, to effect your first conscious relation with God, as you understand Him. Afterward, you will find yourself accepting many things which now seem entirely out of reach. That is growth, but if you are going to grow, you have to begin somewhere. So use your own conception, however limited it may be. 47:1

You need ask yourself but one short question. "Do I now believe, or am I even willing to believe, that there is a Power greater than myself?" As soon as a man can say that he does believe, or is willing to believe, we emphatically assure him that he is on his way. It has been repeatedly proven among us that upon this simple cornerstone a wonderfully effective spiritual structure can be built. 47:2

That was great news to us, for we had assumed we could not make use of spiritual principles unless we accepted many things on faith which seemed difficult to believe. When people presented us with spiritual approaches, how frequently did we all say: "I wish I had what that man has. I'm sure it would work if I could only believe as he believes. But I cannot accept as surely true the many articles of faith which are so plain to him." So it was comforting to learn that we could commence at a simpler level. 47:3

Besides a seeming inability to accept much on faith, we often found ourselves handicapped by obstinacy, sensitiveness, and unreasoning prejudice. Many of us have been so touchy that even casual reference to spiritual things made us bristle with antagonism. This sort of thinking had to be abandoned. Though some of us resisted, we founds no great difficulty in casting aside such feelings. Faced with alcoholic destruction, we soon became as open minded on spiritual matters as we had tried to be on other questions. In this respect alcohol was a great persuader. It finally beat us into a state of reasonableness. Sometimes this was a tedious process; we hope no one will be prejudiced as long as some of us were. 47:4

The reader may still ask why he should believe in a Power greater than himself. We think there are good reasons. Let us have a look at some of them. 48:1

The practical individual of today is a stickler for facts and results. Nevertheless, the twentieth century readily accepts theories of all kinds, provided they are firmly grounded in fact. We have numerous theories, for example, about electricity. Everybody believes them without a murmur of doubt. Why this ready acceptance? 48:2

Simply because it is impossible to explain what we see, feel, direct, and use, without a reasonable assumption as a starting point.

48:3   Everybody nowadays, believes in scores of assumptions for which there is good evidence, but no perfect visual proof. And does not science demonstrate that visual proof is the weakest proof? It is being constantly revealed, as mankind studies the material world, that outward appearances are not inward reality at all. To illustrate:

48:4   The prosaic steel girder is a mass of electrons whirling around each other at incredible speed. These tiny bodies are governed by precise laws, and these laws hold true throughout the material world. Science tells us so. We have no reason to doubt it. When, however, the perfectly logical assumption is suggested that underneath the material world, and life as we see it, there is an All Powerful, Guiding, Creative Intelligence, right there our perverse streak comes to the surface and we laboriously set out to convince ourselves it isn't so. We read wordy books and indulge in windy arguments, thinking we believe this universe needs no God to explain it. Were our contentions true, it would follow that life originated out of nothing, means nothing, and proceeds nowhere.

49:1   Instead of regarding ourselves as intelligent agents, spearheads of God's ever advancing Creation, we agnostics and atheists chose to believe that our human intelligence was the last word, the alpha and the omega, the beginning and end of all. Rather vain of us, wasn't it?

49:2   We, who have traveled this dubious path, beg you to lay aside prejudice, even against organized religion. We have learned that whatever the human frailties of various faiths may be, those faiths have given purpose and direction to millions. People of faith have a logical idea of what life is all about. Actually, we used to have no reasonable conception whatever. We used to amuse ourselves as we cynically dissected spiritual beliefs and practices; we might have observed that many spiritually-minded persons of all races, colors, and creeds were demonstrating a degree of stability, happiness and usefulness which we should have sought ourselves.

50:1   Instead, we looked at the human defects of these people, and sometimes used their shortcomings as a basis of wholesale condemnation. We talked of intolerance, while we were intolerant ourselves. We missed the reality and the beauty of the forest because we were diverted by the ugliness of some of its trees. We never gave the spiritual side of life a fair hearing.

50:2   In the stories which follow you will find wide variation in the way each teller approaches and conceives of the Power which is greater than himself. Whether you agree with a particular approach or conception seems to make little difference. Experience has taught that these are matters about which, for our purpose, we need not be worried. They are questions for each individual to settle for himself.

50:3   On one proposition, however, these men and women are strikingly agreed. Everyone of them has gained access to, and believes in a Power greater than himself. This Power has in each case accomplished the miraculous, the humanly impossible. As a celebrated American statesman puts it, "Let's look at the record."

50:4   Here are one hundred men and women, worldly and sophisticated indeed. They flatly declare to you that since they have come to believe in a Power greater than themselves, to take a certain attitude toward that Power, and to do certain simple things, there has been a revolutionary change in their way of living and thinking. They tell you that in the face of collapse and despair, in the face of the total failure of their human resources, that a new Power, peace, happiness, and sense of direction has flowed into them. This happened soon after they whole-heartedly met a few simple requirements. Once confused and baffled by the seeming futility of existence they will show you the underlying reasons why they were making heavy going of life. Leaving aside the drink question, they tell why living was so unsatisfactory. They will show you how the change came over them. When one hundred people, much like you, are able to say that consciousness of The Presence of God is today the most important fact of their lives, they present a powerful reason why you too should have faith.

This world of ours has made more material progress in the last century than in all the milleniums which sent before. Almost everyone knows the reason. Students of ancient history tell us that the intellect of men in those days was equal to the best of today. Yet in ancient times material progress was painfully slow. The spirit of modern scientific inquiry, research and invention was almost unknown. In the realm of the material, men's minds were fettered by superstition, tradition, and all sorts of fixed ideas. The contemporaries of Columbus thought a round earth preposterous. Others like them came near putting Galileo to death for his astronomical heresies. 51:1

But ask yourself this: are not some of us just as biased and unreasonable about the realm of the spirit as were the ancients about the realm of the material? Even in the present century, American newspapers were afraid to print an account of the Wright Brothers first successful flight at Kittyhawk. Had not all efforts at flight failed before? Did not Professor Langley's absurd flying machine go to the bottom of the Potomac river? Was it not true that the best mathematical minds had proved man could never fly? Had not people said God had reserved this privilege to the birds? Only thirty years later the conquest of the air was almost an old story and airplane travel was in full swing. 51:2

But in most fields our generation has witnessed complete liberation of our thinking. Show any longshoreman a Sunday supplement describing a proposal to explore the moon by means of a rocket and he will say, "I bet they do it — maybe not so long either." Is not our age characterized by the ease with which we discard old ideas for new, by the complete readiness with which we throw away the theory or gadget which does not work for something new which does? 52:1

We had to ask ourselves why we shouldn't apply to our human problems this same readiness to change the point of view. We were having trouble with personal relationships, we couldn't control our emotional natures, we were a prey to misery and depression, we couldn't make a living, we had a feeling of uselessness, we were full of fear, we were unhappy, we couldn't seem to be of real help to other people — was not a basic solution of this bedevilment more important than whether we should see newsreels of lunar flight? Of course it was. 52:2

When we saw others solve their problems by simple reliance upon the Spirit of this universe, we had to stop doubting the power of God. Our ideas did not work. But the God idea did. 52:3

The Wright Brothers' almost childish faith that they could build a machine which would fly was the mainspring of their accomplishment. Without that, nothing could have happened. We agnostics and atheists were sticking to the idea that self-sufficiency would solve our problems. When others showed us that "God-sufficiency" worked with them, we began to feel like those who had insisted the Wrights would never fly. 52:4

Logic is great stuff. We liked it. We still like it. It is not by chance we were given the power to reason, to examine the evidence of our senses, and to draw conclusions. That is one of man's magnificent attributes. We agnostically inclined would not feel satisfied with a proposal which does not lend itself to reasonable 53:1

Page 24.

approach and interpretation. Hence we are at pains to tell why we think
our present faith is reasonable, why we think it more sane and logical
to believe than not to believe, why we say our former thinking was soft
and mushy when we threw up our hands in doubt and said, "We don't know."

53:2   When we became alcoholics, crushed by a self-imposed crisis we
could not postpone or evade, we had to fearlessly face the proposition
that either God is everything or else He is nothing. God either is, or
He isn't. What was our choice to be?

53:3   Arrived at this point, we were squarely confronted with the question of faith. We couldn't duck the issue. Some of us had already walked
far over the Bridge of Reason toward the desired shore of faith. The
outlines and the promise of the New Land had brought lustre to tired
eyes and fresh courage to flagging spirits. Friendly hands had stretched
out in welcome. We were grateful that Reason had brought us so far. But
somehow, we couldn't quite step ashore. Perhaps we had been leaning too
heavily on Reason that last mile and we did not like to lose our
support.

53:4   That was natural, but let us think a little more closely. Without
knowing it, had we not been brought to where we stood by a certain kind
of faith? For did we not believe in our own reasoning? Did we not have
confidence in our ability to think? What was that but a sort of faith?
Yes, we had been faithful, abjectly faithful to the God of Reason. So,
in one way or another, we discovered that faith had been involved all
the time!

54:1   We found too, that we had been worshippers. What a state of mental
gooseflesh that used to bring on! Had we not variously worshipped
people, sentiment, things, money, and ourselves? And then, with a
better motive, had we not worshipfully beheld the sunset, the sea, or
a flower? Who of us had not loved something or somebody? How much did
these feelings, these loves, these worships have to do with pure
reason? Little or nothing, we saw at last. Were not these things the
tissue out of which our lives were constructed? Did not these feelings,
after all, determine the course of our existence? It was impossible to
say we had no capacity for faith, or love, or worship. In one form or
another we had been living by faith and little else.

54:2   Imagine life without faith! Were nothing left but pure reason, it
wouldn't be life. But we believed in life — of course we did. We could
not prove life in the sense that you can prove a straight line is the
shortest distance between two points: yet, there it was. Could we still
say the whole thing was nothing but a mass of electrons, created out of
nothing, meaning nothing, whirling on to a destiny of nothingness? Of
course we couldn't. The electrons themselves seemed more intelligent
than that. At least, so the chemist said.

54:3   Hence, we saw that reason isn't everything. Neither is reason, as
most of us used it, entirely dependable, though it emanate from our best
minds. What about people who proved that man could never fly?

55:1   Yet we had been seeing another kind of flight, a spiritual liberation from this world, people who rose above their problems. They said
God made these things possible, and we only smiled. We had seen spiritual release, but liked to tell ourselves it wasn't true.

55:2   Actually we were fooling ourselves, for deep down in every man, woman,
and child, is the fundamental idea of God. It may be obscured by calamity,
by pomp, by worship of other things, but in some form or other it is there.
For faith in a Power greater than ourselves, and miraculous demonstrations of that power in human lives, are facts as old as man himself.

We finally saw that faith in some kind of God was a part of our make-up, just as much as the feeling we have for a friend. Sometimes we had to search fearlessly, but He was there. He was as much a fact as we were. And we are sure you will find the Great Reality deep down within you. In the last analysis it is only there that He may be found. It was so with us; why not with you? 55:3

We can only clear the ground a bit for you. If our testimony helps sweep away prejudice, enables you to think honestly, encourages you to search diligently within yourself, then you will have joined us on the Broad Highway. With this attitude you cannot fail. The consciousness that you do believe is sure to come to you. 55:4

In this book you will read the experience of a man who thought he was an atheist. His story is so interesting that some of it should be told now. His change of heart was dramatic, convincing, and moving. 55:5

Our friend was a minister's son. He attended church school, where he became rebellious at what he thought an overdose of religious education. For years thereafter he was dogged by trouble and frustration. Business failure, insanity, fatal illness, suicide — these calamities in his immediate family embittered and depressed him. Post-war disillusionment, ever more serious alcoholism, impending mental and physical collapse, brought him to the point of self-destruction. 56:1

One night when confined in a hospital, he was approached by an alcoholic who had known a spiritual experience. Our friend's gorge rose as he bitterly cried out: "If there is a God, He certainly hasn't done anything for me." But later, alone in his room, he asked himself this question: "Is it possible that all the religious people I have known are wrong?" While pondering the answer, he felt as though he lived in hell. Then, like a thunderbolt, a great thought came. It crowded out all else: 56:2

"WHO ARE YOU TO SAY THERE IS NO GOD?" 56:3

This man recounts that he tumbled out of bed to his knees. In a few seconds he was overwhelmed by a conviction of the Presence of God. It poured over and through him with the certainty and majesty of a great tide at flood. The barriers he had built through the years were swept away. He stood in the Presence of Infinite Power and Love. He had stepped from bridge to shore. For the first time, he lived in conscious companionship with his Creator. 56:4

Thus was our friend's cornerstone fixed in place. No later vicissitude has shaken it. His alcoholic problem was taken away. That very night three years ago it disappeared. Save for a few brief moments of temptation, the thought of drink has never returned; and at such times a great revulsion has risen up in him. Seemingly he could not drink even if he would. God had restored his sanity. 56:5

What is this but a miracle of healing? Yet its elements are simple. Circumstances made him willing to believe. He humbly offered himself to his Maker — then he knew. 57:1

Even so has God restored us all to our right minds. To this man, the Revelation was sudden. Some of us grow into it more slowly. But He has come too all who have honestly sought Him. 57:2

Draw near to Him and He will disclose Himself to you! 57:3

Chapter Five

HOW IT WORKS

58:1   Rarely have we seen a person fail who has thoroughly followed our directions. Those who do not recover are people who cannot or will not completely give themselves to this simple program, usually men and women who are constitutionally incapable of being honest with themselves. There are such unfortunates. They are not at fault; they seem to have been born that way. They are naturally incapable of grasping and developing a way of life which demands rigorous honesty. Their chances are less than average. There are those, too, who suffer from grave emotional and mental disorders, but many of them do recover if they have the capacity to be honest.

58:2   Our stories disclose in a general way what we used to be like, what happened, and what we are like now. If you have decided you want what we have and are willing to go to any length to get it —then you are ready to follow directions.

58:3   At some of these you may balk. You may think you can find an easier, softer way. We doubt if you can. With all the earnestness at our command, we beg of you to be fearless and thorough from the very start. Some of us have tried to hold on to our old ideas and the result was nil until we let go absolutely.

58:4   Remember that you are dealing with alcohol — cunning, baffling, powerful! Without help it is too much for you. But there is One who has all power — That One is God. You must find Him now!

59:1   Half measures will avail you nothing. You stand at the turning point. Throw yourself under His protection and care with complete abandon.

59:2   Now we think you can take it! Here are the steps we took, which are suggested as your Program of Recovery:

1. Admitted we were powerless over alcohol — that our lives had become unmanageable.
2. Came to believe that a Power greater than ourselves could re store us to sanity.
3. Made a decision to turn our will and our lives over to the care and direction of God as we understood Him.
4. Made a searching and fearless moral inventory of ourselves.
5. Admitted to God, to ourselves, and to another human being the exact nature of our wrongs.
6. Were entirely willing that God remove all these defects of character.
7. Humbly, on our knees, asked Him to remove our shortcomings — holding nothing back.
8. Made a list of all persons we had harmed, and became willing to make complete amends to them all.
9. Made direct amends to such people wherever possible, except when to do so would injure them or others.

10. Continued to take personal inventory and when we were wrong promptly admitted it.
11. Sought through prayer and meditation to improve our contact with God, praying only for knowledge of His will for us and the power to carry that out.
12. Having had a spiritual experience as the result of this course of action, we tried to carry this message to others, especially alcoholics, and to practice these principles in all our affairs.

You may exclaim, "What an order! I can't go through with it." Do not be discouraged. No one among us has been able to maintain anything like perfect adherence to these principles. We are not saints. The point is, that we are willing to grow along spiritual lines. The principles we have set down are guides to progress. We claim spiritual progress rather than spiritual perfection. [60:1]

Our description of the alcoholic, the chapter to the agnostic, and our personal adventures before and after, have been designed to sell you three pertinent ideas: [60:2]

(a) That you are alcoholic and cannot manage your own life.
(b) That probably no human power can relieve your alcoholism.
(c) That God can and will.

If you are not convinced on these vital issues, you ought to re-read the book to this point or else throw it away!

If you are convinced, you are now at step three, which is that you make a decision to turn your will and your life over to God as you understand Him. Just what do we mean by that, and just what do we do? [60:3]

The first requirement is that you see that any life run on self-will can hardly be a success. On that basis we are almost always in collission[†] with something or somebody, even though our motives may be good. Most people try to live by self-propulsion. Each person is like an actor who wants to run the whole show: is forever trying to arrange the lights, the ballet, the scenery and the rest of the players in his own way. If his arrangements would only stay put, if only people would do as he wishes, the show would be great. Everybody, including himself, would be pleased. Life would be wonderful. In trying to make these arrangements our actor may sometimes be quite virtuous. He may be kind, considerate, patient, generous; even modest and self-sacrificing. On the other hand, he may be mean, egotistical, selfish and dishonest. But, as with most humans, he is more likely to have varied traits. [60:4]

What usually happens? The show doesn't come off very well. He begins to think life doesn't treat him right. He decides to exert himself some more. He becomes, on the next occasion, still more demanding or gracious, as the case may be. Still the play does not suit him. Admitting he may be somewhat at fault, he is sure that other people are more to blame. He becomes angry, indignant, self-pitying. What is his basic trouble? Is he not really a self-seeker even when trying to be kind? Is he not a victim of the delusion that he can wrest satisfaction and happiness out of this world if he only manages well? Is it not evident to all the rest of the players that these are the things he wants? And do not his actions make each of them wish to retaliate, snatching all they can get out of the show? Is he not, even in his best moments, a producer of confusion rather than harmony? [61:1]

Our actor is self-centered — ego-centric, as people like to call it nowadays. He is like the retired business man who lolls in the Florida sunshine in the winter [61:2]

---

† This accurately reflects the language of the original.

Page 28.

complaining of the sad state of the nation; the preacher who sighs over
the sins of the twentieth century; politicians and reformers who are
sure all would be Utopia if the rest of the world would only behave; the
outlaw safe cracker who thinks society has wronged him; and the alcoholic who has lost all and is locked up. Whatever their protestations,
are not these people mostly concerned with themselves, their resentments, or their self-pity?

62:1   Selfishness — self-centeredness! That, we think, is the root of our
troubles. Driven by a hundred forms of fear, self-delusion, self-
seeking, and self-pity, we step on the toes of our fellows and they
retaliate. Sometimes they hurt us, seemingly, without provocation, but
we invariably find that at some time in the past we have made decisions
based on self, which later placed us in a position to be hurt.

62:2   So our troubles, we think, are basically of our own making. They
arise out of ourselves, and the alcoholic is almost the most extreme
example that could be found of self-will run riot, though he usually
doesn't think so. Above everything, we alcoholics must be rid of this
selfishness. We must, or it kills us! God makes that possible. And there
is no way of entirely getting rid of self without Him. You may have
moral and philosophical convictions galore, but you can't live up to
them even though you would like to. Neither can you reduce your self-
centeredness much by wishing or trying on your own power. You must have
God's help.

62:3   This is the how and why of it. First of all, quit playing God
yourself. It doesn't work. Next, decide that hereafter in this drama of
life, God is going to by your Director. He is the Principal; you are to
be His agent. He is the Father, and you are His child. Get that simple
relationship straight. Most good ideas are simple and this concept is
to be the keystone of the new and triumphant arch through which you will
pass to freedom.

63:1   When you sincerely take such a position, all sorts of remarkable
things follow. You have a new Employer. Being all powerful, He must
necessarily provide what you need, if you keep close to Him and perform
His work well. Established on such a footing you become less and less
interested in yourself, your little plans and designs. More and more
you become interested in seeing what you can contribute to life. As you
feel new power flow in, as you enjoy peace of mind, as you discover you
can face life successfully, as you become conscious of His presence,
you begin to lose your fear of today, tomorrow, or the hereafter. You
will have been reborn.

63:2   Get down upon your knees and say to your Maker, <u>as you understand
Him</u>: "God, I offer myself to Thee — to build with me and to do with me
as Thou wilt. Relieve me of the bondage of self, that I may better do
Thy will. Take away my difficulties, that victory over them may bear
witness to those I would help of Thy Power, Thy Love, and Thy Way of
life. May I do Thy will always!" Think well before taking this step. Be
sure you are ready; that you can at last abandon yourself utterly to
Him.

63:3   It is very desirable that you make your decision with an understanding person. It may be your wife, your best friend, your spiritual
adviser, but remember it is better to meet God alone that[†] with one who
might misunderstand. You must decide this for yourself. The wording of
your decision is, of course, quite optional so long as you express the
idea, voicing it without reservation. This decision is only a beginning, though if honestly and humbly made, an effect, sometimes a very
great one, will be felt at once.

63:4   Next we launch out on a course of vigorous action, the first
step of which is a personal housecleaning, which you have never in
all probability attempted. Though your decision is a vital and
crucial step, it can have little permanent effect unless at once
followed by a strenuous effort to face, and to be rid of, the things

[†] This accurately reflects the language of the original.

in yourself which have been blocking you. Your liquor is but a symptom. Let's now get down to basic causes and conditions.

Therefore, you start upon a personal inventory. <u>This is step four</u>. A business which takes no regular inventory usually goes broke. Taking a commercial inventory is a fact-finding and a fact-facing process. It is an effort to discover the truth about the stock-in-trade. Its object is to disclose damaged or unsalable goods, to get rid of them promptly and without regret. If the owner of the business is to be successful, he cannot fool himself about values. 64:1

We do exactly the same thing with our lives. We take stock honestly. First, we search out the flaws in our make-up which have caused our failure. Being convinced that self, manifested in various ways, is what has defeated us, we consider its common manifestations. 64:2

Resentment is the "number one" offender. It destroys more alcoholics than anything else. From it stem all forms of spiritual disease, for we have been not only mentally and physically ill, we have been spiritually sick. When the spiritual malady is overcome, we straighten out mentally and physically. In dealing with resentments, we set them on paper. List people, institutions or principles with whom you are angry. Ask yourself why you are angry. In most cases it will be found that your self-esteem, your pocketbook, your ambitions, your personal relationships, (including sex) are hurt or threatened. So you are sore. You are "burned up." 64:3

On your grudge list set opposite each name your injuries. Is it your self-esteem, your security, your ambitions, your personal, or your sex relations, which have been interfered with? 65:1

Be as definite as this example: 65:2

I'm resentful at:	The Cause	Affects my:
Mr. Brown	His attention to my wife.	Sex relations. Self-esteem (fear)
	Told my wife of my mistress.	Sex relations. Self-esteem (fear)
	Brown may get my job at the office.	Security. Self-esteem (fear)
Mrs. Jones	She's a nut — she snubbed me. She committed her husband for drinking. He's my friend. She's a gossip.	Personal relationship. Self-esteem (fear)
My employer	Unreasonable — Unjust — Overbearing — Threatens to fire me for drinking and padding my expense account.	Self-esteem (fear) Security
My wife	Misunderstands and nags. Likes Brown. Wants house put in her name.	Pride — Personal and sex relations-Security (fear)

Go on through the list back through your lifetime. Nothing counts but thoroughness and honesty. When you are finished consider it carefully. The first thing apparent to you is that this world and its people are quite wrong. To conclude 65:3

Page 30.

that others are wrong is as far as most of us ever get. The usual outcome is that people continue to wrong you and you stay sore. Sometimes it is remorse and then you are sore at yourself. But the more you fight and try to have your way, the worse matters get. Isn't that so? As in war, victors only _seem_ to win. Your moments of triumph are short-lived.

66:1   It is plain that a way of life which includes deep resentment leads only to futility and unhappiness. To the precise extent that we permit these, do we squander the hours that might have been worth while. But with the alcoholic whose only hope is the maintenance and growth of a spiritual experience, this business of resentment is infinitely grave. We find that it is fatal. For when harboring such feelings we shut ourselves off from the sunlight of the Spirit. The insanity of alcohol returns and we drink again. And with us, to drink is to die.

66:2   If we are to live, we must be free of anger. The grouch and the brainstorm are not for us. They may be the dubious luxury of normal men, but for alcoholics these things are poison.

66:3   Turn back to your list, for it holds the key to your future. You must be prepared to look at it from an entirely different angle. You will begin to see that the world and its people really dominate you. In your present state, the wrongdoing of others, fancied or real, has power to actually kill you. How shall you escape? You see that these resentments must be mastered, but how? You cannot wish them away any more than alcohol.

66:4   This is our course: realize at once that the people who wrong you are spiritually sick. Though you don't like their symptoms and the way these disturb you, they, like yourself, are sick, too. Ask God to help you show them the same tolerance, pity, and patience that you would cheerfully grant a friend who has cancer. When a person next offends, say to yourself "This is a sick man. How can I be helpful to him? God save me from being angry. Thy will be done."

67:1   Never argue. Never retaliate. You wouldn't treat sick people that way. If you do, you destroy your chance of being helpful. You cannot be helpful to all people, but at least God will show you how to take a kindly and tolerant view of each and every one.

67:2   Take up your list again. Putting out of your mind the wrongs others have done, resolutely look for your own mistakes. Where have you been selfish, dishonest, self-seeking and frightened? Though a situation may not be entirely your fault, disregard the other person involved entirely. See where _you_ have been to blame. This is your inventory, not the other man's. When you see your fault write it down on the list. See it before you in black and white. Admit your wrongs honestly and be willing to set these matters straight.

67:3   You will notice that the word fear is bracketed alongside the difficulties with Mr. Brown, Mrs. Jones, your employer, and your wife. This short word somehow touches about every aspect of our lives. It is an evil and corroding thread; the fabric of our existence is shot through with it. It sets in motion trains of circumstances which bring us misfortune we feel we don't deserve. But did not we, ourselves, set the ball rolling? Sometimes we think fear ought to be classed with stealing as a sin. It seems to cause more trouble.

68:1   Review your fears thoroughly. Put them on paper, even though you have no resentment in connection with them. Ask yourself why you have them. Isn't it because self-reliance has failed you? Self-reliance was good as far as it went, but it didn't go far enough. Some of us once had great self-confidence, but it didn't fully solve the fear problem, or any other. When it made us cocky, it was worse.

Perhaps there is a better way — we think so. For you are now to go on a different basis; the basis of trusting and relying upon God. You are to trust infinite God rather than your finite self. You are in the world to play the role he assigns. Just to the extent that you do as you think He would have you, and humbly rely on Him, does He enable you to match calamity with serenity. 68:2

You must never apologize to anyone for depending upon your Creator. You can laugh at those who think spirituality the way of weakness, Paradoxically, it is the way of strength. The verdict of the ages is that faith means courage. All men of faith have courage. They trust their God. Never apologize for God. Instead let Him demonstrate, through you, what He can do. Ask Him to remove your fear and direct your attention to what He would have you be. At once, you will commence to outgrow fear. 68:3

Now about sex. You can probably stand an overhauling there. We needed it. But above all, let's be sensible on this question. It's so easy to get way off the track. Here we find human opinions running to extremes — absurd extremes, perhaps. One set of voices cry that sex is a lust of our lower nature, a base necessity of procreation. Then we have the voices who cry for sex and more sex; who bewail the institution of marriage; who think that most of the troubles of the race are traceable to sex causes. They think we do not have enough of it, or that it isn't the right kind. They see its significance everywhere. One school would allow man no flavor for his fare and the other would have us all on a straight pepper diet. We want to stay out of this controversy. We do not want to be the arbiter of anyone's sex conduct. We all have sex problems. We'd hardly be human if we didn't. What can we do about them? 68:4

Review your own conduct over the years past. Where have you been selfish, dishonest, or inconsiderate? Whom did you hurt? Did you unjustifiably arouse jealousy, suspicion or bitterness? Where you were at fault, what should you have done instead? Get this all down on paper and look at it. 69:1

In this way you can shape a sane and sound ideal for your future sex life. Subject each relation to this test — is it selfish or not? Ask God to mould your ideals and help you to live up to them. Remember always that your sex powers are God-given, and therefore good, neither to be used lightly or selfishly nor to be despised and loathed. 69:2

Whatever your ideal may be, you must be willing to grow toward it. You must be willing to make amends where you have done harm, provided that you will not bring about still more harm in so doing. In other words, treat sex as you would any other problem. In meditation, ask God what you should do about each specific matter. The right answer will come, if you want it. 69:3

God alone can judge your sex situation. Counsel with persons is often desirable, but let God be the final judge. Remember that some people are as fanatical about sex as others are loose. Avoid hysterical thinking or advice. 69:4

Suppose you fall short of the chosen ideal and stumble. Does this mean you are going to get drunk? Some people will tell you so. If they do, it will be only a half-truth. It depends on you and your motive. If you are sorry for what you have done, and have the honest desire to let God take you to better things, you will be forgiven and will have learned your lesson. If you are not sorry, and your conduct continues to harm others, you are quite sure to drink. We are not theorizing. These are facts out of our experience. 70:1

To sum up about sex: earnestly pray for the right ideal, for guidance in each questionable situation, for sanity, and for the strength to do the right thing. If 70:2

sex is very troublesome, throw yourself the harder into helping others. Think of their needs and work for them. This will take you out of yourself. It will quiet the imperious urge, when to yield would mean heartache.

70:3   If you have been thorough about your personal inventory, you have written down a lot by this time. You have listed and analyzed your resentments. You have begun to comprehend their futility and their fatality. You have commenced to see their terrible destructiveness. You have begun to learn tolerance, patience and good will toward all men, even your enemies, for you know them to be sick people. You have listed the people you have hurt by your conduct, and you are willing to straighten out the past if you can.

70:4   In this book you read again and again that God did for us what we could not do for ourselves. We hope you are convinced now that He can remove the self-will that has blocked you off from Him. You have made your decision. You have made an inventory of the grosser handicaps you have. You have made a good beginning, for you have swallowed and digested some big chunks of truth about yourself. Are you willing to go on?

Chapter Six

INTO ACTION

Having made your personal inventory, what shall you do about it?   72:1
You have been trying to get a new attitude, a new relationship with your
Creator, and to discover the obstacles in your path. You have admitted
certain defects; you have ascertained in a rough way what the trouble
is; you have put your finger on the weak items in your personal
inventory. Now these are about to be case[†] out. This requires action on
your part, which, when completed, will mean that you have admitted to
God, to yourself, and to another human being, the exact nature of your
defects. This brings us to the fifth step in the Program of Recovery
mentioned in the preceding chapter.

This is perhaps difficult — especially discussing your defects with   72:2
another person. You think you have done well enough in admitting these
things to yourself, perhaps. We doubt that. In actual practice, we
usually find a solitary self-appraisal insufficient. We strenuously
urge you to go much further. But you will be more reconciled to
discussing yourself with another person if we offer good reasons why
you should do so. The best reason first: if you skip this vital step,
you may not overcome drinking. Time after time newcomers have tried to
keep to themselves certain facts about their lives. Trying to avoid
this humbling experience, they have turned to easier methods. Almost
invariably they got drunk. Having persevered with the rest of the
program, they wondered why they fell. The answer is that they never
completed their housecleaning. They took inventory all right, but hung
on to some of the worst items in stock. They only <u>thought</u> they had lost
their egoism and fear; they only <u>thought</u> they had humbled themselves.
But they had not learned enough of humility, fearlessness and honesty,
in the sense we find it necessary, until they told someone else <u>all</u>
their life story.

More than most people, the alcoholic leads a double life. He is very   73:1
much the actor. To the outer world he presents his stage character. This
is the one he likes his fellows to see. He wants to enjoy a certain
reputation, but knows in his heart he doesn't deserve it.

The inconsistency is made worse by the things he does on his sprees.   73:2
Coming to his senses, he is revolted at certain episodes he vaguely
remembers. These memories are a nightmare. He trembles to think someone
might have observed him. As fast as he can, he pushes these memories far
inside himself. He hopes they will never see the light of day. He is
under constant fear and tension — that makes for more drinking.

Psychologists agree with us. Members of our group have spent   73:3
thousands of dollars for examinations by psychologists and psychiatrists. We know but few instances where we have given these doctors a
fair break. We have seldom told them the whole truth. Unwilling to be
honest with these sympathetic men, we were honest with no one else.
Small wonder the medical profession has a low opinion of alcoholics
and their chance for recovery!

You must be entirely honest with somebody if you expect to   73:4
live long or happily in this world. Rightly and naturally, you are
going to think well before you choose the person or persons with
whom to take this intimate and confidential step. If you belong to
a religious denomination which requires confession, you must, and

---

[†] This accurately reflects the language of the original.

of course, will want to go to the properly appointed authority whose duty it is to receive it. Though you have no religious connection, you may still do well to talk with someone ordained by an established religion. You will often find such a person quick to see and understand your problem. Of course, we sometimes encounter ministers who do not understand alcoholics.

74:1   If you cannot, or would rather not do this, search your acquaintance for a close-mouthed, understanding friend. Perhaps your doctor or your psychologist will be the person. It may be one of your own family, but you should not disclose anything to your wife or your parents which will hurt them and make them unhappy. You have no right to save your own skin at another person's expense. Such parts of your story you should tell to someone who will understand, yet be unaffected. The rule is you must be hard on yourself, but always considerate of others.

74:2   Notwithstanding the great necessity for discussing yourself with someone, it may be that you are so situated that there is no suitable person available. If that is so, you may postpone this step, only, however, if you hold yourself in complete readiness to go through with it at the first opportunity. We say this because we are very anxious that you talk to the right person. It is important that he be able to keep a confidence; that he fully understand and approve what you are driving at; that he will not try to change your plan. But don't use this as a mere excuse to postpone.

75:1   When you decide who is to hear your story, waste no time. Have a written inventory. Be prepared for a long talk. Explain to your partner what you are about to do, and why you have to do it. He should realize that you are engaged upon a life-and-death errand. Most people approached in this way will be glad to help; they will be honored by your confidence.

75:2   Pocket your pride and go to it! Illumine every twist of character, every dark cranny of the past. Once you have taken this step, witholding nothing, you will be delighted. You can look the world in the eye. You can be alone at perfect peace and ease. Your fears will fall from you. You will begin to feel the nearness of your Creator. You may have had certain spiritual beliefs, but now you will begin to have a spiritual experience. The feeling that the drink problem has disappeared will come strongly. You will know you are on the Broad Highway, walking hand in hand with the Spirit of the Universe.

75:3   Return home and find a place where you can be quiet for an hour. Carefully review what you have done. Thank God from the bottom of your heart that you know Him better. Take this book down from your shelf and turn to the page which contains the twelve steps. Carefully read the first five proposals and ask if you have omitted anything, for you are building an arch through which you will walk a free man at last. Is your part of the work solid so far? Are the stones properly in place? Have you skimped on the cement you have put into the foundation? Have you tried to make mortar without sand?

76:1   If you can answer to your satisfaction, look at step six. We have emphasized willingness as being indispensable. Are you now perfectly willing to let God remove from you all the things which you have admitted are objectionable? Can He now take them all — every one? If you yet cling to something you will not let go, ask God to help you be willing.

76:2   When you are ready, say something like this: "My Creator, I am now willing that you should have all of me, good and bad. I pray that you now remove from me every single defect of character which stands in the way of my usefulness to you and my fellows. Grant me strength, as I go out from here, to do your bidding. Amen.† You have then completed step seven.

---

† This accurately reflects the language of the original.

Now you need more action without which you will find that "Faith 76:3
without works is dead." Look at steps eight and nine. You have a list
of all persons you have harmed and to whom you are willing to make
complete amends. You made it when you took inventory. You subjected
yourself to a drastic self-appraisal. Now you are to go out to your
fellows and repair the damage you did in the past. You are to sweep away
the debris which has accumulated out of your effort to live on self-will
and run the show yourself. If you haven't the will to do this, ask until
it comes. Remember you agreed at the beginning you would go to any
lengths for victory over alcohol.

You probably still have some misgivings. We can help you dispel 76:4
them. As you look over the list of business acquaintances and friends
you have hurt, you will feel diffident about going to some of them on
a spiritual basis. Let us reassure you. To some people you need not, and
probably should not emphasize the spiritual feature on your first
approach. You might prejudice them. At the moment you are trying to put
your own life in order. But this is not an end in itself. Your real
purpose is to fit yourself to be of maximum service to God and the
people about you. It is seldom wise to approach an individual, who still
smarts from your injustice to him, and announce that you have given your
life to God. In the prize ring, this would be called leading with the
chin. Why lay yourself open to being branded a fanatic or a religious
bore? You may kill a future opportunity to carry a beneficial message.
But he is sure to be impressed with a sincere desire to set right the
wrong. He is going to be more interested in your demonstration of good
will than in your talk of spiritual discoveries.

Don't use this advice as an excuse for shying away from the subject 77:1
of God. When it will serve any good purpose, you should be willing to
announce your convictions with tact and common sense. The question of
how to approach the man you have hated will arise. It may be he has done
you more harm than you have dome[†] him and, though you may have acquired
a better attitude toward him, you are still not too keen about admitting
your faults. Nevertheless, with a person you dislike, we advise you to
take the bit in your teeth. He is an ideal subject upon which to
practice your new principles. Remember that he, like yourself, is sick
spiritually. Go to him in a helpful and forgiving spirit. Be sure to
confess your former ill feeling and express your regret of it.

Under no condition should you criticize such a person or be drawn 77:2
into an argument with him. Simply tell him that you realize you will
never get over drinking until you have done your utmost to straighten
out the past. You are there to sweep off your side of the street,
realizing that nothing worth while can be accomplished until you do so.
Never try to tell him what he should do. Don't discuss his faults. Stick
to your own. If your manner is calm, frank, and open, you will be
gratified with the result.

In nine cases out of ten the unexpected happens. Sometimes the man 78:1
you are calling upon admits his own fault; so feuds of years' standing
melt away in an hour. Rarely will you fail to make satisfactory progress.
Your former enemies will sometimes praise what you are doing and wish
you well. Occasionally, they will cancel a debt, or otherwise offer
assistance. Its should not matter, however, if someone does throw you
out of his office. You have made your demonstration, done your part.
It's water over the dam.

Most alcoholics owe money. Do not dodge your creditors. Tell them 78:2
what you are trying to do. Make no bones about your drinking; they
usually know it anyway, whether you think so or not. Never be afraid of
disclosing your alcoholism on the theory it may cause you financial
harm. Approached in this way, the most ruthless creditor will sometimes
surprise you. Arrange the best deal you can and let these people know
you are sorry your drinking has made you slow to pay. You must lose

---

[†] This accurately reflects the language of the original.

your fear of creditors no matter how far you have to go, for you are liable to drink if you are afraid to face them.

78:3 Perhaps you have committed a criminal offense which might land you in jail if known to the authorities. You may be short in your accounts and can't make good. You have already admitted this in confidence to another person, but you are sure you would be imprisoned or lose your job if it were known. Maybe it's only a petty offence such as padding your expense account. Most of us have done that sort of thing. Maybe you have divorced your wife. You have remarried but haven't kept up the alimony to number one. She is indignant about it, and has a warrant out for your arrest. That's a common form of trouble too.

79:1 Although these reparations take innumerable forms, there are some general principles which we find guiding. Remind yourself that you have decided to go to any lengths to find a spiritual experience. Ask that you be given the strength and direction to do the right thing, no matter what the personal consequence to you. You may lose your position or reputation, or face jail, but you are willing. You have to be. You must not shrink at anything.

79:2 Usually, however, other people are involved. Therefore, you are not to be the hasty and foolish martyr who would needlessly sacrifice others to save himself from the alcoholic pit. A man we know had remarried. Because of resentment and drinking, he had not paid alimony to his first wife. She was furious. She went to court and got an order for his arrest. He had commenced our way of life, had secured a position, and was getting his head above water. It would have been impressive heroics if he had walked up to the Judge and said, "Here I am."

79:3 We thought he ought to be willing to do that if necessary, but if he were in jail, he could provide nothing for either family. We suggested he write his first wife admitting his faults and asking forgiveness. He did, and also sent a small amount of money. He told her that he would try to do in the future. He said he was perfectly willing to go to jail if she insisted. Of course she did not, and the whole situation has long since been adjusted.

80:1 If taking drastic action is going to implicate other people, they should be consulted. Use every means to avoid wide-spread damage. You cannot shrink, however, from the final step if that is clearly indicated. If, after seeking advice, consulting others involved, and asking God to guide you, there appears no other just and honorable solution than the most drastic one, you must take your medicine. Trust that the eventual outcome will be right.

80:2 This brings to mind a story about one of our friends. While drinking, he accepted a sum of money from a bitterly-hated business rival, giving him no receipt for it. He subsequently denied having taken the money and used the incident as a basis for discrediting the man. He thus used his own wrong-doing as a means of destroying the reputation of another. In fact, his rival was ruined.

80:3 He felt he had done a wrong he could not possible make right. If he opened that old affair, he was sure it would destroy the reputation of his partner, disgrace his family and take away his own means of livelihood[†]. What right had he to involve those dependent upon him? How could he possibly make a public statement exonerating his rival?

80:4 He finally came to the conclusion that it was better to take those risks than to stand before his Creator guilty of such ruinous slander. He saw that he had to place the outcome in God's hands or he would soon start drinking again, and all would be lose[†] anyhow. He attended church for the first time in many years. After

---

[†] This accurately reflects the language of the original.

the sermon, he quietly got up and made an explanation. His action met widespread approval, and today he is one of the most trusted citizens of his town. This all happened three years ago.

The chances are that you have serious domestic troubles. We are perhaps mixed up with women in a fashion you wouldn't care to have advertised. We doubt if, in this respect, alcoholics are fundamentally much worse than other people. But drinking does complicate sex relations in the home. After a few years with an alcoholic, a wife gets worn out, resentful, and uncommunicative. How could she be anything else? The husband begins to feel lonely, sorry for himself. He commences to look around in the night clubs, or their equivalent, for something besides liquor. You may be having a secret and exciting affair with "the girl who understands me." In fairness we must say that she may understand, but what are you going to do about a thing like that? A man so involved often feels very remorseful at times, especially if he is married to a loyal and courageous girl who has literally gone through hell for him. 80:5

Whatever the situation, you usually have to do something about it. If you are sure your wife does not know, should you tell her? Not always, we think. If she knows in a general way that you have been wild, should you tell her in detail? Undoubtedly you should admit your fault. Your wife may insist on knowing all the particulars. She will want to know who the woman is and where she is. We feel you ought to say to her that you have no right to involve another person. You are sorry for what you have done, and God willing, it shall not be repeated. More than that you cannot do; you have no right to go further. Though there may be justifiable exceptions, and though we wish to lay down no rule of any sort, we have often found this the best course to take. 81:1

Our design for living is not a one-way street. It is as good for the wife as for the husband. If you can forget, so can she. It is better, however, that you do not needless† name a person upon whom she can vent her natural jealousy. 81:2

There are some cases where the utmost frankness is demanded. Perhaps yours is one of them. No outsider can appraise such an intimate situation. It may be you will both decide that the way of good sense and loving kindness is to let by-gones be by-gones. Each of you might pray about it, having the other one's happiness uppermost in mind. Keep it always in sight that you deal with that most terrible human emotion — jealousy. Good generalship may decide that you and your wife attack the problem on the flank, rather than risk face-to-face combat. You have to decide about that alone with your Creator. 82:1

Should you have no such complication, there is still plenty you should do at home. Sometimes we hear an alcoholic say that the only thing he needs to do is to keep sober. Certainly he needs to keep sober, for there will be no home if he doesn't. But he is yet a long way from making good to the wife or parents whom for years he has so shockingly treated. Passing all understanding is the patience mothers and wives have had with alcoholics. Had this not been so, many of us would have no homes today, would perhaps be dead. 82:2

The alcoholic is like a tornado roaring his way through the lives of others. Hearts are broken. Sweet relationships are dead. Affections have been uprooted. Selfish and inconsiderate habits have kept the home in turmoil. We feel a man is unthinking when he says that sobriety is enough. He is like the farmer who came up out of his cyclone cellar to find his home ruined. To his wife, he remarked, "Don't see anything the matter here, Ma. Ain't it grand the wind stopped blowin'?" 82:3

Yes, there is a long period of reconstruction ahead. You must take the lead. A remorseful mumbling that you are sorry won't fills the bill at all. You ought to 83:1

---

† This accurately reflects the language of the original.

Page 38.

sit down with your family and frankly analyze your past as you now see it, being very careful not to criticize them. Never mind their defects. They may be glaring, but the chances are that your own actions are partly responsible. So clean house with the family, asking each morning in meditation that your Creator show you the way of patience, tolerance kindliness, and love.

83:2   The spiritual life is not a theory. <u>You</u> have to live it. Unless your family expresses a desire to live upon spiritual principles, however, we think you ought to leave them alone. You should not talk incessantly about spiritual matters to them. They will change in time. Your practice will convince them more than your words. Remember that ten or twenty years of drunkenness would make a skeptic out of anyone.

83:3   There may be some wrongs you can never fully right. Don't worry about them if you can honestly say to yourself that you would right them if you could. Some people you cannot see — send them an honest letter. And there may be a valid reason for postponement in some cases. But don't delay if it can be avoided. Be sensible, tactful, and considerate. Be humble without being servile or scraping. As one of God's people you are to stand on your feet; don't crawl on your belly before anyone.

83:4   If you are painstaking about this phase of your development, you will be amazed before you are half through. You are going to know a new freedom and happiness. You will not regret the past nor wish to shut the door on it. You will comprehend the word serenity and know peace. No matter how far down the scale you have gone, you will see how your experience can benefit others. That feeling of uselessness and self-pity will disappear. You will lose interest in selfish things and gain interest in your fellows. Self-seeking will slip away. Your whole attitude and outlook upon life will change. Fear of people and of economic insecurity will leave you. You will intuitively know how to handle situations which used to baffle you. You will suddenly realize that God is doing for you what you could not do for yourself.

84:1   You say these are extravagent promises. They are not. They are being fulfilled among us — sometimes quickly, sometimes slowly. They will materialize in you if you work for them.

84:2   This thought brings us to step ten, which suggests you continue to take personal inventory and continue to set any new mistakes right as you go along. You vigorously commenced this way of life as you cleaned up your past. You have entered the world of Spirit. Your next function is to grow in understanding and effectiveness. This is not an overnight matter. It should continue for your life time. Continue to watch yourself for selfishness, dishonesty, resentment, and fear. When these crop up, ask God at once to remove them. Discuss them with someone immediately. Make amends quickly if you have harmed anyone. Then resolutely turn your thoughts to someone you can help. Love and tolerance of others is your code.

84:3   And you have ceased fighting anything or anyone — even alcohol. For by this time your sanity will have returned. You will seldom be interested in liquor. If tempted, you will recoil from it as you would from a hot flame. You will react sanely and normally. You will find this has happened automatically. You will see that your new attitude toward liquor has been given you without any thought or effort on your part. It just comes! That is the miracle of it. You are not fighting it, neither are you avoiding temptation. You feel as though you had been placed in a position of neutrality. You feel safe and protected. You have not even sworn off. Instead, the problem has been removed. It does not exist for you. You are neither cocky, nor are you afraid. That is our experience. That is how we react so long as we keep in fit spiritual condition.

It is easy to let up on the spiritual program of action and rest on 85:1
your laurels. You are headed for trouble if you do, for alcohol is a
subtle foe. We are not cured of alcoholism. What we really have is a
daily reprieve. Every day is a day when you have to carry the vision of
God's will into all of your activities. "How can I best serve Thee — Thy
will (not mine) be done." These are thoughts which must go with you
constantly. You can exercise your will power along this line all you
wish. It is the proper use of the will.

Much has already been said about receiving strength, inspiration, 85:2
and direction from Him who has all knowledge and power. If you have
carefully followed directions, you have begun to sense the flow of His
Spirit into you. To some extent you have become God-conscious. You have
begun to develop this vital sixth sense. But you must go further and
that means more action.

Step eleven suggests prayer and meditation. Don't by[†] shy on this 85:3
matter of prayer. Better men than we are using it constantly. It works,
if you have the proper attitude and work at it. It would be easy to be
vague about this matter. Yet, we believe we can give you some definite
and valuable suggestions.

When you awake tomorrow morning, look back over the day before. 86:1
Were you resentful, selfish, dishonest, or afraid? Do you owe an
apology? Have you kept something to yourself which should be discussed
with another person at once? Were you kind and loving toward all? What
could you have done better? Were you thinking of yourself most of the
time? Or were you thinking of what you could do for others, of what you
could pack into the stream of life? After you have faced yesterday, ask
God's forgiveness for any wrong. Ask to be shown what to do. Thus you
keep clean as you live each day.

Next, think about the twenty-four hours ahead. Consider your plans 86:2
for the day. Before you begin, ask God to guide your thinking. Especially ask that it be divorced from self-pity, dishonest or self-
seeking motives. Then go ahead and use your common sense. There is
nothing hard or mysterious about this. God gave you brains to use. Clear
your thinking of wrong motives. Your thought life will be placed on a
much higher plane.

In thinking through your day you may face indecision. You may not be 86:3
able to determine which course to take. Here you ask God for inspiration, an intuitive thought or a decision. Relax and take it easy. Don't
struggle. Ask God's help. You will be surprised how the right answers
come after you have practiced a few days. What used to be the hunch or
the occasional inspiration becomes a working part of your mind. Being
still inexperienced and just making your contact with God, it is not
probable that you are going to be divinely inspired all the time. That
would be a large piece of conceit, for which you might pay in all sorts
of absurd actions and ideas. Nevertheless you will find that your
thinking will, as time passes, be more and more on the plane of
inspiration and guidance. You will come to rely upon it. This is not
weird or silly. Most psychologists pronounce these methods sound.

You might conclude the period of meditation with a prayer that you be 87:1
shown all through the day what your next step is to be, that He give you
whatever you need to take care of every situation. Ask especially for
freedom from self-will. Be careful to make no request for yourself only.
You may ask for yourself, however, if others will be helped. Never pray
for your own selfish ends. People waste a lot of time doing that, and it
doesn't work. You can easily see why.

If curcumstances[†] warrant, ask your wife or a friend to join you in morning 87:2
meditation. If you belong to a religious denomination which requires a definite
morning devotion, be sure to attend to that also. If you are not a member of a

† This accurately reflects the language of the original.

religious body, you might select and memorize a few set prayers which emphasize the principles we have been discussing. There are many helpful books also. If you do not know of any, ask your priest, minister, or rabbi, for suggestions. Be quick to see where religious people are right. Make use of what they offer.

87:3   As you go through the day, pause when agitated or doubtful. Be still and ask for the right thought or action. It will come. Remind yourself you are no longer running the show. Humbly say to yourself many times each day "Thy will be done." You will be in much less danger of excitement, fear, anger, worry, self-pity, or foolish decisions. You will become much more efficient. You will not tire easily, for you will not be burning up energy foolishly as you did when trying to arrange life to suit yourself.

88:1   It works — it really does. Try it.

88:2   We alcoholics are undisiplined[†]. So let God discipline you in the simple way we have just outlined.

88:3   But this is not all. There is action and more action. "Faith without works is dead." What works? We shall treat them in the next chapter which is entirely devoted to step twelve.

[†] This accurately reflects the language of the original.

Chapter Seven

WORKING WITH OTHERS

Practical experience shows that nothing will so much insure your own immunity from drinking as intensive work with other alcoholics. It words when other spiritual activities fail. This is our twelfth suggestion: Carry this message to other alcoholics! You can help when no one else can. You can secure their confidence when others fail. Remember they are fatally ill. [89:1]

The kick you will get is tremendous. To watch people come back to life, to see them help others, to watch loneliness vanish, to see a fellowship grow up about you, to have a host of friends — this is an experience you must not miss. We know you will not want to miss it. Frequent contact with newcomers and with each other is the bright spot of our lives. [89:2]

Perhaps you are not acquainted with any drinkers who want to recover. You can easily find some by asking a few doctors, ministers, priests and hospitals. They will be only too glad to have your help. Don't start out an an evangelist or reformer. Unfortunately a lot of prejudice exists. You will be handicapped if you arouse it. Preachers and doctors don't like to be told they don't know their business. They are usually competent and you can learn much from them if you wish, but it happens that because of your own drinking experience you can be uniquely useful to other alcoholics. So cooperate; never criticise. To be helpful should be your only aim. [89:3]

When you discover a prospect for Alcoholics Anonymous, find out all you can about him. If he does not want to stop drinking, don't waste time trying to persuade him. You may spoil a later opportunity. This advice is given for his family also. They must be patient, realizing they are dealing with a sick person. [90:1]

If there is any indication that he wants to stop, have a good talk with the person most interested in him — usually his wife. Get an idea of his behavior, his problems, his background, the seriousness of his condition, and his religious leanings. You need this information to put yourself in his place, to see how you would like him to approach you if the tables were turned. [90:2]

Usually it is wise to wait till he goes on a binge. The family may object to this, but unless he is in a dangerous physical condition, it is better to risk it. Don't deal with him when he is very drunk, unless he is ugly and the family needs your help. Wait for the end of the spree, or at least for a lucid interval. Then let his family or a friend ask him if he wants to quit for good and if he would go to any extreme to do so. If he says yes, then his attention should be drawn to you as a person who has recovered. You should be described to him as one of a fellowship who, as a part of their own recovery, try to help others, and who will be glad to talk to him if he cares to see you. [90:3]

If he does not want to see you, never force yourself upon him. Neither should the family hysterically plead with him to do anything, nor should they tell him much about you. They should wait for the end of his next drinking bout. You might place this book where he can see it in the interval. Here no specific rule can be given. The family must decide these things. But urge them not to be over-anxious, for that might spoil matters. [90:4]

Page 42.

91:1   The family should not try to represent you. When possible, avoid meeting a man through his family. Approach through a doctor or an institution is a better bet. If your man needs hospitalization, he should have it, but not forcibly, unless he is violent. Let the doctor tell him he has something new in the way of a solution.

91:2   When your man is better, let the doctor suggest a visit from you. Though you have talked with the family, leave them out of the first discussion. Under these conditions your prospect will see he is under no pressure. He will feel he can deal with you without being nagged by his family. Call on him while he is still jittery. He will be more receptive when depressed.

91:3   See your man alone, if possible. At first engage in general conversation. After a while, turn the talk to some phase of drinking. Say enough about your drinking habits, symptoms, and experiences to encourage him to speak of himself. If he wishes to talk, let him do so. You will thus get a better idea of how you ought to proceed. If he is not communicative, give him a sketch of your drinking career up to the time you quit. But say nothing, for the moment, of how that was accomplished. If he is in a serious mood, dwell on the troubles liquor has caused you, being careful not to moralize or preach. If his mood is light, tell him humorous stories of your escapades. Get him to tell some of his.

91:4   When he sees you know all about the drinking game, commence to describe yourself as an alcoholic. Tell him how baffled you were, how you finally learned that you were sick as well as weak. Give him an account of the struggles you made to stop. Show him the mental twist which leads to the first drink of a spree. Do this as we have done in the chapter on alcoholism. If he is alcoholic, he will understand you at once. He will match your mental inconsistencies with some of his own.

92:1   If you are satisfied that he is a real alcoholic, you may begin to dwell on the hopeless feature of the malady. Show him, from your own experience, how the queer mental condition surrounding that first drink prevents normal functioning of the will power. Don't at this stage refer to this book, unless he has seen it and wishes to discuss it. And be careful not to brand him an alcoholic. Let him draw his own conclusion. If he sticks to the idea that he can still control his drinking, tell him that possibly he can — if he is not too alcoholic. But insist that if he is severely afflicted, there is little chance he can recover by himself.

92:2   Continue to speak of alcoholism as a sickness, a fatal malady. Talk about the conditions of body and mind which accompany it. Keep his attention focused mainly on your personal experience. If doctors or psychiatrists have pronounced you incurable, be sure and let him know about it. Explain that many are doomed who never realize their predicament. Doctors who know the truth are rightly loath to tell alcoholic patients the whole story unless it wilt serve some good purpose, but you may talk to him about the hopelessness of alcoholism, because you offer a solution. You will soon have your friend admitting he has many, if not all, of the traits of the alcoholic. If his own doctor is willing to tell him that he is alcoholic, so much the better. Even though your protege may not have entirely admitted his condition, he has become very curious to know how you got well. Let him ask you that question, if he will. If he does not ask, proceed with the rest of your story. Tell him exactly what happened to you. Stress the spiritual feature freely. If the man be agnostic or atheist, make it emphatic that he does not have to agree with your conception of God. He can choose any conception he likes, provided it makes sense to him. <u>The main thing is that he be willing to believe in a Power greater than himself and that he live by spiritual principles</u>.

93:1   When dealing with such a person, you had better use everyday language to describe spiritual principles. There is no use arousing any prejudice he may have against certain theological terms and conceptions, about which he may already be confused. Don't raise such issues, no matter what your own convictions are.

Your prospect may belong to a religious denomination. He religious education and training may be far superior to yours. In that case he is going to wonder how you can add anything to what he already knows. But he will be curious to learn why his own religious convictions have not worked, and yours have given you victory. He may be an example of the truth that faith alone is insufficient. To be vital, faith must be accompanied by self sacrifice and unselfish, constructive action. Let him see that you are not there to instruct him in religion. Admit that he probably knows more about it than you do, but call to his attention the fact that however deep his faith and knowledge, there must be something wrong, or he would not drink. Say that perhaps you can help him see where he fails to apply to himself the very precepts he knows so well. For our purpose you represent no particular faith or denomination. You are dealing only with general principles common to most denominations. 93:2

Outline our program of action, telling how you made a self-appraisal, how you straightened out your past, and why you are now endeavoring to be helpful to him. Make it plain he is under no obligation to you, that you hope only that he will try to help other alcoholics when he escapes his own difficulties. Show how important it is that he place the welfare of other people ahead of his own. Make it clear that he is not under pressure, that he needn't see you again, if he doesn't want to. You should not be offended if he wants to call it off, for he has helped you more than you have helped him. If your talk has been sane, quiet and full of human understanding, you have probably made a friend. Maybe you have disturbed him about the question of alcoholism. This is all to the good. The more hopeless he feels, the better. He will be more likely to follow your suggestions. 94:1

Your candidate may give reasons why he need not follow all of your program. He will rebel at the thought of a drastic housecleaning which requires discussion with other people. Do not contradict such views. Tell him you once felt as he does, but you doubt if you would have made much progress had you not taken action. On your first visit tell him about the fellowship of Alcoholics Anonymous. If he shows interest, lend him your copy of this book. 94:2

Unless your friend wants to talk further about himself, do not wear out your welcome. Give him a chance to think it over. If you do stay, let him steer the conversation in any direction he likes. Sometimes a new man is anxious to make a decision and discuss has affairs at once, and you may be tempted to let him proceed. This is almost always a mistake. If he has trouble later, he is likely to say you rushed him. You will be most successful with alcoholics if you do not exhibit any passion for crusade or reform. Never talk down to an alcoholic from any moral or spiritual hilltop, simply lay out your kit of spiritual tools for his inspection. Show him how they worked with you. Offer him friendship and fellowship. Tell him that if he wants to get well you will do anything to help. 95:1

If he is not interested in your solution, if he expects you to act only as a banker for his financial difficulties or a nurse for his sprees, drop him until he changes his mind. This he may do after he gets hurt again. 95:2

If he is sincerely interested and wants to see you again, ask him to be sure to read this book in the interval. After doing that, he is to decide for himself whether he wants to go on. He is not to be pushed or prodded by you, his wife, or his friends. If he is to find God, the desire must come from within. 95:3

If he thinks he can do the job in some other way, or prefers some other spritual[†] approach, encourage him to follow his own conscience. You have no monopoly on 95:4

† This accurately reflects the language of the original.

God; you merely have an approach that worked with you. But point out that we alcoholics have much in common and that you would like, in any case, to be friendly. Let it go at that.

96:1 Do not be discouraged if your prospect does not respond at once. Search out another alcoholic and try again. You are sure to find someone desperate enough to accept with eagerness what you offer. It's a waste of time and poor strategy to keep chasing a man who cannot or will not work with you. If you leave such a person alone, in all likelihood he will begin to run after you, for he will soon become convinced that he cannot recover alone. To spend too much time on any one situation is to deny some other alcoholic an opportunity to live and be happy. One of our fellowship failed entirely with his first half dozen prospects. He often says that if he had continued to work on them, he might have deprived many others, who have since recovered, of their chance.

96:2 Suppose now you are making your second visit to a man. He has read this volume and says he is prepared to go through with the twelve steps of The Program of Recovery. Having had the experience yourself, you can give him much practical advice. Suggest he make his decision with you and tell you his story, but do not insist upon it if he prefers to consult someone else.

96:3 He may be broke and homeless. If he is, try to help him about getting a job. Give him a little financial assistance, unless it would deprive your family or creditors of money they should have. Perhaps you will want to take the man into your home for a few days. But be sure you use discretion. Be certain he will be welcomed by your family, and that he is not trying to impose upon you for money, connections, or shelter. Permit that and you only harm him. You will be making it possible for him to be insincere. You will be aiding in his destruction, rather than his recovery.

97:1 Never avoid these responsibilities, but be sure you are doing the right thing if you assume them. Self-sacrifice for others is the foundation stone of your recovery. A kindly act once in a while isn't enough. You have to act the Good Samaritan every day, if need be. It may mean the loss of many nights' sleep, great interference with your pleasures, interruptions to your business. It may mean sharing your money and your home, counseling frantic wives and relatives, innumerable trips to police courts, sanitariums, hospitals, jails and asylums. Your telephone may jangle at any time of the day or night. Your wife will sometimes say she is neglected. A drunk may smash the furniture in your home, or burn a mattress. You may have to fight with him if he is violent. Sometimes you will have to call a doctor and administer sedatives under his direction. Another time you may have to send for the police or an ambulance.

97:2 This sort of thing goes on constantly, but we seldom allow an alcoholic to live in our homes for long at a time. It is not good for him, and it sometimes creates serious complications in a family.

97:3 Though an alcoholic does not respond, there is no reason why you should neglect his family. You should continue to be friendly to them in every way. The family should be offered your way of life. Should they accept, and practice spiritual principles, there is a much better chance the head of the family will recover. And even though he continues to drink, the family will find life more bearable.

97:4 For the type of alcoholic who is able and willing to get well, little charity, in the ordinary sense of the word, is needed or wanted. The men who cry for money and shelter before conquering alcohol, are on the wrong track. Yet we do go to great extremes to provide each other with these very things, when such action is warranted. This may seem inconsistent, but it is not.

It is not the matter of giving that is in question, but when and how to give. That makes the difference between failure and success. The minute we put our work on a social service plane, the alcoholic commences to rely upon our assistance rather than upon God. He clamors for this or that, claiming he cannot master alcohol until his material needs are cared for. Nonsense. Some of us have taken very hard knocks to learn this truth: job or no job — wife or no wife — we simply do not stop drinking alcohol so long as we place dependence upon other people ahead of dependence on God. 98:1

Burn the idea into the consciousness of every man that he can get well regardless of anyone. No person on this earth can stop his recovery from alcohol, or prevent his being supplied with whatever is good for him. The only condition is that he trust in God and clean house. 98:2

Now, the domestic problem: There may be divorce, seperation†, or just strained relations. When your prospect has made such restitution as he can to his family, and has thoroughly explained to them the new principles by which he is living, he should proceed to put those principles into action at home. That is, if he is lucky enough to have a home. Though his family be at fault in many respects, he should not be concerned about that. He should concentrate on his own spiritual demonstration. Argument and fault-finding are to be avoided like leprosy. In many homes this is a difficult thing to do, but it must be done if any results are to be expected. If persisted in for a few months, the effect on a man's family is sure to be great. The most incompatible people discover they have a basis upon which they can meet. Little by little the family will see their own defects and admit them. These can then be discussed in an atmosphere of helpfulness and friendliness. 98:3

After they have seen tangible results, the family will perhaps want to join in the better way of life. These things will come to pass naturally and in good time, provided, however, the alcoholic continues to demonstrate that he can be sober, considerate, and helpful, regardless or what anyone says or does. Of course, we all fall much below this standard many times. But we must try to repair the damage immediately lest we pay the penalty by a spree. 99:1

If there be divorce or seperation†, there should be no undue haste for the couple to get together. The man should be sure of his ground. The wife should fully understand his new way of life. If their old relationship is to be resumed, it must be on a better basis, since the old one did not work. This means a new attitude and spirit all around. Sometimes it is to the best interests of all concerned that a couple remain apart. Obviously, no rule can be laid down. Let the alcoholic continue his new way of life day by day. When the time for living together has come, it will be apparent to both parties. 99:2

Let no alcoholic say he cannot recover unless he has his family back. This just isn't so. In some cases the wife will never come back for one reason or another. Remind your prospect that his recovery is not dependent upon people. It is dependent upon his relationship with God. We have seen men get well whose families have not returned at all. We have seen others slip when the family came back too soon. 99:3

Both you and the new prospect must day by day walk in the path of spiritual progress. If you persist, remarkable things will happen to you. When we look back, we realize that the things which came to us when we put ourselves in God's hands were better for us than anything we could have planned. Follow the dictates of a Higher Power and you will presently live in a new and wonderful world, no matter what your present circumstances! 100:1

† This accurately reflects the language of the original.

100:2   When working with a man and his family, you must take care not to participate in their quarrels. You may spoil your chance of being helpful if you do. But you may urge upon a man's family that he has been a very sick person and should be treated accordingly. You should warn them against arousing resentment or jealousy. You should point out that his defects of character are not going to disappear overnight. Show them that he has entered upon a period of growth. Ask them to remember, when they are impatient, the blessed fact of his sobriety.

100:3   If you have been successful in solving your own domestic problems, tell the newcomer's family how that was accomplished. In this way you can set them on the right track without becoming critical of them. The story of how you and your wife settled your difficulties is worth any amount of preaching or criticism.

100:4   Assuming we are spiritually fit, we can do all sorts of things alcoholics are not supposed to do. People have said we must not go where liquor is served; we must not have it in our homes; we must shun friends who drink; we must avoid moving pictures which show drinking scenes; we mustn't go into bars; our friends must hide their bottles if we go to their houses; we mustn't think or be reminded about alcohol at all. Experience proves this is nonsense.

101:1   We meet these conditions every day. An alcoholic who cannot meet them, still has an alcoholic mind: there is something the matter with his spiritual status. His only chance for sobriety would be some place like the Greenland Ice Cap, and even there an Eskimo might turn up with a bottle of scotch and ruin everything! Ask any woman who has sent her husband to distant places on the theory he would escape the alcohol problem.

101:2   Any scheme of combatting alcoholism which proposes to shield the sick man from temptation is doomed to failure. If the alcoholic tries to shield himself, he may succeed for a time, but will wind up with a bigger explosion than ever. Our wives and we have tried these methods. These foolish attempts to do the impossible have always failed.

101:3   So our rule is not to avoid a place where there is drinking, _if we have a legitimate reason for being there_. That includes bars, nightclubs, dances, receptions, weddings, even plain ordinary whoopee parties. To a person who has had experience with an alcoholic, this may seem like tempting Providence, but it isn't.

101:4   You will note that we made an important qualification. Therefore, ask yourself on each occasion, "Have I any legitimate social, business, or personal reason for going to this place? Am I going to be helpful to anyone there? Could I be more useful or helpful by being somewhere else?" If you answer these questions satisfactorily, you need have no apprehension. You may go or stay away, whatever seems best. But be sure you are on solid spiritual ground before you start and that your motive in going is thoroughly good. Do not think of what you will get out of the occasion. Think of what you can bring to it. But if you are spiritually shaky, you had better work with another alcoholic instead!

102:1   You are not to sit with a long face in places where there is drinking, sighing about the good old days. If it is a happy occasion, try to increase the pleasure of those there; if a business occasion, go and attend to your business enthusiastically. If you are with a person who wants to eat in a bar, by all means go along. Let your friends know they are not to change their habits on your account. At a proper time and place explain to all your friends why alcohol disagrees with you. If you do this thoroughly, no decent person will ask you to drink. While you were drinking, you were withdrawing from life little by little. Now you are getting back into the life of this world. Don't start to withdraw from life again just because your friends drink liquor.

Your job now is to be at the place where you may be of maximum 102:2
helpfulness to others, so never hesitate to go where there is drinking,
if you can be helpful. You should not hesitate to visit the most sordid
spot on earth on such a mission. Keep on the firing line of life with
these motives, and God will keep you unharmed.

Many of us keep liquor in our homes. We often need it to carry green 102:3
recruits through a severe hangover. Some of us still serve it to our
friends in moderation, provided they are people who do not abuse
drinking. But some of us think we should not serve liquor to anyone. We
never argue this question. We feel that each family, in the light of
their own circumstances, ought to decide for themselves.

We are careful never to show intolerance or hatred of drinking as an 103:1
institution. Experience shows that such an attitude is not helpful to
anyone. Every new alcoholic looks for this spirit among us and is
immensely relieved when he finds we are not witch-burners. A spirit of
intolerance might repel alcoholics whose lives would have been saved,
had it not been for our stupidity. We would not even do the cause of
temperate drinking any good, for not one drinker in a thousand is
willing to be told anything about alcohol by one who hates it.

Someday we hope that Alcoholics Anonymous will help the public to a 103:2
better realization of the gravity of the liquor problem. We shall be of
little use if our attitude is one of bitterness or hostility. Drinkers
will not stand for it.

After all, our troubles were of our own making. Bottles were only a 103:3
symbol. Besides, we have stopped flqhting anybody or anything. We have
to!

Chapter Eight

TO WIVES

104:1   With few exceptions, our book thus far has spoken of men. But what we have said applies quite as much to women. Our activities in behalf of women who drink are on the increase. There is every evidence that women regain their health as readily as men if they follow our suggestions.

104:2   But for every man who drinks others are involved — the wife who trembles in fear of the next debauch; the mother and father who see their son wasting away.

104:3   Among us are wives, relatives, and friends whose problem has been solved, as well as some who have not yet found a happy solution. We shall let the wives of Alcoholics Anonymous address the wives of men who drink too much. What they say will apply to nearly everyone bound by ties of blood or affection to an alcoholic.

- - - -

104:4   As wives of Alcoholics Anonymous, we want you to sense that we understand you as perhaps few can. We want to analyze mistakes we have made and help you to avoid them. We want to leave you with the feeling that no situation is too difficult and no unhappiness too great to be overcome.

104:5   We have traveled a rocky road; there is no mistake about that. We have had long rendezvous with hurt pride, frustration, self-pity, misunderstand, and fear. These are not pleasant companions. We have been driven to maudlin sympathy, to bitter resentment. We have veered from extreme to extreme, ever hoping that one day our loved ones would be themselves once more.

105:1   Our loyalty, and the desire that our husbands hold up their heads and be like other men have begotten all sorts of predicaments. We have been unselfish and self-sacrificing. We have told innumerable lies to protect our pride and our husbands' reputations. We have prayed, we have begged, we have been patient. We have struck out viciously. We have run away. We have been hysterical. We have been terror stricken. We have sought sympathy. We have had retaliatory love affairs with other men.

105:2   Our homes have been battle-grounds many an evening. In the morning we have kissed and made up. Our friends have counseled chucking the men and we have done so with finality, only to be back in a little while, hoping, always hoping. Our men have sworn great solemn oaths they were through drinking forever. We have believed them when no one else could, or would. Then, in days, weeks, or months, a fresh outburst.

105:3   We seldom had friends at our homes, never knowing how or when the men of the house would appear. We could make few social engagements. We came to live almost alone, unwanted by anyone. When we were invited out, our husbands always sneaked so many drinks that they spoiled the occasion. If, on the other hand, they took nothing, their self-pity made them killjoys.

105:4   There was never financial security. Positions were always in jeopardy or gone. An armored car could not have brought the pay envelopes home. The checking account melted like snow in June.

There were other women. How heart breaking was this discovery; 106:1
how cruel to be told they understood our men as we did not!

The bill collectors; the sheriffs; the angry taxi drivers; the 106:2
policemen; the bums; the pals; and even the ladies he brought home
— our husbands thought we were so inhospitable. "Joykiller, nag, wet
blanket" — that's what they said. Next day they would be themselves
again and we would forgive and try to forget.

We have tried to hold the love of our children for their father. 106:3
We have told small tots that father was sick, which was much nearer
the truth than we realized. They struck the children, kicked out door
panels, smashed treasured crockery, and ripped the keys out of
pianos. In the midst of such pandemonium they may have rushed out
threatening to live with the other woman forever. In desperation, we
have even got tight ourselves — the drunk to end all drunks. The
unexpected result was that our husbands seemed to like it.

Perhaps at this point we got a divorce and took the children home 106:4
to father and mother. Then we were severely criticized by our
husband's parents for desertion. Usually we did not leave. We stayed
on and on. We finally sought employment ourselves as destitution
faced us and our families.

We began to ask medical advice as the sprees got closer together. 106:5
The alarming physical and mental symptoms, the deepening pall of
remorse, depression and inferiority that settled down on our loved
ones — these things terrified and distracted us. As animals on a
treadmill, we have patiently and wearily climbed, falling back in
exhaustion after each futile effort to reach solid ground. Most of
us have entered the final stage with its commitment to health
resorts, sanitariums, hospitals, and jails. Sometimes there were
screaming delirium and insanity. Death was often near.

Under these conditions we naturally made mistakes. Some of them 107:1
rose out of ignorance of alcoholism. Sometimes we sensed dimly that
we were dealing with sick men. Had we fully understood the nature of
the alcoholic illness, we might have behaved differently.

How could men who loved their wives and children be so unthink- 107:2
ing, so callous, so cruel? There could be no love in such persons,
we thought. And just as we were being convinced of their heartlessness, they would surprise us with fresh resolves and new attentions.
For a while they would be their old sweet selves, only to dash the
new structure of affection to pieces once more. Asked why they
commenced to drink again, they would reply with some silly excuse,
or none. It was so baffling, so heartbreaking. Could we have been so
mistaken in the men we married? When drinking, they were strangers.
Sometimes they were so inaccessible that it seemed as though a great
wall had been built around them.

And even if they did not love their families, how could they be 107:3
so blind about themselves? What had become of their judgment, their
common sense, their will power? Why could they not see that drink
meant ruin to them? Why was it, when we pointed out these dangers,
that they agreed and then got drunk again immediately?

These are some of the questions which race through the mind 108:1
of every girl who has an alcoholic husband. We hope our book has
answered some of them. But now you will have seen that perhaps your
husband has been living in that strange world of alcoholism where
everything is distorted and exaggerated. You can see that he really
does love you with his better self. Of course, there is such a thing as
incompatibility, but in nearly every instance the alcoholic only seems
to be unloving and inconsiderate; it is usually because he is warped
and sickened that he says and does these appalling things. Today most
of our men are better husbands and fathers than ever before.

108:2   Don't condemn your alcoholic husband no matter what he says or does. He is just another very sick, unreasonable person. Treat him, when you can, as though he had pneumonia. When he angers you, remember that he is very ill.

108:3   There is an important exception to the foregoing. We realize some men are thoroughly bad-intentioned, that no amount of patience will make any difference. An alcoholic of this temperament will be quick to use this chapter as a club over your head. Don't let him get away with it. If you are positive he is one of this type you may feel you had better leave. It is not right to let him ruin your life and the lives of your children, especially when he has before him a way to stop his drinking and abuse if he really wants to pay the price.

108:4   The problem with which you struggle usually falls within one of four categories:

108:5   One: Your husband may be only a heavy drinker. His drinking may be constant or it may be heavy only on certain occasions. He spends too much money for liquor. It slows him up mentally and physically, but he does not see it. Sometimes he is a source of embarrassment to you and his friends. He is positive he can handle his liquor, that it does him no harm, that drinking is necessary in his business. He would be insulted if called an alcoholic. This world is full of people like him. Some will moderate or stop altogether, and some will not. Of those who keep on, a good number will become true alcoholics after a while.

109:1   Two: Your husband is showing lack of control. He is unable to stay on the water wagon, even when he wants to. He often gets entirely out of hand when drinking. He admits this is true, but is obsessed with the idea that he will do better. He has begun to try, with or without your cooperation, various means of moderating or staying dry. He is beginning to lose his friends. His business may suffer somewhat. He is worried at times, and is becoming aware that he cannot drink like other people. He sometimes drinks in the morning, and through the day also, to hold his nervousness in check. He is remorseful after serious drinking bouts and tells you he wants to stop. But when he gets over the spree, he begins to think once more how he can drink moderately next time. This person is in danger. He has the earmarks of a real alcoholic. Perhaps he can still tend to business fairly well. He has by no means ruined everything. As we say among ourselves, "He wants to want to stop."

109:2   Three: This husband has gone much further than husband number two. Though once like number two, he became worse. His friends have slipped away, his home is a near-wreck, and he cannot hold a position. Maybe the doctor has been called in, and the weary round of sanitariums and hospitals has begun. He admits he cannot drink like other people, but does not see why. He clings to the notion that he will yet find a way to do so. He may have come to the point where he desperately wants to stop but cannot. His case presents additional questions which we shall try to answer for you. You can be quite hopeful of a situation like this.

110:1   Four: You may have a husband of whom you completely despair. He has been placed in one institution after another. He is violent, or definitely insane, when drunk. Sometimes he drinks on the way home from the hospital. Perhaps he has had delirium tremens. Doctors shake their heads and advise you to have him committed. Maybe you have already been obliged to put him away. This picture may not be as dark as it looks. Many of our husbands were just as far gone. Yet they got well.

110:2   Let's now go back to husband number one. Oddly enough, he is often difficult to deal with. He enjoys drinking. It stirs his imagination. His friends feel closer over a highball. Perhaps you enjoy drinking with him yourself when he doesn't go too far. You have passed happy evenings together chatting and drinking before your fire. Perhaps you both like parties which would be dull without liquor. We have enjoyed such evenings ourselves; we had a good time. We know all about liquor as a social lubricant. Some, but not all of us, think it has its advantages when reasonably used.

Your husband has begun to abuse alcohol. The first principle of success is that you should never be angry. Even though your husband becomes unbearable, and you have to leave him temporarily, you should, if you can, go without rancor. Patience and good temper are vitally necessary. 111:1

The next rule is that you should never tell him what to do about his drinking. If he gets the idea that you are a nag or a killjoy, your chance of accomplishing anything useful will be zero. He will use that as an excuse to drink some more. He will tell you he is misunderstood. This may lead to lonely evenings for you. He may seek someone to console him — not always another man. 111:2

Be determined that your husband's drinking is not going to spoil your relation with your children or your friends. They need your companionship and your help. It is possible to have a full and useful life, though your husband continues to drink. We know women who are unafraid, even happy, under these conditions. Do not set your heart on reforming your husband. You may be unable to do so, no matter how hard you try. 111:3

We know these suggestions are not impossible to follow, but you will save many a heartbreak if you can succeed in observing them. Your husband will come to appreciate your reasonableness and patience. This will lay the groundwork for a frank and friendly talk about his liquor problem. Try to have him bring up the subject himself. Besure[†] you are not critical during such a discussion. Attempt instead, to put yourself in his place. Let him see that you want to be helpful rather than critical. 111:4

When a discussion does arise, you might suggest he read this book, or at least the chapter on alcoholism. Tell him you have been worried, though perhaps needlessly. You think he ought to know the subject better, as everyone should have a clear understanding of the risk he takes if he drinks much. Show him you have confidence in his power to stop or moderate. Say you do not want to be a wet blanket; that you only want him to take care of his health. Thus you may succeed in interesting him in alcoholism. 111:5

He probably has several alcoholics among his own acquaintances. You might suggest that you both take an interest in them. Drinkers like to help other drinkers. Your husband may be willing to talk to one of them, perhaps over a highball. 112:1

If this kind of approach does not catch your husband's interest, it may be best to drop the subject for a time, but after a friendly talk your husband will usually revive the topic himself. This may take patient waiting, but it will be worth it. Meanwhile you might try to help the wife of another serious drinker. If you act upon these principles, your husband may stop or moderate after a while. 112:2

Suppose, however, that your husband fits the description of number two. The same principles which apply to husband number one should be practiced. But after his next binge, ask him if he would really like to get over drinking for good. Do not ask that he do it for you or anyone else. Just would he _like_ to? 112:3

The chances are he would. Show him your copy of this book and tell him what you have found out about alcoholism. Show him that the writers of the book understand, as only alcoholics can. Tell him some of the interesting stories you have 112:4

---

† This accurately reflects the language of the original.

read. If you think he will be shy of our spiritual remedy, ask him to look at the chapter on alcoholism. Then perhaps he will be interested enough to continue.

113:1   If he is enthusiastic, cooperate with him, though you, yourself, may not yet agree with all we say. If he is lukewarm, or thinks he is not an alcoholic, leave him alone. Never urge him to follow our program. The seed has been planted in his mind. He knows that over a hundred men, much like himself, have recovered. But don't remind him of this after he has been drinking, for he will be angry. Sooner or later, you are likely to find him reading the book once more. Wait until repeated stumbling convinces him he must act, for the more you hurry him, the longer his recovery may be delayed.

113:2   If you have a number three husband, you may be in luck. Being certain he wants to stop, you can go to him with this volume as joyfully as though you had struck oil. He may not share your enthusiasm, but he is practically sure to read the book, and he may go for the program at once. If he does not, you will probably not have long to wait. Again, you must not crowd him. Let him decide for himself. Cheerfully see him through more sprees. Talk about his condition or this book only when he raises the issue. In some cases it may be better to let the family doctor present the book. The doctor can urge action without arousing hostility. If your husband is otherwise a normal individual, your chances are good at this stage.

113:3   You would suppose that men in the fourth classification would be quite hopeless, but that is not so. Many of Alcoholics Anonymous were like that. Everybody had given them up. Defeat seemed certain. Yet often such men have spectacular and powerful recoveries.

114:1   There are exceptions. Some men have been so impaired by alcohol that they cannot stop. Sometimes there are cases where alcoholism is complicated by other disorders. A good doctor or psychiatrist can tell you whether these complications are serious. In any event, see that your husband gets this book. His reaction may be one of enthusiasm. If he is already committed to an institution but can convince you and your doctor that he means business, you should give him a chance to try our method, unless the doctor thinks his mental condition abnormal or dangerous. We make this recommendation with some confidence. About a year ago a certain state institution released six chronic alcoholics. It was fully expected they would all be back in a few weeks. Only one of them has returned. The others had no relapse at all. The power of God goes deep!

114:2   You may have the reverse situation on your hands. Perhaps you have a husband who is at large, but who should be committed. Some men cannot, or will not get over alcoholism. When they become too dangerous, we think the kind thing is to lock them up. The wives and children of such men suffer horribly, but not less than the men themselves.

As a rule, an institution is a dismal place, and sometimes it is not conducive to recovery. It is a pity that chronic alcoholics must often mingle with the insane. Some day we hope our group will be instrumental in changing this condition. Many of our husbands spent weary years in institutions. Though more reluctant than most people to place our men there, we sometimes suggest that it be done. Of course, a good doctor should always be consulted.

114:3   But sometimes you must start life anew. We know women who have done it. If such women adopt our way of life, their road will be smoother.

114:4   If your husband is a drinker, you worry over what other people are thinking. You hate to meet your friends. You draw more and more into yourself. You think everyone is talking about conditions at your home. You avoid the subject of drinking, even with your own parents. You do not know what to tell the children. When your husband is bad, you become a trembling recluse, wishing the telephone had never been invented.

We find that most of this embarrassment is unnecessary. While you 115:1 need not discuss your husband, you can quietly let your friends know what the trouble is. Sometimes it is wise to talk with his employer. But you must be on guard not to embarrass or harm your husband.

When you have carefully explained to such people that he is a sick 115:2 person, little more to blame than other men who drink but manage their liquor better, you will have created a new atmosphere. Barriers which have sprung up between you and your friends will disappear with the growth of sympathetic understanding. You will no longer be self-conscious, nor feel that you must apologize as though your husband were a weak character. He may be anything but that. Your new courage, good nature, and lack of self-consciousness wilt do wonders for your social status.

The same principle applies in dealing with the children. Unless 115:3 they actually need protection from their father, it is best not to take sides in any argument he has with them while drinking. Use your energies to promote a better understanding all around. Then that terrible tension which grips the home of every problem drinker will be lessened.

Frequently you have felt obliged to tell your husband's employer and his friends that he was sick, when as a matter of fact he was tight. Avoid answering these inquiries as much as you can. Whenever possible, let your husband explain. Your desire to protect him should not cause you to lie to people, when they have a right to know where he is and what he is doing. Discuss this with him when he is sober and in good spirits. Ask him to promise that he will not place you in such a position again. But be careful not to be resentful about the last time he did so.

There is another paralyzing fear. You are afraid your husband will 116:1 lose his position; you are thinking of the disgrace and hard times which will befall you and the children. This experience may come to you. Or you may already have had it several times. Should it happen again, regard it in a different light. Maybe it will prove a blessing! It may convince your husband he wants to stop drinking forever. And now you know that he can stop if he will! Time after time, this apparent calamity has been a boon to us, for it opened up a path which led to the discovery of God.

We have elsewhere remarked how much better life is when lived on a 116:2 spiritual plane. If God can solve the age-old riddle of alcoholism, he can solve your problems too. We wives found that, like everybody else, we were afflicted with pride, self-pity, vanity, and all the things which go to make up the self-centered person; and we were not above selfishness or dishonesty. As our husbands began to apply spiritual principles in their lives, we began to see the desirability of doing so too.

At first, some of us did not believe that we needed this help. We 116:3 thought, on the whole, we were pretty good women, capable of being nicer if our husbands stopped drinking. But it was a silly idea that we were too good to need God. Now we try to put spiritual principles to work in every department of our lives. When we do that, we find it solves our problems too: the ensuing lack of fear, worry and hurt feelings is a wonderful thing. We urge you to try our program, for nothing will be so helpful to your husband as the radically changed attitude toward him which God will show you how to have. Go along with your husband if you possibly can.

117:1   If you and your husband find a solution for the pressing problem of drink, you are, of course, going to be very happy. But all problems will not be solved at once. Seed has started to sprout in a new soil, but growth has only begun. In spite of your new-found happiness, there will be ups and downs. Many of the old problems will still be with you. This is as it should be.

117:2   The faith and sincerity of both you and your husband will be put to the test. You must regard these work-outs as part of your education, for thus you will be learning to live as you were intended to live. You will make mistakes, but if you are in earnest, they will not drag you down. Instead, you will capitalize them. A better way of life will emerge when they are overcome.

117:3   Some of the snags you will encounter are irritation, hurt-feelings, resentments. Your husband will sometimes be unreasonable, and you will want to criticize. Starting from a speck on the domestic horizon, great thunderclouds of dispute may gather. These family dissensions are very dangerous, especially to your husband. Often you must carry the burden of avoiding them or keeping them under control. Never forget that resentment is a deadly hazard to an alcoholic. We do not mean that you have to agree with your husband wherever there is an honest difference of opinion. Just be careful not to disagree in a resentful or critical spirit.

118:1   You and your husband will find that you can dispose of serious problems easier than you can the trivial ones. Next time you and he have a heated discussion, no matter what the subject, it should be the privilege of either to smile and say "This is getting serious. I'm sorry I got disturbed. Let's talk about it later." If your husband is trying to live on a spiritual basis, he will also be doing everything in his power to avoid disagreement or contention.

118:2   Your husband knows he owes you more than sobriety. He wants to make good. Yet you must not expect too much. His ways of thinking and doing are the habits of years. Patience, tolerance, understanding, and love are your watchwords. Show him these things in yourself and they will be reflected back to you from him. Live and let live is the rule. If you both show a willingness to remedy your own defects, there will be little need to criticize each other.

118:3   We women carry with us a picture of the ideal man, the sort of chap we would like our husbands to be. It is the most natural thing in the world, once his liquor problem is solved, to feel that he will now measure up to that cherished vision. The chances are he will not, for like yourself, he is just beginning his development. Be patient.

118:4   Another feeling we are very likely to entertain is one of resentment that love and loyalty could not cure our husbands of alcoholism. We do not like the thought that the contents of a book, or the work of another alcoholic, has accomplished in a few weeks the end for which we struggled for years. At such moments we forget that alcoholism is an illness over which we could not possibly have had any power. Your husband will be the first to say it was your devotion and care which brought him to the point where he could have a spiritual experience. Without you he would have gone to pieces long ago. When resentful thoughts come, pause and count your blessings. After all, your family is reunited, alcohol is no longer a problem, and you and your husband are working together toward an undreamed-of future.

119:1   Still another difficulty is that you may become jealous of the attention he bestows on other people, especially alcoholics. You have been starving for his companionship, yet he spends long hours helping other men and their families. You feel he should now be yours. The fact is that he must work with other people to maintain his own sobriety. Sometimes he will be so interested that he becomes really neglectful. Your house is filled with strangers. You may not like some of them. He gets stirred up about their troubles, but not at all about yours. It will do no good if you point that out and urge more attention for yourself. It is a real mistake if you dampen his enthusiasm for alcoholic work. You should join in his efforts as much as you possibly can. Direct some of your thought to the wives of his new alcoholic friends. They need the counsel and love of a woman who has gone through what you have.

It is probably true that you and your husband have been living too much alone, for drinking almost isolated many of us. Therefore, you need fresh interests and a great cause to live for as much as your husband. If you cooperate, rather than complain, you will find that his excess enthusiasm will tone down. Both of you will awaken to a new sense of responsibility for others. You, as well as your husband, must think of what you can put into life, instead of how much you can take out. Inevitably your lives will be fuller for doing so. You will lose the old life to find one much better. 119:2

Perhaps your husband will make a fair start on the new basis, but just as things are going beautifully, he dismays you be† coming home drunk. If you are satisfied he really wants to get over drinking, you need not be alarmed. Though it is infinitely better he have no relapse at all, as has been true with many of our men, it is by no means a bad thing in some cases. Your husband will see at once that he must redouble his spiritual activities if he expects to survive. If he adopts this view, the slip will help him. You need not remind him of his spiritual deficiency — he will know of it. Cheer him up and ask him how you can be still more helpful. 120:1

Even your hatred must go. The slightest sign of fear or intolerance will lessen your husband's chance of recovery. In a weak moment he may take your dislike of his high-stepping friends as one of those insanely trivial excuses to drink. 120:2

Never, never try to arrange his life, so as to shield him from temptation. The slightest disposition on your part to guide his appointments or his affairs so he will not be tempted will be noticed. Make him feel absolutely free to come and go as he likes. This is important. If he gets drunk, don't blame yourself. God has either removed your husband's liquor problem, or He has not. If not, it had better be found out right away. Then you and your husband can get right down to fundamentals. If a repetition is to be prevented, place the problem, along with everything else, in God's hands. 120:3

We realize we have been giving you much direction and advice. We may have seemed "preachy". If that is so, we are sorry, for we ourselves, don't care for people who preach. But what we have related is based upon experience, some of it painful. We had to learn these things the hard way. That is why we are anxious that you understand, that you avoid these unnecessary difficulties. 121:1

So to you out there — who may soon be with us — we say "Good luck and God bless you!" 121:2

---

† This accurately reflects the language of the original.

Chapter Nine

THE FAMILY AFTERWARD

122:1   Our women folk have suggested certain attitudes a wife may take with the husband who is recovering. Perhaps they created the impression that he is to be wrapped in cotton wool and placed on a pedestal. Successful readjustment means the opposite. All members of the family must meet upon the common ground of tolerance, understanding, and love. This involves a process of deflation. The alcoholic, his wife, his children, his "in-laws", each one is likely to have fixed ideas about the family's attitude towards himself or herself. Each is interested in having his or her wishes respected. The more one member of a family demands that the other concede to him, the more resentful they become. This makes for discord and unhappiness.

122:2   Any[†] why? Is it not because each wants to play the lead? Is not each trying to arrange the family show to his liking? Is he not unconsciously trying to see what he can take from the family life, rather than give?

122:3   Cessation of drinking is but the first step away from a highly strained, abnormal condition. A doctor said the other day, "Years of living with an alcoholic is almost sure to make any wife or child neurotic. The entire family is, to some extent, ill." Let families realize, as they start their journey, that all will not be fair weather. Each in his turn will be footsore and will straggle. There will be alluring shortcuts and by-paths down which they may wander and lose their way.

123:1   Suppose we tell you some of the obstacles a family will meet; suppose we suggest how they may be avoided — even converted to good use for others. The family of an alcoholic longs for the return of happiness and security. They remember when father was romantic, thoughtful and successful. Today's life is measured against that of other years and, when it falls short, the family may be unhappy.

123:2   Family confidence in dad is rising high. The good old days will soon be back, they think. Sometimes they demand that dad bring them back instantly! God, they believe, almost owes this recompense on a long overdue account. But the head of the house has spent years in pulling down the structures of business, romance, friendship, health — these things are now ruined or damaged. It will take time to clear away the wreck. Though old buildings will eventually be replaced by finer ones, the new structures will take years to complete.

123:3   Father knows he is to blame; it may take him many seasons of hard work to be restored financially, but he shouldn't be reproached. Perhaps he will never have much money again. But the wise family will admire him for what he is trying to be, rather than for what he is trying to get.

123:4   Now and then the family will be plagued by spectres from the past, for the drinking career of almost every alcoholic has been marked by escapades, funny, humiliating, shameful, or tragic. The first impulse will be to bury these skeletons in a dark closet and padlock the door. The family may be obsessed with the idea that future happiness can be based only upon forgetfulness of the past. Such a view is quite self-centered and in direct conflict with the new way of life.

124:1   Henry Ford once made a wise remark to the effect that experience is the thing of supreme value in life. That is true only if one is willing to turn the past to

---

[†] This accurately reflects the language of the original.

good account. We grow by our willingness to face and rectify errors and convert them into assets. The alcoholic's past thus becomes the principal asset of the family, and frequently it is the only one!

This painful past may be of infinite value to other families still struggling with their problem. We think each family which has been relieved owes something to those which have not, and when the occasion requires, each member of it who has found God, should be only too willing to bring former mistakes, no matter how grievous, out of their hiding places. Showing others who suffer how we were given victory, is the very thing which makes life seem so worth while to us now. Cling to the thought that, in God's hands, the dark past is the greatest possession you have — the key to life and happiness for others. With it you can avert death and misery for them. 124:2

It is possible to dig up past misdeeds so they become a blight, a veritable plague. For example, we know of situations in which the alcoholic or his wife have had love affairs. In the first flush of spiritual experience they forgave each other and drew closer together. The miracle of reconciliation was at hand. Then, under one provocation or another, the aggrieved one would unearth the old affair and angrily cast its ashes about. A few of us have had these growing pains and they hurt a great deal. Husbands and wives have sometimes been obliged to separate for a time until new perspective, new victory over hurt pride, could be rewon. In most cases, the alcoholic survived this ordeal without relapse, but not always. So our rule is that unless some good and useful purpose is to be served, past occurrences are not discussed. 124:3

We families of Alcoholics Anonymous have few secrets. Everyone knows all about everyone else. This is a condition which, in ordinary life, would produce untold grief. There would be scandalous gossip, laughter at the expense of other people, and a tendency to take advantage of intimate information. Among us, these are rare occurrences. 125:1

We do talk about each other a great deal but almost invariably temper such talk by a spirit of love and tolerance. We discuss another's shortcomings in the hope that some new idea of helpfulness may come out of the conversation. Thy cynic might say we are good because we have to be.

Another rule we observe carefully is that we do not relate intimate experiences of another person unless we are sure he would approve. We find it better, when possible, to stick to our own stories, A man may criticize or laugh at himself and it will affect others favorably, but criticism or ridicule of him coming from another often produces the contrary effect. Members of a family should watch such matters carefully, for one careless, inconsiderate remark has been known to raise the very devil. We alcoholics are sensitive people. It takes some of us a long time to outgrow that serious handicap. 125:2

Most alcoholics are enthusiasts. They run to extremes. At the beginning of recovery a man will take, as a rule, one of two directions. He may either plunge into a frantic attempt to get on his feet in business, or he may be so enthralled by his new life that he talks or thinks of little else. In either case certain family problems will arise. With these we have experience galore. 125:3

We pointed out the danger he runs if he rushes headlong at his economic problem. The family will be affected also, pleasantly at first, as they feel their money troubles are to be solved, then not so pleasantly as they find themselves neglected. Dad may be tired at night and pre-occupied by day. He may take small interest in the children and may show irritation when reproved for his delinquencies. If not irritable, he may seem dull and boring, not gay and affectionate, as 126:1

the family would like him to be. Mother may complain of inattention. They are all disappointed, and soon let him feel it. Beginning with such complaints, a barrier arises. He is straining every nerve to make up for lost time. He is striving to recover fortune and reputation and thinks he is doing very well.

126:2   Mother and children don't think so. Having been wantonly neglected and misused in the past, they think father owes them more than they are getting. They want him to make a fuss over them. They expect him to give them the nice times they used to have before he drank, and to show his contrition for what they suffered. But dad doesn't give freely of himself. Resentment grows. He becomes still less communicative. Sometimes he explodes over a trifle. The family is mystified. They criticize, pointing out how he is falling down on his spiritual program.

126:3   This sort of thing must be stopped. Both father and the family are wrong, though each side may have some justification. It is of little use to argue and only makes the impasse worse. The family must realize that dad, though marvelously improved, is still a sick man. They should thank God he is sober and able to be of this world once more. Let them praise his progress. Let them remember that his drinking wrought all kinds of damage that may take long to repair. If they sense these things, they will not take so seriously his periods of crankiness, depression, or apathy, which will disappear when there is tolerance, love, and spiritual understanding.

127:1   The head of the house ought to remember that he is mainly to blame for what befell his home. He can scarcely square the account in his lifetime. But he must see the danger of over-concentration on financial success. Although financial recovery is on the way for many of us, we found we could not place money first. For us, material well-being always followed spiritual progress; it never preceded.

127:2   Since the home has suffered more than anything else, it is well that a man exert himself there. He is not likely to get far in any direction if he fails to show unselfishness and love under his own roof. We know there are difficult wives and families, but the man who is getting over alcoholism must remember they are sick folk too, and that he did much to make them worse.

127:3   As each member of a resentful family begins to see his shortcomings and admits them to the others, he lays a basis for helpful discussion. These family talks will be constructive if they can be carried on without heated argument, self-pity, self-justification, or resentful criticism. Little by little, mother and children will see they ask too much, and father will see he gives too little. Giving, rather than getting, will become the guiding principle.

128:1   Assume now that father has, at the outset, a stirring spiritual experience. Over-night, as it were, he is a changed man. He becomes a religious enthusiast. He is unable to focus on anything else. As soon as his sobriety begins to be taken as a matter of course, the family may look at their strange new dad with apprehension, then with irritation. There is talk about spiritual matters morning, noon and night. He may demand that the family find God for themselves in a hurry, or exhibit amazing indifference to them and say he is above worldly considerations. He tells mother, who has been religious all her life, that she doesn't know what its all about, and that she had better get his brand of spirituality while there is yet time.

128:2   When father takes this tack, the family may react unfavorably. They are jealous of a God who has stolen dad's affections. While grateful that he drinks no more, they do not like the idea that God has accomplished the miracle where they failed. They often forget father was beyond human aid. They do not see why their love and devotion did not straighten him out. Dad is not so spiritual after all, they say.

If he means to right his past wrongs, why all this concern for everyone in the world but his family? What about his talk that God will take care of them? They suspect father is a bit balmy!

He is not so unbalanced as they might think. Many of us have experienced dad's elation. We have indulged in spiritual intoxication. Like gaunt prospectors, belts drawn in over our last ounce of food, our pick struck gold. Joy at our release from a lifetime of frustration knew no bounds. Father sees he has struck something better than gold. For a time he may try to hug the new treasure to himself. He may not see at once that he has barely scratched a limitless lode which will pay dividends only if he mines it for the rest of his life and insists on giving away the entire product. 128:3

If the family cooperates, dad will soon see that he is suffering from a distortion of values. He will perceive that his spiritual growth is lopsided, that for an average man like himself, a spiritual life which does not include his family obligations may not be so perfect after all. If the family will appreciate that dad's current behavoir is but a phase of his development, all will be well. In the midst of an understanding and sympathetic family, these vagaries of dad's spiritual infancy will quickly disappear. 129:1

The opposite may happen should the family condemn and criticize. Dad may feel that for years his drinking has placed him on the wrong side of every argument, but that now he has become a superior person, with God on his side. If the family persists in criticism, this fallacy may take a still greater hold on father. Instead of treating the family as he should, he may retreat further into himself and feel he has spiritual justification for so doing. 129:2

Though the family does not fully agree with dad's spiritual activities, they should let him assume leadership. Even if he displays a certain amount of neglect and irresponsibility towards the family, it is well to let him go as far as he likes in helping other alcoholics. During those first days of convalescence, this will do more to insure his sobriety than anything else. Though some of his manifestations are alarming and disagreeable, dad will be on a firmer foundation than the man who is placing business or professional success ahead of spiritual development. He will be less likely to drink again, and anything is preferable to that. 129:3

Those of us who have spent much time in the world of spiritual make-believe have eventually seen the childishness of it. This dream world has been replaced by a great sense of purpose, accompanied by a growing consciousness of the power of God in our lives. We have come to believe God would like us to keep our heads in the clouds with Him, but that our feet ought to be firmly planted on earth, nevertheless. That is where our fellow travelers are, and that is where our work must be done. These are the realities for us. We have found nothing incompatible between a powerful spiritual experience, and a life of sane and happy usefulness. 130:1

One more suggestion: Whether the family has spiritual convictions or not, they may do well to examine the principles by which the alcoholic member is trying to live. They can hardly fail to approve these simple principles, though the head of the house still fails somewhat in practicing them. Nothing will help the man who is off on a spiritual tangent so much as the wife who adopts the self-same program, making a better practical use of it. 130:2

There will be still other profound changes in the household. Liquor incapacitated father for so many years that mother became head of the house. She met these responsibilities gallantly. By force of circumstances, she was obliged to treat father as a sick or wayward child. Even when he wanted to assert himself, he could not, for his drinking placed him constantly in the wrong. Mother made all the plans 130:3

and gave the directions. When sober, father usually obeyed. Thus mother, through no fault of her own, became accustomed to wearing the family trousers. Father, coming suddenly to life again, often begins to assert himself. This means trouble, unless the family watches for these tendencies in each other and come to a friendly agreement about them.

131:1 Drinking isolates most homes from the outside world, so the family was used to having father around a great deal. He may have laid aside for years all normal activities — clubs, civic duties, sports. When he renews interest in such things, a feeling of jealousy may arise. The family may feel they hold a mortgage on dad, so big that no equity should be left for outsiders. Instead of developing new channels of activity for themselves, mother and children may demand that he stay home and make up the deficiency.

131:2 At the very beginning, the couple ought to frankly face the fact that each will have to yield here and there, if the family is going to play an effective part in the new life. Father will necessarily spend much time with other alcoholics, but this activity should be balanced. New acquaintenances who know nothing of alcoholism might be made and thoughtful consideration given their needs. The problems of the community might engage attention. Though the family has no religious connections, they may do well to make contact with, or take membership in a religious body.

131:3 Alcoholics who have derided religious people will sometimes be helped by such contacts. Being possessed of a spiritual experience, the alcoholic will find he has much in common with these people, though he may differ with them on many matters. If he does not argue and forget that men find God in many ways, he will make new friends, and is sure to find new avenues of usefulness and pleasure. He and his family can be a bright spot in such congregations. He may bring new hope and new courage to many a priest, minister, or rabbi, who gives his all to minister to our troubled world. We intend the foregoing as a helpful suggestion only. So far as we are concerned, there is nothing obligatory about it. As a non-denominational group, we cannot make up people's minds for them. Each individual must consult his own conscience.

132:1 We have been speaking to you of serious, sometimes tragic things. We have been dealing with alcohol in its worst aspect. But we aren't a glum lot. If newcomers could see no joy or fun in our existence, they wouldn't want it. We absolutely insist on enjoying life. We try not to indulge in cynicism over the state of the nations, nor do we carry the world's troubles on our shoulders. When we see a man sinking into the mire that is alcoholism, we give him first and and[†] place everything we have at his disposal. For his sake, we do recount and almost relive the horrors of our past. But those of us who have tried to shoulder the entire burden and trouble of others, find we are soon overcome by them.

132:2 So we think cheerfulness and laughter make for usefulness. Outsiders are sometimes shocked when we burst into merriment over a seemingly tragic experience out of the past. But why shouldn't we laugh? We are the victors, and have been given the power to help others.

132:3 Everybody knows that those in bad health, and those who seldom play, do not laugh much. So let each family play together or separately, as much as their circumstances warrant. We are sure God wants us to be happy, joyous, and released. We cannot subscribe to the belief that this life is a vale of tears, though it once was just that for many of us. But it is clear that we made our own misery. God didn't do it. Avoid then, the deliberate manufacture of misery, and when trouble comes, cheerfully capitalize it as an opportunity to demonstrate His omnipotence.

133:1 Now about health: A body badly burned by alcohol does not often recover over-

[†] This accurately reflects the language of the original.

night, nor do twisted thinking and depression vanish in a twinkling. We are convinced that a spiritual mode of living is a most powerful health restorative. We, who have recovered from serious drinking, are miracles of mental health. But we have also seen remarkable transformations in our bodies. Hardly one of our crowd now shows any mark of dissipation.

But this does not mean that we disregard human health measures. God has abundantly supplied this world with fine doctors, psychologists, and practitioners of various kinds. Do not hesitate to take your health problems to such a person. Most of them give freely of themselves, that their fellows may enjoy sound minds and bodies. Try to remember that though God has wrought miracles among us, we should never belittle a good doctor or psychiatrist. Their services are often indispensable in treating a newcomer and following his case afterward. 133:2

A word about sex relations. Alcohol is so sexually stimulating to some men that they have over-indulged. Couples are occasionally dismayed to find that when drinking is stopped, the man tends to be impotent. Unless the reason is understood, there may be an emotional upset. Some of us had this experience, only to enjoy, in a few months, a finer intimacy than ever. There should be no hesitancy in consulting a doctor or phychologist if this condition persists. We do not know of any case where this difficulty lasted long. 134:1

The alcoholic may find it hard to re-establish friendly relations with his children. Their young minds were impressionable while he was drinking. Without saying so, they may cordially hate him for what he has done to them and to their mother. The poor children are sometimes dominated by a pathetic hardness and cynicism. They cannot seem to forgive and forget. This may hang on for months, long after their mother has accepted dad's new way of living and thinking. 134:2

Father had better be sparing of his correction or criticism of them while they are in this frame of mind. He had better not urge his new way of life on them too soon. In time they will see that he is a new man and in their own way they will let him know it. When this happens, they can be invited to join in morning meditation, then they can take part in the daily discussion without rancor or bias. From that point on, progress will be rapid. Marvelous results often follow such a reunion. 134:3

Whether the family goes on a spiritual basis or not, the alcoholic member must. The others must be convinced by his changed life beyond a shadow of a doubt. He must lead the way. Seeing is believing to most families who have lived with a drinker. 135:1

Here is a case in point: One of our friends is a heavy smoker and coffee drinker. There was no doubt he over-indulged. Seeing this, and meaning to be helpful, his wife commenced to admonish him about it. He admitted he was overdoing these things, but frankly said that he was not ready to stop. His wife is one of those persons who really feel there is something rather sinful about these commodities, so she nagged, and her intolerance finally threw him into a fit of anger. He got drunk. 135:2

Of course our friend was wrong — dead wrong. He had to painfully admit that and mend his spiritual fences. Though he is now a most effective member of Alcoholics Anonymous, he still smokes cigarettes and drinks coffee, but neither his wife nor anyone else stands in judgment. She sees she was wrong to make a burning issue out of such a matter when his more serious ailments were being rapidly cured. 135:3

First things first! We have two little mottoes which are apropos. Here they are: "LIVE AND LET LIVE" and "EASY DOES IT". 135:4

Chapter Ten

TO EMPLOYERS

136:1   One of our friends, whose gripping story you have read, has spent much of his life in the world of big business. He has hired and fired hundreds of men. He knows the alcoholic as the employer sees him. His present views ought to prove exceptionally useful to business men everywhere.

136:2   But let him tell you:

136:3   I was at one time assistant manager of a corporation department employing sixty-six hundred men. One day my secretary came in saying that Mr. B— insisted on speaking with me. I told her to say that I was not interested. I had warned this man several times that he had but one more chance. Not long afterward he had called me from Hartford on two successive days, so drunk he could hardly speak. I told him he was through — finally and forever.

136:4   My secretary returned to say that it was not Mr. B— on the phone; it was Mr. B—'s brother, and he wished to give me a message. I still expected a plea for clemency, but these words came through the receiver: "I just wanted to tell you Paul jumped from a hotel window in Hartford last Saturday. He left us a note saying you were the best boss he ever had, and that you were not to blame in any way."

136:5   Another time, as I opened a letter which lay on my desk, a newspaper clipping fell out. It was the obituary of one of the best salesman I ever had. After two weeks of drinking, he had placed his foot on the trigger of a loaded shotgun — the barrel was in his mouth. I had discharged him for drinking six weeks before.

137:1   Still another experience: A woman's voice came faintly over long distance from Virginia. She wanted to know if her husband's company insurance was still in force. Four days before he had hanged himself in his woodshed. I had been obliged to discharge him for drinking, though he was brilliant, alert, and one of the best organizers I have ever known.

137:2   Here were three exceptional men lost to this world because I did not understand as I do now. Then I became an alcoholic myself! And but for the intervention of an understanding person, I might have followed in their footsteps. My downfall cost the business community unknown thousands of dollars, for it takes real money to train a man for an executive position. This kind of waste goes on unabated. Our business fabric is shot through with it and nothing will stop it but better understanding all around.

137:3   You, an employer, want to understand. Nearly every modern employer feels a moral responsibility for the well-being of his help, and he usually tries to meet these responsibilities. That he has not always done so for the alcoholic is easily understood. To him the alcoholic has often seemed to be a fool of the first magnitude. Because of the employee's special ability, or of his own strong personal attachment to him, the employer has sometimes kept such a man at work long beyond the time he ordinarily would. Some employers have tried every known remedy. More often, however, there is very little patience and tolerance. And we, who have imposed on the best of employers, can scarcely blame them if they have been short with us.

Here,for instance, is a typical example: An officer of one of the   138:1
largest banking institutions in America knows I no longer drink. One
day he told me about an executive of the same bank, who, from his
description, was undoubtedly alcoholic. This seemed to me like an
opportunity to be helpful So I spent a good two hours talking about
alcoholism, the malady. I described the symptoms and supported my
statements with plenty of evidence. His comment was: "Very interesting.
But I'm sure this man is done drinking. He has just returned from a
three-months' leave of absence, had taken a cure, looks fine, and to
clinch the matter, the board of directors told him this was his last
chance."

My rejoinder was that if I could afford it, I would bet him a   138:2
hundred to one the man would go on a bigger bust than ever. I felt this
was inevitable and that the bank was doing a possible injustice. Why not
bring the man in contact with some of our alcoholic crowd? He might have
a chance. I pointed out I had had nothing to drink whatever for three
years, and this in the face of difficulties that would have made nine
out of ten men drink their heads off. Why not at least afford him an
opportunity to hear my story? "Oh no", said my friend, "this chap is
either through with liquor, or he is minus a job. If he has your will
power and guts, he will make the grade."

I wanted to throw up my hands in discouragement, for I saw that my   138:3
banking acquaintance had missed the point entirely. He simply could not
believe that his brother-executive suffered from a deadly malady. There
was nothing to do but wait.

Presently the man did slip and, of course, was fired. Following his   139:1
discharge, our group contacted him. Without much ado, he accepted our
principles and procedure. He is undoubtedly on the high road to recovery. To me, this incident illustrates a lack of understanding and
knowledge on the part of employers — lack of understanding as to what
really ails the alcoholic, and lack of knowledge as to what part
employers might profitably take in salvaging their sick employees.

To begin with, I think you employers would do well to disregard your   139:2
own drinking experience, or lack of it. Whether you are a hard drinker,
a moderate drinker, or a teetotaler, you have but little notion of the
inner workings of the alcoholic mind. Instead, you may have some pretty
strong opinions, perhaps prejudices, based upon your own experiences.
Those of you who drink moderately are almost certain to be more annoyed
with an alcoholic than a total abstainer would be. Drinking occasionally, and understanding your own reactions, it is possible for you to
become quite sure of many things, which, so far as the alcoholic is
concerned, are not always so.

As a moderate drinker, you can take your liquor or leave it alone.
Whenever you want to, you can control your drinking. Of an evening, you
can go on a mild bender, get up in the morning, shake your head, and go
to business. To you, liquor is no real problem. You cannot see why it
should be to anyone else, save the spineless and stupid.

When dealing with an alcoholic, you have to fight an ingrained   139:3
annoyance that he could be so weak, stupid and irresponsible. Even when
you understand the malady better, you may still have to check this
feeling and remember that your employee is very ill, being seldom as
weak and irresponsible as he appears.

Take a look at the alcoholic in your organization. Is he not usually   139:4
brilliant, fast-thinking, imaginative and likeable? When sober, does
he not work hard and have a knack of getting things done? Review his
qualities and ask yourself whether he would be worth retaining, if
sober. And do you owe him the same obligation you feel toward other sick
employees? Is he worth salvaging? If your decision is yes, whether the
reason be humanitarian, or business, or both, then you will wish to know
what to do.

140:1   The first part has to do with you. Can you stop feeling that you are dealing only with habit, with stubborness, or a weak will? If you have difficulty about that I suggest you re-read chapters two and three of this book, where the alcoholic sickness is discussed at length. You, as a business man, know better than most that when you deal with any problem, you must know what it is. Having conceded that your employee is ill, can you forgive him for what he has done in the past? Can you shelve the resentment you may hold because of his past absurdities? Can you fully appreciate that the man has been a victim of crooked thinking, directly caused by the action of alcohol on his brain?

140:2   I well remember the shock I received when a prominent doctor in Chicago told me of cases where pressure of the spinal fluid actually ruptured the brain from within. No wonder an alcoholic is strangely irrational. Who wouldn't be, with such a fevered brain? Normal drinkers are not so handicapped.

140:3   Your man has probably been trying to conceal a number of scrapes, perhaps pretty messy ones. They may disgust you. You may be puzzled by them, being unable to understand how such a seemingly above board chap could be so involved. But you can generally charge these, no matter how bad, to the abnormal action of alcohol on his mind. When drinking, or getting over a bout, an alcoholic, sometimes the model of honesty when normal, will do incredible things. Afterward, his revulsion will be terrible. Nearly always, these antics indicate nothing more than temporary abberations and you should so treat them.

141:1   This is not to say that all alcoholics are honest and upright when not drinking. Of course that isn't so, and you will have to be careful that such people don't impose on you. Seeing your attempt to understand and help, some men will try to take advantage of your kindness. If you are sure your man does not want to stop, you may as well discharge him, the sooner the better. You are not doing him a favor by keeping him on. Firing such an individual may prove a blessing to him. It may be just the jolt he needs. I know, in my own particular case, that nothing my company could have done would have stopped me, for so long as I was able to hold my position, I could not possibly realize how serious my situation was. Had they fired me first, and had they then taken steps to see that I was presented with the solution contained in this book, I might have returned to them six months later, a well man.

141:2   But there are many men who want to stop right now, and with them you can go far. If you make a start, you should be prepared to go the limit, not in the sense that any great expense or trouble is to be expected, but rather in the matter of your own attitude, your understanding treatment of the case.

141:3   Perhaps you have such a man in mind. He wants to quit drinking, and you want to help him, even if it be only a matter of good business. You know something of alcoholism. You see that he is mentally and physically sick. You are willing to overlook his past performances. Suppose you call the man in and go at him like this:

141:4   Hit him point blank with the thought that you know all about his drinking, that it must stop. Say you appreciate his abilities, would like to keep him, but cannot, if he continues to drink. That you mean just what you say. And you should mean it too!

142:1   Next, assure him that you are not proposing to lecture, moralize, or condemn; that if you have done so formerly, it is because you misunderstood. Say, if you possibly can, that you have no hard feeling toward him. At this point, bring out the idea of alcoholism, the sickness. Enlarge on that fully. Remark that you have been looking into the matter. You are sure of what you say, hence your change of attitude, hence your willingness to deal with the problem as though it were a disease. You are willing to look at your man as a gravely-ill person, with this qualification — being perhaps fatally ill, does your man want to get well, and right now? You ask because many alcoholics, being warped and drugged, do not want to quit. But does he? Will he take every necessary step, submit to anything to get well, to stop drinking forever?

If he says yes, does he really mean it, or down inside does he think 142:2 he is fooling you, and that after rest and treatment he will be able to get away with a few drinks now and then? Probe your man thoroughly on these points. Be satisfied he is not deceiving himself or you.

Not a word about this book, unless you are sure you ought to 142:3 introduce it at this juncture. If he temporizes and still thinks he can ever drink again, even beer, you may as well discharge him after the next bender which, if an alcoholic, he is certain to have. Tell him that emphatically, and mean it! Either you are dealing with a man who can and will get well, or you are not. If not, don't waste time with him. This may seem severe, but it is usually the best course.

After satisfying yourself that your man wants to recover and that 142:4 he will go to any extreme to do so, you may suggest a definite course of action. For most alcoholics who are drinking, or who are just getting over a spree, a certain amount of physical treatment is desirable, even imperative. Some physicians favor cutting off the liquor sharply, and prefer to use little or no sedative. This may be wise in some instances, but for the most of us it is a barbaric torture. For severe cases, some doctors prefer a slower tapering-down process, followed by a health farm or sanitarium. Other doctors prefer a few days of de-toxication, removal of poisons from the system by cathartics, belladonna, and the like, followed by a week of mild exercise and rest. Having tried them all, I personally favor the latter, though the matter of physical treatment should, of course, be referred to your own doctor. Whatever the method, its object should be to thoroughly clear mind and body of the effects of alcohol. In competent hands, this seldom takes long, nor should it be very expensive. Your man is entitled to be placed in such physical condition that he can think straight and no longer physically craves liquor. These handicaps must be removed if you are going to give him the chance you want him to have. Propose such a procedure to him. Offer to advance the cost of treatment, if necessary, but make it plain that any expense will later be deducted from his pay. Make him fully responsible; it is much better for him.

When your man accepts your offer, point out that physical treatment 143:1 is but a small part of the picture. Though you are providing him with the best possible medical attention, he should understand that he must undergo a change of heart. To get over drinking will require a trans-formation of thought and attitude. He must place recovery above every-thing, even home and business, for without recovery he will lose both.

Show that you have every confidence in his ability to recover. 143:2 While on the subject of confidence, tell him that so far as you are concerned, this will be a strictly personal matter. His alcoholic derelictions, the treatment about to be undertaken, these will never be discussed without his consent. Cordially wish him success and say you want to have a long chat with him on his return.

To return to the subject matter of this book: It contains, as you 143:3 have seen, full directions by which your employee may solve his problem. To you, some of the ideas which it contains are novel. Perhaps some of them don't make sense to you. Possibly you are not quite in sympathy with the approach we suggest. By no means do we offer it as the last word on this subject, but so far as we are concerned, it has been the best word so far. Our approach often does work. After all, you are looking for results rather than methods. Whether your employee likes it or not, he will learn the grim truth about alcoholism. That won't hurt him a bit, though he does not go for the remedy at first.

144:1   I suggest you draw our book to the attention of the doctor who is to attend your patient during treatment. Ask that the book be read the moment the patient is able — while he is acutely depressed, if possible.

144:2   The doctor should approve a spiritual approach. And besides, he ought to tell the patient the truth about his condition, whatever that happens to be. The doctor should encourage him to acquire a spiritual experience. At this stage it will be just as well if the doctor does not mention you in connection with the book. Above all, neither you, the doctor, nor anyone should place himself in the position of telling the man he must abide by the contents of this volume. The man must decide for himself. You cannot command him, you can only encourage. And you will surely agree that it may be better to withold[†] any criticism you may have of our method until you see whether it works.

144:3   You are betting, of course, that your changed attitude and the contents of this book will turn the trick. In some cases it will, and in others it will not. But we think that if you persist, the percentage of successes will gratify you. When our work spreads and our numbers increase, we hope your employees may be put in personal contact with some of us, which, needless to say, will be more effective. Meanwhile, we are sure a great deal can be accomplished if you will follow the suggestions of this chapter.

144:4   On your employee's return, call him in and ask what happened. Ask him if he thinks he has the answer. Get him to tell you how he thinks it will work, and what he has to do about it. Make him feel free to discuss his problems with you, if he cares to. Show him you understand, and that you will not be upset by anything he wishes to say.

145:1   In this connection, it is important that you remain undisturbed if the man proceeds to tell you things which shock you. He may, for example, reveal that he has padded his expense account, or that he has planned to take your best customers away from you. In fact, he may say almost anything if he has accepted our solution which, as you know, demands rigorous honesty. Charge this off as you would a bad account and start afresh with him. If he owes you money, make terms which are reasonable. From this point on, never rake up the past unless he wants to discuss it.

145:2   If he speaks of his home situation, be patient and make helpful suggestions. Let him see that he can talk frankly with you so long as he does not bear tales or criticize others. With the kind of employee you want to keep, such an attitude will command undying loyalty.

145:3   The greatest enemies of the alcoholic are resentment, jealousy, envy, frustration, and fear. Wherever men are gathered together in business, there will be rivalries, and, arising out of these, a certain amount of office politics. Sometimes the alcoholic has an idea that people are trying to pull him down. Often this is not so at all. But sometimes his drinking will be used as a basis of criticism.

145:4   One instance comes to mind in which a malicious individual was always making friendly little jokes of an alcoholic's drinking exploits. In another case, an alcoholic was sent to a hospital for treatment. Only a few knew of it at first, but within a short time, it was bill-boarded throughout the entire company. Naturally, this sort of thing decreases a man's chance of recovery. The employer should make it his business to protect the victim from this kind of talk if he can. The employer cannot play favorites, but he can always try to defend a man from needless provocation and unfair criticism.

146:1   As a class, alcoholics are energetic people. They work hard and they play hard.

[†] This accurately reflects the language of the original.

Your man will be on his mettle to make good. Being somewhat weakened, and faced with physical and mental readjustment to a life which knows no alcohol, he may overdo. Don't let him work sixteen hours a day just because he wants to. Encourage him to play once in a while. Make it possible for him to do so. He may wish to do a lot for other alcoholics and something of the sort may come up during business hours. Don't begrudge him a reasonable amount of time. This work is necessary to maintain his sobriety.

After your man has gone along without drinking a few months, try to make use of his services with other employees who are giving you the alcoholic run-around — provided, of course, they are willing to have a third party in the picture. Don't hesitate to let an alcoholic who has recovered, but holds a relatively unimportant job, talk to a man with a better position. Being on radically different basis of life, he will never take advantage of the situation.[†]   146:2

You must trust your man. Long experience with alcoholic excuses naturally makes you suspicious. When his wife next calls saying he is sick, don't jump to the conclusion he is drunk. If he is, and is still trying to recover upon our basis, he will presently tell you about it, even if it means the loss of his job. For he knows he must be honest if he would live at all. Let him see you are not bothering your head about him at all, that you are not suspicious, nor are you trying to run his life so he will be shielded from temptation to drink. If he is conscientiously following the Program of Recovery he can go anywhere your business may call him. Do not promote him, however, until you are sure.   146:3

In case he does stumble, even once, you will have to decide whether to let him go. If you are sure he doesn't mean business, there is no doubt you should discharge him. If, on the contrary, you are sure he is doing his utmost, you may wish to give him another chance. But you should feel under no obligation to do so, for your obligation has been well discharged already. In any event, don't let him fool you, and don't let sentiment get the better of you if you are sure he ought to go.   147:1

There is another thing you might do. If your organization is a large one, your junior executives might be provided with this book. You might let them know you have no quarrel with the alcoholics of your organization. These juniors are often in a difficult position. Men under them are frequently their friends. So, for one reason or another, they cover these men, hoping matters will take a turn for the better. They often jeopardize their own positions by trying to help serious drinkers who should have been fired long ago, or else given an opportunity to get well.   147:2

After reading this book, a junior executive can go to such a man and say, "look here, Ed. Do you want to stop drinking or not? You put me on the spot every time you get drunk. It isn't fair to me or the firm. I have been learning something about alcoholism. If you are an alcoholic, you are a mighty sick man. You act like one. The firm wants to help you get over it, if you are interested. There is a way out, and I hope you have sense enough to try it. If you do, your past will be forgotten and the fact that you went away for treatment will not be mentioned. But if you cannot, or will not stop drinking, I think you ought to resign."   147:3

Your junior executive may not agree with the contents of our book. He need not, and often should not, show it to his alcoholic prospect. But at least he will understand the problem and will no longer be misled by ordinary promises. He will be able to take a position with such a man which is eminently fair and square. He will have no further reason for covering up an alcoholic employee.   148:1

It boils right down to this: No man should be fired just because he is alcoholic. If he wants to stop, he should be afforded a real chance. If he cannot, or does not want to stop, he should usually be discharged. The exceptions are few.   148:2

[†] This accurately reflects the language of the original.

148:3   We think this method of approach will accomplish several things for you. It will promptly bring drinking situations to light. It will enable you to restore good men to useful activity. At the same time you will feel no reluctance to rid yourself of those who cannot, or will not, stop. Alcoholism may be causing your organization considerable damage in its waste of money, men and reputation. We hope our suggestions will help you plug up this sometimes serious leak. We do not expect you to become a missionary, attempting to save all who happen to be alcoholic. Being a business man is enough these days. But we can sensibly urge that you stop this waste and give your worth-while man a chance.

148:4   The other day an approach was made to the vice-president of a large industrial concern. He remarked: "I'm mighty glad you fellows got over your drinking. But the policy of this company is not to interfere with the habits of our employees. If a man drinks so much that his job suffers, we fire him. I don't see how you can be of any help to us, for as you see, we don't have any alcoholic problem." This same company spends millions for research every year. Their cost of production is figured to a fine decimal point. They have recreational facilities. There is company insurance. There is a real interest, both humanitarian and business, in the well-being of employees. But alcoholism — well, they just don't have that.

149:1   Perhaps this is a typical attitude. We, who have collectively seen a great deal of business life, at least from the alcoholic angle, had to smile at this gentleman's opinion. He might be shocked if he knew how much alcoholism cost his organization a year. That company may harbor many actual or potential alcoholics. We believe that managers of large enterprises often have little idea how prevalent this problem is. Perhaps this is a guess, but we have a hunch it's a good one. If you still feel your organization has no alcoholic problem, you might well take another look down the line You may make some interesting discoveries.

149:2   Of course, this chapter refers to alcoholics, sick people, deranged men. What our friend, the vice-president, had in mind, was the habitual or whoopee drinker. As to them, his policy is probably sound, but as you see, he does not distinguish between such people and the alcoholic.

Being a business man, you might like to have a summary of this chapter. Here it Is[†]:

One: Acquaint yourself with the nature of alcoholism.

Two: Be prepared to discount and forget your man's past.

Three: Confidentially offer him medical treatment and cooperation, provided you think he wants to stop.

Four: Have the alcohol thoroughly removed from his system and give him a suitable chance to recover physically.

Five: Have the doctor in attendance present him with this book, but don't cram it down his throat.

Six: Have a frank talk with him when he gets back from his treatment, assuring him of your full support, encouraging him to say anything he wishes about himself, and making it clear the past will not be held against him.

Seven: Ask him to place recovery from alcoholism ahead of all else.

Eight: Don't let him overwork.

Nine: Protect him, when justified, from malicious gossip.

Ten: If, after you have shot the works, he will not stop, then let him go.

149:3   It is not to be expected that you give your alcoholic employee a disproportionate amount of time and attention. He is not to be made a favorite. The right kind of man, the kind who recovers, will not want this sort of thing. He will not impose upon you. Far from it. He will work like the devil, and thank you to his dying day.

149:4   Today, I own a little company. There are two alcoholic employees, who produce as

---

[†] This accurately reflects the language of the original.

much as five normal salesmen. But why not? They have a better way of life, and they have been saved from a living death. I have enjoyed every moment spent in getting them straightened out. You, Mr. Employer, may have the same experience!*

* See appendix — The Alcoholic Foundation. We may be able to carry on a limited correspondence.

Chapter Eleven

A VISION FOR YOU

151:1   For most normal folks, drinking means conviviality, companionship, and colorful imagination. It means release from care, boredom, and worry. It is joyous intimacy with friends, and a feeling that life is good. But not so with us in those last days of heavy drinking. The old pleasures were gone. They were but memories. Never could we recapture the great moments of the past. There was an insistent yearning to enjoy as we once did and a heartbreaking obsession that some new miracle of control would enable us to do it. There was always one more attempt — and one more failure.

151:2   The less people tolerated us, the more we withdrew from society, from life itself. As we became subjects of King Alcohol, shivering denizens of his mad realm, the chilling vapor that is loneliness settled down. It thickened, ever becoming blacker. Some of us sought out sordid places, hoping to find understanding companionship and approval. Momentarily we did — then would come oblivion and the awful awakening to face the hideous Four Horsemen — Terror, Bewilderment, Frustration, Despair. Unhappy drinkers who see this page will understand!

151:3   Now and then a serious drinker, being dry at the moment says, "I don't miss it at all. Feel better. Work better. Having a better time." As ex-alcoholics, we smile at such a sally. We know our friend is like a boy whistling in the dark to keep up his spirits. He fools himself. Inwardly he would give anything to take half a dozen drinks and get away with them. He will presently try the old game again, for he isn't happy about his sobriety. He cannot picture life without alcohol. Some day he will be unable to imagine life either with alcohol or without it. Then he will know loneliness such as few do. He will be at the jumping-off place. He will wish for the end.

152:1   We have shown you how we got out from under. You say: "Yes, I'm willing. But am I to be consigned to a life where I shall be stupid, boring and glum, like some righteous people I see? I know I must get along without liquor, but how can I? Have you a sufficient substitute?"

152:2   Yes, there is a substitute, and it is vastly more than that. It is a Fellowship in Alcoholics Anonymous. There you will find release from care, boredom, and worry. Your imagination will be fired. Life will mean something at last. The most satisfactory years of your existence lie ahead. Thus we find The Fellowship, and so will you.

152:3   "How is that to come about?" you say. "Where am I to find these people?"

152:4   You are going to meet these new friends in your own community. Near you alcoholics are dying helplessly like people in a sinking ship. If you live in a large place, there are hundreds. These are to be your companions. High and low, rich and poor, these are future Fellows of Alcoholics Anonymous. Among them you will make lifelong friends. You will be bound to them with new and wonderful ties, for you will escape disaster together and you will commence shoulder to shoulder your common journey. Then you will know what it means to give of yourself, that others may survive and rediscover life. You will learn the full meaning of "Love thy neighbor as thyself."

153:1   It may seem incredible that these men are to become happy, respected, and useful once more. How can they rise out of such misery, bad repute and hopelessness? The practical answer is that since these things have happened among us, they can happen again. Should you wish them above all else, and should you be willing to make use of our experience, we are sure they will come. The age of miracles is still with us. Our own recovery proves that!

Our hope is that when this chip of a book is launched on the world tide of alcoholism, defeated drinkers will seize upon it, following its directions. Many, we are sure, will rise to their feet and march on. They will approach still other sick ones and so the Fellowship of Alcoholics Anonymous may spring up in each city and hamlet, havens for those who must find a way out. 153:2

In the chapter "Working With Others" you gathered an idea of how to approach and aid others to health. Suppose now that through you several families have adopted your way of life. You will want to know more of how to proceed from that point. Perhaps the best way of treating you to a glimpse of your future will be to describe the growth of the Fellowship among us. Here is a brief account: 153:3

Nearly four years ago, one of our number made a journey to a certain western city. From the business standpoint, his trip came off badly. Had he been successful in his enterprise, he would have been set on his feet financially, which, at the time, seemed vitally important. But his venture wound up in a law suit and bogged down completely. The proceding† was shot through with much hard feeling and controversy. 153:4

Bitterly discouraged, he found himself in a strange place, discredited and almost broke. Still physically weak, and sober but a few months, he saw that his predicament was dangerous. He wanted so much to talk with someone, but whom? 154:1

One dismal afternoon he paced a hotel lobby wondering how his bill was to be paid. At one end of the room stood a glass covered directory of local churches. Down the lobby a door opened into an attractive bar. He could see the gay crowd inside. In there he would find companionship and release. Unless he took some drinks, he might not have the courage to scrape an acquaintance, and would have a lonely week-end. 154:2

Of course, he couldn't drink, but why not sit hopefully at a table, a bottle of ginger ale before him? Then after all, had he not been sober six months now? Perhaps he could handle, say, three drinks — no more! Fear gripped him. He was on thin ice. Again it was the old, insidious insanity — that first drink. With a shiver, he turned away and walked down the lobby to the church directory. Music and gay chatter still floated to him from the bar. 154:3

But what about his responsibilities — his family and the men who would die because they would not know how to get well, ah — yes, those other alcoholics? There must be many such in this town. He would phone a clergyman. His sanity returned, and he thanked God. Selecting a church at random from the directory, he stepped into a booth and lifted the receiver. 154:4

Little could he foresee what that simple decision was to mean. How could any one guess that life and happiness for many was to depend on whether one depressed man entered a phone booth or a bar? His call to the clergyman led him presently to a certain resident of the town, who, though formerly able and respected, was then nearing the nadir of alcoholic despair. It was the usual situation: home in jeopardy, wife ill, children distracted, bills in arrears, and reputation damaged. He had a desperate desire to stop, but saw no way out; for he had earnestly tried many avenues of escape. Painfully aware of being somehow abnormal, the man did not fully realize what it means to be alcoholic. 155:1

† This accurately reflects the language of the original.

155:2   When our friend told his experience, the man agreed that no amount of will power he might muster could stop his drinking for long. A spiritual experience, he conceded, was absolutely necessary, but the price seemed high upon the basis suggested. He told how he lived in constant worry about creditors and others who might find out about his alcoholism. He had, of course, the familiar alcoholic obsession that few knew of his drinking. Why, he argued, should he lose the remainder of his business, so bringing still more suffering to his family, by foolishly admitting his plight to his creditors and those from whom he made his livelihood? He would do anything, he said, but that.

155:3   Being intrigued, however, he invited our friend to his home. Some time later, and just as he thought he was getting control of his liquor situation, he went on a roaring bender. For him, this was the spree that ended all sprees. He saw that he would have to face his problems squarely, that God might give him mastery.

156:1   One morning he took the bull by the horns and set out to tell those he feared what his trouble had been. He found himself surprisingly well received, and learned that many knew of his drinking. Stepping into his car, he made the rounds of people he had hurt. He trembled as he went about, for this might mean ruin, particularly to a person in his line of business.

156:2   At midnight he came home exhausted, but very happy. He has not had a drink since. As we shall see, he now means a great deal to his community, and the major liabilities of thirty years of hard drinking have been repaired in less than four.

156:3   But life was not easy for the two friends. Plenty of difficulties presented themselves. Both saw that they must keep spiritually active. One day they called up the head nurse of a local hospital. They explained their need and inquired if she had a first class alcoholic prospect.

156:4   She replied, "Yes, we've got a corker. He's just beaten up a couple of nurses. Goes off his head completely when drinking. But he's a grand chap when sober though he's been in here six times in the last four months. Understand he was once a well-known lawyer in town, but just now we've got him strapped down tight."

156:5   Here was a prospect all right, but, by the description, none too promising. The use of spiritual principles in such cases was not so well understood as it is now. But one of the friends said, "Put him in a private room. We'll be down."

157:1   Two days later, a future Fellow of Alcoholics Anonymous stared glassily at the strangers beside his bed. "Who are you fellows, and why this private room? I was always in a ward before."

157:2   Said one of the visitors, "We're giving you a treatment for alcoholism."

157:3   Hopelessness was written large on the man's face as he replied: "Oh, but that's no use. Nothing would fix me. I'm a goner. The last three times, I got drunk on the way home from here. I'm afraid to go out the door. I can't understand it."

157:4   For an hour, the two friends told him about their drinking experiences. Over and over, he would say: "That's me. That's me. I drink like that."

157:5   The man in the bed was told of the acute poisoning from which he suffered, how it deteriorates the body of an alcoholic and warps his mind. There was much talk about the mental state preceding the first drink.

157:6   "Yes, that's me," said the sick man, "the very image. You fellows know your stuff all right, but I don't see what good it'll do. You fellows are somebody. I was once, but I'm a nobody now. From what you tell me, I know more than ever I can't stop." At this both the visitors burst into a laugh. Said the future Fellow Anonymous: "Damn little to laugh about that I can see."

The two friends spoke of their spiritual experience and told him about the course of action they carried out. 157:7

He interrupted: "I used to be strong for the church, but that won't fix it. I've prayed to God on hangover mornings and sworn that I'd never touch another drop, but by nine oclock I'd be boiled as an owl." 157:8

Next day found the prospect more receptive. He had been thinking it over. "Maybe you're right," he said. "God ought to be able to do anything." Then he added, "He sure didn't do much for me when I was trying to fight this booze racket alone." 158:1

On the third day the lawyer gave his life to the care and direction of his Creator, and said he was perfectly willing to do anything necessary. His wife came, scarcely daring to be hopeful, but she thought she saw something different about her husband already. He had begun to have a spiritual experience. 158:2

That afternoon he put on his clothes and walked from the hospital a free man. He entered a political campaign, making speeches, frequenting men's gathering places of all sorts, often staying up all night. He lost the race by only a narrow margin. But he had found God — and in finding God had found himself. 158:3

That was in June, 1935. He never drank again. He too, has become a respected and useful member of his community. He has helped other men recover, and is a power in the church from which he was long absent. 158:4

So, you see, there were three alcoholics in that town, who now felt they had to give to others what they had found, or be sunk. After several failures to find others, a fourth turned up. He came through an acquaintance who had heard the good news. He proved to be a devil-may-care young fellow whose parents could not make out whether he wanted to stop drinking or not. They were deeply religious people, much shocked by their son's refusal to have anything to do with the church. He suffered horribly from his sprees, but it seemed as if nothing could be done for him. He consented, however, to go to the hospital, where he occupied the very room recently vacated by the lawyer. 158:5

He had three visitors. After a bit, he said: "The way you fellows put this spiritual stuff makes sense. I'm ready to do business. I guess the old folks were right after all." So one more was added to the Fellowship. 159:1

All this time our friend of the hotel lobby incident remained in that town. He was there three months. He now returned home, leaving behind his first acquaintance, the lawyer, and the devil-may-care chap. These men had found something brand new in life. Though they knew they must help other alcoholics if they would remain sober, that motive became secondary. It was transcended by the happiness they found in giving themselves for others. They shared their homes, their slender resources, and gladly devoted their spare hours to fellow-sufferers. They were willing, by day or night, to place a new man in the hospital and visit him afterward. They grew in numbers. They experienced a few distressing failures, but in those cases, they made an effort to bring the man's family into a new way of living, thus relieving much worry and suffering. 159:2

A year and sic† months later these three had succeeded with seven more. Seeing much of each other, scarce an evening passed that someone's home did not shelter a little gathering of men and women, happy in their release, and constantly thinking 159:3

---

† This accurately reflects the language of the original.

how they might present their discovery to some newcomer. In addition to these casual get-togethers, it became customary to set apart one night a week for a meeting to be attended by anyone or everyone interested in a spiritual way of life. Aside from fellowship and sociability, the prime object was to provide a time and place where new people might bring their problems.

160:1 Outsiders became interested. One man and his wife placed their large home at the disposal of this strangely assorted crowd. This couple has since become so fascinated that they have dedicated their home to the work. Many a distracted wife has visited this house to find loving and understanding companionship among women who knew their problem, to hear from the lips of men like their husbands what had happened to them, to be advised how her own wayward mate might be hospitalized and approached when next he stumbled.

160:2 Many a man, yet dazed from his hospital experience, has stepped over the threshold of that home into freedom. Many an alcoholic who entered there came away with an answer. He succumbed to that gay crowd inside, who laughed at their misfortune and understood him. Impressed by those who visited him at the hospital, he capitulated entirely, when, later, in an upper room of this house, he heard the story of some man whose experience closely tallied with his own. The expression on the faces of the women, that indefinable something in the eyes of the men, the stimulating and electric atmosphere of the place, conspired to let him know that here was haven at last.

160:3 The very practical approach to his problems, the absence of intolerance of any kind, the informality, the genuine democracy, the uncanny understanding which these people had were irresistable. He and his wife would leave elated by the thought of what they could now do for some stricken acquaintance and his family. They knew they had a host of new friends; it seemed they had known these strangers always. They had seen miracles, and one was to come to them. They had visioned The Great Reality — their loving and All Powerful Creator.

161:1 Now, this house will hardly accommodate its weekly visitors, for they number sixty or eighty as a rule. Alcoholics are being attracted from far and near. From surrounding towns, families drive long distances to be present. A community thirty miles away has fifteen Fellows of Alcoholics Anonymous. Being a large place, we think that some day its Fellowship will number many hundreds.

161:2 But life among Alcoholics Anonymous is more than attending meetings and visiting hospitals. Cleaning up old scrapes, helping to settle family differences, explaining the disinherited son to his irate parents, lending money and securing jobs for each other, when justified — these are everyday occurrences. No one is too discredited. nor has sunk too low to be welcomed cordially — if he means business. Social distinctions, petty rivalries and jealousies — these are laughed out of countenance. Being wrecked in the same vessel, being restored and united under one God, with hearts and minds attuned to the welfare of others, the things which matter so much to some people no longer signify much to them. How could they?

161:3 Under only slightly different conditions, the same thing is taking place in several eastern cities. In one of these there is a well-known hospital for the treatment of alcoholic and drug addiction. Four years ago one of our number was a patient there. Many of us have felt, for the first time, the Presence and Power of God within its walls. We are greatly indebted to the doctor in attendance there, for he, although it might prejudice his own work, has told us his belief in our work.

162:1 Every few days this doctor suggests our approach to one of his patients. Understanding our work, he can do this with an eye to selecting those who are willing and able to recover on a spiritual basis. Many of us, former patients, go there to help.

Then, in this eastern city there are informal meetings such as we have described to you, where you may see thirty or forty, there are the same fast friendships, there is the same helpfulness to one another as you find among our western friends. There is a good bit of travel between East and West and we foresee a great increase in this helpful interchange.

Some day we hope that every alcoholic who journeys will find a Fellowship of Alcoholics Anonymous at his destination. To some extent this is already true. Some of us are salesmen and go about. Little clusters of twos and threes and fives of us have sprung up in other communities, through contact with our two larger centers. Those of us who travel drop in as often as we can. This practice enables us to lend a hand, at the same time avoiding certain alluring distractions of the road, about which any traveling man can inform you. {162:2}

Thus we grow. And so can you, though you be but one man with this book in your hand. We believe and hope it contains all you will need to begin. {162:3}

We know what you are thinking. You are saying to yourself: "I'm jittery and alone. I couldn't do that." But you can. You forget that you have just now tapped a source of power so much greater than yourself. To duplicate, with such backing, what we have accomplished is only a matter of willingness, patience and labor. {163:1}

We know a former alcoholic who was living alone in a large community. He had lived there but a few weeks when he found that the place probably contained more alcoholics per square mile than any city in the country. This was only a few days ago at this writing. The authorities were much concerned. He got in touch with a prominent psychiatrist who has undertaken certain responsibilities for the mental health of the community. The doctor proved to be able and exceedingly anxious to adopt any workable method of handling the situation. Agreeing with many competent and informed physicians, he said he could do little or nothing for the average alcoholic. So, he inquired, what did our friend have on the ball? {163:2}

Our friend proceeded to tell him. And with such good effect that the doctor agreed to a test among his patients and certain other alcoholics from a clinic which he attends. Arrangements were also made with the chief psychiatrist of a large public hospital to select still others from the stream of misery which flows through that institution. {163:3}

So our fellow worker will soon have friends galore. Some of them may sink and perhaps never get up, but if our experience is a criterion, more than half of those approached will become Fellows of Alcoholics Anonymous. When a few men in this city have found themselves, and have discovered the joy of helping others to face life again, there will be no stopping until everyone in that town has has† his opportunity to recover — if he can and will. {163:4}

Still you may say: "But I will not have the benefit of contact with you who write this book." We cannot be sure. God will determine that, so you must remember that your real reliance is always upon Him. He will show you how to create the Fellowship you crave.* {164:1}

Our book is meant to be suggestive only. We realize we know only a little. God will constantly disclose more to you and to us. Ask him in your morning meditation what you can do each day for the man who is still sick. The answers will come, if your own house is in order. But obviously you cannot transmit something you haven't got. See to it that your relationship with Him is right, and great events will come to pass for you and countless others. This is the Great Fact for us. {164:2}

Abandon yourself to God as you understand God. Admit your faults to him and {164:3}

---

† This accurately reflects the language of the original.

Page 76.

and[†] your fellows. Clear away the wreckage of your past. Give freely of what you find, and join us. We shall be with you, in the Fellowship of The Spirit, and you will surely meet some of us as you trudge the Road of Happy Destiny.

164:4   May God bless you and keep you — until then.

* See appendix — The Alcoholic Foundation. It may be we shall be able to carry on a limited correspondence.

[†] This accurately reflects the language of the original.

THE ALCOHOLIC FOUNDATION

In our text we have shown the alcoholic how he can recover but we realize that many will want to write us directly.

To receive these inquiries, to administer royalties from this book and such other funds as may come to hand, a Trust has been created known as The Alcoholic Foundation. Three Trustees are members of Alcoholics Anonymous, the other four are well-known business and professional men who have volunteered their services. The Trust states these four (who are not of Alcoholics Anonymous) or their successors, shall always constitute a majority of the Board of Trustees.

We must frankly state however, that under present conditions, we may be unable to reply to all inquiries, as our members, in their spare time, will attend to most of the correspondence. Nevertheless we shall strenuously attempt to communicate with those men and women who are able to report that they are staying sober and working with other alcoholics. Once we have such an active nucleus, we can then refer to them those inquiries which originate in their respective localities. Starting with small but active centers created in this fashion, we are confident that fellowships will spring up and grow very much as they have among us. Meanwhile, we hope the Foundation will become more useful to all.

The Alcoholic Foundation is our only agency of its kind. We have agreed that all business engagements touching on our alcoholic work shall have the approval of its trustees. People who state they represent The Alcoholic Foundation should be asked for credentials and if unsatisfactory, these ought to be checked with the Foundation at once. We welcome inquiry by scientific, medical and religious societies.

This volume is published by the Works Publishing Company, organized and financed mostly by small donations of our members. This company donates the customary royalties from each copy of Alcoholics Anonymous to The Alcoholic Foundation.

To order this book, send your check or money order for $3.50 to:

The Works Publishing Company,
17 William Street,
Newark, N. J.

I N D E X — (2)

PERSONAL STORIES

* * * * *

THE DOCTOR'S NIGHTMARE

I was born in a small New England village of about 7,000   171:2
souls. The general moral standard was, as I recall it, far
above the average. No beer or liquor was sold in the neighborhood, except at the State liquor agency where perhaps one
might procure a pint if he could convince the agent that he
really needed it. Without this proof the expectant purchaser
would be forced to depart empty handed with none of what I
later came to believe was the great panacea for all human
ills. Men who had liquor shipped in from Boston or New York by
express were looked upon with great distrust and disfavor by
most of the good townspeople. The town was well supplied with
churches and schools in which I pursued my early educational
activities.

My father was a professional man of recognized ability and   171:3
both my father and mother were most active in church affairs.
Both father and mother were considerably above the average in
intelligence.

Unfortunately for me, I was the only child, which perhaps   172:1
engendered the selfishness which played such an important part
in bringing on my alcoholism.

From childhood through high school, I was more or less   172:2
forced to go to church, Sunday School and evening service,
Monday night Christian Endeavor and sometimes to Wednesday
evening prayer meeting. This had the effect of making me
resolve that when I was free from parental domination, I would
never again darken the doors of a church. This resolution I
kept steadfastly for the next forty years, except when circumstances made it seem unwise to absent myself.

After high school came four years in one of the best   172:3
colleges in the country where drinking seemed to be a major
extra-curricular activity. Almost everyone seemed to do it. I
did it more and more, and had lots of fun without much grief,
either physical or financial. I seemed to be able to snap back
the next morning better than most of my fellow drinkers, who
were cursed (or perhaps blessed) with a great deal of morning
after nausea. Never once in my life have I had a headache,
which fact leads me to believe that I was an alcoholic almost
from the start. My whole life seemed to be centered around
doing what I wanted to do, without regard for the rights,
wishes, or privileges of anyone else; a state of mind which
became more and more predominant as the years passed. I was
graduated with "summa cum laude" in the eyes of the drinking
fraternity, but not in the eyes of the Dean.

The next three years I spent in Boston, Chicago and Montreal   172:4
in the employ of a large manufacturing concern, selling railway supplies, gas engines of all sorts, and many other items
of heavy hardware. During these years, I drank as much as my
purse permitted, still without paying too great a penalty,
although I was beginning to have morning "jitters" at times.
But I lost only a half day's work during these three years.

173:1   My next move was to take up the study of medicine, entering one of the largest universities in the country. There I took up the business of drinking with much greater earnestness than I had previously shown. On account of my enormous capacity for beer, I was elected to membership in one of the drinking societies, and soon became one of the leading spirits. Many mornings I have gone to classes, and even though fully prepared, I would turn and walk back to my fraternity house because of my jitters, not daring to enter the classroom for fear of making a scene should I be called on for recitation.

173:2   This went from bad to worse until sophomore spring when, after a prolonged period of drinking, I made up my mind that I could not complete my course, so I packed my grip and went South and spent a month on a large farm owned by a friend of mine. When I got the fog out of my brain, I decided that quitting school was very foolish and that I had better return and continue my work. When I reached school, I discovered the faculty had other ideas on the subject. After much argument they allowed me to return and take my exams, all of which I passed creditably. But they were much disgusted and told me they would attempt to struggle along without my presence. After many painful discussions, they finally gave me my credits and I migrated to another of the leading universities of the country and entered as a Junior that Fall.

174:1   There my drinking became so much worse that the boys in the fraternity house where I lived felt forced to send for my father, who made a long journey in the vain endeavor to get me straightened around. This had little effect however for I kept on drinking and used a great deal more hard liquor than in former years.

174:2   Coming up to final exams I went on a particularly strenuous spree. When I went in to write the examinations, my hand trembled so I could not hold a pencil. I passed in at least three absolutely blank books. I was, of course, soon on the carpet and the upshot was that I had to go back for two more quarters and remain absolutely dry, if I wished to graduate. This I did, and proved myself satisfactory to the faculty, both in deportment and scholastically.

174:3   I conducted myself so creditably that I was able to secure a much coveted internship† in a Western City, where I spent two years. During these two years I was kept so busy that I hardly left the hospital at all. Consequently, I could not get into any trouble.

174:4   When these two years were up, I opened my office downtown. Then I had some money, all the time in the world, and considerable stomach trouble. I soon discovered that a couple of drinks would alleviate my gastric distress, at least for a few hours at a time, so it was not at all difficult for me to return to my former excessive indulgence.

174:5   By this time I was beginning to pay very dearly physically, and in hope of relief voluntarily incarcerated myself at least a dozen

---

† This accurately reflects the language of the original.

times in one of the local sanitariums. I was between Scylla and Charybdis now, because if I did not drink my stomach tortured me, and if I did, my nerves did the same thing. After three years of this, I wound up in the local hospital where they attempted to help me, but I would get my friends to smuggle me in a quart, or I would steal the alcohol about the building, so that I got rapidly worse.

Finally my father had to send a doctor out from my home town who managed to get me back there some way and I was in bed about two months before I could venture out of the house. I stayed about town a couple of months more and returned to resume my practice. I think I must have been thoroughly scared by what had happened, or by the doctor, or probably both, so that I did not touch a drink again until the country went dry. `175:1`

With the passing of the Eighteenth Amendment I felt quite safe. I knew everyone would buy a few bottles, or cases, of liquor as their exchequers permitted, and it would soon be gone. Therefore it would make no great difference, even if I should do some drinking. At that time I was not aware of the almost unlimited supply the government made it possible for us doctors to obtain, neither had I any knowledge of the bootlegger who soon appeared on the horizon. I drank with moderation at first, but it took me only a relatively short time to drift back into the old habits which had wound up so disastrously before. `175:2`

During the next few years, I developed two distinct phobias. One was the fear of not sleeping, and the other was the fear of running out of liquor. Not being a man of means, I knew that if I did not stay sober enough to earn money, I would run out of liquor. Most of the time, therefore, I did not take the morning drink which I craved so badly, but instead would fill up on large doses of sedatives to quiet the jitters, which distressed me terribly. Occasionally, I would yield to the morning craving, but if I did, it would be only a few hours before I would be quite unfit for work. This would lessen my chances of smuggling some home that evening, which in turn would mean a night of futile tossing around in bed followed by a morning of unbearable jitters. During the subsequent fifteen years I had sense enough never to go to the hospital if I had been drinking, and very seldom did I receive patients. I would sometimes hide out in one of the clubs, of which I was a member, and had the habit at times of registering at a hotel under a fictitious name. But my friends usually found me and I would go home if they promised that I should not be scolded. `175:3`

If my wife were planning to go out in the afternoon, I would get a large supply of liquor and smuggle it home and hide it in the coal bin, the clothes chute, over door jambs, over beams in the cellar and in cracks in the cellar tile. I also made use of old trunks and chests, the old can container, and even the ash container. The water tank on the toilet I never used, because that looked too easy. I found out later that my wife inspected it frequently. I used to put eight or twelve ounce bottles of alcohol in a fur lined `176:1` glove and toss it onto the back airing porch when winter days got dark enough. My bootlegger had hidden it at the back steps where I could get it at my convenience. Sometimes I would bring it in my pockets, but there[†] were inspected, and that became too risky. I used also to put it up in four ounce bottles and stick several in my stocking tops. This worked nicely until my wife and I went to see Wallace Beery in "Tugboat Annie", after which the pant-leg and stock-racket[†] were out!

177:1   I will not take space to relate all my hospital or sanitarium experiences.

177:3   For the benefit of those experimentally inclined, I should mention the so-called beer experiment. When beer first came back, I thought that I was safe. I could drink all I wanted of that. It was harmless; nobody ever got drunk on beer. So I filled the cellar full, with the permission of my good wife. It was not long before I was drinking at least a case and a half a day. I put on thirty pounds weight in about two months, looked like a pig, and was uncomfortable from shortness of breath. It then occurred to me that after one was all smelled up with beer nobody could tell what had been drunk, so I began to fortify my beer with straight alcohol. Of course, the result was very bad, and that ended the beer experiment.

177:2   During all this time we became more or less ostracized by our friends. We could not be invited out because I would surely get tight and my wife dared not invite people in for the same reason. My phobia for sleeplessness demanded that I get drunk every night, but in order to get more liquor for the next night, I had to stay sober during the day, at least up to four oclock. This routine went on with few interruptions for seventeen years. It was really a horrible night-mare, this earning money, getting liquor, smuggling it home, getting drunk, morning jitters, taking large doses of sedatives to make it possible for me to earn more money, and so on ad nauseam. I used to promise my wife, my friends, and my children that I would drink no more — promises which seldom kept me sober even through the day, though I was very sincere when I made them.

178:1   About the time of the beer experiment I was thrown in with a crowd of people who attracted me because of their seeming poise, health, and happiness. They spoke with great freedom from embarrassment, which I could never do, and they seemed very much at ease on all occasions and appeared very healthy. More than these attributes, they seemed to be happy. I was self conscious and ill at ease most of the time, my health was at the breaking point, and I was thor-oughly miserable. I sensed they had something I did not have, from which I might readily profit. I learned that it was something of a spiritual nature, which did not appeal to me very much, but I thought it could do no harm. I gave the matter much time and study for the next two and a half years, but still got tight every night nevertheless. I read everything I could find, and talked to everyone who I thought knew anything about it.

[†] This accurately reflects the language of the original.

My good wife became deeply interested and it was her 178:2
interest that sustained mine, though I at no time sensed
that it might be an answer to my liquor problem. How my wife
kept her faith and courage during all those years, I'll
never know, but she did. If she had not, I know I would have
been dead a long time ago. For some reason, we alcoholics
seem to have the gift of picking out the world's finest
women. Why they should be subjected to the tortures we
inflicted upon them, I cannot explain.

About this time a lady called up my wife one Saturday 179:1
afternoon, saying she wanted me to come over that evening
to meet a friend of hers who might help me. It was the day
before Mother's Day and I had come home plastered, carrying
a big potted plant which I set down on the table and
forthwith went upstairs and passed out. The next day she
called again. Wishing to be polite, though I felt very
badly, I said, "Let's make the call," and extracted from my
wife a promise that we would not stay over fifteen minutes.

We entered her house at exactly five oclock and it was 179:2
exactly eleven fifteen when we left. I had a couple of
shorter talks with this man afterward, and stopped drinking
abruptly. This dry spell lasted for about three weeks, when
I went to Atlantic City to attend several days' meeting of
a National Society of which I was a member. I drank all the
Scotch they had on the train and bought several quarts on my
way to the hotel. This was on Sunday. I got tight that
night, stayed sober Monday till after the dinner and then
proceeded to get tight again. I drank all I dared in the
bar, and then went to my room to finish the job. Tuesday I
started in the morning, getting well organized by noon. I
did not want to disgrace myself, so I then checked out. I
bought some more liquor on the way to the depot. I had to
wait some time for the train. I remember nothing from then
until I woke up at a friend's house, in a nearby town. These
good people notified my wife, who sent my newly-made friend
over to get me in my car. He came and got me home and to bed,
gave me a few drinks that night, and one bottle of beer the
next morning.

That was June 10, 1935, and that was my last drink. As 180:1
I write nearly four years have passed.

The question which might naturally come into your mind 180:2
would be: what did the man do or say that was different from
what others had done or said? It must be remembered that I
had read a great deal and talked to everyone who knew, or
thought they knew, anything about the subject of alcoholism. This man was a man who had experienced many years of
frightful drinking, who had had most all the drunkard's
experience known to man, but who had been cured by the very
means I had been trying to employ, that is to say, the
spiritual approach. He gave me information about the subject of alcoholism which was undoubtedly helpful. <u>Of far
more importance was the fact that he was the first living
human with whom I had ever talked, who knew what he was
talking about in regard to alcoholism from actual experience. In other words, he talked my language</u>. He knew all the
answers, and certainly not because he had picked them up in
his reading.

180:3   It is a most wonderful blessing to be relieved of the terrible curse with which I was afflicted. My health is good and I have regained my self-respect and the respect of my colleagues. My home life is ideal and my business is as good as can be expected in these uncertain times.

180:4   I spend a great deal of time passing on what I learned to others who want and need it badly. I do it for four reasons:

1. Sense of duty.
2. It is a pleasure.
3. Because in so doing I am paying my debt to the man who took time to pass it on to me.
4. Because every time I do it I take out a little more insurance for myself against a possible slip.

181:1   Unlike most of our crowd, I did not get over my craving for liquor much during the first two and one-half years of abstinence. It was almost always with me. But at no time have I been anywhere near yielding. I used to get terribly upset when I saw my friends drink and knew I could not, but I schooled myself to believe that though I once had the same privilege, I had abused it so frightfully that it was withdrawn. So it doesn't behoove me to squawk about it, for after all, nobody ever used to throw me down and pour any liquor down my throat.

181:2   If you think you are an atheist, an agnostic, a skeptic, or have any other form of intellectual pride which keeps you from accepting what is in this book, I feel sorry for you. If you still think you are strong enough to beat the game, that is your affair. But if you really and truly want to quit drinking liquor for good and all, and sincerely feel that you must have some help, we know that we have an answer for you. It never fails if you go about it with one half the zeal you have been in the habit of showing when getting another drink.

181:3   Your Heavenly Father will never let you down!

* * * *

THE UNBELIEVER

Dull . . . listless . . . semicomatose . . . I lay on my bed in a famous hospital for alcoholics. Death or worse had been my sentence.

What was the difference? What difference did anything make? Why think of those things which were gone — why worry about the results of my drunken escapades? What the hell were the odds if my wife had discovered the mistress situation? Two swell boys . . . sure . . . but what difference would a corpse or an asylum imprisoned father make to them? . . thoughts stop whirling in my head . . . that's the worst of this sobering-up process . . . the old think tank is geared in high-high . . . what do I mean high-high . . . where did that come from . . . oh yes, that first Cadillac I had, it had four speeds . . . had a high-high gear . . . insane asylum . . . how that bus could scamper . . . yes . . . even then liquor probably poisoned me. What had the little doctor said this morning . . . thoughts hesitate a moment . . . stop your mad turning . . . what was I thinking about . . . oh yes, the doctor.

This morning I reminded Doc this was my tenth visit. I had spent a couple of thousand dollars on these trips and those that I had financed for the plastered play girls who also couldn't sober up. Jackie was a honey until she got plastered and then she was a hellion. Wonder what gutter she's in now. Where was I? Oh . . . I asked the doctor for God's sake to tell me the truth. He owed it to me for the amount of money I had spent. He faltered. Said I'd been drunk that's all. God! Didn't I know that?

But Doc, you're evading. Tell me honestly what is the matter with me. I'll be all right did you say? But Doc, you've said that before. You said once that if I stopped for a year I would be over the habit and would never drink again. I didn't drink for over a year, but I did start to drink again.

Tell me what is the matter with me. I'm an alcoholic? Ha, ha and ho, ho! As if I didn't know that! But aside from your fancy name for a plain drunk, tell me why I drink. You say a true alcoholic is something different from a plain drunk? What do you mean . . . let me have it cold . . . brief and with no trimmings.

An alcoholic is a person who has an allergy to alcohol? Is poisoned by it? One drink does something to the chemical make-up of the body? That drink does something to the nerves and in a certain number of hours another drink is medically demanded? And so the vicious cycle is started? An ever smaller amount of time between drinks to stop those screaming, twitching, invisible wires called nerves?

I know that history Doc . . . how the spiral tightens . . . a drink . . . unconscious . . . awake . . . drink . . . unconscious . . . poured into the hospital . . . suffer the agonies of hell . . . the shakes . . . thoughts running wild . . . brain unleashed . . . engine without a governor. But hell Doc, I don't want to drink! I've got one of the stubbornest will powers known in business. I stick at things. I get them done. I've stuck on the wagon for months. And not been bothered by it . . . and then suddenly, incomprehensibly, an empty glass in my hand and another spiral started. How did the Doc explain that one?

He couldn't. That was one of the mysteries of true alcoholism. A famous medical foundation had spent a fortune trying to segregate the reasons for the alcoholic as compared to the plain hard, heavy drinker. Had tried to find the cause. And all they had been able to determine as a fact was that the majority of the alcohol in every drink taken by the alcoholic went to the fluid in which the brain floated. Why a man ever started when he knew those things was one of the things that could not be fathomed. Only the damn fool public believed it a matter of weak will power. Fear . . . ostracism . . . loss of family . . . loss of position . . . the gutter . . . nothing stopped the alcoholic.

For Christ's sake, Doc! What do you mean — nothing! What! An incurable disease? Doc, you're kidding me! You're trying to scare me into stopping! What's that you say? You wish to God you were? What are those tears in your eyes Doc? What's that? Forty years you've spent at this alcoholic business and you have yet to see a true alcoholic cured? Your life defeated and wasted? Oh, come, come Doc . . . what would some of us do without you? If even to only sober up. But Doc . . . let's have it. What is going to be my history from here on out? Some vital organ will stop or the mad house with a wet brain? How soon? Within two years? But, Doc, I've got to do something about it! I'll see doctors . . . I'll go to sanitariums. Surely the medical profession knows something about it. So little, you say? But why? Messy. Yes, I'll admit there is nothing messier than an alcoholic drunk.

What's that Doc? You know a couple of fellows that were steady customers here that haven't been drunk for about ten months? You say they claim they are cured? And they make an avocation of passing it on to others? What have they got? You don't know . . . and you don't believe they are cured . . . well why tell me about it? A fine fellow you say, plenty of money, and you're sure it isn't a racket . . . just wants to be helpful . . . call him up for me will you, Doc?

How Doc had hated to tell me. Thoughts stop knocking at my door. Why can't I get drunk like other people, get up next morning, toss my head a couple of times and go to work? Why do I have to shake so I can't hold the razor? Why does every little muscle inside me have to feel like a crawling worm? Why do even my vocal cords quiver so words are gibberish until I've had a big drink? Poison! Of course! But how could anyone understand such a necessity for a drink that it has to be loaded with pepper to keep it from bouncing? Can any mortal understand such secret shame in having to have a drink as to make a person keep the bottles hidden all over the house. The morning drink . . . shame and necessity . . . weakness . . . remorse. But what do the family know about it? What do doctors know about it? Little Doc was right, they know nothing. They just say "Be strong" — "Don't take that drink" — "Suffer it through."

What the hell do they know about suffering? Not sickness. Not a belly ache - oh yes, your guts get so sore that you cannot place your hands on them . . . oh sure, every time you go you twist and writhe in pain. What the hell does any non-alcoholic know about suffering? Thoughts . . . stop this mad merry-go-round. And worst of all this mental suffering — the hating yourself — the feeling of absurd, irrational weakness — the unworthiness. Out that window! Use the gun in the drawer! What about poison? Go out in a garage and start the car. Yeah, that's the way out . . . but then people'll say "He was plastered." Jesus! I can't leave that story behind. That's worse than cowardly.

Isn't there some one who understands? Thoughts . . . please, oh please, stop . . . I'm going nuts . . . or am I nuts now? Never . . . never again will I take another drink, not even a glass of beer . . . even that starts it. Never . . . never . . . never again . . . and yet I've said that a dozen times and inexplicably I've found an empty glass in my hand and the whole story repeated.

My Lord, the tragedy that sprang out of her eyes when I came home with a breath on me . . . and fear. The smiles wiped off the kids' faces. Terror stalking through the house. Yes . . . that changed it from a home into a house. Not drunk yet, but they knew what was coming. Mr. Hyde was moving in.

And so I'm going to die. Or a wet brain. What was it that fellow said who was here this afternoon? Damn fool thought . . . get out of my mind. Now I know I'm going nuts. And science knows nothing about it. And psychiatrists. I've spent plenty with them. Why should they feed on us who are suffering? Thoughts, go away! No . . . I don't want to think about what that fellow said this afternoon.

He's trying . . . idealistic as hell . . . nice fellow, too. Oh, why do I have to suffer with this revolving brain? Why can't I sleep? What was it he said? Oh yes, came in and told about his terrific drunks, his trips up here, this same thing I'm going through. Yes, he's an alcoholic all right. And then he told me he knew he was cured. Told me he was peaceful . . . (I'll never know peace again) . . . that he didn't carry constant fear around with him. Happy because he felt free. But it's screwy. He said so himself. But he did get my confidence when he started to tell what he had gone through. It was so exactly like my case. He knew what this torture is. He raised my hopes so high; he looked as though he had something. I don't know, I guess I was so sold that I expected him to spring some kind of a pill and I asked him desperately what it was.

And he said "God."

And I laughed.

A ball bat across my face would have been no greater shock. I was so high with hope and expectation. How can a man be so heartless? He said that it sounded screwy but it worked, at least it had with him . . . said he was not a religionist . . . in fact didn't go to church much . . . my ears came up at that . . . his unconventionality attracted me . . . said that some approaches to religion were screwy . . . talked about how the simplest truth in the world had been all balled up by complicating it . . . that attracted me . . . oh, for God's sake get out of my mind . . . what a fine religious bird I'd be . . . imagine the glee of the gang at me getting religion . . . phooey . . . thoughts, please slow down . . . why don't they give me something to go to sleep . . . lay down in green pastures . . . the guy's nuts . . . forget him.

And so it's the nut house for me . . . glad mother is dead, she won't have to suffer that . . . if I'm going nuts maybe it'd be better to be crazy the way he is . . . at least the kids wouldn't have the insane father whisper to carry through life . . . life's cruel . . . the puny-minded, curtain hiding gossips . . . didn't you know his father was committed for insanity? What a sly label to hang on those boys . . . damn the gossiping, reputation-shredding, busybodies who put their noses into other people's business.

He'd laid in this same dump . . . suffered . . . gone through hell . . . made up his mind to get well . . . studied alcoholism . . . Jung . . . Blank Medical Foundation . . . asylums . . . Hopkins . . . many said incurable disease . . . impossible . . . nearly all known cures had been through religion . . . revolted him . . . made a study of religion . . . more he studied the more it was bunk to him . . . not understandable . . . self-hypnotism crap . . . and then the thought hit him that people had it all twisted up. They were trying to pour everyone into moulds, put a tag on them, tell them what they had to do and how they had to do it, for the salvation of their own souls. When as a matter of fact people were through worrying about their souls, they wanted action right here and now. A lot of tripe had been built up around the simplest and most beautiful ideas in the world.

And how did he put the idea . . . bunk . . . bunk . . . why in hell am I still thinking about him . . . in hell . . . that's good . . . I am in hell. He said: "I came to the conclusion that there is SOMETHING. I know not what It is, but It is bigger than I. If I will acknowledge It, if I will humble myself, if I will give in and bow in submission to that SOMETHING and then try to lead a life as fully in accord with my idea of good as possible, I will be in tune." And later the word good contracted in his mind to God.

But, mister, I can't see any guy with long white whiskers up there just waiting for me to make a plea . . . and what did he answer . . . said I was trying to complicate it . . . why did I insist on making It human . . . all I had to do was believe in some power greater than myself and knuckle down to It . . . and I said maybe, but tell me mister why are you wasting your time up here? Don't hand me any bunk about it being more blessed to give than to receive . . . asked him what this thing cost and he laughed. He said it wasn't a waste of time . . . in doping it out he had thought of something somebody had said. A person never knew a lesson until he tried to pass it on to someone else. And that he had found out every time he tried to pass this on it became more vivid to him. So if we wanted to get hard boiled about it, he owed me, I didn't owe him. That's a new slant . . . the guy's crazy as a loon . . . get away from him brain . . . picture me going around telling other people how to run their lives . . . if I could only go to sleep . . . that sedative don't seem to take hold.

He could visualize a great fellowship of us . . . quietly, semi-secretly passing this from alcoholic to alcoholic . . . nothing orga-nized . . . not ministers . . . not missionaries . . . what a story . . . thought we'd have to do it to get well . . . some kind of a miracle had happened in his life . . . common sense guy at that . . . his plan does fire the imagination.

Told him it sounded like self hypnotism to me and he said what of it . . . didn't care if it was yogi-ism, self-hypnotism, or anything else . . . four of them were well. But it's so damn hypocritical . . . I get beat every other way and then I turn around and lay it in God's lap . . . damned if I ever would turn to God . . . what a low-down, cowardly, despicable trick that would be . . . don't believe in God anyway . . . just a lot of hooey to keep the masses in subjugation . . . world's worst inquisitions have been practiced in His name . . . and he said . . . do I have to turn into an inquisitionist . . . if I don't knuckle down, I die . . . why the low-down missionary . . . what a bastardly screw to put on a person . . . a witch burner, that's what he is . . . the hell with him and all his damn theories . . . crap . . . witch burner.

Sleep, please come to my door . . . that last was the eight hundred and eighty fifth sheep over the fence . . . guess I'll put in some black ones . . . sheep . . . shepherds . . . wise men . . . what was that story . . . hell there I go back on that same line . . . told him I couldn't understand and I couldn't believe anything I couldn't understand. He said he supposed then that I didn't use electricity. No one actually understood where it came from or what it was. Nuts to him. He's got too many answers. What did he think the nub of the whole thing was? Subjugate self to some power above . . . ask for help . . . mean it . . . try to pass it on. Asked him what he was going to name this? Said it would be fatal to give it any kind of a tag . . . to have any sort of formality.

I'm going nuts . . . tried to get him into an argument about miracles . . . about immaculate conception . . . about stars leading three wise men . . . Jonah and the whale. He wanted to know what difference those things made . . . he didn't even bother his head about them . . . if he did, he would get tight again. So I asked him what he thought about the Bible. Said he read it, and used those things he agreed with and understood. He didn't take the Bible literally as an instruction book, for there was no nonsense you could not make out of it that way. If ministers could only just advise people and not try to tell them what they <u>had</u> to do, he figured religion would be more successful with fellows like us . . . figured most preachers tried to pour people into some mould of their own.

Thought I had him when I asked about the past sins I had committed. Guess I've done everything in the book . . . I supposed I would have to adopt the attitude that all was forgiven . . . here I am pure and clean as the driven snow . . . or else I was to go through life flogging myself mentally . . . bah. But he had the answer for that one too. Said he couldn't call back the hellish things he had done, but he figured life might be a ledger page. If he did a little good here and there, maybe the score would be evened up some day. On the other hand, if he continued as he had been going there would be nothing but debit items on the sheet. Kind of common sense.

This is ridiculous . . . have I lost all power of logic . . . would I fall for all that religious junk . . . let's see if I can't get to thinking straight . . . that's it . . . I'm trying to do too much thinking . . . just calm myself . . . quietly . . . quiet now . . . relax every muscle . . . start at the toes and move up . . . insane . . . wet brain . . . those boys . . . what a mess my life is . . . mistress . . . how I hate her . . . ah . . . I know what's the matter . . . that fellow gave me an emotional upset . . . I'll list every reason I couldn't accept his way of thinking. After laughing at this religious stuff all these years I'd be a hypocrite. That's one. Second, if there was a God, why all this suffering? Wait a minute, he said that was one of the troubles, we tried to give God some form. Make It just a Power that will help. Third, it sounds like the Salvation Army. Told him that and he said he was not going around singing on any street corners. Simply, if he heard of a guy suffering the torments, he told him his story and belief.

There I go thinking again . . . just started to get calmed down . . . sleep . . . boys . . . insane . . . death . . . mistress . . . life all messed up . . . business. Now listen, take hold . . . what am I going to do? NEVER . . . that's final and in caps. Never . . . that's net[†] no discount. Never. . . never . . . and my mind is made up. NEVER am I going to be such a cowardly low down son of a bitch as to acknowledge any God. The two faced, gossiping Babbitts can go around with their sanctimonious Christ mouthings, their miserable worshipping, their Bible quotations, their holier-than-thou attitudes, their nicy-nice Christian, Sunday worshipping, Monday robbing actions, but never will they find me acknowledging God. Let me laugh. . . I'd like to shriek with insane glee . . . my mind's made up . . . insane, there it is again.

- - - - - - - -

Brrr, this floor is cold on my knees . . . why are the tears running like a river down my cheeks . . . God, have mercy on my soul!

* * * * *

---

† This accurately reflects the language of the original.

THE EUROPEAN DRINKER

I was born in Europe, in Alsace to be exact, shortly after it had become German and practically grew up with "good Rhine wine" of song and story. My parents had some vague ideas of making a priest out of me and I attended for some years the Franciscan school at Basle, Switzerland, just across the border, about six miles from my home. But, although I was a good Catholic, the monastic life had little appeal for me.

Very early I became apprenticed to harness-making and acquired considerable knowledge of upholstering. My daily consumption of wine was about a quart, but that was common where I lived. Everybody drank wine. And it is true that there was no great amount of drunkenness. But I can remember, in my teens, that there were a few characters who caused the village heads to nod pityingly and sometimes in anger as they paused to say, "That sot, Henri" and "Ce pauvre Jules", who drank too much. They were undoubtedly the alcoholics of our village.

Military service was compulsory and I did my stretch with the class of my age, goose-stepping in German barracks and taking part in the Boxer Rebellion in China, my first time at any great distance from home. In foreign parts many a soldier who has been abstemious at home learns to use new and potent drinks. So I indulged with my comrades in everything the Far East had to offer. I cannot say, however, that I acquired any craving for hard liquor as a result. When I got back to Germany I settled down to finish my apprenticeship, drinking the wine of the country as usual.

Many friends of my family had emigrated to America, so at 24 I decided that the United States offered me the opportunity I was never likely to find in my native land. I came directly to a growing industrial city in the middle west, where I have lived practically ever since. I was warmly welcomed by friends of my youth who had preceded me. For weeks after my arrival I was feted and entertained in the already large colony of Alsatians in the city, among the Germans in their saloons and clubs. I early decided that the wine of America was very inferior stuff and took up beer instead.

I soon found work at my trade in harness-making. It was still an age of horses. But I discovered that harness and saddle-making in America was different than anything I had known. Every man in the shop was a specialist and instead of having a variety of jobs to do every day I was compelled to sit all day long at a bench doing the same thing endlessly. I found it very monotonous and, wanting a change, I found it when I got work as an upholsterer in a large furniture store.

Fond of singing, I joined a German singing society which had good club headquarters. There I sat in the evenings, enjoying with my friends our memories of the "old country," singing the old songs we all knew, playing simple card games for drinks and consuming great quantities of beer.

At that time I could go into any saloon, have one or two beers, walk out and forget about it. I had no desire whatever to sit down at a table and stay a whole morning or afternoon drinking. Certainly at that time I was one of those who "can take it or leave it alone". There had never been any drunkards in my family. I came of good stock, of men and women who drank wine all their lives as a beverage, and while they occasionally got drunk at special celebrations, they were up and about their business the next day.

Prohibition came. Having regard for the law of the land, I resigned myself to the will of the national legislators and quit drinking altogether, not because I had found it harmful, but because I couldn't get what I was accustomed to drink. You can all remember that in the first few months after the change, a great many men, who had formerly been used to a few beers every day or an occasional drink of whiskey, simply quit all alcoholic drinks. For the great majority of us, however, that condition didn't last. We saw very early that prohibition wasn't going to work. It wasn't very long before home-brewing was an institution and men began to search feverishly for old recipe books on wine-making.

But I hardly tasted anything for two years and started in business for myself, founding a mattress factory which is today an important industrial enterprise in our city. I was doing very well with that and general upholstering work and there was every indication that I would be financially independent by the time I reached middle age. By this time I was married and was paying for a home. Like most immigrants I wanted to be somebody and have something and I was very happy and contented as I felt success crown my efforts. I missed the old social times, of course, but had no definite craving even for beer.

Successful home-brewers among my friends began to invite me to their homes. I decided that if these fellows could make it I would try it myself and so I did. It wasn't very long until I had developed a pretty good brew with uniformity and plenty of authority. I knew the stuff I was making was a lot stronger than I had been used to, but never suspected that steady drinking of it might develop a taste for something even stronger.

It wasn't long before the bootlegger was an established institution in this as in other towns. I was doing well in business and in going around town I was frequently invited to have a drink in a speakeasy. I condoned my domestic brewing and the bootleggers and their business. More and more I formed the habit of doing some of my business in the speakeasy and after a time did not need that as an excuse. The "speaks" usually sold whiskey. Beer was too bulky and it couldn't be kept in a jug under the counter ready to be dumped when John Law would come around. I was now forming an entirely new drinking technique. Before long I had a definite taste for hard liquor, knew nausea and headaches I had never known before, but as in the old days, I suffered them out. Gradually, however, I'd suffer so much that I simply had to have the morning-after drink.

I became what is called a periodical drinker. I was eased out of the business I had founded and was reduced to doing general upholstery in a small shop at the back of my house. My wife upbraided me often and plenty when she saw that my "periodicals" were gradually losing me what business I could get. I began to bring bottles in. I had them hidden away in the house and all over my shop in careful concealment. I had all the usual experiences of the alcoholic for I was certainly one by this time. Sometimes, after sobering up after a bout of several weeks, I would righteously resolve to quit. With a great deal of determination, I would throw out full pints — pour them out and smash the bottles — firmly resolved never to take another drink of the stuff. I was going to straighten up.

In four or five days I would be hunting all over the place, at home and in my workshop for the bottles I had destroyed, cursing myself for being a damned fool. My "periodicals" became more frequent until I reached the point where I wanted to devote all my time to drinking, working as little as possible and then only when the necessity of my family demanded it. As soon as I had satisfied that, what I earned as an upholsterer went for liquor. I would promise to have jobs done and never do them. My customers lost confidence in me to the point where I retained what business I had only because I was a well-trained and reputedly fine craftsman. "Best in the business, when he's sober," my customers would say and I still had a following who would give me work though they deplored my habits because they knew the job would be well done when they eventually got it.

I had always been a good Catholic, possibly not so devoted as I should have been, but fairly regular in my attendance at services. I had never doubted the existence of the Supreme Being but now I began to absent myself from my church where I had formerly been a member of the choir. Unfortunately, I had no desire to consult my priest about my drinking. In fact I was scared to talk to him about it, for I feared the kind of talk he would give me. Unlike many other Catholics who frequently take pledges for definite periods — a year, two years or for good, I never had any desire to "take a pledge" before the priest. And yet, realizing at last that liquor really had me, I wanted to quit. My wife wrote away for advertised cures for the liquor habit and gave them to me in coffee. I even got them myself and tried them. None of the various cures of this kind were any good.

My experiences differ very little from the experiences of other alcoholics but if ever a man was firmly in the grip of a power that could lead only to ruin and disgrace, I was that man.

I had the usual array of friends who tried to stop me in my drinking career. I can hear them yet. Kindly for the most part, yet blind and almost wholly without understanding, they had the approach that every alcoholic knows:

"Can't you be a man?"

"You can cut it out."

"You've got a good wife; you could have the best business
in town. What's the matter with you anyway?"

Every alcoholic has heard those familiar phrases from well-meaning friends. And they were my friends, too. In their way they did what they could, helped me at different times to get on my feet after a particularly bad time, aided me in unraveling my tangled business affairs, suggested this and suggested that. They all wanted to help me. But none of them knew how. Not one of them had the answer I wanted.

My wife got talking to a local merchant one day. He was knows[†] as a deeply religious man. He was undoubtedly a fundamentalist with strong leanings toward evangelistic preaching. He knew me and something of my reputation. My wife asked him to help her if he could. So he came to see me, bringing a friend along. He found me drunk and in bed. This man had never been an alcoholic and his approach to me was the familiar one of the emotional seeker after souls. Well, there I was, lying in an alcoholic stupor with occasional flashes of emotional self-pity, in pretty much the same condition as the drunk who plunges to the sawdust at the appeal of a religious orator.

Good, honest and sincere man, he prayed at my bedside and I promised to go to church with him to hear an evangelist. He didn't wait for me to come to his office, he came after me. I heard the evangelist but was not impressed. The service was entirely foreign to what I had been accustomed to in my religious observance since childhood. I have no doubt of the preacher's sincerity and seek not at all to belittle his work, but I was unaffected. So I got no answer.

[†] This accurately reflects the language of the original.

There are alcoholics who have been without any consciousness of God all their lives; there are some who are actual haters of the idea of a Supreme Being; there are others, like myself, who have never given up a belief in the Almighty, but who have always felt that God is afar off. And that's the way I felt. I had a closer sense of God during the mass at church, a feeling of his presence, but in everyday life He seemed to be at a distance from me and more as a righteous judge, than an all-wise, pitying father to the human race.

Then occurred the event that saved me. An alcoholic came to see me who is a doctor. He didn't talk like a preacher at all. In fact his language was perfectly suited to my understanding. He had no desire to know anything except whether I was definite about my desire to quit drinking. I told him with all the sincerity at my command that I did. Even then he went into no great detail about how he and a crowd of alcoholics with whom he associated had mastered their difficulty. Instead he told me that some of them wanted to talk to me and would be over to see me.

This doctor had imparted his knowledge to just a few other men at that time — not more than four or five — a group that now numbers more than seventy persons. And, because as I have discovered since, it is part of the "treatment" that these men be sent to see and talk with alcoholics who want to quit, he kept them busy. He had already imbued them with his own spirit until they were ready and willing at all times to go where sent, and as a doctor he well knew that this mission and duty would strengthen them as it later helped me. The visits from these men impressed me at once. Where preaching and prayers had touched me very little, I was immediately impressed with desire for further knowledge of these men.

"There must be something to it," I said to myself. "Why would these busy men take the time to come to see me? They understand my problem. Like me, they've tried this remedy and that remedy but never found one. But whatever it is they are using now, it seems to keep them sober."

Certainly I could see they were sober. The third man who came to see me had been one of the greatest business-getters his company had ever employed. From the top of the heap in a few years he had skidded to becoming a shuffling customer, still entering the better barrooms but welcomed by neither mine[†] host nor his patrons. His own business was practically gone, he told me, when he discovered the answer.

"You've been trying man's ways and they always fail," he told me. "You can't win unless you try God's way."

I had never heard of the remedy expressed in just this language. In a few sentences he made God seem personal to me, explained Him as a being who was interested in me, the alcoholic, and that all I needed to do was to be willing to follow His way for me; that as long as I followed it I would be able to overcome my desire for liquor.

Well, there I was, willing to try it, but I didn't know how, except in a vague way. I knew somehow that it meant more than just going to church and living a moral life. If that was all, then I was a little doubtful that it was the answer I was looking for.

He went on talking and told me that he had found the plan has a basis of love and the practice of Christ's injunction, "Love thy neighbor as thyself." Taking that as a foundation, he reasoned that if a man followed that rule he could not be selfish. I could see that. And he further said that God could not accept me as a sincere follower of his Divine Law unless I was ready to be thoroughly honest about it.

[†] This accurately reflects the language of the original.

That was perfectly logical. My church taught that. I had always known that in theory. We talked, too, about personal purity. Every man has his problem of this kind but we didn't discuss it very much. My visitor well knew, that as I tried to follow God's plan I would get to studying these things out for myself.

We talked things over a long time. I saw readily that I couldn't afford to quibble. I already believed in God, had always done so. Was I ready to surrender my will to His, to let Him guide me daily? That's what it came to.

That day I gave my will to God and asked to be directed. But I have never thought of that as something to do and then forget about. I very early came to see that there had to be a continual renewal of that simple deal with God; that I had perpetually to keep the bargain. So I began to pray; to place my problems in God's hands.

For a long time I kept on trying, in a pretty dumb way at first, I know, but very earnestly. I didn't want to be a fake. And I began putting in practice what I was learning every day. It wasn't very long until my doctor friend sent me to tell another alcoholic what my experience had been. This duty together with my weekly meetings with my fellow alcoholics and my daily renewal of the contract I originally made with God have kept me sober when nothing else ever did.

I have been sober for three years now. The first few months were hard. Many things happened: business trials, little worries and feelings of general despondency came near driving me to the bottle, but I made progress. As I go along the new way I seem to get strength daily to be able to resist more easily. And when I get upset, cross-grained and out of tune with my fellowman I know that I am out of tune with God. Searching where I have been at fault, it is not hard to discover and get right again, for I have proven to myself and to many others who know me that God can keep a man sober if he will let Him.

Being a Catholic, it is natural that I should attend my own church which I do regularly. I partake of its sacraments which have a new and deeper meaning to me now. I realize what it is to be in the presence of God right in my own home and I realize it deeply when I am at church. For when a man is truly trying to do God's will, instead of his own, he is very conscious of being in the presence of God always, wherever he may be.

* * * * * *

A FEMINE† VICTORY

To my lot falls the rather doubtful distinction of being the only "lady" alcoholic in our particular section. Perhaps it is because of a desire for a "supporting cast" of my own sex that I am praying for inspiration to tell my story in a manner that may give other women who have this problem the courage to see it in its true light and seek the help that has given me a new lease on life.

When the idea was first presented to me that I was an alcoholic, my mind simply refused to accept it. Horrors! How disgraceful! What humiliation! How preposterous! Why, I loathed the taste of liquor — drinking was simply a means of escape when my sorrows became too great for me to endure. Even after it had been explained to me that alcoholism is a disease, I could not realize that I had it. I was still ashamed, still wanted to hide behind the screen of reasons made up of "unjust treatment", "unhappiness", "tired and dejected", and the dozens of other things that I thought lay at the root of my search for oblivion by means of whiskey or gin.

In any case, I felt quite sure that I was not an alcoholic. However, since I have faced the fact, and it surely is a fact, I have been able to use the help that is so freely given when we learn how to be really truthful with ourselves.

The path by which I have come to this blessed help is long and devious. It has been through the mazes and perplexities of an unhappy marriage and divorce, and a dark time of separation from my grown children, and a readjustment of life at an age when most women feel pretty sure of a home and security.

But I have reached the source of help. I have learned to recognize and acknowledge the underlying cause of my disease: selfishness, self-pity and resentment. A few short months ago those three words applied to me would have aroused as much indignation in my heart as the word alcoholic. The ability to accept them as my own has been derived from trying, with the un-ending help of God, to live with certain goals in mind.

Coming to the grim fact of alcoholism, I wish I could present the awful reality of its insidiousness in such a way that no one could ever again fail to recognize the comfortable, easy steps that lead down to the edge of the precipice, and show how those steps suddenly disappeared when the great gulf yawned before me. You couldn't possibly turn and get back to solid earth again that way.

The first step is called — "The first drink in the morning to pull you out of a hangover."

I remember so well when I got onto that step — I had been drinking just like most of the young married crowd I knew. For a couple of years it went on, at parties and at "speakeasies", as they were then called, and with cocktails after matinees. Just going the rounds, and having a good time.

Then came the morning when I had my first case of jitters. Someone suggested a little of the "hair of the dog that bit me". A half hour after that drink I was sitting on top of the world, thinking how simple it was to cure shaky nerves. How wonderful liquor was, in only a few minutes my head had stopped shaking, my spirits were back to normal and all was well in this very fine world.

Unfortunately, there was a catch to it — I was an alcoholic. As time went on

---

† This accurately reflects the language of the original.

the one drink in the morning had to be taken a little earlier — it had to be followed by a second one in an hour or so, before I really felt equal to getting on with the business of living.

Gradually I found at parties the service was a little slow; the rest of the crowd being pretty happy and carefree after the second round. My re-action was inclined to be just the opposite. Something had to be done about that so I'd just help myself to a fast one, sometimes openly, but as time went on and my need became more acute, I often did it on the quiet.

In the meantime, the morning-after treatment was developing into something quite stupendous. The eye-openers were becoming earlier, bigger, more frequent, and suddenly, it was lunch time! Perhaps there was a plan for the afternoon — a bridge or tea, or just callers. My breath had to be accounted for, so along came such alibis as a touch of grippe or some other ailment for which I'd just taken a hot whiskey and lemon. Or "someone" had been in for lunch and we had just had a couple of cocktails. Then came the period of brazening it out — going to social gatherings well fortified against the jitters; next the phone call in the morning — "Terribly sorry that I can't make it this afternoon, I have an awful headache"; then simply forgetting that there were engagements at all; spending two or three days drinking, sleeping it off, and waking to start all over again.

Of course, I had the well known excuses: my husband was failing to come home for dinner or hadn't been home for several days; he was spending money which was needed to pay bills; he had always been a drinker; I had never known anything about it until I was almost thirty years old and he gave me my first drink. Oh, I had them all down, letter perfect — all the excuses, reasons and justifications. What I did not know was that I was being destroyed by selfishness, self-pity and resentment.

There were the swearing-off periods and the "goings on the wagon" — they would last anywhere from two weeks to three or four months. Once, after a very severe illness of six weeks' duration (caused by drinking), I didn't touch anything of an alcoholic nature for almost a year. I thought I had it licked that time, but all of a sudden things were worse off than ever. For you can't cure this thing through fear!

Next came the hospitalization, not a regular sanitarium, but a local hospital where my doctor would ship me when I'd get where I had to call him in. That poor man — I wish he could read this for he would know then it was no fault of his I wasn't cured. He told me, the last time he took care of me, that I was his only failure!

When I was divorced, I thought the cause had been removed. I felt that being away from what I had considered injustice and ill-treatment would solve the problem of my unhappiness. In a little over a year I was in the alcoholic ward of a public hospital!

It was there that L.... came to me. I had known her very slightly ten years before. My ex-husband brought her to me hoping that she could help. She did. From the hospital I went home with her.

There, her husband told me the secret of his rebirth. It is not really a secret at all, but something free and open to all of us. He asked me if I believed in God or some power greater than myself. Well, I did believe in God, but at that time I hadn't any idea what He is. As a child I had been taught my "Now I lay me's" and "Our Father which art in Heaven". I had been sent to Sunday School and taken to church. I had been baptized and confirmed. I had been taught to realize there is a God and to "love" him. But though I had been taught all these things, I had never learned them.

When B... (L's husband) began to talk about God, I felt pretty low in my mind. I thought God was something that I, and lots of other people like me, had to worry along without. Yet I had always had the "prayer habit". In fact I used to say in my mind "Now, if God answers this prayer, I'll know there is a God." It was a great system, only somehow it didn't seem to work!

Finally B...put it to me this way: "You admit you've made a mess of things trying to run them your way, are you willing to make a decision? Are you willing to say: "Here it is God, all mixed up. I don't know how to un-mix it, I'll leave it to you." Well, I couldn't quite do that. I wasn't feeling very well, and I was afraid I'd make a decision and later when the fog wore off, I'd want to back out. So we let it rest a few days. L and B sent me to stay with some friends of theirs out of town — I'd never seen them before. The man of that house, P.... had made his decision three months before. After I had been there a few days, I saw that P... and his wife had something that made them mighty hopeful and happy. But I got a little uneasy going into a perfect stranger's home and staying day after day. I said this to P... and his reply was: "Why, you don't know how much it is helping me to have you here." Was that a surprise! Always before that when I was recovering from a tailspin I'd been just a pain in the neck to everyone. So, I began to sense in a small way just what these spiritual principles were all about.

Finally I very self-consciously and briefly asked God to show me how to do what He wanted me to do. My prayer was just about as weak and helpless a thing as one could imagine, but it taught me how to open my mouth and pray earnestly and sincerely. However, I had not quite made the grade. I was full of fears, shames, and other "bug-a-boos" and two weeks later an incident occurred that put me on the toboggan again. I seemed to feel that the hurt of that incident was too great to endure without some "release". So I forsook Spirit in favor of "spirits" and that evening I was well on the way to a long session with my old enemy "liquor". I begged the person in whose home I was living not to let anyone know, but she, having good sense, got in touch right away with those who had helped me before and very shortly they had rallied round.

I was eased out of the mess and in a day or two I had a long talk with one of the group. I dragged out all my sins of commission and ommission, I told everything I could think of that might be the cause of creating a fear situation or a remorse situation, or a shame situation. It was pretty terrible, I thought then to lay myself bare that way, but I know now that such is the first step away from the edge of the precipice.

Things went very well for quite a while, then came a dull rainy day. I was alone. The weather and my self-pity began to cook up a nice dish of the blues for me. There was liquor in the house and I found myself suggesting to myself "Just one drink will make me feel so much more cheerful." Well, I got the Bible and "Victorious Living" and sitting down in full view of the bottle of whiskey, I commenced to read. I also prayed. But I didn't say "I must not take that drink because I owe it to so and so not to." I didn't say "I won't take that drink because I'm strong enough to resist temptation." I didn't say "I must not" or "I will not" at all. I simply prayed and read and in half an hour I got up and was absolutely free of the urge for a drink.

It might be very grand to be able to say "Finis" right here, but I see now I hadn't gone all the way I was intended to go. I was still coddling and nursing my my two pets, self-pity and resentment. Naturally, I came a cropper once more. This time I went to the telephone (after I had taken about two drinks) and called L to tell her what I had done. She asked me to promise that I would not take another drink before someone came to me. Well, I had learned enough about truthfulness to refuse to give that promise. Had I been living after the old pattern, I would have been ashamed to call for help. In fact I should not have wanted help. I should have tried to hide the fact that I was drinking and continued until I again wound up behind the "eight ball." I was taken back to B's home where I stayed for three weeks. The drinking ended the morning after I got there, but the suffering continued for some time. I felt desperate and I questioned my ability to really avail myself of the help that the others had received and applied so successfully. Gradually, however, God began to clear my channels so that real understanding began to come. Then was the time when full realization and acknowledgement came to me. It was realization and acknowledgement of the fact that I was full of self-pity and resentment, realization of the fact that I had not fully given my problems to God. I was still trying to do my own fixing.

That was more than a year ago. Since then, although circumstances are no different, for there are still trials and hardships and hurts and disappointments and disillusionments, the two sins of self-pity and resentment are being forgiven and eliminated. In this past year I haven't been tempted once. I have no more idea of taking a drink to aid me through a difficult period than I would if I had never drank. But I know absolutely that the minute I close my channels with sorrow for myself, or being hurt by, or resentful toward anyone, I am in horrible danger.

I know that my victory is none of my human doing. I know that I must keep myself worthy of Divine help. And the glorious thing is this: I am free, I am happy, and perhaps I am going to have the blessed opportunity of "passing it on". I say in all reverence — Amen.

* * * * *

OUR SOUTHERN FRIEND

Two rosy-cheeked children stand at the top of a long hill as the glow of the winter sunset lights up the snow-covered country-side. "Its time to go home" says my sister. She is the eldest. After one more exhilarating trip on the sled, we plod homeward through the deep snow. The light from an oil lamp shines from an upstairs window of our home. We stamp the snow from our boots and rush in to the warmth of the coal stove which is supposed to heat upstairs as well. "Hello dearies", calls Mother from above, "get your wet things off".

"Where's Father?" I ask, having gotten a whiff of sausage cooking through the kitchen door and thinking of supper.

"He went down to the swamp," replies Mother. "He should be home soon."

Father is an Episcopal minister and his work takes him over long drives on bad roads. His parishioners are limited in number, but his friends are many, for to him race, creed, or social position make no difference. It is not long before he drives up in the old buggy. Both he and old Maud are glad to get home. The drive was long and cold but he was thankful for the hot bricks which some thoughtful person had given him for his feet. Soon supper is on the table. Father says grace, which delays my attack on the buckwheat cakes and sausage. What an appetite!

A big setter lies asleep near the stove. He begins to make queer sounds and his feet twitch. What is he after in his dreams? More cakes and sausage. At last I am filled. Father goes to his study to write some letters. Mother plays the piano and we sing. Father finishes his letters and we all join in several exciting games of parchesi. Then Father is persuaded to read aloud some more of "The Rose and the Ring."

Bed-time comes. I climb to my room in the attic. It is cold so there is no delay. I crawl under a pile of blankets and blow out the candle. The wind is rising and howls around the house. But I am safe and warm. I fall into a dreamless sleep.

- - - - -

I am in church. Father is delivering his sermon. A wasp is crawling up the back of the lady in front of me. I wonder if it will reach her neck. Shucks! It has flown away. Ho, hum, maybe the watermelons are ripe in Mr. Jones patch. That's an idea! Benny will know, but Mr. Jones will not know what happened to some of them, if they are. At last! The message has been delivered.

"Let your light so shine before men that they may see your good works-------." I hunt for my nickel to drop in the plate so that mine will be seen.

Father comes forward in the chancel of the church. "The peace of God which passes all understanding, keep your hearts and minds-------." Hurray! Just a hymn and then church will be over until next week!

- - - - -

I am in another fellow's room at college. "Freshman", said he to me, "do you ever take a drink?" I hesitated. Father had never directly spoken to me about drinking and he never drank any, so far as I knew. Mother hated liquor and feared a drunken man. Her brother had been a drinker and had died in a state hospital for the insane. But his life was unmentionable, so far as I was concerned. I had never had a drink but I had seen enough merriment in the boys who were drinking to be interested. I would never be like the village drunkard at home. How a lot of people despised him! Just a weakling!

"Well," said the older boy, "Do you?"

"Once in a while," I lied. I could not let him think I was a sissy.

He poured out two drinks. "Here's looking at you," said he. I gulped it down and choked. I didn't like it, but I would not say so. No, never! A mellow glow stole over me. Say! This wasn't so bad after all. In fact, it was darn good. Sure I'd have another. The glow increased. Other boys came in. My tongue loosened Everyone laughed loudly.[†] I was witty. I had no inferiorities. Why, I wasn't even ashamed of my skinny legs! This was the real thing!

A haze filled the room. The electric light began to move. Then two bulbs appeared. The faces of the other boys grew dim. How sick I felt. I staggered to the bathroom--------------. Shouldn't have drunk so much or so fast. But I knew how to handle it now. I'd drink like a gentleman after this.

And so I met John Barleycorn. The grand fellow who at my call made me "a hale fellow, well met", who gave me such a fine voice, as we sang "Hail, hail, the gangs all here", and "Sweet Adeline", who gave me freedom from fear and feelings of inferiority. Good old John! He was my pal, all right.

- - - - -

Final exams of my senior year and I may somehow graduate. I would never have tried, but Mother counts on it so. A case of measles saved me from being kicked out during my Sophomore year. Bells, bells, bells! Class, library, laboratory! Am I tired!

But the end is in sight. My last exam and an easy one. I gaze at the board with its questions. Can't remember the answer to the first. I'll try the second. No soap there. Say this is getting serious! I don't seem to remember anything. I concentrate on one of the questions. I don't seem to be able to keep my mind on what I am doing. I get uneasy. If I don't get started soon, I won't have time to finish. No use. I can't think.

Oh! An idea! I leave the room, which the honor system allows. I go to my room. I pour out half a tumbler of grain alcohol and fill it with ginger ale. Oh, boy! Now back to the exam. My pen moves rapidly. I know enough of the answers to get by. Good old John Barleycorn! He can certainly be depended on. What a wonderful power he has over the mind! He has given me my diploma!

- - - - -

Underweight! How I hate that word. Three attempts to enlist in the service, and three failures because of being skinny. True, I have recently recovered from pneumonia and have an alibi, but my friends are in the war, or going, and I am not. To hell with it all! I visit a friend who is awaiting orders. The atmosphere of "eat, drink, and be merry" prevails and I absorb it. I drink a lot every night.

[†] This accurately reflects the language of the original.

I can hold a lot now, more than the others.

I am examined for the draft and pass the physical exam. What a dirty deal! Drafted! The shame of it. I am to go to camp on November 13th. The Armistice is signed on the 11th and the draft is called off. Never in the service! The war leaves me with a pair of blankets, a toilet kit, a sweater knit by my sister, and a still greater inferiority.

- - - - -

It is ten oclock of a Saturday night. I am working hard on the books of a subsidiary company of a large corporation. I have had experience in selling, collecting, and accounting, and am on my way up the ladder.

Then the crack-up. Cotton struck the skids and collections went cold. A twenty three million dollar surplus wiped out. Offices closed up and workers discharged. I, and the books of my division have been transferred to the head office. I have no assistance and am working nights, Saturdays and Sundays. My salary has been cut. My wife and new baby are fortunately staying with relatives. What a life! I feel exhausted. The doctor has told me that if I don't give up inside work, I'll have tuberculosis. But what am I to do? I have a family to support and have no time to be looking for another job.

Oh, well. I reach for the bottle which I just got from George, the elevator boy.

- - - - -

I am a traveling salesman. The day is over and business has been not so good. I'll go to bed. I wish I were home with the family and not in this dingy hotel.

Well — well — look who's here! Good old Charlie! It's great to see him. How's the boy? A drink? You bet your life! We buy a gallon of "corn" because it is so cheap. Yet I am fairly steady when I go to bed.

Morning comes. I feel horribly. A little drink will put me on my feet. But it takes others to keep me there.

I see some prospects. I am too miserable to care if they give me an order or not. My breath would knock out a mule, I learn from a friend. Back at the hotel and more to drink. I come to early in the morning. My mind is fairly clear, but inwardly I am undergoing torture. My nerves are screaming in agony. I go to the drug store and it is not open. I wait. Minutes are interminable. Will the store never open? At last! I hurry in. The druggist fixes me up a bromide. I go back to the hotel and lie down. I wait. I am going crazy. The bromides have no effect. I get a doctor. He gives me a hypodermic. Blessed peace!

And I blame this experience on the quality of the liquor.

- - - - -

I am a real estate salesman. "What is the price of that house," I ask the head of the firm I work for. He names me a price. Then he says, "That is what the builders are asking, but we will add on $500.00 and split it, if you can close the deal." The prospect signs the contract for the full amount. My boss buys the property and sells to the prospect. I get my commission and $250.00 extra and everything is Jake. But is it? Something is sour. So let's have a drink!

I become a teacher in a boy's school. I am happy in my work. I like the boys and we have lots of fun, in class and out.

An unhappy mother comes to me about her boy, for she knows I am fond of him. They expected him to get high marks and he has not the ability to do it. So he altered his report card from fear of his father. And his dishonesty has been discovered. Why are there so many foolish parents, and why is there so much unhappiness in these homes?

The doctors bills are heavy and the bank account is low. My wife's parents come to our assistance. I am filled with hurt pride and self-pity. I seem to have no sympathy for my illness and no appreciation of the love behind the gift.

I call the boot-legger and fill up my charred keg. But I do not wait for the charred keg to work. I get drunk. My wife takes the children away for the night. Her father comes to sit with me. He never says an unkind word. He is a real friend but I do not appreciate him.

- - - - -

We are staying with my wife's father. Her mother is in critical condition at a hospital. The wind is moaning in the pine trees. I cannot sleep. I must get myself together. I sneak down stairs and get a bottle of whiskey from the cellaret. I pour drinks down my throat. My father-in-law appears. "Have a drink?" I ask. He makes no reply, and hardly seems to see me. His wife dies that night.

- - - - -

Mother has been dying of cancer for a long time. She is near the end and now in a hospital. I have been drinking a lot for some time, but never get drunk. Mother must never know. I see her about to go.

I return to the hotel where I am staying and get gin from the bell-boy. I drink and go to bed; I take a few the next morning and go see my mother once more. I cannot stand it. I go back to the hotel and get more gin. I drink steadily. I come to at three in the morning. The indescribable torture has me again. I turn on the light. I must get out of the room or I shall jump out of the window. I walk miles. No use. I go to the hospital, where I have made friends with the night superintendent. She puts me to bed and gives me a hypodermic. Oh, wonderful peace!

- - - - -

Mother and Father die the same year. What is life all about anyway? The world is crazy. Read the newspapers. Everything is a racket. Education is a racket. Medicine is a racket. Religion is a racket. How could there be a loving God who would allow so much suffering and sorrow? Bah! Don't talk to me about religion. For what were my children ever born? I wish I were dead!

- - - - -

I am at the hospital to see my wife. We have another child. But she is not glad to see me. I have been drinking while the baby was arriving. Her father stays with her.

- - - - -

My parents estates are settled at last. I have some money. I'll try farming. It will be a good life. I'll farm on a large scale and make a good thing of it. But the deluge descends. Lack of judgment, bad management, a hurricane, and the depression create debts in ever-increasing number. But the stills are operating throughout the country-side.

- - - - -

It is a cold, bleak day in November. I have fought hard to stop drinking. Each battle has ended in defeat. I tell my wife I cannot stop drinking. She begs me to go to a hospital for alcoholics which has been recommended. I say I will go. She makes the arrangements, but I will not go. I'll do it all myself. This time I'm off of it for good. I'll just take a few beers now and then.

- - - - -

It is the last day of October, a dark, rainy morning. I come to in a pile of hay in a barn. I look for liquor and can't find any. I wander to a stable and drink five bottles of beer. I must get some liquor. Suddenly I feel hopeless, unable to go on. I go home. My wife is in the living room. She had looked for me last evening after I left the car and wandered off into the night. She had looked for me this morning. She has reached the end of her rope. There is no use trying any more, for there is nothing to try. "Don't say anything," I say to her. "I am going to do something."

- - - - -

I am in the hospital for alcoholics. I am an alcoholic. The insane asylum lies ahead. Could I have myself locked up at home? One more foolish idea. I might go out West on a ranch where I couldn't get anything to drink. I might do that. Another foolish idea. I wish I were dead, as I have often wished before. I am too yellow to kill myself. But maybe---------. The thought stays in my mind.

- - - - -

Four alcoholics play bridge in a smoke-filled room. Anything to get my mind from myself. The game is over and the other three leave. I start to clean up the debris. One man comes back, closing the door behind him.

He looks at me. "You think you are hopeless, don't you?" he asks.

"I know it", I reply.

"Well, you're not," says the man. "There are men on the streets of New York today who were worse than you, and they don't drink anymore."

"What are you doing here?" I ask.

"I went out of here nine days ago saying that I was going to be honest, and I wasn't." he answers.

A fanatic, I thought to myself, but I was polite. "What is it?" I enquire.

Then he asks me if I believe in a power greater than myself, whether I call that power God, Allah, Confucius, Prime Cause, Divine Mind, or any other name. I tell him that I believe in electricity and other forces of nature, but as for a God, if there is one, he has never done anything for me. Then he asks me if I am willing to right all the wrongs I have ever done to anyone, no matter how wrong I thought they were. Am I willing to be honest with myself about myself and tell someone about myself, and am I willing to think of other people instead of myself and of their needs; to get rid of the drink problem?

"I'll do anything," I reply.

"Then all of your troubles are over" says the man and leaves the room. The man is in bad mental shape certainly. I pick up a book and try to read, but cannot concentrate. I get in bed and turn out the light. But I cannot sleep. Suddenly a thought comes. Can all the worthwhile people I have known be wrong about God? Then I find myself thinking about myself, and a few things that I had wanted to forget. I begin to see I am not the person I had thought myself, that I had judged myself by comparing myself to others, and always to my own advantage. It is a shock.

Then comes a thought that is like A Voice. "Who are you to say there is no God?" It rings in my head, I can't get rid of it.

I get out of bed and go to the man's room. He is reading. "I must ask you a question," I say to the man. "How does prayer fit into this thing?"

"Well," he answers, "you've probably tried praying like I have. When you've been in a jam you've said, 'God, please do this or that' and if it turned out your way that was the last of it and if it didn't you've said 'There isn't any God' or 'He don't do anything for me'. Is that right?"

"Yes" I reply.

"That isn't the way" he continued. "The thing for you to do is to say 'God here I am and here are all my troubles. I've made a mess of things and can't do anything about it. You take me, and all my troubles, and do anything you want with me.' Does that answer your question?"

"Yes, it does" I answer. I return to bed. It didn't make sense. Suddenly I felt a wave of utter hopelessness sweep over me. I was in the bottom of hell. And there a tremendous hope was born. It might be true.

I tumbled out of bed onto my knees. I know not what I said. But slowly a great peace came to me. I felt lifted up. I believed in God. I crawled back into bed and slept like a child.

Some men and women came to visit my friend of the night before. He invites me to meet them. They are a joyous crowd. I have never seen people that joyous before. We talk. I tell them of the Peace, and that I believe in God. They tell me what I must do to live. I think of my wife. I must write her. One girl suggests that I phone her. What a wonderful idea.

My wife hears my voice and knows I have found the answer to life. She comes to New York. I get out of the hospital and we visit some of these new-found friends. What a glorious time we have!

- - - - -

I am home again. I have lost the fellowship. Those that understand me are far away. The same old problems and worries surround me. Members of my family annoy me. Nothing seems to be working out right. I am blue and unhappy. Maybe a drink—I put on my hat and dash off in the car.

Get into the lives of other people, is one thing the fellows in New York had said. I go to see a man I had been asked to visit and tell him my story. I feel much better. Much better! I have forgotten about a drink.

- - - - -

I am on a train, headed for a city. I have left my wife at home, sick, and I have been unkind to her in leaving. I am very unhappy. Maybe a few drinks when I get to the city will help. A great fear seizes me. I talk to the stranger in the seat with me. The fear and the insane idea is taken away.

- - - - -

Things are not going so well at home. I am learning that I cannot have my own way as I used to. I blame my wife and children. Anger possesses me, anger such as I have never felt before. I will not stand for it. I pack my bag and leave. I stay with understanding friends.

I see where I have been wrong in some respects. I do not feel angry any more. I return home and say I am sorry for my wrong. I am quiet again. But I have not seen yet, that I should do some constructive acts of love without expecting any return. I shall learn this after some more explosions.

- - - - -

I am blue again. I want to sell the place and move away. I want to get where I can find some alcoholics to help, and where I can have some fellowship. A man calls me on the phone. Will I take a young fellow who has been drinking for two weeks to live with me? Soon I have others who are alcoholics and some who have other problems.

I begin to play God. I feel that I can fix them all. I do not fix anyone, but I am getting part of a tremendous education and I have made some new friends.

- - - - -

Nothing is right. Finances are in bad shape. I must find a way to make some money. The family think of nothing but spending. People annoy me. I try to read. I try to pray. Gloom surrounds me. Why has God left me? I mope around the house. I will not go out and I will not enter into anything. What is the matter? I cannot understand. I will not be that way.

I'll get drunk! It is a cold-blooded idea. It is premeditated. I fix up a little apartment over the garage with books and drinking water. I am going to town to get some liquor and food. I shall not drink until I get back to the apartment. Then I shall lock myself in and read. And as I read, I shall take little drinks at long intervals. I shall get myself "mellow" and stay that way.

I get in the car and drive off. Halfway down the driveway a thought strikes me. I'll be honest anyway. I'll tell my wife what I am going to do. I back up to the door and go into the house. I call my wife into a room where we can talk privately. I tell her quietly what I intend to do. She says nothing. She does not get excited. She maintains a perfect calm.

When I am through speaking, the whole idea has become absurd. Not a trace of fear is in me. I laugh at the insanity of it. We talk of other things. Strength has come from weakness.

I cannot see the cause of this temptation now. But I am to learn later that it began with the desire for my own material success becoming greater than the interest in the spiritual welfare of my fellow man. I learn more of that foundation stone of character, which is honesty. I learn that when we act upon the highest conception of

honesty which is given us, our sense of honesty becomes more acute.
     I learn that honesty is truth, and the truth shall make us free!

- - - - -

     Sensuality, drunkeness, and worldliness produce harmony within a man for a time, but their power is a decreasing one. God produces harmony in those who receive His Spirit and follow its dictates.
     Today as I become more harmonized within, I become more in tune with all of God's wonderful creation. The singing of the birds, the sighing of the wind, the patter of raindrops, the roll of thunder, the laughter of happy children, add to the symphony with which I am in tune. The heaving ocean, the driving rain, autumn leaves, the stars of heaven, the perfume of flowers, music, a smile, and a host of other things tell me of the glory of God.
     There are periods of darkness, but the stars are shining, no matter how black the night. There are disturbances, but I have learned that if I seek patience and open-mindedness, understanding will come. And with it, direction by the Spirit of God. The dawn comes and with it more understanding, the peace that passes understanding, and the joy of living that is not disturbed by the wildness of circumstances or people around me. Fears, resentments, pride, worldly desires, worry, and self-pity no longer possess me. Ever-increasing are the number of true friends, ever-growing is the capacity for love, ever-widening is the horizon of understanding. And above all else comes a greater thankful-ness to, and a greater love for Our Father in heaven.

A BUSINESS MAN'S RECOVERY

The S. S. "Falcon" of the Red D. Line, bound from New York to Maracaibo, Venezuela, glided up the bay, and docked at the wharf in the port of La Guayra on a hot tropical afternoon early in 1927. I was a passenger on that boat bound for the oil fields of Maracaibo as an employee of the X Oil Company, under a two year contract at a good salary and maintenance. There I hoped to buckle down to two years of hard work, and save some money, but above all to avoid any long, continued drinking that would interfere with my work, because that had cost me too many jobs in the past.

Not that I was going to give up drinking entirely; no, such a step would be too drastic. But down here in the oil fields, with a bunch of hard working, hard drinking good fellows, I, too, would learn how to handle my liquor and not let it get the best of me again. Such an environment would surely do the trick, would surely teach me to drink moderately with the best of them and keep me away from those long, disastrous sprees. I was still young, I could make the grade, and this was my chance to do it. At last I had the real answer, and my troubles were over!

Red and I, who had become bosom shipboard companions on the way down from New York, stood at the rail watching the activity on the dock incident to getting the vessel secured alongside. Red was also on his way to Maracaibo to work for the same company, and we agreed that so long as we were going to be here overnight, we might as well go ashore together and look the town over.

Red was a swell fellow who might take a drink now and then, who might even get drunk once in a while, but he could handle his liquor and did not go to any great excesses. Thousands of other fellows like him, who have been my drinking companions from time to time, were in no way responsible for the way I drank, or what I did, or the way liquor affected me.

So off we went, Red and I, to do the town — and do it we did. After a few drinks we decided there wasn't much else to do in town except to make a round of the cantinas, have a good time, get back to the ship early and get a good night's rest. So what harm would a little drinking do now, I reasoned. Especially with one full day and two nights ahead to get over it.

We visited every cantina along the straggling main street of La Guayra, and feeling high, wide and handsome, Red and I decided to return to the ship. When we rolled down to the dock we found that our ship had been berthed off from the wharf about thirty feet and that it was necessary to take a tender out to her. No such ordinary method would satisfy Red and myself, so we decided to climb the stern hawser hand over hand to get on board. The flip of a coin decided that I would go first; so off I started, hand over hand, up the hawser.

Now even a good experienced sailor, perfectly sober, would never attempt such a foolhardy feat and, as was to be expected, about half way up the hawser I slipped and fell into the bay with a loud splash. I remember nothing more until next morning. The captain of the boat said to me "Young man, it is true that God looks after drunken fools and little children. You probably don't know it, but this bay is infested with man-eating sharks and usually a man overboard is a goner. How close you were to death, you don't realize, but I do."

Yes, I was lucky to be saved! But it wasn't until ten years later, after I had time and time again tempted Fate by going on protracted benders that I was really saved — not until after I had been fired from job after job, tried the patience of my family to the breaking point, alienated what might have been many, many good, lasting friendships, taken my dear wife through more sorrow and heartaches than any one woman should bear in a lifetime; after doctors, hospitals, psychiatrists, rest cures, changes of scenery and all the other paraphernalia that go with the alcoholic's futile attempts to quit drinking. Finally I dimly began to get the realization that during twenty years of continual drinking every expedient I had tried, (and I had tried them all) had failed me. I hated to admit the fact even to myself, that I just couldn't lick booze. I was licked. I was desparate[†]. I was scared.

I was born in 1900, my father was a hardworking man who did the very best he could to support his family of four on a small income. Mother was very good to us, kind, patient, and loving. As soon as we were old enough my mother sent us to Sunday School and it so happened that as I grew older I took quite an active interest in Sunday School, becoming successively a teacher and later Superintendent of a small Sunday School in uptown New York.

When the United States entered the World War in April 1917, I was under age but, like most other youngsters of that period, wanted very much to get into the fray. My parents, of course, would not hear of this but told me to be sensible and wait until I was eighteen. Being young and restless, however, and fired by the military spirit of the times, I ran away from home to join the Army in another city.

There I joined up. I didn't get into any of the actual hostilities at the front, but later, after the Armistice, served with the United States forces occupying the Rhineland, working my way up to a good non-commissioned rank.

While serving abroad I started to drink. This, of course, was entirely my own choice. Drinking by a soldier during those times was viewed with a degree of indulgence by both superiors and civilians. It seems to me, as I recall it now, that even then I wasn't satisfied to drink like the normal fellow.

Most of the United States Army of Occupation were sent back home in 1921 but my appetite for travel had been whetted, and having heard terrible stories of Prohibition in the United States, I wanted to remain in Europe where "a man could raise a thirst."

Subsequently I went to Russia, then to England, and back to Germany; working in various capacities, my drinking increasing and my drunken escapades getting worse. So back home in 1924 with the sincere desire to stop drinking and the hope that the Prohibition I had heard so much about would enable me to do it — in other words — that it would keep me away from it.

I secured a good position, but it wasn't long before I was initiated into the mysteries of the speakeasy to such an extent that I soon found myself once more jobless. After looking around for some time, I found that my foreign experience would help me in securing work in South America. So, full of hope once more, resolved that at last I was on the wagon to stay, I sailed for the tropics. A little over a year was all the company I then worked for would stand of my continual drinking and ever-lengthening benders. So they had me poured on a boat and shipped back to New York.

This time I was really through. I promised my family and friends, who helped

---

[†] This accurately reflects the language of the original.

me get along while looking for another job, that I would never take another drink as long as I lived — and I meant it. But alas!

After several successive jobs in and around New York had been lost, and it isn't necessary to tell you the cause, I was sure that the only thing that would enable me to get off the stuff was a change of scenery. With the help of patient, long-suffering friends, I finally persuaded an oil company that I could do a good job for them in the oil fields of Maracaibo.

But it was the same thing all over again!

Back to the United States again. I really sobered up for a while — long enough to establish a connection with my present employers. During this time I met the girl who is now my wife. At last here was the real thing — I was in love. I would do anything for her. Yes, I would give up drinking. I would never, never do anything to even remotely affect the happiness that now came into my life. My worries were over, my problem was solved. I had sown my wild oats and now I was going to settle down to be a good husband and live a normal happy life.

And so we were married.

Supported by my new found happiness, my abstinence this time lasted about six months. Then a New Year's party we gave started me off on a long bender. The thing about this episode that is impressed on my mind is how earnestly and sincerely I then promised my wife that I would absolutely and positively this time give up drinking — and again I meant it.

No matter what we tried, and my wife helped me in each new experiment to the best of her ability and understanding, failure was always the result, and each time greater hopelessness.

The next step was doctors, a succession of them, with occasional hospitalization. I remember one doctor who thought a course of seventy-two injections, three a week, after two weeks in a private hospital, would supply the deficiency in my system that would enable me to stop drinking. The night after the seventy-second injection I was paralyzed drunk and a couple of days later talked myself out of being committed to the City Hospital.

My long-suffering employers had a long talk with me and told me that they were only willing to give me one last final chance because during my short periods of sobriety I had shown them that I could do good work. I knew they meant it and that it was the last chance they would ever give me.

I also knew that my wife couldn't stand it much longer.

Somehow or other I felt that I had been cheated — that I had not really been cured at the Sanitarium even though I felt good physically. So I talked it over with my wife who said there must be something somewhere that would help me. She persuaded me to go back to the Sanitarium and consult Dr.---, which thank God I did.

He told me everything had been done for me that was medically possible but that unless I made a decision I was licked. "But doctor," I said, "I have decided time and time again to quit drinking and I was sincere each time, but each time I slipped again and each time it got worse." The doctor smiled and said, "Yes, yes, I've heard that story hundreds of times. You really never made a decision, you just declarations.[†] You've got to make a decision and if you really want to quit drinking I know of some fellows who can help you. Would you like to meet them?"

[†] This accurately reflects the language of the original.

Would a condemned man like a reprieve? Of course I wanted to meet them. I was so scared and so desperate that I was willing to try anything. Thus it was that I met that band of life-savers, Alcoholics Anonymous.

The first thing Bill told me was that I was a hopeless alcoholic and that nothing that I could do for myself would help me to be otherwise — that the only possible way, providing I really wanted to quit, was to let a Greater Power do it for me.

He told me his own story, which paralleled mine in most respects, and then said that for three years he had had no trouble. It was plain to see that he was a supremely happy man — that he possessed a happiness and peacefulness I had for years envied in men.

What he told me made sense because I knew that everything that I, my wife, my family and my friends had tried had failed. I had always believed in God even though I was not a devout church-goer. Many times in my life I had prayed for the things I wanted God to do for me, but it had never occurred to me that He, in His Infinite Wisdom knew much better than I what I should have, and be, and do, and that if I simply turned the decision over to Him, I would be led along the right path.

At the conclusion of our first interview, Bill suggested that I think it over and come back to see him within a few days if I was interested. Fully realizing the utter futility with which my own efforts had met in the past, and somehow or other sensing that delay might be dangerous, I was back to see him the next day.

At first it seemed a wild, crazy idea to me, but because of the fact that everything else I had tried had failed, because everything seemed so hopeless, and because it worked with these fellows who all had been through the same hell that I had been through, I was willing, at least, to have a try.

To my utter astonishment, when I did give their method a fair trial, it not only worked, but was so amazingly easy and simple that I said to them "Where have you been all my life?"

That was in February, 1937, and life took on an entirely different meaning. It was plain to see that my wife was radiantly happy. All of the differences that we seemed to have been having, all of the tenseness, the worry, confusion, the hectic days and nights that my drinking had poured into our life together, vanished. There was peace. There was real love. There was kindness and consideration. There was everything that goes into the fabric of a happy normal existence together.

My employers, of course, as the writers of these stories, must remain anonymous. But I would be very thoughtless if I did not take this opportunity to acknowledge what they did for me. They kept me on, giving me chance after chance, hoping I suppose, that some day I would find the answer, although they themselves did not know what it might be. They do now, however.

A tremendous change took place in my work, in my relationship with my employers, in my association with my co-workers and in my dealings with our customers. Crazy as the idea seemed when broached to me by these men who had found it worked, God did come right into my work when permitted, as He had come into the other activities connected with my life.

With this sort of lubricant the wheels turned so much more smoothly that it seemed as if the whole machine operated on a much better basis than heretofore. Promotion that I had longed for previously, but hadn't deserved, was given to me. Soon another followed; more confidence, more trust, more responsibility and finally a key executive position in that same organization which so charitably kept me on in a minor position through the period of my drunkenness.

You can't laugh that off. Come into my home and see what a happy one it is. Look into my office, it is a happy human beehive of activity. Look into any phase of my life and you will see joy and happiness, a sense of usefulness in the scheme of things, where formerly there was fear, sorrow and utter futility.

* * * * *

A DIFFERENT SLANT

I probably have one of the shortest stories in this whole volume and it is short because there is one point I wish to get over to an occasional man who may be in my position.

Partner in one of this country's nationally known concerns, happily married with fine children, sufficient income to indulge my whims and future security from the financial standpoint should paint a picture in which there would be no possibility of a man becoming an alcoholic from the psychological standpoint. I had nothing to escape from and I am known as a conservative, sound business man.

I had missed going to my office several times while I tapered off and brought myself to sobriety. This time, though, I found I could not taper off, I could not stop and I had to be hospitalized. That was the greatest shock I ever had to my pride. Such a blow that I made the firm resolve to never again taste as much as one glass of beer. Careful thought and analysis went into that decision.

The doctor at this hospital told me vaguely of the work of a group of men who called themselves Alcoholics Anonymous and asked if I wanted one of them to call upon me. I knew I needed no outside help, but in order to be polite to the doctor and hoping he would forget it, I assented.

I was embarrassed when a chap called at my house one evening and told me about himself. He quickly sensed my slight resentment and made it plain to me that none of the crowd were missionaries, nor did they feel it their duty to try to help anyone who did not want help. I think I closed the talk by saying I was glad I was not an alcoholic and sorry he had been bothered by me.

Within sixty days after leaving the hospital the second time, I was pounding at his door, willing to do anything to conquer the vicious thing that had conquered me.

The point I hope I have made is — Even a man with everything from the material standpoint, a man with tremendous pride and the will power to function in all ordinary circumstances can become an alcoholic and find himself as hopeless and helpless as the man who has a multitude of worries and troubles.

* * * * *

TRAVELER, EDITOR, SCHOLAR

The annual post-game banquet was winding up. The last rolling "R" of the speaker's hearty Caledonian accent died away sonorously. The company of students and alumni, all Scots, began to adjourn to the spacious bar for stronger stuff than the comparatively innocuous wines on the tables. A goal-scorer in a soccer game between my school and its centuries-old rival, I rated some popularity and the admiration of the moment expressed in famous ales and whiskey and soda. I was the son of a clergyman and just past sixteen years of age.

Waking in my hotel room the next day, I groaned. I didn't want to see or talk to anyone. Then someone raised my head and put a glass to my lips. "What you need is 'a hair of the dog that bit you', get this into you."

The smell of the stuff sickened me. I grimaced, gulped the draught down and fell back on the bed. Somehow it stayed down and in about fifteen minutes I began to feel better and, managed to eat a fair breakfast. That was my first experience of the "morning after" drink.

Back to college and my apprenticeship to a well-known lawyer, the students in their various clubs and societies, tippled enormously. I gave up the law but stayed in school to graduate. Through these college years in a city of well over a million inhabitants I learned all the better barrooms. Burns and Byron and other colorful profligates were the literary idols in the gang of "bloods" with whom I was a popular figure. I thought I was a gay dog and this was the life.

With nothing but a liberal arts education, very definitely estranged from my family and already married, soon after graduation I became a bookmaker's clerk on the British racing circuits, far better off financially than the average professional man. I moved in a gay crowd in the various "pubs" and sporting clubs. My wife traveled with me, but with a baby coming I decided to settle in a large city where I got a job with a commission agent which is a polite term for a hand-book operator. My job was to collect bets and betting-slips in the business section, a lucrative spot. My boss, in his way, was "big business". Drinking was all in the day's work.

One evening, the book, after checking up, was very definitely in the red for plenty through a piece of studied carelessness on my part, and my boss, very shrewd and able, fired me with a parting statement to the effect that once was enough. With a good stake I sailed for New York. I knew I was through among the English "bookies."

Tom Sharkey's brawling bar on 14th Street and the famous wine-room at the back were headquarters for me. I soon ran through my stake. Some college friends got me jobs when I finally had to go to work, but I didn't stick to them. I wanted to travel. Making my way to Pittsburgh, I met other former friends and got a job in a large factory where pieceworkers were making good money. My fellow-workers were mostly good Saturday night drinkers and I was right with them. Young and able to travel with the best of them, I managed to hold my job and keep my end up in the barrooms.

One of my keenest memories is of meeting Jack London who came in unannounced one night to our favorite saloon, made a rousing speech, and later set up the drinks all evening.

I quit the factory and got a job on a small newspaper, going from that to a Pittsburgh daily, long ago defunct. Following a big drunk on that sheet where I was doing leg-work and rewrite, a feeling of nostalgia made me buy a ticket for Liverpool and I returned to Britain.

During my visit there, renewing acquaintance with former friends I soon spent most of my money. I wanted to roam again and through relatives got a supercargo job on an Australian packet which allowed me to visit my people in Australia where I was born. But I didn't stay long. I was soon back in Liverpool. Coming out of a pub near the Cunard pier I saw the Lusitania standing out in the middle of the Mersey. She had just come in and was scheduled to sail in two days. In my mind's eye I saw Broadway again and Tom Sharkey's bar; the roar of the subway was in my ears. Saying goodbye to my wife and baby, I was treading Manhattan's streets in a little more than a week. Again I spent my bankroll, by no means as thick as the one I had when I first saw the skyline of Gotham. I was soon broke, this time without trainfare to go anywhere. I got my first introduction to "riding the rods and making a blind."

In my early twenties the hardships of hobo life did not discourage me but I had no wish to become just a tramp. Forced to detrain from an empty gondola on the other side of Chicago by a terrific rainstorm which drenched me to the skin, I hit the first factory building I saw for a job. That job began a series of brief working spells, each one ending in a "drunk" and the urge to travel. My migrations extended for over a year as far west as Omaha. Drifting back to Ohio, I landed on a small newspaper and later was impressed into the direction of boy-welfare work at the local "Y". I stayed sober for four years except for a one-night carousel in Chicago. I stayed so sober that I used to keep a quart of medicinal whiskey in my bureau which I used to taper off the occasional newspaper alcoholics who were sent to see me.

Lots of times, vain-gloriously, I used to take the bottle out, look at it and say, "I've got you licked."

The war was getting along. Curiour[†] about it, feeling I was missing something, absolutely without any illusions about the aftermath, with no pronounced feeling of patriotism, I joined up in a Canadian regiment, serving a little over two years. Slight casualties, complicated however by a long and serious illness, were my only mishaps. Remarkably enough, I was a very abstemious soldier. My four years of abstinence had something to do with it, but soldiering is a tough enough game for a sober man, and I had no yen for full-pack slogging through mud with a cognac or vin rouge hangover.

Discharged in 1919, I really made up for my dry spell. Quebec, Toronto, Buffalo, and finally Pittsburgh, were the scenes of man-sized drunks until I had gone through my readjusted discharge pay, a fair sum.

I again became a reporter on a Pittsburgh daily. I applied for a publicity job and got it. My wife came over from Scotland and we started housekeeping in a large Ohio city.

The new job lasted five years. Every encouragement was given me with frequent salary increases, but the sober times between "periods" became shorter. I myself could see deterioration in my work, from being physically and mentally affected by liquor, although I had not yet reached the point where all I wanted was more to drink. Successive Monday morning hangovers, which despite mid-week resolutions to do better, came with unfailing regularity, eventually causing me to quit my job. Washington D. C. and news-gathering agency work followed with many parties. I

† This accurately reflects the language of the original.

couldn't stand the pace. My drinking was never the spaced doses of the careful tippler; it was always gluttonous.

Returning to the town I had left three months before, I became editor of a monthly magazine, soon had additional publicity and advertising accounts and the money rolled in. The strain of overwork soon led me to the bottle again. My wife made several attempts to get me to stop and I had the usual visits from persons who would always ask me "Why?" — as if I knew! Offered the job of advertising manager for an eastern automotive Company, I moved to Philadelphia to begin life anew. In three months John Barleycorn had me kicked out.

I did six years of newspaper, advertising and trade journal work with many, many drunks of drab and dreary hue woven into the pattern of my life. I visited my family just once in that time. An old avocation, the collection of first editions, rare books and Americana, fascinated me between times. I had some financial success through no ability of my own, and, when jobless and almost wiped out in 1930, I began to trade and sell my collection and much of the proceeds went to keep my apartment stocked with liquor and almost every night saw me helpless to bed.

I tried to help myself. I even began to go the rounds of the churches. I listened to famous ministers — found nothing. I began to know the inside of jails and workhouses. My family would have nothing to do with me, in fact couldn't, because I couldn't spare any of my money which I needed for drink to support them. My last venture, a book shop, was hastened to closed doors by my steady intoxication. Then I had an idea.

Loading a car with good old books to sell to collectors, librarians, universities and historical societies, I started out to travel the country. I stayed sober during the trip except for an occasional bottle of beer because funds barely met expenses. When I hit Houston, Texas, I found employment in a large bookstore. Need I say here that in a very short time I was walking along a prairie highway with arm extended and thumb pointed? In the two succeeding years I held ten different jobs ranging from newspaper copy-desk and rewrite, to traffic director for an oil field equipment company. Always in between there were intervals of being broke, riding freights and hitch-hiking interminable distances from one big town to another in three states. Now on a new job I was always thinking about payday and how much liquor I could buy and the pleasure I could have.

I knew I was a drunkard. Enduring all the hangover-hells that every alcoholic experiences, I made the usual resolutions. My thoughts sometimes turned to the idea that there must be a remedy. I have stood listening to street-corner preachers tell how they did beat the game. They seemed to be happy in their fashion, they and the little group of supporters, but always pride of intellect stopped me from seeking what they evidently had. Sniffing at emotional religion I walked away. I was an honest agnostic but definitely not a hater of the church or its adherents. What philosophy I had was thoroughly paganistic — all my life was devoted to a search for pleasure. I wanted to do nothing except what it pleased me to do and when I wanted to do it.

Federal Theatre in Texas gave me an administrative job which I held for a year, only because I worked hard and productively when I worked, and because my very tolerant chief ascribed my frequent lapses to a bohemian temperament. When it was closed through Washington edict I began with Federal Writers in San Antonio. In those days my system was always to drink up my last pay check and believe that necessity would bring the next job. A friend who knew I would soon be broke mounted guard over me when I left my job of writing the histories of Texas cities and put me aboard a bus for the town I had left almost five years before.

In five years a good many persons had forgotten that I had been somewhat notorious. I had arrived drunk but promised my wife I would keep sober, and I knew I could get work if I did. Of course, I didn't keep sober. My wife and family stood by me for ten weeks and then, quite justifiably, ejected me. I managed to maintain myself with odd jobs, did ten weeks in a social rescue institution and at length wound up in a second-hand bookstore in an adjacent town as manager. While there I was called to the hospital in my home town to see a former partner who had insisted that I visit him. I found my friend was there for alcoholism and now he was insisting that he had found the only cure. I listened to him, rather tolerantly. I noticed a Bible on his table and it amazed me. I had never known him to be anything but a good healthy pagan with a propensity for getting into liquor jams and scrapes. As he talked I gathered vaguely, (because he was a faltering beginner then just as I am now) that to be relieved of alcoholism I would have to be different.

Some days later, after he had been discharged, a stranger came into my shop in the nearby town. He introduced himself and began to tell me about a group of some 60 former drinkers and drunkards who met once a week, and he invited me to go with him to the next meeting. I thanked him, pleaded business engagements and promised I'd go with him at some future date.

"Anyhow, I'm on the wagon now," I said. "I'm doing a job I like and it's quiet where I live, practically no temptations. I don't feel bothered about liquor."

He looked at me quizzically. He knew too well that didn't mean a thing just as I knew in my heart that it would be only a question of time — a few days, a week, or even a month, it was inevitable — till I would be off on another bender. The time came just a week later. And as I look back on the events of two months, I can clearly see that I had been circling around, half-afraid of encountering the remedy for my situation, half-wanting it, deferring fulfillment of my promise to get in touch with the doctor I had heard about. An accident while drunk laid me low for about three weeks. As soon as I could get up and walk I started to drink again and kept it up until my friend of the hospital, who, in his first try at the new way of life had stubbed his toe in Chicago but had come back to the town to take counsel and make a new start, picked me up and got me into a hospital.

I had been drinking heavily from one state of semi-coma to another and it was several days before I got "defogged" but subconsciously I was in earnest about wanting to quit liquor forever. It was no momentary emotionalism born of self-pity in a maudlin condition. I was seeking something and I was ready to learn. I did not need to be told that my efforts were and would be unavailing if I did not get help. The doctor who came to see me almost at once did not assail me with any new doctrines; he made sure that I had a need and that I wanted to have that need filled and little by little I learned how my need could be met. The story of Alcoholics Anonymous fascinated me. Singly and in groups of two or three, they came to visit me. Some of them I had known for years, good two-fisted drinkers who had disappeared from their former haunts. I had missed them myself from the barrooms of the town.

There were business and professional men, factory workers. All sorts were represented and their relation of experiences and how they had found the only remedy, added to their human existence as sober men, laid the foundation of a very necessary faith. Indeed, I was beginning to see that I would require implicit faith, like a small child, if I was going to get anywhere or so it appeared as I lay in that hospital. The big thing was that these men were all sober and evidently had something I didn't have. Whatever it was, I wanted it.

I left the hospital on a meeting night. I was greeted warmly, honestly and with a true ring of sincerity by everyone present. That night I was taken home by a former alcoholic and his wife. They did not show me to my room and wish me a good night's rest. Instead, over coffee cups, this man and his wife told me what had been done for them. They were earnest and obviously trying to help me on the road I had chosen. They will never know how much their talk with me has helped. The hospitality of their home and their fine fellowship were mine freely.

I had never, since the believing days of childhood, been able to conceive an authority directing the universe. But I had never been a flippant, wise-cracking sneerer at the few persons I had met who had impressed me as Christian men and women, or at any institutions whose sincerity of purpose I could see. No conviction was necessary to establish my status as a miserable failure at managing my own life. I began to read the Bible daily and to go over a simple devotional exercise as a way to begin each day. Gradually I began to understand.

I cannot say that my taste for liquor has entirely disappeared. It has been that way with some, but it has not been with me and may never be. Neither can I honestly say that I have forgotten the "fleshpots of Egypt." I haven't. But I also can remember the urge of the Prodigal Son to return to his Father that he might taste of the husks that the swine did eat.

Formerly in the acute mental and physical pain during the remorse-ful periods succeeding each drunk, I found my recollection of the misery I had gone through a bolsterer of resolution and afterward, perhaps, a deterrent for a time. But in those days I had no one to whom I might take my troubles. Today I have. Today I have someone who will always hear me; I have a warm fellowship among men who understand my problems; I have tasks to do and am glad to do them, to see others who are alcoholics and to help them in any way I can to become sober men.

* * * * *

THE BACK-SLIDER

When I was graduated from high-school the World War was on in full blast. I was too young for the army but old enough to man a machine for the production of the means of wholesale destruction. I became a machine-hand at high wages. Machinery appealed to me anyway, because I had always wanted to be a mechanical engineer. Keen to learn as many different operations as possible, I insisted on being transferred from one operation to another until I had a good practical knowledge of all machines in a standard machine shop. With that equipment I was ready to travel for broader experience and in seven years had worked in the leading industrial centers in the eastern states, supplementing my shop work with night classes in marine engineering.

I had the good times of the period but confined my drinking to weekends, with an occasional party after work in the evenings. But I was unsettled and dissatisfied, and in a sense disgusted with going from job to job and achieving nothing more than a weekly pay envelope. I wasn't particularly interested in making a lot of money, but I wanted to be comfortable and independent as soon as possible.

So I married at that time, and for a while it seemed that I had found the solution to my urge for moving around. Most people settle down when they marry and I thought I'd have the same experience, that my wife and I would chose a place where we could establish a home and bring up a family. I had the dream of wearing carpet slippers in a life of comparative ease by the time I was forty. It didn't work out that way. After the newness of being married had worn off a little the old wander business got me again.

In 1924 I brought my wife to a growing city in the middle west where work was always plentiful. I had been in and out of it several times before and I could always get a job in the engineering department of its largest industrial plant. I early acquired the spirit of the organization which had a real reputation for constructive education of its workers. It encouraged ambition and aided latent talent to develop. I was keen about my work and strove always to place myself in line for promotion. I had a thorough knowledge of the mechanical needs of the plant and when I was offered a job in the purchasing department's mechanical section I took it.

We were now resident in sort of a workers' paradise, a beautifully landscaped district where employees were encouraged to buy homes from the company. We had a boy about two years after I started with the company and with his advent I began to take marriage seriously. My boy was going to have the best I could give him. He would never have to work through the years as I had done. We had a very nice circle of acquaintance where we lived, nice neighbors and my colleagues in the engineering department and later in purchasing were good people, many of them bent on getting ahead and enjoying the good things of life while they climbed. We had nice parties with very little drinking, just enough to give a little Saturday night glow to things — never enough to get beyond control.

Fateful and fatal came the month of October in the year 1929. Work slowed down. Reassuring statements from financial leaders maintained our confidence that industry would soon be on an even keel again. But the boat kept rocking. In our organization, as in many others, the purchasing department found its work lessened by executive order. Personnel was cut down. Those who were left went around working furiously at whatever there was to do, looking furtively at each other wondering who would be next to go. I wondered if the long hours of overtime with no pay would be recognized in the cutting down program. I lay awake lots of nights just like any other man who sees what he has built up threatened with destruction.

I was laid off. I took it hard for I had been doing a good job and I thought as a man often will, that it might have been somebody else who should get the axe. Yet there was a sense of relief. It had happened. And partly through resentment and partly from a sense of freedom I went out and got pretty well intoxicated. I stayed drunk for three days, something very unusual for me, who had very seldom lost a day's work from drinking.

My experience soon helped me to a fairly important job in the engineering department of another company. My work took me out of town quite a bit, never at any great distance from home, but frequently overnight. Sometimes I wouldn't have to report at the office for a week, but I was always in touch by phone. In a way I was practically my own boss and being away from office discipline I was an easy victim to temptation. And temptation certainly existed. I had a wide acquaintance among the vendors to our company who liked me and were very friendly. At first I turned down the countless offers I had to take a drink, but it wasn't long before I was taking plenty.

I'd get back into town after a trip, pretty well organized from my day's imbibing. It was only a step from this daily drinking to successive bouts with absence from my route. I would phone and my chief couldn't tell from my voice whether I had been drinking or not, but gradually learned of my escapades and warned me of the consequences to myself and my job. Finally when my lapses impaired my efficiency and some pressure was brought to bear on the chief, he let me go. That was in 1932.

I found myself exactly back where I had started when I came to town. I was still a good mechanic and could always get a job as an hourly rated machine operator. This seemed to be the only thing which offered and once more I discarded the white collar for the overalls and canvas gloves. I had spent more than half a dozen good years and had got exactly nowhere, so I did my first really serious drinking. I was good for at least ten days or two weeks off every two months I worked, getting drunk and then half-heartedly sobering up. This went on for almost three years. My wife did the best she could to help me at first, but eventually lost patience and gave up trying to do anything with me at all. I was thrown into one hospital after another, got sobered up, discharged and ready for another bout. What money I had saved dwindled and I turned everything I had into cash to keep on drinking.

In one hospital, a Catholic Institution, one of the sisters had talked religion to me and had brought a Priest in to see me. Both were sorry for me and assured me that I would find relief in Mother Church. I wanted none of it. "If I couldn't stop drinking of my own free will, I was certainly not going to drag God into it," I thought.

During another hospital stay a minister whom I liked and respected came to see me. To me, he was just another non-alcoholic who was unable, even by the added benefit and authority of the cloth, to do anything for an alcoholic.

I sat down one day to figure things out. I was no good to myself, my wife, or my growing boy. My drinking had even affected him; he was a nervous, irritable child, getting along badly at school, making poor grades because the father he knew was a sot and an unpredictable one. My insurance was sufficient to take care of my wife and child for a fresh start by themselves and I decided that I'd simply move out of the world for good. I took a killing dose of bichloride of mercury.

They rushed me to the hospital. The emergency physicians applied the immediate remedies but shook their heads. There wasn't a chance, they said. And for days it was touch and go. One day the chief resident physician came in on his daily rounds. He had often seen me there before for alcoholism.

Standing at my bedside he showed more than professional interest, tried to buoy me up with the desire to live. He asked me if I would really like to quit drinking and have another try at living. One clings to life no matter how miserable. I told him I would and that I would try again. He said he was going to send another doctor to see me, to help me.

This doctor came and sat beside my bed. He tried to cheer me up about my future, pointed out I was still a young man with the world to lick and insisted that I could do it if I really wanted to stop drinking. Without telling me what it was, he said he had an answer to my problem and condition that really worked. Then he told me very simply the story of his own life, a life of generous tippling after professional hours for more than three decades until he had lost almost everything a man can lose, and how he had found and applied the remedy with complete success. He felt sure I could do the same. Day after day he called on me in the hospital and spent hours talking to me and gradually leading me to make an important decision.

He simply asked me to make a practical application of beliefs I already held theoretically but had forgotten all my life. I believed in a God who ruled the universe. The doctor submitted to me the idea of God as a father who would not willingly let any of his children perish and suggested that most, if not all of our troubles, come from being completely out of touch with the idea of God, with God Himself. All my life, he said, I had been doing things of my own human will as opposed to God's will and that the only certain way for me to stop drinking was to submit my will to God and let him handle my difficulties.

I had never looked on my situation in that way, had always felt myself very remote indeed from a Supreme Being. "Doc", as I shall call him hereinafter, was pretty positive that God's law was the Law of Love and that all my resentful feelings which I had fed and cultivated with liquor were the result of either conscious or unconscious, it didn't matter which, disobedience to that law. Was I willing to submit my will? I said I would try to do so. While I was still at the hospital his visits were supplemented by visits from a young fellow who had been a heavy drinker for years but had run into "Doc" and had tried his remedy.

At that time, the group of ex-alcoholics in this town, which has now grown to considerable proportions, numbered only Doc and two other fellows. To help themselves and compare notes they met once a week in a private house and talked things over. As soon as I came from the hospital I went with them. The meeting was without formality. Taking love as the basic command I discovered that my faithful attempt to practice a law of love led me to clear myself of certain dishonesties.

I went back to my job. New men came and we were glad to visit them. I found that new friends helped me to keep straight and the sight of every new alcoholic in the hospital was a real object lesson to me. I could see in them myself as I had been, something I had never been able to picture before.

Now I come to the hard part of my story. It would be great to say I progressed to a point of splendid fulfillment, but it wouldn't be true. My later experience points a moral derived from a hard and bitter lesson. I went along peacefully for two years after God had helped me quit drinking. And then something happened. I was enjoying the friendship of my ex-alcoholic fellows and getting along quite well in my work and in my small social circle. I had largely won back the respect of my former friends and the confidence of my employer. I was feeling fine — too fine. Gradually I began to take the plan I was trying to follow apart. After all, I asked myself, did I really have to follow any plan at all to stay sober? Here I was, dry for two years and getting along all right. It wouldn't hurt if I just carried on and missed a meeting or two. If not present in the flesh I'd be there in spirit, I said in excuse, for I felt a little bit guilty about staying away.

And I began to neglect my daily communication with God. Nothing happened — not immediately at any rate. Then came the thought that I could stand on my own feet now. When that thought came to mind — that God might have been all very well for the early days or months of my sobriety but I didn't need him now — I was a gone coon. I got clear away from the new life I had been attempting to lead. I was in real danger. It was just a step from that kind of thinking to the idea that my two years training in total abstinence was just what I needed to be able to handle a glass of beer. I began to taste. I became fatalistic about things and soon was drinking deliberately knowing I'd get drunk, stay drunk, and what would inevitably happen.

My friends of the group came to my aid. They tried to help me, but I didn't want help. I was ashamed and preferred not to see them come around. And they knew that so long as I didn't want to quit, as long as I preferred my own will instead of God's will, the remedy simply could not be applied. It is a striking thought that God never forces anyone to do his will, that his help is ever available but has to be sought in all earnestness and humility.

This condition lasted for months, during which time I had voluntarily entered a private institution to get straightened out. On the last occasion when I came out of the fog, I asked God to help me again. Shamefaced as I was, I went back to the fellowship. They made me welcome, offered me collectively and individually all the help I might need. They treated me as though nothing had happened. And I feel that it is the most telling tribute to the efficacy of this remedy that during my period of relapse I still knew this remedy would work with me if I would let it, but I was too stubborn to admit it.

That was a year ago. Depend upon it I stay mighty close to what I have proven to be good for me. I don't dare risk getting very far away. And I have found that in simple faith I get results by placing my life in God's hands every day, by asking Him to keep me a sober man for 24 hours, if I try to do His will. He has never let me down yet.

* * * * *

HOME BREWMEISTER

Strangely enough, or by some queer quirk, I became acquainted with the "hilarious life just at the time in my life when I was beginning to really settle down to a common-sense, sane, domestic life.[†] My wife became pregnant and the doctor recommended the use of Porter Ale...so...I bought six gallon crock[†] and a few bottles, listened to advice from amateur brewmeisters, and was off on my beer manufacturing career on a small scale (for the time being). Somehow or other, I must have misunderstood the doctor's instructions, for I not only made the beer for my wife, I also drank it for her.

As time went on, I found that it was customary to open a few bottles whenever visitors dropped in. That being the case, it didn't take me long to figure out that my meager manufacturing facilities were entirely inadequate to the manufacture of beer for social and domestic consumption. From that point on, I secured crocks of ten gallon capacity and really took quite an active interest in the manufacture of home brew.

We were having card parties with limburger and beer quite regularly. Eventually, of course, it came to beer with no time for cards, what with all the hilarity that could be provoked with a few gallons of beer, there seemed to be no need of bridge or poker playing for entertainment. Well...we all know how those things go. The parties waxed more liquid and hilarious as time went on, and eventually I discovered that a little shot of liquor now and then between beers had the tendency to put me in a whacky mood much quicker than having to down several quarts of beer to obtain the same results. The inevitable result of the above mentioned discovery was that I soon learned that beer made a very good wash for whiskey. That discovery so intrigued me, that I stayed on that diet almost entirely for the balance of my extended drinking career. Yes sir, the old Boilermaker and his Helper. The last day of my drinking career, I drank 22 of them between 10 and 12 A.M. and I shall never know how many more followed them until I was poured into bed that night.

I was getting along fairly well with my party drinking for quite some time however, but eventually I began to visit beer joints in between parties. A night or so a week in a joint, and a party or so a week at home or with friends, along with a little lone drinking, soon had me preparing for the existence of a top flight drunkard.

Three years after I started on my drinking career, I lost my first job. At that time, I was living out of town, so I moved back to the home town and made a connection in a responsible position with one of the larger companies in the finance business. Up to this point I had spent six years in the business and had enjoyed the reputation of being very successful.

My new duties were extremely confining and my liquor consumption began to increase at this time. Upon leaving the office in the evening, my first stop would be a saloon about a block from the office. However, as there happened to be several saloons within that distance, I didn't find it necessary to patronize the same place each evening. It doesn't pay to be seen in the same place at the same hour every day, you know.

The general procedure was to take 4 or 5 shots in the first place I stopped at.

[†] This accurately reflects the language of the original.

This would get me feeling fit, and then I would start for home and fireside, thirteen miles away. Well...on the way home numerous places must be passed. If I were alone I would only stop at four or five of them, but only one or two in the event I had my mistrusting wife with me.

Eventually I would arrive home for a late supper, for which, of course, I had absolutely no relish. I would make a feeble attempt at eating supper but never met with any howling success. I never enjoyed any meal, but I ate my lunch at noon for two reasons: first, to help get me out of the fog of the night before, and second, to furnish some measure of nourishment. (My enjoyment of meals now is an added feature to the Seven Wonders of the World to me. I can still hardly believe it). Eventually, the noon meal was also dispensed with.

I cannot remember just when I became the victim of insomnia, but I do know that the last year and a half I never went to bed sober a single night. I couldn't sleep. I had a mortal fear of going to bed and tossing all night. Evenings at home were an ordeal. As a result, I would fall off in a drunken stupor every night

How I was able to discharge my duties at the office during those horrible mornings, I will never be able to explain. Handling customers, dealers, insurance people, dictation, telephoning, directing new employees, answering to superiors, etc. However, it finally caught up with me, and when it did, I was a mental, physical, and nervous wreck.

Finally, I arrived at the stage where I couldn't quite make it to the office some mornings. Then I would send an excuse of illness. But the firm became violently ill with my drunkenness and their course of treatment was to remove their ulcer in the form of me from their payroll, amid much fanfare and very personal and slighting remarks and insinuations.

During this time, I had been threatened, beaten, kissed, praised and damned alternately by relatives, family, friends and strangers, but of course it all went for naught. How many times I swore off in the morning and got drunk before sunset I don't know. I was on the toboggan and really making time.

After being fired, I lined up with a new finance company that was just starting in business, and took the position of business promotion man, contacting automobile dealers. WOW::::[†] was that something??? While working in an office, there was some semblance of restraint, but, oh boy, when I got on the outside with this new company without supervision, did I go to town???

I really worked for several weeks, and having had a fairly wide acquaintance with the dealer trade, it was not difficult for me to line enough of them up to give me a very substantial volume of business with a minimum of effort.

Now I was getting drunk all the time. It wasn't necessary to report to the office in person every day, and when I did go in, it was just to make an appearance and bounce right out again. Was that a merry-go-round for the eight months that it lasted???

Finally this company also became ill and I was once more looking for a job. Then I learned something else. I learned that a person just can't find a job hanging in a dive or barroom all day and all night, as jobs don't seem to turn up in those places. I became convinced of that because I spent most of my time there and nary a job turned up. By this time, my chances of getting lined up in my chosen business were shot. Everyone had my number and wouldn't hire me at any price.

[†] This accurately reflects the language of the original.

I have omitted details of transgressions that I made when drunk for several reasons. One is that I don't remember too many of them, as I was one of those drunks who could be on his feet and attend a meeting or a party, engage in a conversation with people and do things that any nearly normal person would do, and the next day, not remember a thing about where I was, what I did, who I saw, or how I got home. (That condition was a distinct handicap to me in trying to vindicate myself with the not so patient wife).

I also committed other indiscretions of which I see no particular point in relating. Anyone who is a rummy or is close to rummies knows what all those things amount to without having to be told about them.

Things eventually came to the point where I had no friends. I didn't care to go visiting unless the parties we might visit had plenty of liquor on hand and I could get stinking drunk. Fact is, that I was always well on my way before I would undertake to go visiting at all. (Naturally, this condition was also a source of great delight to my wife).

After holding good positions, paying better than average income for over ten years, I was in debt, had no clothes to speak of, no money, no friends, and no one any longer tolerating me but my wife. My son had absolutely no use for me. Even some of the saloon-keepers where I had spent so much time and money, requested that I stay away from their places. Finally, an old business acquaintance of mine, whom I hadn't seen for several years offered me a job. I was on that job a month and drunk most of the time.

Just at this time my wife heard of a doctor in another city who had been very successful with drunks. She offered me the alterative of going to see him or her leaving me for good and all. Well...I had a job, and I really wanted desperately to stop drinking, but couldn't, so I readily agreed to visit the doctor she recommended.

That was the turning point of my life. My wife accompanied me on my visit and the doctor really told me some things that in my state of jitters nearly knocked me out of the chair. He talked about himself, but I was sure it was me. He mentioned lies, deceptions, etc. in the course of his story in the presence of the one person in the world I wouldn't want to know such things. How did he know all this? I had never seen him before, and at the time hoped to hell I would never see him again. However, he explained to me that he had been just such a rummy as I, only for a much longer period of time.

He advised me to enter the particular hospital to which staff he was connected and I readily agreed. In all honesty though, I was skeptical, but I wanted so definitely to quit drinking that I would have welcomed any sort of physical torture or pain to accomplish the result.

I made arrangements to enter the hospital three days later and promptly went out and got stiff for three days. It was with grim foreboding and advanced jitters that I checked in at the hospital. Of course, I had no hint or intimation as to what the treatment was to consist of. Was I to be surprised!

After being in the hospital for several days, a plan of living was outlined to me. A very simple plan that I find much joy and happiness in following. It is impossible to put on paper all the benefits I have derived...physical, mental, domestic, spiritual, and monetary.

This is no idle talk. It is the truth.

From a physical standpoint, I gained 16 pounds in the first two months I was off liquor. I eat three good meals a day now, and really enjoy them. I sleep like a baby, and never give a thought to such a thing as insomnia. I feel as I did when I was fifteen years younger.

Mentally...I know where I was last night, the night before, and the nights before that. Also, I have no fear of anything. I have self confidence and assurance that cannot be confused with the cockeyness or noise-making I once possessed. I can think clearly and am guided much in my thinking and judgement by my spiritual development which grows daily.

From a domestic standpoint, we really have a home now. I am anxious to get home after work. My wife is ever glad to see me come in. My youngster has adopted me. Our home is always full of friends and visitors (no home brew as an inducement).

Spiritually...I have found a Friend who never lets me down and is ever eager to help. I can actually take my problems to Him and He DOES give me comfort, peace, and radiant happiness.

From a monetary standpoint...in the past nine months, I have reduced my reckless debts to almost nothing, and have had money to get along comfortably. I still have my job, and just prior to the writing of this narrative, I received an advancement.

For all of these blessings, I thank Him.

* * * * *

THE SEVEN MONTH SLIP.

At fourteen years of age, when I should have been at home under the supervision of my parents, I was in the United States army serving a one year enlistment. I found myself with a bunch of men none too good for a fourteen year old kid who passed easily for eighteen. I transferred my hero-worshipping to these men of the world. I suppose the worst damage done in that year in the army barracks was the development of an almost unconscious admiration for their apparently jolly sort of living.

Once out of uniform I went to Mexico where I worked for an oil company. Here I learned to take on a good cargo of beer and hold it. Later I rode the range in the Texas cow country and often went to town with the boys to "whoop it up on payday". By the time I returned to my home in the middle west I had learned several patterns of living, to say nothing of a cock-sure attitude that I needed no advice from anyone.

The next ten years are sketchy. During this time I married and established my own home and everything was lovely for a time. Soon I was having a good time getting around the law in speakeasies. Oh yes, I out-smarted our national laws but I was not quite successful in evading the old moral law.

I was working for a large industrial concern and had been promoted to a supervisional job. In spite of big parties, I was for three or four years able to be on the job the next morning. Then gradually the hangovers became more persistent and I found myself not only needing a few shots of liquor before I could go to work at all, but finally found it advisable to stay at home and sober up by the taper-off method. My bosses tried to give me some good advice. When that didn't help the[†] tried more drastic measures, laying me off without pay. They covered up my too frequent absences many times in order to keep them from the attention of the higher officials in the company.

My attitude was that I could handle my liquor whenever I wanted to go about it seriously, and I considered my absences no worse than those of other employees and officials who were getting away with murder in their drinking.

One does not have to use his imagination much to realize that this sort of drinking is hard on the matrimonial relationship. After proving myself neither faithful nor capable of being temperate, my wife left me and obtained a judicial separation. This gave me a really good excuse to get drunk.

In the years 1933 and 1934 I was fired several times, but always got my job back on my promises to do better. On the last occasion I was reduced to the labor gang in the plant. I made a terrific effort to stay sober and prove myself capable of better things. I succeeded pretty well and one day I was called into the production chief's office and told I had met with the approval of the executive department and to be ready to start on a better job.

This good news seemed to justify a mild celebration with a few beers. Exactly four days later I reported for work only to find that they too knew about the "mild" celebration and that they had decided to check me out altogether. After a time I went back and was assigned to one of the hardest jobs in the factory. I was in bad shape physically and after six months of this, I quit, going on a drunk

---

† This accurately reflects the language of the original.

with my last pay check.

Then I began to find that the friends with whom I had been drinking for some time seemed to disappear. This made me resentful and I found myself many times feeling that everybody was against me. Bootleg joints became my hangouts. I sold my books, car, and even clothing in order to buy a few drinks.

I am certain that my family kept me from gravitating to flophouses and gutters. I am eternally thankful to them that they never threw me out or refused me help when I was drinking. Of course I didn't appreciate their kindness then, and I began to stay away from home on protracted drinking spells.

Somehow my family heard of two men in town who had found a way to quit drinking. They suggested that I contact these men but I retorted "If I can't handle my liquor with my own will power then I had better jump over the viaduct."

Another of my usual drinking spells came on. I drank for about ten days with no food except coffee before I was sick enough to start the battle back to sobriety with the accompanying shakes, night sweats, jittery nerves, and horrible dreams. This time I felt that I really needed some help. I told me[†] mother she could call the doctor who was the center of the little group of former drinkers. She did.

I allowed myself to be taken to a hospital where it took several days for my head to clear and my nerves to settle. Then, one day I had a couple of visitors, one a man from New York and the other a local attorney. During our conversation I learned that they had been as bad as myself in this drinking, and that they had found relief and had been able to make a come-back. Later they went into more detail and put it to me very straight that I'd have to give over my desires and attitudes to a power higher than myself which would give me new desires and attitudes.

Here was religion put to me in a different way and presented by three past-masters in liquor guzzling. On the strength of their stories I decided to give it a try. And it worked, as long as I allowed it to do so.

After a year of learning new ways of living, new attitudes and desires, I became self-confident and then careless. I suppose you would say I got to feeling too sure of myself and Zowie! First it was a beer on Saturday nights and then it was a fine drunk. I knew exactly what I had done to bring myself to this old grief. I had tried to handle my life on the strength of my own ideas and plans instead of looking to God for the inspiration and the strength.

But I didn't do anything about it. I thought "to hell with everybody. I'm going to do as I please." So I floundered around for seven months refusing help from any quarter. But one day I volunteered to take another drunk on a trip to sober him up. When we got back to town we were both drunk and went to a hotel to sober up. Then I began to reason the thing out. I had been a sober, happy man for a year, living decently and trying to follow the will of God. Now I was unshaven, unkept[†], ill-looking, bleary-eyed. I decided then and there and went back to my friends who offered me help and who never lectured me on my seven month failure.

That was more than a year ago. I don't say now that I can do anything. I only know that as long as I seek God's help to the best of my ability, just so long will liquor never bother me.

* * * * *

[†] This accurately reflects the language of the original.

MY WIFE AND I

Coming from a farm boyhood with the common education of the little red schoolhouse, I had worked during the war and afterwards for seven years at high wages in a booming industrial town, had saved considerable money and finally married an able, well-educated woman who had an unusual gift of common sense and far more than the average business vision, a true helpmate in every way.

In our early twenties, we were both ambitious and had boundless faith in our ability to succeed. We talked over the future all the time, exchanged ideas and really planned our way in life. Just working in a factory, even at highly-paid piece work, and saving out of my wages did not seem to us to be the best way to do. We talked things over and decided to strike out for ourselves. Our first venture, a neighborhood grocery store, prospered. Another neighborhood store, in an ideal location at a nearby summer resort, looked good to us. We bought it and started in to make it go. Then came a business slump affecting the whole country. With fewer customers I had lots of time on my hands and was getting to like high-powered home brew and the potent liquors of prohibition days entirely too well. That didn't help the business. We finally shut up shop.

Jobs were scarce, but by persistence I again found a factory job. In a few months the factory closed down. We had again accumulated a small stake and since the job situation showed no improvement, we thought we would try business again.

This time we opened a restaurant in a semi-rural section and for a time all went well. My wife opened up in the morning, did all the baking and cooking and waited on trade. I relieved her later in the day and stayed open late to catch every possible bit of business. Our place became a regular hang-out for groups of late-comers who showed up with a bottle every now and then.

I told myself that I was one man who could handle my liquor because I was always on my feet at closing time. I talked knowingly about "spacing my drinks," about taking only a measured shot, and about the folly of gulping down big drinks. Yes sir, I was never going to be one of those "rummies" who let liquor get the best of them. Young and strong, I could throw off the effects of the previous night's drinking and stand the nausea the following morning, even abstaining from taking a drink until the afternoon. But before long the idea of suffering for a few hours didn't seem so good.

The morning drink became the first act of the daily routine. I had now become a "regular". I had my regular remedy — a stiff shot to start the day and no waiting till a specified time. I used to wait for the need, soon I was craving the stuff so much that I didn't wait for that. My wife could see that it was gripping me. She warned me, gently at first, with quiet seriousness. Was I going to pave the way to losing this business just when it needed to be nursed along? We began to run behind. My wife, anxious for the goal we had set out to reach, and seeing the result if I didn't brace up, talked straight from the shoulder. We had words. I left in a passion.

Our seperation† lasted a week, I did a lot of thinking, and went back to my wife. Quieter, somewhat remorseful, we talked things over. Our situation was worse than I had anticipated. We got a buyer for the place and sold out. We still had some money left.

† This accurately reflects the language of the original.

I had always been a natural mechanic, handy with tools. We moved back into town with a slim bankroll and, still determined never to be a factory hand again, I looked around and finding a workshop location with a house adjacent I started a sheet-metal shop. I had chosen a very difficult time to start up. My business practically vanished on account of the depression.

There were no jobs of any kind. We fell far behind on our rent and other obligations. Our cupboard was often bare. With every penny needed for food and shelter and wearing old clothes with nothing new except what our two youngsters needed, I didn't touch a drop for two years. I went after business. I slugged doorbells all over the town asking for jobs. My wife rang bells with me, taking one side of the street while I worked the other. We left nothing undone to keep going, but we were still far behind, so far that at the low point we could see eviction and our belongings in the street.

I braced myself to talk to our landlord who was connected with a large real estate firm managing many properties. We were behind six months in our rent and they saw that the only way to get their back rent was to give me a couple of small jobs. My wife learned to use the tools to shape and fashion material when I was doing the installation work. The real estate firm liked my work and began to give me more jobs. In those grim days, with babies to feed, I couldn't spend what little money came in for drink. I stayed sober. My wife and I even started back to church, began paying our dues.

They were thin years, those depression years. For three years in succession, Christmas in our little family was just the 25th of December. Our customers saw us as two earnest young people trying to get along and as times improved a little we began to get better jobs. Now we could hire some competent workmen and bought a car and a few small trucks. We prospered and moved into a better-equipped house.

My pockets, which hadn't jingled for years, now held folding money. The first greenbacks grew into a roll with a rubber band around it. I became well-known to real estate firms, business men and politicians. I was well-liked, popular with everyone. Following a prosperous season came a quiet period. With time on our hands I had a drinking spell. It lasted for a month, but with the aid of my wife, I checked myself in time. "Remember how we lost the store! Remember our restaurant!" my wife said. Yes, I could remember. Those times were too recent and their memory too bitter. I solemnly swore off and once more climbed aboard the wagon, this time for nine long months.

Business kept up. It became evident that by careful handling we might eventually have something pretty good, sufficient income to provide a good living for us all and ensure a good education for our children.

My business is seasonal. Fall and early winter are rush times. The first few months of the year are quiet. But though business slackened, I got around making contracts, lining up future work and meeting people who would be able to put work in my way. Not yet sensing any great danger, in spite of past experiences, I seldom refused the invitations of business friends to have a drink. In a short time I was drinking every day and eventually much more than I had ever done before for I always had a roll in my pocket.

At first I was even more jolly than usual when I came home in the evening to my wife and family. But the joking good fellow who was the husband and father they had known, gave place to a man who slammed the door when he came in. My wife, genuinely alarmed now as week after week went past without any sign that I was going quit,[†] tried to reason with me, but the old arguments didn't work this time.

[†] This accurately reflects the language of the original.

Summer came on with its demand for roof repairs and spouting installations. My wife often started the men to work in the morning, did shop jobs, kept the books and, in addition ran the house and looked after the family.

For eight months my daily routine was steady drinking. Even after slumping in bed late at night in a semi-stupor, I would get up at all hours and drive to some all-night spot where I could get what I wanted. I was going to have a good time in spite of hell and high water.

I became increasingly surly when at home. I was the boss. I was master in my own house, wasn't I? I became morose, with few lucid moments between drinks. I would listen to no arguments and certainly attempts to reason with me were futile. Unknown to me, my wife influenced some of my friends and business associates to drop in casually. They were mostly non-drinkers and generally ended up by mildly upbraiding me.

"A fine lot of Job's comforters," I would say. I felt that everybody was against me, thought bitterly of my wife as being of little help and told myself I wasn't getting the breaks, that everybody was making a mountain out of a molehill and so, to hell with everything! I still had money and with money I could always buy bottled happiness. And still my wife kept trying. She got our pastor to talk to me. It was no good.

Drinking and staying drunk without cessation, even my splendid constitution began to give way. My wife called doctors who gave me temporary relief. Then my wife left me after a bitter quarrel, taking the children with her. My pride was hurt and I began to regard myself as an injured husband and an unappreciated father who, deep in his heart, just doted on his children. I went to see her and demanded to see them. I up and told her that I didn't care whether she came back or not, that I wanted the children. My wife, wise woman, thought she still had a chance to save me, save our home for the children. She threw aside her sense of injury, spoke right up to me and said she was coming back, that forbidding her the house wouldn't work, that she had helped me get what I had and was going to cross its threshold and resume its management. She did just that. When she opened the door she was appalled at the sight of it, curtains down, dishes and utensils unwashed, dirty glasses and empty bottles everywhere.

Every alcoholic reaches the end of the tether some day. For me there came a day when physically and mentally unable to make my way to a saloon for a drink. I went to bed. I told my wife for the first time that I wanted to quit drinking but couldn't. I asked her to do something for me; I had never done this before. I realized that I needed help. Somehow in talking with a lady doctor, my wife had heard of another doctor who in some mysterious way had stopped drinking after thirty years and had been successful in helping a few other alcoholics to become sober men. As a last resort, my wife appealed to this doctor, who insisted on a certain situation before he could help; his experience had taught him that unless that situation existed nothing could be done for the alcoholic.

"Does your husband want to stop drinking, or is he merely temporarily uncomfortable? Has he come to the end of the road?" he asked my wife.

She told him that for the first time I had expressed a desire to quit, that I had asked her in desperation to try to do something — anything, to help me stop. He said he would see me the following morning.

With every part of my being craving a drink, I could hardly sit still when I got up to await the visit from the man she had talked to on the phone, but something kept me in the house. I wanted to hear what this fellow had to offer and since he was a medical man I had some pre-conceived notions ready for him when he came. I was pretty jittery when my wife opened the door to admit a tall, somewhat brusque professional man who, from his speech, was obviously an Easterner. I don't know what I had expected, but his salutation, designed to shake me up I can now see, had almost the same effect as the hosing with cold water in a turkish bath.

"I hear you're another "rummy" he said as he smiled and sat down beside me. I let him talk. Gradually he drew me out until what I did tell him gave him a picture of my experience. And then he put it to me plainly. "If you are perfectly sure that you want to quit drinking for good, if you are serious about it, if you don't merely wish to get well so that you can take up drinking again at some future date, you can be relieved," he said.

I told him that I had never wanted anything as much in my life as to be able to quit using liquor, and I meant every word of it.

"The first thing to do with your husband," he said, turning to my wife, "is to get him to a hospital and have him "defogged." I'll make the necessary arrangements."

He didn't go into any further explanation, not even to my wife. That evening I was in a hospital bed. The next day the doctor called. He told me that several former alcoholics were now dry as a result of following certain prescribed course of action and that some of them would be in to see me.[†] My wife came to see me faithfully. She, too, had been learning, perhaps more quickly than I was doing, through talking with the doctor who by this time was getting down to brass tacks with me. My friend was the human agency employed by an all-wise Father to bring me into a pathway of life.

It is an easy matter to repeat and orally affirm a faith. Here were these men who visited me and they, like myself, had tried everything else and although it was plain to be seen none of them were perfect, they were living proof that the sincere attempt to follow the cardinal teachings of Jesus Christ was keeping them sober. If it could do that for others, I was resolved to try it, believing it could do something for me also.

I went home after four days, my mind clear, feeling much better physically and, what was far more important, with something better than just Will Power to aid me. I got to know others of the little group of alcoholics whose human center was my doctor. They came to our home. I met their wives and families. They invited my wife and myself to their homes. I learned that it would be well to begin the day with morning devotion which is the custom in our house now.

It was almost a year when I began to get a little careless. One day I hoisted a few drinks, arriving home far from sober. My wife and I talked it over, both knowing it had happened because I had stopped following the plan. I acknowled[†] my fault to God and asked His help to keep to the course I had to follow.

Our home is a happy one. My children no longer hide when they see me coming. My business has improved. And — this is important — I try to do what I can for my fellow alcoholics. In our town there are some 70 of us, reading[†] and willing to spend our time to show the way to sobriety and sanity to men who are like what we used to be.

* * * * *

[†] This accurately reflects the language of the original.

A WARD OF THE PROBATE COURT

At about the time of my graduation from high school, a state university was established in our city. On the call for an office assistant, I was recommended by my superintendent, and got the position. I was rather his choice and pride, but a few years later, I met him in a nearby city and "panhandled" him for two "bucks" for drinks.

I grew with this institution and advanced in position. I took a year off for attendance at an engineering college. At college I refrained from any hilarious celebrating or drinking.

War was declared. I was away from home on business at the State Capitol where my mother couldn't raise objections and I enlisted. Overseas I was on five fronts from Alsace up to the North Sea. Upon relief from the lines — back in the rest-area, "vin rouge" and "cognac" helped in the let down from trying circumstances. I was introduced to the exhilaration of intoxication. The old spirit, "What the hell?" "Heini may have you tagged," didn't help toward any moderation in drinking then. We had many casualties but one of the real catastrophies was the loss of a pal, a lieutenant who died from the D.T.'s over there, after it was all over. This didn't slow me up and back in the States I had a big fling before returning home.

My plans were to cover up with my mother and the girl I was to marry, that I had become addicted to alcohol. But I exposed the fact on the day our engagement was announced. On the way I met a training camp buddy, got drunk and missed the party. Booze had got over its first real blow on me. I saw her briefly that night but didn't have the guts to face her people. The romance was over.

To forget, I engaged in a super-active life in social, fraternal and civic promotion in my community. This all outside my position in the President's Office of the State University. I became a leader — the big flash in the pond. I organized and was first commander of the American Legion Post — raised funds and built a fine memorial Club House. Was Secretary of Elks, Eagles, Chamber of Commerce, City Club and active as an operator and officer in political circles. I was always a good fellow and controlled my drinking, indulging only in sprees in private clubs or away from home.

I was deposed from the executive position at the college by a political change in the governorship of the State. I knew the salesmanager of the Securities Division of a large Utility corporation in Wall Street, and started out to sell securities. The issues and the market were good and I had a fine opportunity. I was away from home and I began to drink heavily. To get away from my drinking associates, I managed to be transferred to another city, but this didn't help. Booze had me, my sales and commissions diminished, I remained almost in a continuous stupor on my drawing account until I was released.

I braced up, got sober, and made a good connection with a steamship agency, a concern promoting European travel and study at most all important universities in Europe. Those were the bath-tub gin days and for drinking in and about my office, I held out in this position for only a year.

I was now engaged to be married and fortunately I got another position as salesman for a large corporation. I worked hard, was successful and drinking became periodical. I was married and my wife soon learned that I was no social drinker. I tried hard to control it, but could not. There were many separations and she would return home. I would make pledges and a sincere effort and then my top would blow off again. I began here to take sanitarium treatments to satisfy my wife and my folks.

I had a great capacity for drink and work. With the help of turkish baths, bromo-seltzer and aspirin, I held to the job. I became top-notcher in the entire sales force of the country. I was assigned to more special territory and finally into the market of keenest competition. I was top rate in salary, won bonus awards and was bringing in the volume. But there was always the drawback my excessive drinking made at times. I was called in once, twice, and warned. Finally I wasn't to be tolerated any longer, although I was doing a good job. I had lasted five and a half years.

I lost my wife along with my job and fine income. This was a terrible jolt. I tried for a hook-up, but I had a black-eye marring a good record. I became discouraged and depressed. I sought relief with booze. There began the four black years of my life.

I had returned home to the community where I had been so prominent. These were book-let days still and I hung out at the clubs with bars. I got so I would last on a job but a few days, just until I could get an advance for drinks. I began to get entangled with the law — arrested for driving while intoxicated and drunken and disorderly conduct.

My folks heard of the cure at the State Hospital. I was picked up drunk and sent there by the Probate Court. I was administered paralde-hyde and came to in a receiving ward among lunatics. I was transferred to another ward of less violent cases and I found a little group of alcoholics and "junkers" (dope addicts). I learned from them the seri-ousness of being a ward of the Probate Court. I felt then if I ever got released the old devil alcohol would never get me in a jam like this again. In times of great distress such as this, I would pray to God for help.

I was fortunate and was released after eleven days and nights barred up in the laughing academy — "bug-house". That was enough. I wanted no more of it. I took a job as manager of a club and put myself to the old acid test. I was going to really assert my will power. I even tended bar part of the time, but never imbibed a bit. This lasted about three months.

I went to an annual convention of my overseas division and came to locked up in a cheap hotel room, new shoes, suit coat, hat and purse missing. I must have slipped badly.

Then followed much drinking and trouble. After a few arrests for intoxication, the law decided another sojourn to the State Hospital would tame me. They jumped the stay this time from eleven days to eleven weeks. It was getting tough for me. I came out in good physical condition and held a fear of getting probated again, thinking the seige might be eleven months. I got another job and stayed dry for about two months and off to the races again.

I became terribly weak — couldn't eat and tried to get nourishment from booze and mostly only bootleg at that. One time, I just made it into a hospital and another time a police patrol took me to the hospital instead of the jail. I suffered badly from insomnia. As many as three shots in the arm had no effect.

I would get in shape and back at it again. I was going to battle it to the finish. The time came when I was to be paid my soldier's bonus. I had the limit or maximum coming. Friends advised my folks to send me to a Veterans Hospital before I got this money in my hands. I was probated again, held in a county jail for two weeks and sent again to the asylum. This was my summer resort for three months. I was on the waiting list for the Veterans Hospital but I got into such wonderful physical condition from eating and working out of doors that I was released.

I reached home full of resentment against my folks for their having my money tied up under a guardian-ship. I went out and got saturated and landed in jail — I had been free from the asylum about eight hours. Behind the bars again so soon — this was bad. However, I was freed again next day and this was my last confinement with the law. I began to use my head, I continued to drink but kept under cover or hid in the "jungles" with the bums.

In a few months an old friend came along. He located me a few times in saloons. We had been drinking pals in the early days, particularly at the Elk's Lodge. He had heard of my predicament. He himself had quit drinking and looked fine. He encouraged me to visit him in a nearby city.

I wanted to quit drinking, but hadn't much faith in ever getting away from it. I agreed to go into a hospital as the patient of a doctor who had been an alcoholic for many years and was now a new man.

It is almost uncanny — in just eight days I left there a different person. This doctor in plain words was a wonderful guy — he spent many hours with me telling me his experience with alcohol. Others of his group, which was then small, visited me — told me their stories. They were all strangers to me, but treated me as a friend. I was impressed with their interest and fellowship. I learned the secret. They had a religious experience. I was willing, and renewed my acquaintance with God and acknowledged him as a reality.

I found it easy. I came to life and have been free now for two years. I hope never to take another drink. I am building up a reputation again and nearly every day am complimented on my appearance.

I have a new outlook on life. I look forward to each day with happiness because of the real enjoyment it is to me to be sane, sober, and respectable. I was existing really from one drink until the next, with no perception about circumstances, conditions, or even nature's elements. My acquaintance with God — lost and forgotten when I was a young man — is renewed. God is all-loving and all-forgiving. The memories of my past are being dimmed by the life I now aspire to.

* * * * *

RIDING THE RODS.

Fourteen years old and strong, I was ready — an American Whittington who knew a better way to get places than by walking. The "clear the way" whistle of a fast freight thundering over the crossing on the tracks a mile away was a siren call. Sneaking away from my farm home one night, I made my way to the distant yards. Ducking alonw[†] a lane between two made-up trains that seemed endless, I made my way to the edge of the yards. Here and there I passed a silent, waiting figure. Then a little group talking among themselves. Edging in, I listened eagerly. I had met my first hoboes. Then[†] talked of places I had never heard of. This town was good. A fellow could get by on the Bowery all winter if he knew the ropes; that other town was "hostile"; thirty days for "vag" awaited you in another if you didn't hit the cinders before the road "bulls" fine-combed the train.

Then they noticed me. Somehow a new kid is always an object of interest to the adventurers of the rails. "Where ya makin' for, Kid?"

I had heard one of them mention "Dee-troit" and it seemed as good an answer as any. I had no plans, just wanted to get away — anywhere — just away!

"That Michigan Manifest will be along any minute now; I think she's moving." The tall hobo who had spoken grabbed me by the arm. "Come on, kid. We'll help you."

On came the long train, headlight gleaming. Car after car passed, all loaded, doors carded and sealed. Then three empties. The tall hobo began to run, picked me up and pushed me through the open door of the second car, got in himself and helped his buddy aboard.

Suddenly I felt big. I had got[†] away! The two hoboes talked, the tall one about getting work in Detroit, the other arguing for staying on the road. Then the one who had boosted me up began to quiz me. I told him I had run away from the farm. In a sort of halting way he told me not to get the train habit or it would get me until I would always want to be moving. The rocking motion of the car as the train increased speed became a cradle song in my ears. I fell asleep.

It was way past dawn when I awoke. My two companions were already sitting up and talking. The day wore on. We passed through small towns. Soon the train was threading its way between factories and huge warehouses, crossing tracks with brisk clatter, coming into a large railway yard. Brakes went on. They helped me off. We were in Detroit.

My hobo friends parted at a street corner. The tall one took me along right into town and got a room for both of us with "Mother Kelly," a kindly Irish landlady if there ever was one. "Sit tight, kid," he said. "I'll see you through as much as I can. Me to find a job."[†]

He got a job. For almost two years he looked after me. He was always vigilant, steering me past the snares and pitfalls that are always in the path of a growing boy. This hobo, Tom Casey, who never talked much about himself or his experiences except as a warning illustration of "What not to do", made me start a bank account and keep it growing. It is to him I owe the fact that I didn't become a "road kid", that I never became a hobo. Came a day when he left me. The road was calling him, he explained, although that never seemed to me to be the reason. I never saw Tom

---

[†] This accurately reflects the language of the original.

Casey again, but from this man I received my first lesson in the guiding and compelling principle of the Good Life. "Love thy neighbor as thyself."

I was city-wise by this time, uncontaminated to be sure, thanks to my friend. No longer a "boy rube in the big town." I found a job quickly enough but I missed Tom. I began to hang around pool rooms and it was inevitable that I soon learned to handle a schooner of beer and an occasional "shot". Jobs were plentiful. If I didn't feel right in the morning after a night with the "corner gang" I didn't go to work. I lost jobs. My bank account dwindled, disappeared entirely. My new barroom friends were little help. I was broke.

It was summer and the park benches, hard and uncomfortable as they were, appealed to me more than the squalid "flops" of the city's slums. So I slept out a few nights. Young and full of energy, I hunted for work. The war was on and work was easy to get. I became a machine-shop hand, progressing rapidly from drill-press to milling machine to lathe. I could quit a job one day and have a new one the next with more money. Soon I again had a good boarding-house, clothes and money. But I never started another bank account. "Plenty of time for that," I thought. My week-ends were spent in my conception of "a good time", finally becoming regular carousals and debauches over Saturday and Sunday. I had the usual experiences of being slipped a "Mickey Finn" and getting slugged and rolled for my money. These had no deterrent effect. I could always get jobs and live comfortably again in a few weeks. Soon, however, I tired of the weary routine of working and drinking. I began to dislike the city. Somehow my boyhood days on the farm didn't seem to be so bad at a distance.

No, I didn't go home, but found work not too far away. I still drank. I soon got restless and took a freight for a Michigan city, arriving there broke late at night. I set out to look for friends. They helped me find work. Slowly I began to climb the industrial job ladder once more and eventually achieved a responsible position as a machine setter in a large plant. I was sitting on top of the world again. The sense of accomplishment I had now told me that I had earned the right to have enjoyable week-ends once more. The week-ends began to extend to Tuesday and Wednesday until I frequently worked only from Thursday to Saturday with the bottle always in my mind. In a vague sort of way I had set a time to quit drinking but that was at least fifteen years away and "What the hell!" I said to myself. "I'm going to have a good time while I'm young."

Then I was fired. Piqued, I drank up my last pay check and when I got sober again found another job — then another — and another in quick succession. I was soon back on the park benches. And once more I got a break when everything seemed dark. An old friend volunteered to get me a job driving a bus. He said he would buy me a uniform and give me the hospitality of his home if I would promise to quit drinking. Of course I promised. I had been working about three days when the bus line superintendent called me into his office.

"Young fellow," he said, "In your application you stated that you don't use alcoholic liquors. Now, we always check a man's references and three of the firms you have worked for say you're a highly capable man, but you have the drink habit."

I looked at him. It was all true, I admitted, but I had been out of work such a long time that I had welcomed this job as an opportunity to redeem myself. I told him what I had promised my friend, that I was sincerely doing my best and not drinking a drop. I asked him to give me a chance.

"Somehow I think you are in earnest," he said. "I believe you mean it. I'll give you a chance and help you to make good."

He shook my hand in friendship and encouragement. I strode from his office with high hope. "John Barleycorn will never make a bum out of me again," I told myself with determination.

For three months I drove my route steadily with never a hitch. My employers were satisfied. I felt pretty good. I was really on the wagon this time, wasn't I?

Yes indeed, I was on the wagon for good.

I soon repaid my debt to my friend for his stake in me and even saved a little money. The feeling of security increased. It was summer and, hot and tired at the end of the day, I began to stop in at a speakeasy on my way home. Detroit beer was good then, almost like old-time pre-prohibition stuff. "This is the way to do it," I would say to myself. "Stick to beer. After all, it's really a food and it sure hits the spot after a trick of wheeling that job around in this man's town. It's the hard liquor that gets a man down. Beer for mine."

Even then with all the hard lessons of bitter experience behind me I did not realize that thinking along that line was a definite red light on my road in life — a real danger signal.

The evening glass of beer led, as usual, to the night when I didn't get away from the bar until midnight. I began to need a bracer in the morning. Beer, I knew from experience was simply no good as a bracer — all right as a thirst quencher perhaps, but lacking action and authority the next morning. I needed a jolt.

The morning jolt became a habit. Then it got to be several jolts until I was generally pretty well organized when I started to work. Spacing my drinks over the day I managed not to appear drunk, just comfortable as I drove along the crowded thoroughfares of the city. Then came the accident.

On one of the avenues a man darted from between parked cars right in my path. I swung the bus sharply over to keep from hitting him but couldn't quite make it. He died in the hospital. Passenger and sidewalk witnesses absolved me completely. Even if I had been completely sober I couldn't have cleared him. The company investigation immediately after the accident showed me blameless but my superiors knew I had been drinking. They fired me — not for the accident — but for drinking on the job.

Well, once more I felt I had enough of city life and found a job on an upstate farm. While there I met a young school-teacher, fell in love with her and she with me. We were married. Farm work was not very remunerative for a young couple so we went successively to Pontiac, Michigan and later to an industrial city in Ohio. For economy's sake we had been living with my wife's people, but somehow we never seemed able to get ahead. I was still drinking but not so much as formerly, or so it seemed to me.

The new location seemed ideal — no acquaintances, no entanglements, no boon companions to entice me. I made up my mind to leave liquor alone and get ahead. But I forgot one boon companion, one who was always at my elbow, one who followed me from city to farm and back to city. I had forgotten about John Barleycorn.

Even so, the good resolutions held for a time — new job, comfortable home and understanding helpmate, they all helped. We had a son and soon came another. We began to make friends and moved in a small social circle of my fellow-workers and their wives and families. Those were still bootleg days. Drinks were always available but nobody seemed to get very drunk. We just had a good time, welcome surcease after a week of toil. Here were none of the rowdy debauches that I had known, I had discovered "social drinking" how to "drink like a gentleman and hold my liquor." There is no point in reiterating the recurrence of experience already described. The "social drinking" didn't hold up. I became the bootlegger's first morning customer. How I ever managed to hold the job I had I don't know. I began to receive the usual warnings from my superiors. They had no effect. I had now come to an ever-deepening realization that I was a drunkard, that there was no help for me.

I told my wife that. She sought counsel of her friends and my friends. They came and talked with me. Reverend gentlemen, who knew nothing of my problem, pointed me to the age-old religious formula. I would have none of it. It left me cold. Now, with hope gone, I haunted the mean thoroughfares of speakeasy districts, with my mind on nothing but the next drink. I managed to work enough to maintain a slim hold on my job. Then I began to reason with myself.

"What good are you?" I would say. "Your wife and children would be better off if they never saw you again. Why don't you get away and never come back? Let them forget about you. Get away — get away anywhere — that's the thing to do."

That night, coatless and hatless, I hopped a freight for Pittsburgh. The following day I walked the streets of the Smoky City. I offered to work at a roadside stand for a meal. I got the meal, walked on, sat down by the roadside to think.

"What a heel I've turned out to be!" I soliloquized. "My wife and two kids back there — no money — what can they do? I should have another try at it. Maybe I'll never get well, but at least I can earn a dollar or two now and then — for them."

I took another freight back home. Despite my absence, my job was still open. I went to work, but it was no go. I would throw a few dollars at my wife on payday and drink up what was left. I hated my surroundings, hated my job, my fellow-workers — the whole town. I tried Detroit again, landing there with a broken arm. How I got it I'll never know for I was far gone in drink when I left. My wife's relatives returned me to my home in a few days. I became morose, mooning around the house by myself. Seeing me come home, my wife would leave a little money on the table, grab the children and flee. I was increasingly ugly. Now, all hope was gone entirely. I made several attempts on my life. My wife had to hide any knives and hammers. She feared for her own safety. I feared for my mind — feared that I was breaking — that I would end up insane. Finally the fear got so terrible that I asked my wife to have me "put away" legally. There came a morning when, alone in my room, I began to wreck it, breaking the furniture, destroying everything in sight. Desperate, my wife had to employ the means I had suggested to her in the depths of alcoholic despair. Loath to have me committed to the state asylum, still trying to save something from the wreckage of my life and hers, she had me placed in a hospital, hoping against hope to save me.

I was placed under restraint. The treatment was strenuous — no alcohol — just bromides and sleeping potions. The nights were successions of physical and mental agony. It was weeks before I could sit still for any length of time. I didn't want to talk to anyone and cared less to listen. That gradually wore off and one day I fell into casual conversation with another patient — another alcoholic. We began to compare notes. I told him frankly that I was in despair, that no thinking I had ever been able to do had shown me a way of escape, that all my attempts to try will power (well meaning persons had often said, "Why don't you use your will power? — as if will power were a faculty one could turn on and off like a faucet!) had been of no avail.

"Being in here and getting fixed up temporarily," I told him bitterly, "is no good. I know that only too well. I can see nothing but the same old story over again. I'm simply unable to quit. When I get out of here I'm going to blow town."

My fellow-patient and new found acquaintance looked at me a long time in silence and finally spoke. From the most unexpected quarter in the world, from a man who was in the same position I was in, from a fellow-alcoholic, came the first ray of hope I had seen.

"Listen fellow," he said, looking at me with ten times the earnestness of the many good citizens and other well-intentioned persons who had tried their best to help me. "Listen to me. I know a way out. I know the only answer. And I know it works."

I stared at him in amazement. There were several mild mental cases in the place and, little as I knew about their exhibitions of tendencies, I knew that even in a normal conversation, strange ideas might be expected. Was this fellow perhaps a little balmy — a wee bit off? Here was a man, an admitted alcoholic like myself, trying to tell me he knew the remedy for my situation. I wanted to hear what he had to suggest but made the reservation that he was probably a little "Nutty". At the same time I was ready to listen, like any drowning man, to grasp at even a straw.

My friend smiled, he knew what I was thinking. "Yes," he continued. "Forget that I'm here. Forget that I'm just another "rummy". But I had the answer once — the only answer."

He seemed to be recalling his very recent past. Looking at me earnestly, his voice impressive in its sincerity, he went on. "For more than a year before coming here I was a sober man, thoroughly dry. I wasn't just on the wagon. I was dry! And I would still be dry if I had stuck to the plan which kept me sober all that time."

Let me say here that he later went back to the very plan he told me about and has since been sober for more than a year for the second time.

He told me his own story briefly and went on to tell me of a certain cure for alcoholism — the only certain cure. I had anticipated hearing of some new treatment, some newly discovered panacea that I had not heard of, something which no doubt combined drugs and mental healing. But it was neither one nor the other; it was certainly not a mixture of any kind.

He spoke of a group of some 30 men in my town who were ready to take me by the hand and call me by my first name. They would call me "Friend" without canting or ranting. He told me they met once a week to talk over their experiences, how they tried to help each other, how they spent their time in helping men like me.

"I know it sounds strange, incredible, maybe," he said. "I slipped, got drunk after being sober for a year, but I'm going back to try again. I know it works."

Helpless, without faith in myself or anyone else, entirely doubtful that the fellow really had something, I began to ask questions. I had to be interested or go crazy.

"How do you go about this — where do I have to go?" I asked.

"You don't have to go anywhere," he said. "Someone will come to you." He didn't go into any detail, just told me that much and little more. I did some thinking that afternoon. Calling one of the nurses I asked her to get in touch with my wife and have her come to see me that evening.

She came during visiting hours. She expected, I know, to hear me plead for instant release from the place. I didn't talk about that. In my lame way I told her the story. It made little impression.

"It doesn't sound right," she said. "If this plan — and for the life of me I don't quite get it from what you've told me — if this plan is successful, why is this fellow back here himself?"

I was stumped. I was too ignorant about the thing myself to be capable of explaining it clearly to her. "I don't know," I said. "I'll admit it sounds queer, the way this fellow is and all that, but somehow I feel there's something to it. Anyhow, I want to know more about it."

She went away skeptically. But the next day I had a visitor, a doctor who had been himself an alcoholic. He told me little more about the plan. He was kindly, didn't offer any cut and dried formula to overcome my life-long difficulty. He presented no religious nostrums, suggested no saving rituals. Later he sent some of the other ex-alcoholics of the group to see me.

A few days later my fellow-alcoholic was released, and shortly afterward I was allowed to go home also. Through the man who had first told me of the plan I was introduced to several other members of the group of former alcoholics. They told me their experiences. Many were men of former affluence and position. Some had hit even lower levels than I had.

The first Wednesday evening after my release found me a somewhat shame-faced but intensely curious attendant at a meeting in a private home in this city. Some forty others were present. For the first time I saw a fellowship I had never known in actual operation. I could actually feel it. I learned that this could be mine, that I could win my way to sobriety and sanity if I would follow a few precepts, simple in statement, but profound and far-reaching in their effect if followed. It penetrated to my inner consciousness that the mere offering of lip-service wasn't enough. Still ignorant, still a little doubting, but in deadly earnest, I made up my mind to make an honest effort to try.

That was two years ago. The way has not been easy. The new way of living was strange at first, but all my thoughts were on it. The going was sometimes slow; halting were my steps among the difficulties of the path. But always, when troubles came, when doubts assailed and temptation was strong and the old desire returned, I knew where to go for aid. Helping others also strengthened me and helped me to grow.

Today I have achieved, through all these things, a measure of happiness and contentment I had never known before. Material success has mattered little. But I know that my wants will be taken care of.

I expect to have difficulties every day of my life; I expect to encounter stops and hindrances, but now there is a difference. I have a new and tried foundation for every new day.

* * * * *

ACE FULL — SEVEN — ELEVEN.

High school studies irked me early. I was an imaginative kid and when a small carnival came to town it seemed pretty glamorous to me. Not very big, skinny and looking like a victim of malnutrition, I made an admirable "Cigarette Fiend" for one of the side-shows, as one of the concession men told me when he propositioned me. I had a dandy hacking cough and looked very convincing on the platform as the spieler told the crowd how many hundred coffin-nails I smoked every day, how doctors had given me up and I sure surely[†] marked for the Grim Reaper. At every telling point in the ballyhoo, I would cough as if I would croak any minute. I was tickled. I was fooling the people.

That idea of fooling the people, which had its start with the carnival side-show, later dominated my whole life. I was a smart guy living by my wits, making my living by beating the other fellow. Thrown among carnival folks, I soon acquired their ways. I learned to take on a drink or two occasionally and on one night in a middle-western town got so loaded I woke up the next morning in a pig-pen. How I got there I don't even remember. I had been sick during the night and I've often wondered why the pigs tolerated me. Shortly afterward I quit the show and returned home.

My father was a pharacist[†] so I studied to follow in his footsteps, however, on the eve of taking the state board examination, I was ordered to report for military service. Army life contributed to the formation of my character in an important way. Like most of the boys, I didn't expect to be lucky enough to be alive when hostilities were over, so I began to live from day to day. In time of war the soldier is a gambler and tomorrow is something he is never quite sure about.

I was never more than ordinarily lucky and I knew that I couldn't get all the money I wanted by depending on luck, so I began to master the art of manipulating dice and cards. I became passionately interested in the basic arts of the profession of crooked gambling. Conscience bothered me somewhat at first, but the voice was stilled as I was soon making more money than the commanding officer of the encampment. Soon I had a house with a lady in charge outside of government property and laid in a stock of liquor and beer. My place became so popular that I was making money such as I hadn't dreamed of. I was the only real, genuine "doughboy" — I was making the dough and plenty of it.

The war ended and I returned home. I had experienced easy living and I certainly couldn't see a future of rolling pills and making up prescriptions from medical latin. I had plenty of money and in my home town began to know and be known by the gambling fraternity, the town sports, the bookies and operators. But something kept me from making any connection with that crowd professionally in my home town. I knew how hurt my people would be, so I lit out for pastures new.

Downstate was a hell-roaring river town with almost a century old reputation for being a gambler's paradise. It was practically never a closed town except in sporadic elections of reform administrations. I allied myself with one of the best known operators in a saloon, dealing poker, craps and blackjack. I made plenty of money. I developed a strong habit of stimulating myself with liquor.

Even that exciting existence dulled after a time and I felt I ought to see the country so, finding myself a clever and congenial partner, I took to riding the

---

[†] This accurately reflects the language of the original.

"name trains" from coast to coast, always with the best the Pullman company could offer. I had an excellent wardrobe, the best-looking baggage I could get — all the essentials for the front so necessary in the profession of a train-sharper. Prohibition was now with us, and the kind of whiskey I drank was $20.00 and more by the quart. Our plan of operation was in the best technique, based on the opening of offering something for nothing which is sure-fire appeal to human cupidity.

Traveling eventually became tiresome. I went home once more. I was now very definitely a professional but I didn't have to tie up with any outfit in particular. Working when the mood seized me, drinking steadily every day, I did not escape the fate of every gambler, getting into trouble with the authorities now and then, but always getting by because I well knew the value of protection, which was just a business proposition with me and thoroughly justifiable.

For the first time in my life, however, money failed me when I was incarcerated for eight months after hiring the best available mouth-piece and placing the needful where it seemed it might do me good to the tune of more than $5,000. Even when I went behind the bars I still had plenty left. Through influence I became cook for the superintendent of the prison which opened the way to liquor for me, and I managed to be comfortably jingled most of the time I was in the pen.

When I was out on the bricks again, I decided to give my home town a wide berth for a while and went to one of the largest cities in the country to resume operations.

I wasn't much given to contemplation. Long ago I had dropped any idea that there was a God. If I ever gave any thought to myself being in this world for any other purpose than to make all the money I possibly could, I do not recall it.

I drank heavily with sober periods few and far between. In this city I operated for four years during which time I was steadily slipping in any control over liquor I might once have had. I had my first experience of hospitals, taken there helpless from continued drinking. The best medical talent in the city was always in attendance. Hospital followed hospital and I finally went from one sanitarium to another. My business still gave me a considerable income. My economic position was not bad. By this time I had married but that had no steadying influence on me.

Back I went to my home town and then my troubles really started. My domestic situation became very disagreeable. Gambling even almost lost its appeal for me and that had been my life. I quit everything to take up drinking seriously. I knew that I was a drunkard, had no hope of ever overcoming the desire for liquor, now far more necessary to continued existence than the food I ate. My wife heard of a cure at a state institution — the state insane asylum to be frank — and, unknown to me, got a court order to have me sent there. Two deputies hauled me out of bed one day and took me to the county jail for temporary lodgement. I had many friends and even the law didn't want me to be sent to the bughouse. I got as far as the county jail twice for brief periods, being released on my promise to do something about drinking. I didn't do anything about it. When I got out all I wanted was liquor.

So eventually to the bughouse I went, assigned to the alcoholic ward. I spent four months there. During that time I had no trouble getting liquor because I still had money. Again I was released. Once out, I wrecked my car, driving while intoxicated, and it seemed that I might get a stiff jail sentence so when it was suggested that I might avoid that by going back to the asylum, I accepted.

The bughouse had no terrors for me. I knew I could always get a supply of liquor and stay half stupefied most of the time. In the institution I became a nuisance to officials, attendants, and doctors. I had been in and out of the place so often that even the sincere professional medical men and psychologists had given me up. Suggestion, kindness, everything had been tried. They now regarded me as incorrigible, said nothing could be done for or with me and discharged me in a very short time.

In two months I was back again. This time I was treated like any insane person, was punished for infractions, any breaches of discipline. I could still get all the liquor I wanted through my financial reserve and that was all I cared about.

I used to talk with another inmate about this drinking business. He was a man who had lost one good job after another, had fallen from a good professional position to the status of a hobo. This fellow knew and had lived in almost every railroad jungle from coast to coast and had finally been slammed into the bughouse because his family didn't want to read about his death someday as a friendless wanderer. To me he confessed that he had tried for years to quit. I told him I had long ago discovered I couldn't and that now I didn't give a damn. But this time when I was sent back to the asylum, he wasn't there.

About the middle of my last confinement I was surprised by a visit from this fellow. He had kept me in mind and had come a considerable distance to see me. I was half-drunk when he called on me and didn't have even the haziest idea of what he was talking about. But he asked me if I would try to follow instructions if he was successful in getting me out. Half-heartedly I told him I would, but I had no intention of cooperating. I merely wanted to get out, where I could have free access to what money I had and make a real job of drinking.

Shortly after that, my sister visited me and persuaded the authorities to let me go. They were glad to do so, being sick and tired of me. They were glad of the short respite they thought my absence would give them, I guess.

When I got home, doped with sedatives I was put to bed and managed to get a little rest. The next day my former fellow-inmate and recent visitor came from a neighboring town to see me. I was very nervous and jittery and my mind was continually on the bottle while he talked. My natural distrust for all human beings seemed diminished a little while he was talking, for I knew his story and we had something in common. He was pretty definite in his statements and finally elicited from me a promise to try to follow a certain plain† which he now proposed to explain to me. He stressed the fact that his drinking career had been very similar to mine and much more miserable because it had made a homeless bum out of him whereas I had never been in straitened financial circumstances. I told him I would give it a trial if at all possible and invited him to keep on talking.

He began by pointing out what I couldn't dispute, that I had no faith in anything, man or God, that all my life I had lived as I pleased without any moral scruples or misgivings whatever. I admitted that I had.

"What you need is a definite religious experience," he said.

"That's the bunk." I said. "I knew there was some angle like this. Count me out. If I've got to turn around and join a church and sing hymns and holler 'Amen' when some long-bearded jasper, who spends six days out of the week skinning suckers, legally begins to pray in meeting, I don't want any part of it."

"You don't have to do that," he said. "And, anyway, the long-bearded slicker is no concern of yours. Your problem is yourself."

† This accurately reflects the language of the original.

My friend was new to this job of helping the other fellow, but I couldn't get away from the fact that he was now sober and that he had got that way and was being kept that way by a religious experience. He made me a proposition.

"I'll come for you Wednesday night," he said. "I'll take you to where a bunch of guys who used to be pickled practically all the time meet every week. You can see and listen and judge for yourself."

With my friend I attended that meeting. I was cordially received. I knew a good many of them and listened attentively, but I say quite honestly it left me cold. Not that it was like a church service. No, it wasn't like that at all. When some stories had been told it ended up with the Lord's Prayer, then everybody sat around and visited. I was beginning to get a little scared. Now, I thought, is when they'll put the works to a guy; along about this time one of these mugs is going to get me in a corner and ask me about my soul.

Nothing of the sort happened. They invited me back again. Others asked if they could come to see me, when I'd be in and so forth. My pal stuck pretty close to me that week. Some of the gang turned up at my home and told me how they had been helped to quit drinking. I went back to the next meeting and the next and the next again. Gradually I began to see what it was all about. I listened carefully for I was now definitely interested. More or less unconsciously I was seeking for something. I didn't know it then, but I think I was surely seeking God. Now, I didn't find God suddenly. You must remember that God was never in any of my plans. The former cynical, gambler-slicker who didn't even believe much that there was honor among thieves, gradually learned that Love is the law of God. I, who had strictly followed the injunction that you should never give a sucker an even break, had to learn that God demands we be honest if we are to follow his teachings.

I am writing this in the Thanksgiving season. It is a great privilege to have the fine human friendship and association of this gang of former drunks. It is an even greater privilege when I can be of service in helping some guy to a remedy which is for the taking.

But if friends and fellowship were to disappear tomorrow I don't think I would be dismayed. Back of all that there is the knowledge that I have a Divine Father — that as long as I try to walk as He has laid down for me to do throughout my life, nothing of ill can befall me, that if I wish I can be sober for the rest of my days.

I have a simple little job on which I make less in a month that I formerly made in a day, but that doesn't worry me. I know there is something far better than mere dollars. There isn't a gambling house of note that wouldn't be glad to have me as an operator, for the owners know I'm capable, that I can bring and keep business. In fact, some who know, think I would be a greater asset than ever for they have confidence that I would make an honest accounting of receipts.

No, I don't have much money nowadays, but I don't need any. I am quite sure that God doesn't want me to go back to the green tables and the shaded lights again. It might even be possible that I could go back to my former profession and stay sober, but I doubt it. Accustomed to coldly calculating the odds all my life, I'm of the opinion that they would be definitely against me.

His Will must be my bet — There's no other way!

* * * * *

THE SALESMAN

I learned to drink in a workmanlike manner when the law of the land said I couldn't and what started out as a young man's fun became a habit which in its later existence laid me by the heels many a time and almost finished my career.

'Teen years were uneventful with me. I was raised on a farm but saw little future in farming. I was going to be a business man, took a business college course, acquired a truck and stand in the city market of a nearby town, and started off. I brought produce from my folks' place and sold it to city customers and there were plenty of them with bulging pocketbooks.

Back of me was the normal life of a farmer's son. My parents were unusually understanding people. My father was a life-long comrade till the day of his death. The business theory I had learned in college was now being practiced and I was equipped beyond many of my competitors to be materially successful. Soon I had expanded until I was represented in all the city markets and also in another city. In 1921 we had the forerunner of the later depression and my customers disappeared. Successively I had to close my stands and was finally wiped out altogether. Being a young man of affairs, I had begun to do a little business and social drinking and now with time on my hands, I seemed to do more of it.

Following a year of factory work, during which time I got married, I got a job with a grocer as clerk. My grocer-employer was an expert wine-maker and I had free access to his cellar. The work was monotonous in the extreme, behind a counter all day when I had been used to driving around attending to business, meeting people and building for what I thought was a great future. I mark, too, as a milestone, the death of my father, whom I missed greatly.

I kept hitting the wine, with just occasional use of liquor. Leaving the grocery I went back into the produce business and out among people, went back to liquor again and got my first warning to quit before it got me.

I was anxious to get with a concern which would give me an opportunity to build up again, and landed a job with a nationally known biscuit company. I was assigned to a good business region, covering several important towns, and almost at once began to earn real money. In a very short time I was the star salesman of the company, winning a reputation as a business-getter. Naturally I drank with my better customers for on my route I had many stops where that was good business. But I had things rather well under control and in the early days on this job I seldom wound up my day's work with any visible effects of drinking.

I had a private brewery at home which was now producing 15 gallons a week most of which I drank myself. It is typical of the attitude I had toward alcohol at that time that, when a fire threatened total destruction of my home and garage, I rushed to the cellar and rescued my most precious possessions — a keg of wine and all the beer I could carry, and got pretty indignant when my better half suggested that I had better get some of the needed effects out of the house before it burned down.

My home-brewing gradually became a bore and I began to carry home bottles of powerful bookleg† whiskey, starting with half a pint every night and winding up with a quart as my daily after-supper allowance. For a time I kept on the job spacing

---

† This accurately reflects the language of the original.

my drinks en route and very little of them in the morning hours. I just couldn't wait until I got home to drink. In a very short time I became an all-day drinker.

Chain-store managers and quantity buyers were both my guests and hosts and every now and then we had prodigious parties. Finally, in a re-organization shake-up resulting in new district managers with a pretty poor territory deal for me, I gave the company two weeks notice and quit. I had bought a home but in the year and a half following I had little income and finally lost that. I became satisfied with just enough to live on and buy the liquor I wanted. Then I landed in the hospital when my car was hit by a truck. My car was ruined entirely. That loss and my injuries plus the recriminations of my wife sort of sobered me up. When I got out of the hospital I stayed sober for six weeks and had made up my mind to quit.

I went back in the business where I had been a successful salesman, but with another company. When I started with this concern I talked things over with my wife and made her some very solemn promises. I wasn't going to touch another drop of liquor.

By this time prohibition was a thing of the past and saloons and clubs where I was well known as a good customer and a good spender became my patrons. I rolled up business until I was again a star, but after the first four months on the new job I began to slip. It is not unusual in the drinking experience of any man that after a time of sobriety he comes to the conclusion that he "can handle it". In no time at all liquor again became the most important thing in my life and every day became like another, steady drinking in every saloon and club on my route. I would get to headquarters every night in a top-heavy condition, just able to maintain equilibrium. I began to get warnings and was repeatedly fired and taken on again. My wife's parents died about this time in unfortunate circumstances. All my troubles seemed to be piling up on me and liquor was the only refuge I knew.

Some nights I wouldn't go home at all and when I did go home I was displeased when my wife had supper ready and equally angry when she didn't. I didn't want to eat at all and frequently when I underestimated my consumption of the amount of liquor I brought home, I made extra trips back to town to renew the supply. My morning ration when I started out was five double whiskies before I could do any business at all. I would go into a saloon, trembling like a leaf, haggard in appearance and deathly sick, I would down two double whiskies, feel the glow and become almost immediately transformed. In half an hour I would be able to navigate pretty well and start out on my route. My daily reports became almost illegible and finally, following arrest for driving while intoxicated and on my job at that, I got scared and stayed sober for several days. Not long afterward I was fired for good.

My wife suggested I go to my old home in the country, which I did. Continued drinking convinced my wife I was a hopeless case and she entered suit for divorce. I got another job, but didn't stop drinking. I kept on working although my physical condition was such as to have required extensive hospitalization. For years I hadn't had a peaceful nights' sleep and never knew a clear head in the morning. I had lost my wife, and had become resigned to going to bed some night and never waking again.

Every drunkard has one or two friends who haven't entirely given up hope for him, but I came to the point where I had none. That is, none but my Mother, and she, devoted soul, had tried everything with me. Through her, people came to me and talked, but nothing they said — some were ministers and others good church members — helped me a particle. I would agree with them when they were with me and as fast as they went away, I'd go after my bottle. Nothing suggested to me seemed to offer a way out.

But I was getting to a place where I wanted to quit drinking but didn't know how. My Mother heard of a doctor who had been having marked success with alcoholics. She asked me if I'd like to talk to him and I agreed to go with her.

I had known, of course, of the various cures and after we had discussed the matter of my drinking fairly thoroughly, the doctor suggested that I go into the local hospital for a short time. I was very skeptical, even after the doctor hinted there was more to his plan than medical treatment. He told me of several men whom I knew who had been relieved and invited me to meet a few of them who got together every week. I promised I would be on deck at their next meeting but told him I had little faith in any hospital treatments. Meeting night, I was as good as my word and met the small group. The doctor was there but somehow I felt quite outside of the circle. The meeting was informal, nevertheless I was little impressed. It is true they did no psalm singing, but I just didn't care for anything religious. If I had thought of God at all in the years of drinking, it was with a faint idea that when I came to die I would sort of fix things up with him.

I say that the meeting did not impress me. However, I could see men whom I had known as good hard-working drunkards apparently in their right minds, but I just couldn't see where I came into the picture. I went home, stayed sober for a few days, but was soon back to my regular quota of liquor every day.

Some six months later, after a terrific binge, in a maudlin and helpless state, I made my way to the doctor's home. He gave me medical treatment and had me taken to the home of one of my relatives. I told him I had come to the point where I was ready for the remedy, the only remedy. He sent two of the members of the group to see me. They were both kindly to me, told me what they had gone through and how they had overcome their fight with liquor. They made it very plain that I had to seek God, that I had to state my case to him and ask for help. Prayer was something I had long forgotten. I think my first sincere utterance must have sounded pretty weak. I didn't experience any sudden change, and the desire for liquor wasn't taken away overnight, but I began to enjoy meeting these people and began to exchange the liquor habit for something that has helped me in every way. Every morning I read a part of the Bible and ask God to carry me through the day safely.

There is another part I want to talk about — a very important part. I think I would have had much more difficulty in getting straightened out if I hadn't been almost immediately put to work. I don't mean getting back on my job as salesman. I mean something that is necessary to my continued happiness. While I was still shakily trying to rebuild my job of selling, the doctor sent me to see another alcoholic who was in the hospital. All the doctor asked me to do was tell my story. I told it, not any too well perhaps, but as simply and as earnestly as I knew how.

I've been sober for two years, kept that way by submitting my natural will to the Higher Power and that is all there is to it. That submission wasn't just a single act, however. It became a daily duty; it had to be that. Daily I am renewed in strength and I have never come to the point where I have wanted to say, "Thanks God, I think I can paddle my own canoe now," for which I am thankful.

I have been reunited with my wife, making good in business, paying off debts and making restoration as I am able. I wish I could find words to tell my story more graphically. My former friends and employers are amazed and see in me a living proof that the remedy I have used really works. I have been fortunate to be surrounded with friends ever ready to help, but I firmly believe any man can get the same result if he will sincerely work at it God's way.

* * * * *

FIRED AGAIN

In my school work I was somewhat of a shirker. I could usually get somebody else to do most of my work, which certainly didn't help me much. I became evasive, sneaky and guileful at an early age. I was also a rather accomplished liar, seeming to prefer lying when telling the truth would have been more to my advantage.

It was not until I became interested in engineering that I had any real conception of the neccessity for honesty and truthfulness, and it was not until this time that I began to understand that practically everything we do is subject to check and double-check somewhere along the line.

It seems to me that I never did do things normally. When I learned to dance I had to go dancing every night in the week if possible; when I worked or studied I wanted no interruptions or distractions. Wherever I worked I wanted to be the highest paid man in the place or I was irritated; and of course when I drank I could never seem to stop until I was saturated. I was usually hard to get along with as a boy; if the others wouldn't play my way I'd go home.

The town we lived in when I was a child was rather new and raw, people† largely by immigrants who seemed to be constantly getting married with free drinks and eats for anybody who cared to come. We kids usually managed to get to these celebrations, and although supposed to have soda pop we could get ourselves one or two beers. With this sort of background and more money than was good for me, it was fairly easy to start getting drunk before I was sixteen.

After I left home I earned rather decent salaries but was never satisfied with my position, salary, or the treatment accorded me by my employer. I very seldom stayed on one job for more than six months until I was married at the age of 28, at which time I had already begun to lose jobs because of my drinking. Whenever things went wrong I knew that a few drinks would make everything rosy, my fears, doubts and worries would vanish and I would always promise myself that the next time I would stop short of getting plastered. Somehow things seldom worked out that way though.

I was irritated by the efforts of so many doctors, ministers, lawyers, employers, relatives and friends who remonstrated with me, none of whom knew from personal experience what I was up against. I'd fall down, get up, work a while, get my debts paid (at least the most pressing ones) drink moderately for a few days or weeks, but eventually get myself so messed up in tanglefoot that I'd lose another job. In one year (1916) I quit two jobs because I thought I'd be discharged anyhow and was fired outright from five more, which is more jobs than many men have in a lifetime. Had I remained sober, any one of them would have led to advancement because they were with growing companies and in my chosen field of engineering.

After being discharged for the fifth time that year, I drank more than ever, cadging drinks and meals where I could, and running up a large rooming-house account. My brother took me home and my folks talked me into going to a sanitarium for thirty days. This place was operated by a physician who was a personal friend of the family and I was his only patient at the time. The doctor did his best, saw that I got into good physical condition, tried to straighten out the mental quirks he thought partly responsible for my drinking, and I left with the firm resolve never to drink again.

---

† This accurately reflects the language of the original.

Before I left the sanitarium I answered an advertisement for an engineer in a small Ohio town and after an interview, obtained the position. In three days after leaving the sanitarium I had a job I liked at a satisfactory salary in a small town with basic living costs (board, room and laundry) amounting only to about 15% of my salary. I was all set, sober, working in a congenial atmosphere for a firm that had more profitable business than they knew what to do with. I made some beautiful plans. I could save enough in a few years to complete my formal education and there were no saloons in the town to trip me up. So what? So at the end of the week I was drunk again for no particular reason at all that I could understand. In about three months I was out of a job again, but in the meantime two things of major importance had happened. I had fallen in love and war had been declared.

I had learned my lesson. I knew definitely that I couldn't take even one drink. I wanted to get married so I planned very earnestly to get another job, stay sober, and save some money. I went to Pittsburgh on Sunday, called on a manufacturer of rolling-mill equipment and on Monday, got a position and went to work. I was first paid at the end of the second week, was drunk before the end of the day and couldn't be bothered with going to work the next Monday.

Why did I take that first drink? I honestly don't know. Anyhow I nearly went crazy that summer and really developed some sort of mental disturbance. The night clerk of the small hotel where I was staying saw me go out about three in the morning in pajamas and slippers and had a policeman take me back into my room. I suppose he was used to screwy drunks or he would have taken me to jail instead. I stayed there a few days and sweated the alcohol out of my system, went to the office to collect the balance of my salary, paid my room rent, and found I had just enough money to get home. So home I went, sick, broke, discouraged and dispairing[†] of ever attaining a normal, happy life.

After two or three weeks of idleness at home, I obtained a subordinate position with a former employer, doing the lowest grade of drafting work on an hourly basis. I kept reasonably sober for several months, went to see my fiancee one or two weekends, was advanced rapidly in salary and responsibility, had a date set for the wedding and then inadvertently learned that one of the men working under my direction was receiving about forty dollars more per month than I was, which burnt me up to such an extent I quit after an argument, took my money, packed my personal effects, left them at the corner drug store, and went downtown and got plastered. Knowing that I would be greeted with tears, sorrowful sympathy and more grief when I got home, I stayed away until I was again destitute.

I was really worried sick about my drinking so father again advanced the money for treatment. This time I took a three-day cure and left with the firm resolve never to drink again, got a better position then I'd had before and actually did keep sober for several months, saved some money, paid my debts and again made plans to get married. But the desire for a drink was with me constantly after the first week or two, and the memory of how sick I had been from liquor and the agonies of the treatment I had undergone faded into the background. I had only begun to restore the confidence of my associates, family, friends and myself before I was off again without any excuse this time. The wedding was again postponed and it looked very much as though it would never take place. My employer did not turn me loose but I was in another nice jam nevertheless. After considerable fumbling around mentally as to what to do I went back to the three-day cure for the second time.

After this treatment I got along a little better, was married in the spring of 1919 and did very little drinking for several years. I got along very well with my work, had a happy home life, but when away from home with little likelihood of

---

[†] This accurately reflects the language of the original.

being caught at it, I'd go on a mild binge. The thought of what would happen if my wife caught me drinking served to keep me reasonably straight for several years. My work became increasingly more important. I had many outside interests and drinking became less of a factor in my life, but I did continue to tipple some during my out-of-town trips and it was because of this tendency that things finally became all snarled up at home.

I was sent to New York on business and later stopped at a night club where I had been drunk before. I certainly must have been very tight and it is quite likely that I was "Mickey Finned" for I woke up about noon the next day in my hotel without a cent. I had to borrow money to get home on but didn't bother to start back till several days later. When I got there I found a sick child, a distracted wife and had lost another job paying $7,000 a year. This, however, was not the worst of it. I must have given my business card to one of the girls at the night club for she started to send me announcements of another clip-joint where she was employed and writing me long hand "come on" notes, one of which fell into my wife's hands. I'll leave what happened after that to the reader's imagination.

I went back into the business of getting and losing jobs and eventually got to the point where I didn't seem to have any sense of responsibility to myself or to my family. I'd miss important family anniversaries, forget to come home for Christmas and in general wouldn't go home until I was exhausted physically and flat broke. About four years ago I didn't come home on Christmas Eve but arrived there about six oclock on Christmas morning, minus the tree I had promised to get, but with an enormous package of liquor on board. I took the three-day cure again with the usual results, for about three weeks later I went to a party and decided a few beers wouldn't hurt me; however I didn't get back to work for three days and a short while later had lost my job and was again at the bottom of things. My wife obtained employment on a relief basis and I finally got straightened out with my employer who placed me in another position in a nearby city which I also lost by the end of the year.

So it went until about a year ago when a neighbor happened to hear me trying to get into the house and asked my wife whether I had been having some drinking difficulties. This, of course, disturbed my wife but our neighbor was not just inquisitive. She had heard of the work of an ex-alcoholic doctor who was busily engaged in passing on the benefits he had received from another who had found the answer to his difficulties with liquor. As a result of this my wife saw the doctor. Then I talked with him, spent a few days in a local hospital and haven't had a drink since.

While in the hospital about twenty men called on me and told me of their experiences and the help they had received. Of the twenty I happened to know five, three of whom I had never seem† completely sober. I became convinced then and there that if these men had learned something that could keep them sober, I also could profit from the same knowledge. Before leaving the hospital, two of these men, convinced of my sincerity of purpose, imparted to me the necessary knowledge and mental tools which have resulted in my complete sobriety for thirteen months, and an assurance that I need never, so long as I live, drink anything of an alcoholic nature if I kept on the right track.

My health is better, I enjoy a fellowship which gives me a happier life than I have ever known, and my family joins me in a daily expression of gratitude.

* * * * *

---

† This accurately reflects the language of the original.

THE FEARFUL ONE.

When I was 21, I was taken suddenly and violently ill and was ill for seven years. As a result of this illness I was left with a poorish nervous system and a curious phobia. As this has a large place in my story, I will try to explain it clearly. After I had been ill some months, I gew[†] strong enough to get out of doors a little each day, but found I couldn't get farther than the nearest corner without becoming totally panic stricken. As soon as I turned back home the panic would vanish. I gradually overcame this particular phase of the trouble by setting myself longer distances to walk each day. Similarly I learned later to take short street car rides, then longer ones, and so forth, until I appeared to be doing most of the things other people do daily. But the things I did not have to do each day, or at least frequently, remained unconquered and a source of great but secret embarrassment to me.

So I went on for years, planning always to sidestep the things I was afraid of, but concealing my fear from everyone. Those years of illness were not all total invalidism. I made a good living part of the time, but was continually falling down and having to get up and start over again. The whole process gave me a licked feeling, especially when, towards the end of my twenties, I had to give up the presidency of a small company which was just turning the corner to real success. Shortly after this, I was successfully operated on and became a physically well man. But the surgeon did not remove the phobia, that remained with me.

During the period of my illness I was not especially interested in liquor. I was not a teetotaler, but I was just a "social drinker". However, when I was about thirty, my mother died. I went to pieces as I had become very dependent on my parents through my illness. When I began to get on my feet again I discovered that whiskey was a fine relief from the terrific nervous headaches I had developed. Long after the headaches were gone, however, I kept discovering other difficulties for which whiskey was a grand cure. During the ensuing ten years I once, by sheer will power, remained dry for five weeks.

I had many business opportunities during those ten years which, although I tried to keep them in my grasp, slipped through my fingers. A lovely wife came and went. She tried her best and our baby's birth put me on my mettle for all of six months, but after that, worse and more of it. When my wife finally took the baby and left, did I square my shoulders and go to work to prove to her and to the world that I was a man? I did not. I stayed drunk for a solid month.

The next two years were simply a drawn-out process of less and less work and more and more liquor. They ended eventually at the home of a very dear friend whose family were out of town. I had been politely but firmly kicked out of the house where I had been boarding, and although I seemed to be able to find money to buy drinks with, I couldn't find enough to pay advance room rent anywhere.

One night, sure my number was up, I chucked my "pride" and told this friend a good deal of my situation. He was a man of considerable means and he might have done what many men would have done in such a case. He might have handed me fifty dollars and said that I ought to pull myself together and make a new start. I have thanked God more than once that that was just what he did not do.

[†] This accurately reflects the language of the original.

Instead, he took me out, bought me three more drinks, put me to bed and yanked me bodily out of town the next noon to a city 200 miles away and into the arms of one of the most extraordinary group of men in the United States. Here, while in the hospital, men with clear eyes and happy faces came to see me and told me the story of their lives. Some of them were hard to believe, but it didn't take a lot of brain work to see they had something I could use. And it was so simple. The sum and substance of it seemed to be that if I would turn to God, it was very probable that He could do a better job with my life than I had.

When I got out of the hospital, I was invited to stay in the home of one of the fellows. Here I found myself suddenly and uncontrollably seized with the ole† panic. I was in a strange house, in a strange city, and fear gripped me. I shut myself in my room. I couldn't sit down, I couldn't stand up, I couldn't lie down, I couldn't leave because I had nowhere to go and no money to take me. Any attempt at reasoning accomplished nothing.

Suddenly in this maelstrom I grasped at a straw. Maybe God would help me — just maybe, mind you. I was willing to give Him a chance, but with considerable doubt. I got down on my knees — something I hadn't done in thirty years. I asked Him if He would let me hand over all these fears and this panic to Him. I lay down on the bed and went to sleep like a baby. An hour later I awoke to a new world. I could scarcely credit my senses, but that terrible phobia which had wrecked my life for eighteen years, was gone. Utterly gone. And in its place was a power and fearlessness which is a bit hard to get accustomed to.

All that happened nearly six months ago. In those six months a new life has opened before me. It isn't that I have been cured of an ordinarily incurable disease. I have found a joy in living that has nothing to do with money or material success. I know that incomparable happiness that comes from helping some other fellow get straightened out. Don't get me wrong. We are not a bunch of angels. None of us has any notion of becoming such. But we know that we can never go completely back to old ways because we are traveling upward through service to others and in trying to be honest, decent and loving toward the world, instead of sliding and slipping around in a life of drinking, cheating, lying and doing what we like.

* * * * *

† This accurately reflects the language of the original.

TRUTH FREED ME!

In May 1936, after a prolonged period of alcoholism, my friends, my associates, my superiors, and those people who really loved me in spite of embarrassments too numerous to mention, finally left me because they had come to the conclusion that I didn't have any idea of doing or trying to do the right thing.

I was a spineless individual who didn't care a rap for anyone or anything — I was hopeless and knew it — and then in my extremity, The Divine Comforter, "Truth" came to me in a barroom where I had spent the major portion of six weeks.

The Divine Comforter, in my experience, came in the guise of a former drinking companion whom I had assisted home on several occasions. Because of physical infirmities brought about by alcoholic excess, he had been unable to walk a distance of three blocks to his home unassisted, when I law[†] saw him. Now he approached me, and to my amazement he was sober and appeared greatly improved in physical condition.

He induced me to take a ride with him, and as we rode along told me of the marvelous thing that had come into his life. He had more than a practical idea of my difficulties, he also had a logical and practical idea as to how they might be overcome.

He started the conversation by explaining true alcoholism and stated very bluntly that I was an alcoholic. This was news to me in spite of the face[†] that I had promised everybody East of the Mississippi, if they would take time to listen, that I was through with drink. At the time I made these promises, I honestly wanted to quit drinking, but for some unknown reason hadn't seemed able to. He told me why I failed.

He then suggested that accompany him to a local doctor who had been helpful to him.[†] It took forty-eight hours of persuasion and quite a few drinks to fortify myself, but I finally agreed to go. The doctor turned out to be one who had been an alcoholic himself, and in gratitude for the release he had found and because he understood the true meaning of the phrase "Brotherly Love" was spending a great portion of his time helping unfortunate individuals like myself.

With the help and advice of these two individuals and two or three associates, I was able, for the first time in two and a half years, to stay sober for six weeks, and then disastrously tried the beer experiment. For some time I couldn't get hold of myself, but gradually came out of hiding and exposed myself again to this influence which had been so helpful.

July 2, 1936, I again contacted the two individuals, and since that day I have never had a drink. However, because of the difficulties I encountered as the result of the beer experiment, I was unable for some time to find reality in this new way of life. I was doubtful, fearful, full of self-pity, afraid to humiliate myself.

This unreality lasted until December 11th, when I was faced with the absolute necessity of raising a sum of money. For the first time came the realization that I was faced with a difficulty from which I seemed unable to extricate myself. Of course, I took time out to bemoan the fact that "after all I'd done, this had to

---

† This accurately reflects the language of the original.

happen to me" but on the advice of my wife, I reluctantly went to a banker.

I told him my story completely. I went to him believing that my need was money. I went there as a last resort to attempt to pry it loose to meet my needs. My need was not money, but again I had been led to the proper source. After having related my story to the banker, who knew my reputation not only as an alcoholic but as an individual who didn't pay his bills, he said, "I know something of what you are trying to do, and I believe you are on the right track. Are you right with the Father who knows your needs before you ask? If so, you are not dependent upon this bank or any individual in it, or any rules by which we operate, because your help comes from an ever present and all powerful Father. I am going to do everything I can to secure this loan for you. However, I don't want anything that happens here to throw you off the track, I want you to leave here feeling that you have done everything you could to secure these funds, and go about your business. Your business is business with God's work. I don't know whether that calls for you to go and collect a bill, sell some new contract, or to sit quietly and pray, but your Father knows and if you will but permit Him, He will direct you."

I had again found reality. My needs were met from another entirely unexpected source.

The manifestations of this ever present Power in my experience since 1936 are too numerous to mention. Let it suffice to say that I am profoundly grateful for the opportunities I have had of seeing and knowing "TRUTH".

* * * * *

SMILE WITH ME, AT ME.

At the age of eighteen I finished high school and during my last year there my studies were dropping away to be replaced by dancing, going out nights and thinking of a good time as most of the boys of my age did. I secured a job with a well known telegraph company which lasted about a year, due to the face[†] I thought I was too clever for a $7.00 a week job which did not supply me with enough money for my pleasures, such as taking girls out, etc. I was not at all satisfied with my small wages.

Now, I was a very good violinist at the time and was offered jobs with some well known orchestras, but my parents objected to my being a professional musician although my last year in high school was mostly spent playing for dances and giving exhibition dances at most of the fraternity affairs. Now naturally I was far from satisfied with my seven dollars a week wages, so when I came across a boy neighbor of mine on the subway one night (by the way I read in the newspaper that this same boy died four days ago) he told me he was a host in a celebrated Restaurant and Cabaret, and that his salary ran $14.00 per week and he made $50.00 a week in tips. Well, think of being paid for dancing with the carefree ladies of the afternoon and receiving all that sum, and me working for only $7.00 per. The following day I went straight uptown to Broadway and never did go back to my old job.

This was the beginning of a long stretch of high-flying as I thought, only to find out when I was forty one years old to be very low-flying. I worked in this restaurant until I was twenty one, then we went into the world war. I joined the navy. My enlistment pleased the owner of my cabaret so much that he offered me a good job at the end of my federal service.

The day I walked in to his establishment with my release from active duty, he said, "You are my assistant manager from now on." Well, this pleased me as you can imagine and my hat from then on would not fit.

Now, all this time my taste for liquor was constantly growing although it was no habit and I had no craving. In other words, if I had a date and wanted to drink with the girl friend I would, otherwise I would not think of it at all.

In six months time I found I was too good for this job and a competitive restauranteer or a chain of the best well-known night clubs offered me a better position which I accepted. This night life was starting to tell and show its marks and together with the slump in that sort of business at the time, I decided to apply for a job with a well known ballet master who drilled many choruses for Broadway shows.

I was this man's assistant and I really had to work very hard for the little money I received, sometimes twelve hours or more a day, but I got the experience and honor which was just what I was looking for. This was one time when my work interfered with my drinking. This job came to an end one evening when I was drinking quite heavily. A certain prominent actress inquired of Professor X, my boss, if I would be interested to sign an eighty week contract for a vaudeville tour. It seems she could use me as a partner in her act. Now, a very nice woman, Miss J. who was office clerk and pianist for the boss, overheard the conversation and told both Mr. X and Miss Z that I would not be interested.

[†] This accurately reflects the language of the original.

On hearing this I went out and drank enough to cause plenty of trouble, slapping Miss J. and doing an all round drunk act in the studio.

This was the end of my high-flying among the white lights. I was only twenty four years old and I came home to settle down; in fact I had to. I was broke both financially and in spirit.

Being a radio operator in the navy, I became interested in amateur radio. I got a federal license and made a transmitting radio set and would often sit up half the night trying to reach out all over the country. Broadcasting radio was just in its infancy then, so I began to make small receiving sets for my friends and neighbors. Finally I worked up quite a business and opened a store, then two stores, with eleven people working for me.

Now here is where Old Barleycorn showed his hidden strength. I found that in order to have a paying business I had to make friends, not the kind I was used to, but ordinary, sane, hard working people. In order to do this I should not drink, but I found that I could not stop.

I will never forget the first time I realized this. Every Saturday, my wife and I (before we were married) would go to some tavern. I would take a bottle of wine, gin, or the like, and we would spend an evening dancing, drinking, etc. (This was fourteen years ago).

I was practically a pioneer in the radio business and that must account for people putting up with me as they did. However, within three years time I had lost both stores, I won't say entirely due to my drinking, but at least if I had been physically and mentally fit, I could have survived and kept a small business going.

Now from this time up to about a year ago, I drifted from one job to another. I peddled brushes, did odd jobs such as painting, and finally got established with a well known piano company as assistant service manager.

Then came the big crash of 1929 and this particular company abolished their radio department. For two years I worked for one of my old competitors who owned a radio store. He put up with my drinking until I was in such a physical breakdown that I had to quit.

All this time my troubles at home were getting worse. My whole family blamed my failure on the alcoholic question and so the usual arguments would start the instant I came in the house. This naturally made me go out and drink some more. If I had no money, I would borrow, beg, or even steal enough for a bottle.

My wife fortunately went to business which was our only salvation. Our little boy was six years old at the time and due to the fact we needed someone to care for him during the day we moved in with my family. Now the trouble did start, because I not only had my wife to face every evening, but three of the elders of the family.

My wife did everything for me she possibly could. First she got in touch with a well known psychiatrist and I went faithfully to him for a few months. This particular doctor was such a nervous individual, I thought he had the St. Vitus dance and I really thought he needed some kind of treatment more than I did. He advised hospitalization from three months to a year.

Well, this was all out of order as far as I was concerned. In the first place I had an idea that my wife wanted to put me away in a state institution where maybe I would be stuck for the rest of my life. In the second place, I wanted to go, if anywhere, to a private institution and that was far beyond our financial means. In the third place, I knew that that would be no cure, because I reasoned that it would be like taking candy out of a young child's reach. The instant I would come out a free man I would go right back to old Alky again. In this one thing I found out later I was perfectly right.

What I thought and wanted at the time was "not to want, to want to take a drink." This phrase is a very important link in my story. I knew this could only be done by myself, but how could I accomplish it? Well, this was the main question.

The point was always that when I did drink, I wanted all the time not to, and that alone wasn't enough. At the time I felt like a drink, I did not want to take it at all, but I had to, it seemed. So if you can grasp what I mean, I wished I would not want that drink. Am I nuts, or do you get me?

To get back to the doctor. If anything, these visits made me worse, and worst of all, everyone told me I wanted to drink and that was all there was to that. After going to as many as six or eight other doctors, some of my own friends advised my wife to make her plans for the future as I was a hopeless case, had no backbone, no will power, and would end up in the gutter.

Well, here I was, a man with much ability, a violinist, a radio engineer, a ballet master, and at this point took up hair dressing, so that added one more to the list. Can you beat it? I knew there must be some way out of all this mess. Everyone told me to stop my drinking, but none could tell me how, until I met a friend and believe me he turned out to be a true friend, something I never had until this past year.

One morning, after one of my escapades, my wife informed me I was to go with her to a public hospital or she would pack up and leave with our boy. My father, being a physician for forty years, put me in a private New York hospital. I was there ten days and was put in physical shape, and above everything else put on the right path to recovery and happiness.

My friend first asked me if I really wanted to stop drinking, and if I did, would I do anything no matter what it was in order to? I knew there was only one thing left to do if I wished to live and not enter an insane asylum where I knew I would eventually wind up.

Making up my mind that I would, he said, "Fine". And went on to explain the simple steps to take. After spending an hour or two with me that day he returned two days later and went into the subject more thoroughly. He explained he had been in the same hospital with the same malady and after taking these steps after his discharge had not taken a drink in three years and also there were about sixty others that had this same experience. All these fellows got together on Sunday evenings and brought their wives and everybody spent a very pleasant time together.

Well, after I met all these people, I was more than surprised to find a very interesting, sociable, and friendly crowd. They seemed to take more interest in me than all of my old fraternity brothers or Broadway pals had ever done.

There were no dues or expenses whatsoever. I went along for about fourteen weeks, partly keeping these rules, and so one afternoon I thought it would do no harm to take a couple of drinks and no more. Saying to myself, "I have this thing in hand now, I can be a moderate drinker." Here I made a fatal mistake. After all my past experience, again I thought I could handle the situation only to find out one week later it was the same old thing. I repeated the same thing over again and

and[†] another week again.

Finally I was back at the hospital, although I went under protest. My wife had expected to take two weeks vacation in the country with me, but instead had to use this money for the hospital expenses. During my one week stay, I held this as a grudge against her. The result was I got drunk three days after I was discharged from the hospital. And she left me for two weeks. During this period of time I drank heavily, being upset not only over her absense[†], but perfectly at sea as to how I could ever get back on my feet and make a new start again.

There was no mistake about it there was something that I failed to do in those simple steps. So I carefully went over each day as best I could since my first drink after the fourteen weeks of sobriety, and found I had slipped away from quite a few of some of the most important things which I should do in order to keep sober.

Certainly I was down now — ashamed to face my new friends — my own family giving me up as lost and everyone saying, "The system didn't work, did it?"

This last remark was more than too much for me. Why should this fellowship of hard working fellows be jeopardized by me? It worked for them. As a matter of fact, not one who has kept faithfully to it has ever slipped.

One morning, after a sleepless night worrying over what I could do to straighten myself out, I went to my room alone — took my Bible in hand and asked Him, the One Power, that I might open to a good place to read — and I read. "For I delight in the law of God after the inward man. But I see a different law in my members, warring against the law of my mind and bringing me into captivity under the law of sin which is in my members. Wretched man that I am! Who shall deliver me out of the body of this death?"

That was enough for me — I started to understand. Here were the words of Paul a great teacher. When then if I had slipped?[†] Now, I could understand.

From that day I gave and still give and always will, time everyday to read the word of God and let Him do all the caring. Who am I to try to run myself or anyone else?

* * * * *

[†] This accurately reflects the language of the original.

Word definitions
as found in:

Webster's Universal Unabridged Dictionary of the English Language.
World Syndicate Publishing Company of Cleveland, Ohio and New York, N.Y.

Published in 1937, one year prior to the writing of *Alcoholics Anonymous*.
(A few definitions are from other contemporary dictionaries as noted.)

Aberrations
Plural of: Aberration
(àb´e-râ´shen) noun.
1) The act of wandering from the right way; deviation from truth or moral recitude; deviation from a straight line.
2) Partial alienation of mind; mental wandering.

Abide
Abide (e-bìd´) verb.
1) To bear or endure; to bear patiently; as, I cannot *abide* his impertinence.
Note: In general, *abide by*, signifies to adhere to; as to *abide by* a bargain, a promise, or a friend; or to suffer the consequences; as to *abide by* the event.

Abjectly
Derived from: Abject
(àb´jèkt´) adjective.
1) Sunk to a low condition; applied to persons or things.
2) Worthless; mean; despicable; low in estimation without hope or regard.
Synonyms: Low, contemptible, pitiful.

Acute
Acute (e-kyoot´) adjective.
1) In medicine, sharp; severe; coming speedily to a crisis; said of disease; the opposite of chronic.
Synonyms: Keen, penetrating, shrewd, sagacious, piercing, pointed, sharp.

Admonish
Admonish (àd-mòn´îsh) verb, transitive.
1) To warn or notify of a fault; to reprove with mildness.
2) To council against wrong practices; to caution or advise.
3) To instruct or direct; to guide; to inform or acquaint with; as, *admonished* by his ear.
Synonyms: Caution, rebuke, counsel, censure, advise, reprove, forewarn, warn.

Aggrieved
Derived from: Aggrieve (e-grêv´) verb.
1) To give pain or

sorrow; to afflict.
2) To bear hard upon; to oppress or injure in one's rights; to vex or harass by civil or political injustice.

Aghast
Aghast (à-gàst´) adjective.
1) Struck with amazement; stupefied with sudden fright or horror.

Agnostic
Agnostic (àg-nòs´tîk) noun.
1) One who holds the doctrine of agnosticism (the doctrine that God is unknown and unknowable; because god has not revealed himself to man; because finite mind cannot comprehend God; because absolute God cannot come into intimacy nor make himself known to finite mind).

Alibis
Plural of: Alibi (àl´e-bì´) noun.
1) In law, a plea showing that the person charged with the offense was in another place at the time it was committed.
2) The fact of being elsewhere at the time of an offense charged.

Alloy
Alloy (àl´oi´) noun.
1) Figuratively, that which detracts from the value of anything; as, no happiness is without *alloy*.
2) To reduce or abate by mixture; as, to *alloy* pleasure with misfortunes.

Alluring
Alluring (à-loor´ing) adjective.
1) Inviting; having the quality of attracting or tempting.

Alpha
Alpha (àl´fa) noun.
1) The first letter of the Greek alphabet, corresponding to A; used to denote first, beginning or chief.

Altruistic
Derived from: Altruism (àl´true-îz´em) noun.

1) A term first employed by the Positivists, or followers of the French philosopher Comte, to signify devotion to others or humanity; the opposite of *selfishness*.

Amends
Amends (e-mèndz´) plural noun.
1) Compensation for an injury; recompense; satisfaction; equivalent; as the happiness of a future life will more than make *amends* for the miseries of this.
Synonyms: Reparation, restitution, restoration, compensation.

Annihilation
Annihilation (e-nì´e-lâ´shen) noun.
1) The act of reducing to nothing, or non-existence; or the act of destroying the form or combination of parts under which a thing exists, so that the name can no longer be applied to it.
2) The state of being reduced to nothing.

Antagonism
Antagonism (àn-tàg´e-nîz´em) noun.
1) The act of antagonizing or opposing; the characteristic quality of temper of persons opposed.
2) The state of being antagonized, as between persons, forces, or things acting in opposition to each other; contrariety or disagreement, as between conflicting principles.

Antipathy
Antipathy (àn-tîp´e-thê) noun.
1) Inherent aversion or antagonism of feeling; repugnancy; revulsion; as, *antipathy* to snakes; *antipathy* to an offensive person.
2) Any object of repugnancy or idiosyncratic aversion.
Note: Antipathy is regularly followed by *to*, sometimes by *for*, etc. and is opposed to *sympathy*.
Synonyms: Abhorrence,

aversion, contrariety, detestation, dislike, hatred, opposition, repugnance.

Apathy
Apathy (àp´e-thê) noun.
1) Want of feeling, privation of passion or insensibility to pain; applied either to the body or the mind. As applied to the mind it is stoicism, a calmness of mind incapable of being ruffled by pleasure, pain or passion.

Aprópós
Aprópós (àp´re-po´) adjective.
1) Opportunely; seasonably; pertinently.
2) By the way; to the purpose; a word used to introduce an incidental observation, suited to the occasion, though not strictly belonging to the narration.

Aptitudes
Plural of: Aptitude (àp´tî-tood´) noun.
1) A natural or acquired disposition for a particular purpose, or tendency toward particular action or effect; as, oil has an *aptitude* to burn; men acquire an *aptitude* for particular vices.
2) Fitness; suitableness.

Arbiter
Arbiter (är´bî-ter) noun.
1) One who has the power of judging; one whose power of deciding and governing is not limited.
Synonyms: Arbitrator, adjudicator, umpire, referee, judge.

Armistice
Armistice (är´mî-stîs) noun.
1) A cessation of arms, for a short time, by convention; a truce; a temporary suspension of hostilities by agreement of the parties.

Arrears
Derived from: Arrear (e-rîr´) noun.
1) That which is behind in payment, or remains unpaid, though due. It is

generally used in the plural ; as, the *arrears* of rent, wages, or taxes; and it implies part of the money already paid.

Ascertained
Derived from: Ascertain (às´er-tân´) verb, transitive.
1) To make certain; to define or reduce to precision, by removing obscurity or ambiguity; to determine.
Synonyms: Find out, discover, determine, detect, discern, learn.

Askance
Askance (e-skàns´) adverb.
1) Sideways; obliquely; out of the corner of the eye; hence, distrustfully; with suspicion; as, the regarded us *askance*.

Avocation
Avocation (àv´o-kâ´shen) noun.
1) The business which calls aside. The word is generally used for the smaller affairs of life, or occasional calls which summon a person to leave his ordinary or principle business.

Balked
Derived from: Balk (bôk) verb.
1) To turn aside or stop in one's course; as, the horse *balked*; he *balked* in his speech.
2) To leave untouched generally; to omit; to pass over; to neglect; to shun.

Balmy
Balmy (bä´mê) adjective.
1) Silly; weak-minded; half-witted [Slang.]
From The New Century Dictionary, D. Appleton-Century Co. 1944.

Bedevilments
Derived from: Bedevil (bî-dèv´el) noun.
1) Vexatious confusion or bewilderment.

Belladonna
Belladonna (bèl´e-dòn´e) noun.
1) A European plant of the nightshade family (*Atropa belladonna*). It is a perennial herb, poisonous in all its parts, containing the alkaloid atropin. The plant received its name from the use of its products by ladies as cosmetics. The extracts of root and leaf are largely used medicinally, being anodyne and anti-spasmodic, and in optical surgery to dilate

the pupil and temporarily atrophize the muscles. Also called *deadly nightshade*.

Belligerent
Belligerent (be-lîj´er-ent) adjective.
1) Hostile; addicted to war; bellicose; warlike in attitude or intention; threatening war.

Blight
Blight (blìt) noun.
1) That which frustrates or impairs one's ambition, brings to naught one's plans, or ruins one's expectations.

Bogged
Derived from: Bog (bog) verb, transitive.
1) To sink or submerge in mud or mire; as, to *bog* a horse and wagon.

Brainstorm
Brainstorm (brân´stôrm´) noun.
1) *Brain storm.* In pathology, a period when there is an abnormally rapid breaking down of brain cells, resulting in violent derangement of the mind.

Bristle
Bristle (brîs´el) verb.
1) To stiffen the bristles of; to erect in defiance or anger, like the bristles of a hog; as, to *bristle* the crest.
2) To raise the head and show anger or defiance; as, a man *bristles* up.

Calamity
Calamity (ke-làm´î-tê) noun.
1) Any great misfortune or cause of misery; generally applied to events producing extensive evils either to persons or communities.
2) A condition of distress; a time of adversity; misery.
Synonyms: Disaster, misfortune, mischance, mishap.

Camaraderie
Camaraderie (kä´me-rä´de-rê) noun.
1) Intimate, loyal and spontaneous comradeship; good-fellowship.

Capitalize
Derived from: Capital (kàp´î-tl) noun.
1) Resources; any source of profit or advantage.
From The New Century Dictionary, D. Appleton-Century Co. 1944.

Capitulated
Derived from: Capitulate (ke-pîch´e-lât´) verb, intransitive.
1) To surrender, as an army or garrison, to an enemy, by treaty, in which the terms of surrender are specified and agreed to by the parties.

Carom
Carom (kàr´em) noun.
1) A shot in billiards in which the cue-ball strikes successively two or more balls; also, the stroke used in making such a shot, termed in England a *cannon*.

Catapulted
Derived from: Catapult (kàt´e-pùlt´) noun.
1) A military engine used by the ancient Greeks and Romans for throwing stones, darts, and arrows. Later, the engine assumed the form of a gigantic crossbow and was called a *ballista*.

Centric
Centric (sèn´trîk) adjective.
1) Placed in the center or middle.

Cessation
Cessation (sè-sâ´shen) noun.
1) A ceasing; a stop; the act of discontinuing motion or action of any kind, whether temporary or final.
Synonyms: Stop, rest, pause, intermission.

Chicanery
Chicanery (shî-kâ´ne-rê) noun.
1) Sophistry; mean or unfair artifices used in contest or discussion; chicane.
Synonyms: Sophistry, caviling, quibble, trickery, stratagem.

Chronic
Chronic (kròn´îk) adjective.
1) Pertaining to time; having a reference to time.
2) Continuing a long time, as a disease. *Chronic disease*; one which is inveterate or of long continuance, in distinction from an *acute* disease, which speedily terminates.

Cipher
Cipher (sì´fer) noun.
1) Figuratively, something of no value or consequence; essentially a person of no weight, influence,

usefulness, or decided character.

Civic
Civic (sîv´îk) adjective.
1) Literally, pertaining to a city or citizen; relating to civil affairs or honors.

Clemency
Clemency (klèm´en-sê) noun.
1) Mildness of temper, as shown by a superior to an inferior; disposition to spare or forgive; mercy; leniency.
Synonyms: Mercy, lenity, compassion, mildness, gentleness, tenderness.

Cocky
Cocky (cock´ee) adjective.
1) Pert or forward; conceited; snobbish. [Slang.]

Commence
Commence (ke-mèns´) verb.
1) To begin; to enter upon; to perform the first act of; as, to *commence* operations.
Synonyms: Begin, start, set about, originate.

Communicative
Communicative (ke-myoo´nî-kâ´tîv) adjective.
1) Inclined to communicate; ready to impart to others.

Condemn
Condemn (ken-dèm´) verb, transitive.
1) To pronounce utterly wrong; to utter a sentence of disapprobation against; to censure; to blame. The word often expresses more than *censure* or *blame*, conveying the idea of utter rejection; as to *condemn* heretical opinions; to *condemn* one's conduct.
2) To witness against; to show or prove to be wrong, or guilty.
Synonyms: Blame, censure, upbraid, convict, sentence, adjudge, reprove, doom, reprobate, reproach.

Conscience
Conscience (kòn´shens) noun.
1) Internal or self-knowledge, or judgment of right and wrong; or the faculty, power, or principle within a person which decides on the lawfulness or unlawfulness of his actions and affections, and approves or condemns them.
2) Consciousness;

knowledge of our own actions or thoughts.

Consigned
Derived from: Consign (ken-sìn´) verb.
1) To give, send, or set over; to transfer or deliver into the possession of another, or into a different state, with the sense of fixedness in that state, or permanence of possession; as, at death the body is consigned to the grave.
Synonyms: Commit, intrust, make over, transfer, deliver, resign.

Console
Console (ken-sol´) verb, transitive.
1) To comfort; to cheer (the mind) in distress or depression; to alleviate (grief), and give refreshment to (the mind or spirits); to give (some one) contentment or moderate happiness, by relieving from distress.
Synonyms: Comfort, solace, soothe, cheer, sustain, encourage, support.

Consternation
Consternation (kòn´ster-nâ´shen) noun.
1) Amazement or horror that confounds; excessive terror, wonder, or surprise.
Synonyms: Dismay, alarm, terror, panic, overwhelming fear, horror.

Constitutionally
Derived from: Constitutional (kòn´stî-too´she-nel) adjective.
1) Of, pertaining to, or inherent in, the constitution, or in the natural frame of body or mind; as, a constitutional infirmity; constitutional ardor or dullness.

Consummation
Consummation (kòn´se-mâ´shen) noun.
1) Completion; end; perfection of a work, process, or scheme; the act of consummating.

Consumption
Consumption (ken-sùmp´shen) noun.
1) The act of consuming; waste; destruction; as, the consumption of fuel, of food, of time, etc.
Synonyms: Decay, decline, waste, destruction.

Contemporaries
Plural of: Contemporary (ken-tèm´pe-rèr´ê)

noun.
1) One who lives at the same time with another; as, Socrates and Plato were contemporaries.

Contempt
Contempt (ken-tèmpt´) noun.
1) The act of despising; the act of viewing or considering and treating as mean, vile, and worthless; disdain; hatred of what is mean or deemed vile.
Synonyms: Disdain, scorn, derision, mockery, contumely, neglect, disregard, slight.

Contention
Contention (ken-tèn´shen) noun.
1) Strife; struggle; a violent effort to obtain something; contest; quarrel.
2) Strife in words or debate; quarrel; angry contest; controversy; as, contention over property.
3) Something contended for in a debate or other argument; the argument in support of it.
Synonyms: Struggle, contest, litigation, controversy, quarrel, conflict, feud, dissension, variance, disagreement, debate, competition, emulation, discord.

Contingent
Contingent (ken-tîn´jent) adjective.
1) Dependent on an uncertain issue; of doubtful occurrence; incidental; casual; conditional.
Synonyms: Incidental, accidental, casual, fortuitous.

Contrition
Contrition (ken-trîsh´en) noun.
1) Penitance; deep sorrow for sin; grief of heart for having done wrong.
Synonyms: Penitence, sorrow, repentance, compunction, remorse.

Convalescence
Convalescence (kòn´ve-lès´ens) noun.
1) Renewal of health; the insensible recovery of health and strength after disease; the state of a body renewing its vigor after sickness or weakness; also, the period occupied in such recovery or renewal.

Conviviality
Conviviality (ken-vîv´ê-àl´î-tê) noun.
1) The good humor or

mirth indulged in at entertainments of a convivial character.
2) A convivial spirit or disposition.

Cordially
Derived from: Cordial (kôr´jel) adjective.
1) Proceeding as from the heart (the ancients believing the heart the source of affection); hearty; sincere; not hypocritical; warm; affectionate; as, we give our friends a cordial reception.

Countenance
Countenance (koun´te-nens) noun.
1) Out of countenance: abashed (expressed astonishment).
From Abbott's Ready Reference Dictionary, Western Printing & Lithographing. Co. 1938.

Crave
Crave (krâv) verb.
1) To call for, as a gratification; to long for; to require or demand, as a passion or appetite; as, the stomach or appetite craves food.
Synonyms: Desire, entreat, beseech, implore, adjure, request, supplicate, solicit, ask.

Criterion
Criterion (krì-tîr´ê-en) noun.
1) A standard of judging; any established law, rule, principle, or fact, by which facts, propositions, opinions, and behavior are compared, in order to discover their truth or falsehood, or by which a correct judgment may be formed; spelled also, rarely, criterium.
Synonyms: Rule, measure, test, standard.

Crusade
Crusade (kroo-sâd´) noun.
1) An enterprise projected in a spirit of enthusiasm and conducted with earnestness against some social or economic wrong; as, a crusade against the slave-trade; a crusade against impure milk.

Crux
Crux (krùks, kruks) noun.
1) Anything that puzzles, vexes, or tries, in the highest degree.

Cynically
Derived from: Cynical (sîn´î-kel) adjective.

1) In a snarling, captious, or morose manner.

Cynicism
Cynicism (sîn-î´sîzm) noun.
1) The practice of a cynic; a morose contempt of the pleasures and arts of life.

Czar
Czar (zär) noun.
1) A king; a chief; specifically, a title of the emperor of Russia; also spelled tsar, tzar.

Debacle
Debacle (dî-bä´kel) noun.
1) A breaking up of ice in a river; a violent rush of waters, carrying along debris; hence, a general break-up, rout or overthrow.
From The New Century Dictionary, D. Appleton-Century Co. 1944.

Debauch
Debauch (dî-bôch´) noun.
1) Excess in eating or drinking; intemperance; drunkenness; gluttony; lewdness.
2) A time or period of debauchery.

Defects
Plural of: Defect (dê´fèkt´) noun.
1) Want or absence of something necessary or useful toward perfection; fault, imperfection; lack; as, a defect in the plan.
2) Any natural want or imperfection, whether physical or moral; mistake; blemish; deformity; as, a defect in timber; a defect of memory.
Synonyms: Fault, blemish, flaw, speck, imperfection, spot, stain.

Deflation
Deflation (dî-flâ´shen) noun.
1) To reduce (currency, prices etc.) from an inflated condition.
From The New Century Dictionary, D. Appleton-Century Co. 1944.

Delirium
Delirium (dî-lîr´ê-em) noun.
1) A temporary disordered state of the mental faculties occurring during illness, either of a febrile or of an exhausting nature; wandering of the mind. Delirium tremens; an affection of the brain induced by the exces-

sive and prolonged use of intoxicating liquors.
Synonyms: Madness, mania, aberration, frenzy, lunacy, insanity.

Demoralization
Derived from: Demoralize (dî-môr´e-lìz´) verb, transitive.
1) To lower the tone or spirit of; to render distrustful and hopeless; as, hunger and cold *demoralized* the army.
2) To confuse or disorder mentally; as, the examiner's questions *demoralized* the applicant.

Denial
Denial (dî-nì´el) noun.
1) The act of denying, contradicting, refusing, or disowning; an assertion that a declaration or fact stated is not true; negation; contradiction; opposed to *affirmation*.
2) A rejection or refusing to acknowledge; a disowning; a refusing to receive or embrace; as, a *denial* of the faith or the truth.
Synonyms: Disavowal, renunciation, contradiction, dissent, rejection, abnegation.

Denizens
Plural of: Denizen (dèn´î-zen) noun.
1) A stranger admitted to residence in a foreign country; specifically, in English law, an alien who is made a subject by the king's letters patent, holding a middle state between an alien and a natural-born subject.
2) A dweller; as, the *denizens* of air.

Denomination
Denomination (dî-nòm´e-nâ´shen) noun.
1) A society or collection of individuals called by the same name; a sect; as, the Universalist *denomination*.

Deportment
Deportment (dî-pôrt´ment) noun.
1) Carriage; manner of acting in relation to the duties of life; behavior; demeanor; conduct; management.

Deranged
Deranged (dî-rânj´d) adjective.
1) Disordered in mind; insane.

Derelictions
Plural of: Dereliction (dèr´e-lîk´shen) noun.

1) Neglect; unfaithfulness.
2) The state of leaving with an intention not to reclaim or resume; an utter forsaking; abandonment.

Derided
Derived from: Deride (dî-rìd´) verb, transitive.
1) To laugh at in contempt; to turn to ridicule or make sport of; to mock; to treat with scorn by laughter.
Synonyms: Ridicule, mock, taunt.

Destitution
Destitution (dès´tî-too´shen) noun.
1) The state of being destitute or of being deprived of anything; want; poverty; indigence; as, the fire caused much *destitution*.
Synonyms: Indigence, poverty, want, privation, distress, need, deficiency, pauperism.

Diffident
Diffident (dîf´î-dent) adjective.
1) Having or showing diffidence (Distrust of oneself; lack of self reliance; want of confidence in one's own power, ability, or correctness.)
Synonyms: Modest, reserved, retiring, humble, bashful, hesitating, doubtful, suspicious.

Diligently
Derived from: Diligent (dîl´e-jent) adjective.
1) Steadily applied; prosecuted with care and constant effort; careful; assiduous; as, make *diligent* search.
2) Steady in application to business; constant in effort or exertion to accomplish what is undertaken; assiduous; attentive; industrious; not idle or negligent; applied to persons.
Synonyms: Active, assiduous, sedulous, laborious, persevering, attentive, industrious, indefatigable, unremitting, untiring, careful.

Disconcerted
Derived from: Disconcert (dîs´ken-sûrt´) verb, transitive.
1) To throw into disorder or confusion; to undo, as a scheme or plan; to defeat; to frustrate; as, the emperor *disconcerted* the plans of his enemy.
2) To unsettle the mind of; to discompose; to disturb the self-

possession of; to confuse.

Discord
Discord (dîs´kôrd´) noun.
1) Disagreement; want of concord or harmony; said of persons or things. Applied to persons, difference of opinions; variance; opposition; contention; strife; any disagreement which produces angry passions, disputes, litigation, or war.
Synonyms: Disagreement, discordance, variance, difference, opposition, dissension, contention, strife, rupture, clashing, dissonance.

Discretion
Discretion (dî-skrèsh´en) noun.
1) The quality of being discreet; prudence; that discernment which enables a person to judge critically of what is correct and proper, united with caution; nice discernment and judgment, directed by circumspection, and primarily regarding one's own conduct.
2) Liberty or power of acting without other control than one's own judgment; as, the management of affairs was left to the *discretion* of the president.
Synonyms: Sagacity, circumspection, wariness, prudence, caution.

Disease
Disease (dî-zêz´) noun
1) Pain; uneasiness; distress.
2) Any morbid state of the body generally, or of any particular organ or part of the body; the cause of pain or uneasiness; distemper; malady; sickness; disorder; any state of a living body in which the natural functions of the organs are interrupted or disturbed, either by defective or preternatural action, without a disruption of parts by violence, which is called a *wound*. The word is also applied to the disorders of other animals, as well as to those of man, and to any derangement of the vegetative functions of plants.
3) Any disorder, depraved condition or element, moral, mental, social, political, etc.; as, a political foundation

laid in *disease* and corruption.
Synonyms: Distemper, ailment, malady, disorder, sickness, illness, indisposition, complaint, infirmity.
Also:
Disease: verb, transitive.
1) To interrupt or impair any or all the natural and regular functions of (the several organs of a living body); to afflict with pain or sickness; to make morbid; used chiefly in the past participle; as, a *diseased* body; a *diseased* stomach.
2) To pain; to make uneasy.

Disillusionment
Derived from: Disillusion (dîs´î-loo´zhen) verb, transitive.
1) To free from that which deludes or is illusory.

Disinherited
Derived from: Disinherit (dîs´în-hèr´ît) verb, transitive.
1) To cut off from hereditary right; to deprive of an inheritance; to prevent, as an heir, from coming into possession of any property or right which by law or custom would devolve on him in the course of descent; as, a father sometimes *disinherits* his children by will.

Disposition
Disposition (dîs´pe-zîsh´en) noun.
1) Temper or natural constitution of the mind; as, an amiable or an irritable *disposition*.
2) Inclination; propensity; the temper or frame of mind as directed to particular objects; humor; as, the *disposition* of a person to undertake a particular work; the *dispositions* of men toward each other; a *disposition* friendly to any design.
Synonyms: Inclination, tendency.

Disproportionate
Disproportionate (dîs´pre-pôr´she-nît) adjective.
1) Not proportioned; unsymmetrical; unsuitable to something else, in bulk, form, or value; inadequate; as, in a perfect form of the body, none of the limbs are *disproportionate*; it is wisdom not to undertake a work with *disproportionate* means.

Dissensions
Plural of: Dissension (dĭ-sèn´shen) noun.
1) Disagreement in opinion, usually a disagreement which is violent, producing warm debates or angry words; contention in words; strife; discord; quarrel; breach of friendship and union.
Synonyms: Contention, discord, dispute, disagreement, strife, quarrel.

Dissipation
Dissipation (dĭs´e-pâ´shen) noun.
1) Distracted attention; that which diverts and calls off the mind from any subject.
2) A dissolute, irregular course of life; a wandering from object to object in pursuit of pleasure; a course of life usually attended with careless and exorbitant expenditures of money, and indulgence in vices, which impair or ruin both health and fortune.

Doggerel
Doggerel (dô´ger-el) noun.
1) A loose, irregular kind of poetry; rime trivial in sentiment and poor in execution.

Dubious
Dubious (doo´bê-es) adjective.
1) Doubtful; wavering or fluctuating in opinion; not determined; as, the mind is in a *dubious* state.
2) Uncertain; of which the truth is not known; causing doubt; not clear; as, a *dubious* signal.
3) Of doubtful propriety; questionable; causing suspicion; as, *dubious* methods.

Emanate
Emanate (èm´e-nât´) verb, intransitive & transitive.
1) To issue from a source; to flow forth; as, light *emanates* from the sun.
2) To proceed, as from a source or fountain; to take rise; as, the powers of government in republics *emanate* from the people.

Embittered
Derived from: Embitter (èm-bĭt´er) verb, transitive.
1) To render unhappy, as by wrong or disappoint-ment; to fill with distress or anguish.

Eminently
Derived from: Eminent (èm´e-nent) adjective.
1) In a high degree; in a degree to attract observation; in a degree to be conspicuous and distinguished from others; as, to be *eminently* learned or useful.

Ensuing
Derived from: Ensue (èn-soo´) verb, intransitive.
1) To follow as a consequence of premises; as, this result *ensues*.
2) To follow in a train of events or course of time; to succeed; to come after; as, he spoke, and silence *ensued*; the *ensuing* age or years.

Environs
Environs (èn-vì´renz) noun.
1) The parts or places which surround another place, or lie in its neighborhood; as, the *environs* of a city or town.

Epoch
Epoch (ê´pòk´) noun.
1) In chronology, a fixed point of time from which succeeding years are numbered; a point from which computation of years begins; any fixed time or period; era; date; as, the exodus from Egypt and the Babylonish captivity are remarkable *epochs* in the history of the Jews.

Eradicated
Derived from: Eradicate (î-ràd´î-kât´) verb, transitive.
1) To destroy thor-oughly; to extirpate; as, to *eradicate* errors, false principles, vice, or disease.
Synonyms: Extirpate, uproot, exterminate, destroy, annihilate.

Erroneous
Erroneous (î-ro´nê-es) adjective.
1) Wrong; false; mistaken; not conform-able to truth; erring from truth or justice; liable to mislead; as, an *errone-ous* opinion; *erroneous* doctrine.

Exchequers
Plural of: Exchequer (èks´chèk´er) noun.
1) A state treasury; hence, pecuniary property in general; funds; as, my *exchequer* is very low.

Exonerating
Derived from: Exonerate (îg-zòn´e-rât´) verb, transitive.
1) To relieve, as of a charge or blame resting on one; to clear of something that lies upon the character as an imputation; as, to *exonerate* oneself from blame or from the charge of avarice.
Synonyms: Absolve, clear, justify, acquit, exculpate, relieve.

Fallacious
Fallacious (fe-lâ´shes) adjective.
1) Deceptive; deceitful; wearing a false appear-ance; misleading; producing an error or mistake; sophistical; of the nature of, pertaining to, or embodying a fallacy.
Synonyms: Deceitful, fraudulent, delusive.

Fettered
Derived from: Fetter (fèt´er) verb.
1) Anything that confines or restrains from motion; that which destroys liberty and freedom.

Fictitious
Fictitious (fĭk-tîsh´es) adjective.
1) Feigned; imaginary; not real.
2) Counterfeit; false; not genuine; as, *fictitious* fame.

Finite
Finite (fì´nìt´) adjective.
1) Having a limit; limited; bounded; opposed to *infinite*.

Flank
Flank (flàngk) noun.
1) The side of an army, or of any division of an army, as of a brigade, regiment or battalion; the extreme right or left; thus, to attack in flank is to attack on the side.

Forebodings
Derived from: Forebode (fôr-bod´) verb.
1) To foretell; to prognosticate.
2) To foresee; to be prescient of; to feel a secret premonition of.
Synonyms: To foretell, predict, prognosticate, augur, presage, portend, betoken.

Forthwith
Forthwith (fôrth-wĭth´) adverb.
1) Immediately; without delay; directly.
2) In law, as soon as the thing required may reasonably be done, commonly within twenty-four hours.

Frailties
Plural of: Frailty (frâl´tê) noun.
1) Weakness of resolution; infirmity; liableness to be deceived or seduced.
2) A foible or infirmity resulting from some weakness; a fault.
3) Frailness; infirmity of body.
Synonyms: Frailness, infirmity, imperfection, foible, failing.

Frank
Frank (fràngk) adjective.
1) Open; ingenuous; candid; free in uttering real sentiments; not reserved; using no disguise.
Synonyms: Candid, honest, plain, open, sincere.

Futile
Futile (fyoot´l) adjec-tive.
1) Trifling; of no weight or importance; answer-ing no valuable purpose; worthless; of no effect.

Futility
Derived from: Futile (fyoot´l) adjective.
See definition of *futile* above.

Gallantly
Derived from: Gallant (gàl´ent) adjective.
1) Brave; high spirited; courageous; heroic; magnanimous; of a noble bearing.

Gastric
Gastric (gàs´trîk) adjective.
1) Pertaining to the stomach; abdominal.

Gaunt
Gaunt (gônt) adjective.
1) Vacant; hollow; empty; as, an animal after long fasting; hence, lean; meager; thin; slender.

Gay
Gay (gâ) adjective.
1) Merry; airy; jovial; sportive; frolicsome. It denotes more life and animation than *cheerful*.
2) Inflamed or merry with liquor; intoxicated; dissipated. [Colloquial.]
Synonyms: Merry, lively, blithe, sprightly, sportive, hilarious.

Gorge
Gorge (gôrj) noun.
1) A sensation of constriction in the muscles of the throat,

due to disgust, anger or the like; as, his *gorge* rose.

Grenadier
Grenadier (grèn´e-dîr´) noun.
1) Originally, one who threw grenades. Only soldiers of long service and acknowledged bravery were selected for this duty. When hand-grenades went out of general use, the name was still retained for the company, the members of which were of great height and were distinguished by a particular dress, as for instance the high bearskin cap. In the British and French armies the grenadier company was the first of each battalion.

Grievous
Grievous (grê´ves) adjective.
1) Heavy; oppressive; hard to be borne; burdensome; as, a *grievous* load of taxes.

Hamlet
Hamlet (hàm´lît) noun.
1) A small village; a little cluster of houses in the country; especially in England, one which has no church.

Hemorrhage
Hemorrhage (hèm´er-îj) noun.
1) A discharge of blood from the blood-vessels.

Heresies
Plural of: Heresy (hèr´î-sê) noun.
1) In law, an offense against Christianity, consisting in a denial of some of its essential doctrines, publicly avowed, and obstinately maintained.

Highball
Highball (hì´bôl´) noun.
1) A drink consisting of whisky, brandy, or other spirit diluted with soda-water, ginger ale, or some effervescing mineral water. [Slang.]

Humbly
Derived from: Humble (hùm´bel) adjective.
1) To reduce to a low state; as, the power of Rome was *humbled* but not subdued.
2) To mortify or make ashamed; as, one may be *humbled* without having true humility.
3) To make humble or lowly in mind; to abase the pride of; to reduce

the arrogance and self-dependence of; to give a low opinion of the moral worth of; in a religious sense, to make meek and submissive to the divine will; often used reflexively.
Synonyms: Humiliate, lower, mortify, disgrace, degrade.

Humility
Humility (hyoo-mîl´î-tê) noun.
1) Freedom from pride and arrogance; humble-ness of mind; a modest estimate of one's own worth; also, self-abasement; penitence for sin.
2) An act of submission.

Hydrotherapy
Hydrotherapy (hì´dre-thèr´e-pê) noun.
1) The water-cure, a mode of treating diseases by the copious and frequent use of pure water, both internally and externally. This system is said to increase the cutaneous exhalation to a very large amount, and thus to draw off speedily from the blood certain deleterious matters.

Illness
Illness (ill´ness) noun.
1) Badness; unfavorableness; as, the *illness* of the weather. [Obscure.]
2) Disease; indisposi-tion; sickness; as, he has recovered from his *illness*.
3) Wickedness; iniquity. [Obscure.]
Synonyms: Disease, disorder, distemper, indisposition, malady, sickness ailment.

Impeccable
Impeccable (îm-pèk´e-bel) adjective.
1) Faultless or irre-proachable.
From The New Century Dictionary, D. Appleton-Century Co. 1944

Imperative
Imperative (îm-pèr´e-tîv) adjective.
1) Not to be avoided or evaded; that must be obeyed; obligatory; binding; as, an *impera-tive* task.

Imperious
Imperious (îm-pîr´ê-es) adjective.
1) Commanding; urgent; pressing; as, an *imperious* love; *imperi-ous* circumstances; *imperious* appetite.
Synonyms: Imperative,

commanding, pressing.

Impotent
Impotent (îm´pe-tent) adjective.
1) Wholly lacking in sexual power.
From The New Century Dictionary, D. Appleton-Century Co. 1944

Inexplicable
Inexplicable (în-èk´splî-ke-bel) adjective.
1) Not capable of being rendered plain and intelligible; as, an *inexplicable* mystery.

Infinitum
Derived from: Infinity (în-fîn´î-tê) noun.
1) Unlimited extent of time, space or quantity; boundlessness.

Insidious
Insidious (în-sîd´ê-es) adjective.
1) Lying in wait; hence watching an opportunity to ensnare or entrap; deceitful; sly; treacher-ous.
Synonyms: Artful, crafty, cunning, deceitful, tricky, deceptive.

Jag
Jag (jàg) noun.
1) Sufficient liquor to cause intoxication; hence a state of intoxication. [Slang.]

Keystone
Keystone (kê´ston´) noun.
1) The stone at the top or middle of an arch or vault, which, being wider at the top than at the bottom, enters like a wedge and binds the work; sometimes being projecting and orna-mented.
2) In a system, that which holds the several parts together; the supporting fact or principle.

Killjoy
Killjoy (kîl´joi´) noun.
1) A destroyer of joy; an agent of gloom or low spirits.

Lucid
Lucid (loo´sîd) adjec-tive.
1) Bright with the radiance of intellect; not darkened or confused by delirium or madness; marked by the regular operations of reason; as, the *lucid* intervals of a deranged man.

Lucrative
Lucrative (loo´kre-tîv) adjective.

1) Gainful; profitable; making increase of money or good; as, a *lucrative* trade; *lucrative* business or office.

Lunacy
Lunacy (loo´ne-sê) noun.
1) A form of insanity intermittent with lucid intervals; formerly supposed to be influence by the phases of the moon, or periodical in the month; hence mental impairment as opposed to idiocy.

Lustre
Lustre *alternate spelling of:* Luster (lùs´ter) noun & verb.
1) Brightness; splendor; brilliancy; gloss; as, the *luster* of the sun and stars; the *luster* of silk.

Maelstrom
Maelstrom (mâl´strem) noun.
1) A celebrated whirlpool on the coast of Norway; figuratively a resistless agent of destruction to all within its reach; as, the *maelstrom* of vice.

Majesty
Majesty (màj´î-stê) noun.
1) Loftiness of appear-ance; dignity; grandeur; dignity of aspect or manner; the quality or state of a person or thing which inspires awe or reverence in the beholder.

Malicious
Malicious (me-lîsh´es) adjective.
1) Proceeding from extreme hatred or ill will; dictated by malice; as, a *malicious* report.
Synonyms: Malevolent, malignant, mischievous, spiteful.

Marshalled
Marshalled (mär´shel-d) verb, transitive.
1) To dispose in order; to arrange in a suitable manner; as, to *marshal* an army.

Martyr
Martyr (mär´ter) noun.
1) One who suffers death or great loss in defense of any cause; as, a man dies a *martyr* to his political prin-ciples, or to the cause of liberty.

Maudlin
Maudlin (môd´lîn) adjective.
1) Drunk; fuddled; approaching intoxicated;

stupid.
2) Affected with excessive sentimentality; gushy.

Meditation
Meditation (mèd´î-tâ´shen) noun.
1) The act of meditating; close or continued thought; the turning or revolving of a subject in the mind; serious contemplation; mental reflection; often specifically, thought devoted to religious subjects.

Millenniums
Plural of: Millennium (me-lèn´ê-em) noun.
1) An aggregate of a thousand years.

Morass
Morass (me-ràs´) noun.
1) Any stretch of troublesomely muddy ground. [Now chiefly literary.]
    From The New Century Dictionary, D. Appleton-Century Co. 1944.

Morbid
Morbid (môr´bîd) adjective.
1) Diseased; sickly; not sound and healthful; as, a morbid constitution; a morbid sensibility.
2) Of, due to, or characteristic of disease.

Murmur
Murmur (mûr´mer) noun.
1) A complaint half suppressed or uttered in a low, muttering voice.

Musket
Musket (mùs´kît) noun.
1) A kind of smooth-bore firearm formerly used by the infantry in military operations. It succeeded the harquebus, and has been supplanted in modern warfare by the rifle.

Nadir
Nadir (nâ´der) noun.
1) Figuratively, any lowest point; as, the nadir of national strength.

Ne'er
Ne'er (nâr) adverb.
1) A contraction of never.

Neurotic
Neurotic (nu-ròt´îk) adjective.
1) Related to the nerves; seated in the nerves; as, a neurotic disease.

Neutrality
Neutrality (noo-tràl´î-tê) noun.
1) The state or condition of being neutral or of being unengaged in disputes or contests between others; the state of taking no part in either side.

Nil
Nil (nîl) noun.
1) Nothing; as, his liabilities were $5,000 and assets nil.

Nominal
Nominal (nòm´e-nel) adjective.
1) Titular; existing in name only; as, a nominal distinction or difference is a difference in name, and not in reality.

Nonchalant
Nonchalant (nòn´she-länt´) adjective.
1) Indifferent; cool; unconcerned.

Oasis
Oasis (o-â´sîs) noun.
1) Originally, the name of a fertile spot in the Libyan Desert where there is a spring or well and more or less vegetation, but now applied to any fertile tract in the midst of a waste; often used figuratively.

Obstinacy
Obstinacy (òb´ste-ne-sê) noun.
1) A fixedness in opinion or resolution that cannot be shaken at all, or not without great difficulty; firm an (usually but not necessarily) unreasonable adherence to an opinion, purpose , or system; stubbornness.
Synonyms: Firmness, resoluteness, inflexibility, persistency, stubbornness.

Omega
Omega (o-mèg´e) noun.
1) The name of the last letter in the Greek alphabet, as alpha is the first. Hence, in Scripture, Alpha and Omega denotes the first and last, the beginning and the ending.

Ominous
Ominous (òm´e-nes) adjective.
1) Foreboding or presaging evil; indicating a future evil event; inauspicious.
Synonyms: Suggestive, threatening, foreboding.

Omnipotence
Derived from: Omnipotent (òm-nîp´e-tent) adjective.
1) Almighty; possessing unlimited power; all-powerful; applied to the Deity.

Ordained
Derived from: Ordain (ôr-dân´) verb, transitive.
1) To invest with ministerial sacerdotal functions; to introduce and establish or settle in the pastoral office with the customary forms and solemnities; as, to ordain a minister of the gospel.

Ostracized
Derived from: Ostracize (òs´tre-sîz´) verb, transitive.
1) To cast out or banish; to exclude; to subject to ostracism in social, political, or public life.

Panacea
Panacea (pàn´e-sê´e) noun.
1) A remedy for all diseases; a universal medicine; a catholicon or cure-all.

Pandemonium
Pandemonium (pàn´de-mo´nê-em) noun.
1) An uproar; a riotous assemblage; great confusion and noise.

Paradoxically
Derived from: Paradox (pàr´e-dòks´) noun.
1) A tenet or proposition contrary to received opinion; something seemingly absurd, yet true in fact; a statement or phenomenon apparently at variance with or in opposition to established principles yet demonstrably true.
Synonyms: Contradiction, enigma, mystery, absurdity, ambiguity.

Pathological
Derived from: Pathology (pàth´àl-ò-gee) noun.
1) That part of medicine which explains the nature of diseases, their causes and symptoms; the doctrine of the causes and nature of diseases, comprehending nosology, etiology, symptomatology, and therapeutics. The word is used also to indicate any condition produced by disease.

Persevere
Persevere (pûr´se-vîr´) verb, intransitive.
1) To persist in any business or enterprise undertaken; to pursue steadily any design or course commenced; not to give over or abandon what is undertaken.
Synonyms: Continue, persist, insist, pursue.

Pertinent
Pertinent (pûr´tn-ent) adjective.
1) Related to; just to the purpose; adapted to the end proposed; apposite; relevant; not foreign to the thing intended; as, he used an argument not pertinent to his subject or design; the discourse abounds with pertinent remarks; he gave pertinent answers to the questions.
2) Regarding; concerning; belonging; with to.
Synonyms: Apposite, appropriate, relevant, fitting, proper, suitable.

Phenomena
Plural of: Phenomenon (fî-nòm´e-nòn) noun.
1) A visible manifestation or appearance, or one which in any way directly falls under our notice; a fact or occurrence presented to our observation either in the external world or in the human mind; an appearance produced by the action of the different forces upon matter; as, natural phenomena; mental phenomena; the phenomena of light, heat, or electricity.
2) A strange and striking appearance of any nature; something not common, as an unusual appearance in the sky, or a person possessing unusual powers; as, an electrical phenomenon; a musical phenomenon.

Plight
Plight (plìt) noun.
1) Condition; state; predicament; generally, a risky or dangerous state; a distressed condition; as, to be in a wretched plight.
Synonyms: Situation, condition, state, predicament, dilemma, difficulty.

Pneumonia
Pneumonia (nu-mon´ye) noun.
1) In medicine, an inflammation of the lungs; inflammation of the tissues of the lungs as distinguished from inflammation of the bronchial tubes and from inflammation of the serous covering of the lungs.

Pomp
Pomp (pòmp) noun.
1) Ostentation of magnificence, grandeur, or power; parade; splendor.
Synonyms: Grandeur, splendor, magnificence, ostentation, display, pageantry.

Pot
Pot (pòt) noun.
1) A cup; a mug.
2) The quantity contained in a pot; as, a *pot* of ale, usually about a quart.

Powerless
Powerless (pou´er-lîs) adjective.
1) Destitute of power, force, or energy; weak; impotent; not able to produce any effect.

Prayer
Prayer (prâr) noun.
1) The act or practice of praying to or supplicating the Divine Being; the offering to God of adoration, confession, supplication, and thanksgiving; communion with God in devotional exercises.
2) A solemn petition addressed to the Supreme Being; a supplication to God for blessings or mercies, together with a confession of sins, and thanksgiving for mercies or blessings received.
3) The words of a supplication; the form of words used in praying; especially, a formula of prayer used in divine worship, whether private or public.

Precepts
Plural of: Precept
(prê-sèpt´) noun.
1) In a general sense, any commandment or order intended as an authoritative rule of action; but applied particularly to commands respecting moral conduct; as, the Ten Commandments are so many *precepts* for the regulation of our moral conduct.
Synonyms: Doctrine, law, principle, instruction, injunction, maxim.

Precipitates
Plural of: Precipitate
(prî-sîp´î-tât´) verb.
1) To urge or press with eagerness or violence; to hasten; to bring to a crisis; as, to *precipitate* a flight.
2) To hurry blindly or rashly.

Preposterous
Preposterous
(prî-pòs´ter-es) adjective.
1) Contrary to nature, reason, or common sense; utterly absurd or ridiculous; totally opposed to the nature of things; foolish; perverse.
Synonyms: Absurd, foolish, irrational.

Procreation
Derived from: Procreate
(pro´krê-ât´) verb.
1) The act of begetting; generation and production of young.

Procured
Derived from: Procure
(pro-kyoor´) verb.
1) To obtain, as by effort, labor, or purchase; to get; to gain; to come into possession of; as, we *procure* favors by request; we *procure* money by borrowing; we *procure* titles to estates by purchase.
2) To cause to come on; to bring on; to attract; as, modesty *procures* love and respect.
3) To cause; to bring about; to effect; to contrive and effect.

Prodded
Derived from: Prod (pròd) verb, transitive.
1) To prick or punch with something sharp and pointed; to poke; to goad.

Prodigious
Prodigious (pre-dîj´es) adjective.
1) Very great; huge; enormous in size, quantity, extent, etc.; as, a mountain of *prodigious* size; a *prodigious* mass.
Synonyms: Enormous, monstrous, vast, huge, immense, amazing, extraordinary, marvelous, miraculous, astonishing.

Prodigy
Prodigy (pròd´e-jê) noun.
1) Any development out of the ordinary course of nature, and so extraordinary as to excite wonder or astonishment; a person or animal of extraordinary attainments.
Synonyms: Wonder, portent, marvel, monster, enormity, miracle.

Proffered
Derived from: Proffer
(pròf´er) verb, transitive.
1) To offer for accep-

tance; to make an offer of, as to *proffer* a gift; to *proffer* services; to *proffer* friendship.

Prophesied
Derived from: Prophesy
(pròf´î-sì´) verb.
1) To utter predictions; to make declaration of events to come.

Prosaic
Prosaic (pro-zâ´îk) adjective.
1) Dull; uninteresting; lacking animation or imagination; ordinary; commonplace; as, a *prosaic* person; a *prosaic* play.
Synonyms: Dull, tedious, commonplace, prolix, prosy, matter-of-fact.

Protégé
Protégé (pro´te-zhâ´) noun.
1) One under the care and protection of another.

Protestations
Plural of: Protestation
(pròt´î-stâ´shen) noun.
1) A solemn declaration of a fact, opinion, or resolution, especially of dissent; a protest.

Providence
Providence
(pròv´î-dens) noun.
1) In theology, the care and superintendence which God exercises over his creatures.

Provocation
Provocation
(pròv´e-kâ´shen) noun.
1) Incitement.
2) Anything that excites anger; the cause of resentment.

Psychiatric
Derived from: Psychiatry
(sî-kì´e-trê) noun.
1) The treatment of mental disorders.

Queer
Queer (kwîr) adjective.
1) Strange; odd; behaving, acting, or appearing in a manner other than the ordinary, normal, or usual manner; singular; droll; original; peculiar; as, a *queer* manner.
Synonyms: Odd, whimsical, quaint, strange, crotchety, singular, eccentric, droll, erratic, unique.

Queried
Derived from: Query
(kwîr´ê) verb, transitive.
1) To seek by questioning; to endeavor to ascertain by inquiry; as, to *query* a motive.

2) To express doubt concerning; to express a desire to examine into the truth or correctness of; to mark with a query.

Rabbi
Rabbi (ràb´ì) noun.
1) A title bestowed on Jewish teachers and doctors of the law, signifying master or lord.

Rancor
Rancor (ràng´ker) noun.
1) The deepest malignity or spite; deep-seated and implacable malice; inveterate enmity.
Synonyms: Enmity, ill will, harshness, spite, hatred, malevolence.

Recompense
Recompense
(rèk´em-pèns´) noun.
1) An equivalent returned for anything given, done, or suffered; compensation; reward; amends; as, a *recompense* for services, for damages, for loss, etc.
Synonyms: Compensation, satisfaction, remuneration, reward.

Reconciled
Derived from: Reconcile
(rèk´en-sìl´) verb.
1) To bring to a state of acquiescence, content, or quiet submission; generally used reflexively and followed by *to*; as, to *reconcile* oneself *to* a loss.

Reconciliation
Reconciliation
(rèk´en-sìl´ê-â´shen) noun.
1) The act of reconciling; the state of being reconciled; the renewal of friendship between parties at variance.
Synonyms:
Reconciliment, reunion, adjustment, appeasement, pacification, expiation, atonement.

Rectify
Rectify (rèk´te-fì´) verb, transitive.
1) To make right; to correct, as that which is wrong, erroneous, or false; to amend; as, to *rectify* errors or abuses; to *rectify* the will, the judgment, opinions; to *rectify* disorders.
Synonyms: Amend, correct, improve, refine, purify, adjust.

Remonstrances
Plural of: Remonstrance
(rî-mòn´strens) noun.
1) The act of remonstrating or expostulating; a strong representation of reasons or

facts against something complained of or opposed; expostulation; hence, a paper or document containing such representation or expostulation.

Rendezvous
Rendezvous (rän´dâ-voo´) verb.
1) In general, to come or bring together.
From The New Century Dictionary, D. Appleton-Century Co. 1944.

Reparation
Reparation (rèp´e-râ´shen) noun.
1) The act of making amends; indemnification for loss or damage; as, he ought to make some *reparation*; also, the thing done or given as indemnity; satisfaction.
Synonyms: Compensation, recompense, atonement, indemnity, satisfaction, remuneration, restitution, repair.

Reprieve
Reprieve (rî-prêv´) noun.
1) Respite; interval of ease or relief.

Reproached
Derived from: Reproach (rî-proch´) verb, transitive.
1) To upbraid; to suggest blame for anything; as, a man's conscience will *reproach* him for a criminal, mean, or unworthy action.
2) To treat with scorn or contempt.
Synonyms: Reprove, rebuke, upbraid, revile, condemn, blame, accuse.

Reproved
Derived from: Reprove (rî-proov´) verb, transitive.
1) To blame; to censure; to condemn; to disapprove.
2) To charge with a fault; to chide; to reprehend.
Synonyms: Rebuke, reprimand, reprehend.

Resentment
Resentment (rî-zènt´ment) noun.
1) Displeasure caused by a wrong done to oneself or friends; a deep sense of wrong; anger.
Synonyms: Anger, wrath, ire, indignation.

Resolutely
Derived from: Resolute (rèz´e-loot´) adjective.
1) With fixed purpose; firmly; steadily; with steady perseverance; boldly; firmly.

Revulsion
Revulsion (rî-vùl´shen) noun.
1) A sudden and violent change, particularly of feeling.
2) A drawing or holding back or away from; violent separation.

Rigorous
Rigorous (rîg´er-es) adjective.
1) Exact; strict; scrupulously accurate; as, a *rigorous* definition or demonstration.
2) Severe; exact; strict; without abatement or relaxation; as, a *rigorous* execution of law; an enforcement of *rigorous* discipline.
Synonyms: Inflexible, unyielding, austere, inclement, harsh, stern.

Ruinous
Ruinous (roo´e-nes) adjective.
1) Destructive; baneful; pernicious; bringing or tending to bring ruin; as, a *ruinous* practice.

Sane
Sane (sâne) adjective.
1) Mentally sound; not deranged; having the regular exercise of reason and other faculties of the mind.

Sanity
Sanity (sàn´î-tê) noun.
1) The quality or state of being sane; healthiness of body or mind; especially of mind; saneness.

Sally
Sally (sàl´ê) noun.
1) An act of levity or extravagance; wild gaiety; frolic which goes beyond ordinary rules; as, a *sally* of youth; a *sally* of levity.

Samaritan
Samaritan (se-màr´î-tn) noun.
1) *Good Samaritan*; a model of charity and benevolence, as shown in the parable given in Luke x. 30-37.

Sanitarium
Sanitarium (sàn´î-târ´ê-em) noun.
1) An institution for the care and treatment of invalids; a resort having natural aids for curing the sick.

Sash
Sash (sàsh) noun.
1) A frame for holding the glass of a window.

Scheme
Scheme (skêm) noun.
1) A combination of various things into one view, design, or purpose; a system; a plan.
Synonyms: Plan, project, contrivance, purpose, device, plot.

Scoff
Scoff (skòf) verb.
1) To act with insolent ridicule, mockery, or contumelious language; to manifest contempt or derision; usually followed by *at*.

Sentiment
Sentiment (sèn´te-ment) noun.
1) A particular feeling or disposition of mind as regards some person or thing; a thought prompted by passion of feeling.

Serenity
Serenity (se-rèn´î-tê) noun.
1) The quality or condition of being serene; clearness and calmness; quietness; peace.
2) Calmness of mind; evenness of temper; undisturbed state; coolness.

Slander
Slander (slàn´der) noun.
1) A false tale or report maliciously uttered, and tending to injure the reputation of another; in law, specifically, oral defamation published without justification; when written it is *libel*.

Slyly
Derived from: Sly (slì) adjective.
1) Artful in performing things secretly, and escaping observation or detection; usually implying some degree of meanness; artfully cunning; applied to persons; as a *sly* man or boy.

Sober
Sober (so´ber) adjective.
1) Temperate in the use of spirituous liquors; habitually temperate; as, a *sober* man.
2) Not intoxicated or overpowered by spirituous liquors; not drunken; as, he is *sober* at times.
3) Not mad or insane; not wild, visionary, or heated with passion; self-possessed.
4) Regular; calm; thoughtful; as, *sober* judgement; a man in his

sober senses.
Synonyms: Abstemious, abstinent, temperate, moderate, sedate, serious.

Sobriety
Sobriety (so-brì´î-tê) noun.
1) Habitual soberness or temperance in the use of spirituous liquors; as, a man of *sobriety*.
2) Freedom from intoxication.
3) Habitual freedom from enthusiasm, inordinate passion, or overheated imagination; coolness; the *sobriety* of age.
Synonyms: Soberness, temperance, abstemiousness, gravity, steadiness, sedateness.

Sordid
Sordid (sôr´dîd) adjective.
1) Filthy; foul; dirty; gross. [Obscure.]
2) Vile; base; mean; as, *sordid* mortals.

Spectres
Spectre
alternate spelling of:
Specter (spèk´ter) noun.
1) An apparition; the appearance of a person who is dead; a ghost.

Steerage
Steerage (stîr´îj) noun.
1) In passenger-ships, the quarters allotted to the passengers paying the lowest rate of fare.

Sublime
Sublime (se-blìm´) adjective.
1) Striking the mind with a sense of grandeur or power, physical or moral.

Subtle
Subtle (sùt´l) adjective.
1) Characterized by artful cunning; sly; crafty; insinuating; wily.

Succumbed
Derived from: Succumb (se-kùm´) verb, intransitive.
1) To sink or give way without resistance; to yield; to submit.

Suffices
Derived from: Suffice (se-fìs´) verb.
1) To be enough or sufficient; to be equal to the end proposed; to be adequate or satisfactory.

Sumptuous
Sumptuous (sùmp´choo-es) adjective.
1) Costly; expensive; splendid; magnificent.

Supplanted
Derived from: Supplant
(se-plànt´) verb,
transitive.
1) To remove or displace
by stratagem; to
displace and take the
place of.

Tallied
Derived from: Tally
(tàl´ê) verb.
1) To correspond; to
agree; as, the accounts
tally.

Tangent
Tangent (tàn´jent)
adjective & noun.
1) *Figuratively:* Merely
touching; slightly
connected; divergent or
digressive.
   *From The New Century
Dictionary, D. Appleton-
Century Co. 1944.*

Tangible
Tangible (tàn´je-bel)
adjective.
1) Perceptible by the
touch; corporeal; tactile.
2) Real; definite;
palpable apprehensible
by the mind; clear;
evident.

Tedious
Tedious (tê´dê-es)
adjective.
1) Wearisome; tiresome
from continuance.
Synonyms: Wearisome,
tiresome, fatiguing.

Temperament
Temperament
(tèm´pre-ment) noun.
1) That individual
peculiarity of physical
organization by which
the manner of acting,
feeling, and thinking of
each person is perma-
nently affected; also, the
mental disposition
dependent upon and due
to that physical
organization.

Temperance
Temperance
(tèm´per-ens) noun.
1) Moderation; particu-
larly, habitual modera-
tion in regard to the
indulgence of the natural
appetites and passions;
restrained or moderate
indulgence; as, temper-
ance in eating and
drinking; specifically,
total abstinence from
intoxicating liquors.

Temporizes
Derived from: Temporize
(tèm´pe-rìz´) verb,
intransitive.
1) To delay; to procras-
tinate.

Threadbare
Threadbare (thrèd´bâr´)
adjective.

1) Worn out; trite;
hackneyed; having no
novelty or interest.

Tidings
Tide (tid´ingz) plural
noun.
1) News; advice;
information; intelli-
gence; account of what
has taken place, and
was not before known.

Trifle
Trifle (trì´fel) noun.
1) A thing of very little
value or importance; a
trivial matter; a
triviality; hence,
nonsense; absurdity.

Triumphant
Triumphant (trì´um-fant)
adjective.
1) Of supreme magnifi-
cence and beauty;
glorious.

Trolley
Trolley (tròl´ê) noun.
1) On an electric
railway, a car propelled
by a motor receiving its
current from a wire.

Trudge
Trudge (trùj) verb,
intransitive.
1) To travel on foot; to
walk wearily; to jog or
drag along; to travel or
march with labor.

Unabated
Unabated (ùn´e-bâ´tîd)
adjective.
1) Not lessened,
decreased, destroyed or
mitigated.

Unsalable
Unsalable
(un´sâl-a-´bul) adjective.
1) Not capable of being
sold; not being in good
demand.

Utopia
Utopia (yoo-to´pê-e)
noun.
1) An imaginary island
described by Sir Thomas
More in a work of the
same title published in
1516, in which the
inhabitants lived in the
enjoyment of social and
political perfection.
2) Any place or state
ideally perfect, whether
real or imaginary.

Vagaries
Plural of: Vagary
(vâ´ge-rê) noun.
1) A wandering of the
thought; a freak; a whim;
a whimsical purpose; as,
foolish *vagaries*.

Veritable
Veritable (vèr´î-te-bel)
adjective.

1) True; agreeable to
fact; genuine; real;
authentic; actual; also,
truthful.

Vestiges
Plural of: Vestige
(vès´tîj) noun.
1) A track or footstep;
trace; hence, a mark,
impression or appear-
ance of something which
is no longer present or in
existence.
Synonyms: Trace, mark,
sign, token.

Vicarious
Vicarious (vì-kâr´ê-es)
adjective.
1) Deputed; delegated;
as, *vicarious* power or
authority.
2) Acting for another;
filling the place of
another; as, a *vicarious*
agent or officer.
3) Substituted in the
place of another; as, a
vicarious sacrifice.

Vicissitude
Vicissitude
(vî-sîs´î-tood´) noun.
1) A passing from one
state or condition to
another; irregular
change; revolution;
mutation; as, the
vicissitudes of fortune.

Virtuous
Virtuous (vûr´choo-es)
adjective.
1) Morally good; acting
in conformity to the
moral law; practicing the
moral duties and
abstaining from vice; as,
a *virtuous* man.

Whoopee
Whoopee
(hwup´ê, wup´ê, hwoo´pê)
interjection.
1) Uproarious festivity:
often in 'to make
whoopee.' [Slang, U.S.]
   *From The New Century
Dictionary, D. Appleton-
Century Co. 1944.*

Wrought
Wrought (rôt) verb,
intransitive.
1) Past tense and past
participle of *work*.

Zeal
Zeal (zêl) noun.
1) Passionate ardor for
any person or cause;
intense and eager
pursuit or endeavor.

Word Index

Not Indexed:

Frequency

Word	Freq.	Word	Freq.
a	1034	they	234
about	137	this	343
all	176	through	49
an	179	time	91
and	995	to	1497
any	61	too	44
are	355	up	78
as	294	us	232
at	193	was	322
be	500	way	83
been	138	we	1097
but	287	were	160
by	139	what	139
can	169	what's	2
could	112	when	147
did	57	where	48
do	154	which	158
does	39	who	175
doesn't	13	whose	11
each	43	will	342
for	387	with	313
from	130	would	174
get	52	wouldn't	7
go	70	you	538
got	28	your	206
had	312		
has	171		
have	473		
he (lower case)	891		
here	34		
he's	5		
him (lower case)	277		
his (lower case)	393		
how	97		
I	398		
i'd	3		
if	303		
i'll	1		
i'm	11		
in	587		
is	583		
it	469		
its	28		
it's	5		
i've	2		
know	60		
like	82		
man	116		
may	243		
men	81		
more	114		
much	86		
no	153		
not	394		
of	1239		
on	221		
one	140		
or	257		
other	91		
our	377		
out	103		
put	22		
so	174		
some	128		
such	96		
take	65		
than	82		
that	646		
that's	7		
the	1607		
their	116		
them	124		
then	72		
there	183		
these	134		

Dates

1929 3_3 4_1
1932 5_3
1934 8_2
1935 153_4 158_4
1939 163_2

A

Word Index

Word Index

moving 55_5 101_0

Mr. 21_1 65_2 67_3 136_3 136_4

Mrs. 65_2 67_3

multiplies 16_3

multitude 28_3

mumbling 83_1

murmur 48_2

mushy 53_1

music 10_1

musing 8_4

musket 1_2

must 10_1 14_1 20_3 21_1 29_3 33_1 43_3 44_3 62_2 66_3 69_3 73_4 74_0 74_1 75_0 78_2 79_1 80_1 81_0 82_2 83_1 83_2 85_1 85_2 86_1 89_2 90_4 93_2 95_3 99_0 99_1 99_2 100_1 100_4 101_0 111_2 113_1 114_3 115_1 115_2 117_3 118_2 120_1 127_0 127_1 127_2 130_1 135_1 141_4 143_1 144_2 146_3 152_1 153_2 154_4 156_3 159_2 164_1

muster 155_2

musty 11_5

my 1_1 1_4 2_1 2_2 3_0 3_1 3_2 3_3 4_2 4_3 5_1 5_2 5_4 5_5 6_6 6_0 6_1 7_0 7_1 7_3 7_4 8_0 8_1 8_2 8_3 9_5 10_1 10_4 11_3 11_6 12_1 12_4 12_5 12_6 13_2 13_3 13_4 13_5 14_3 14_6 15_1 16_1 16_3 36_1 36_2 40_2 40_3 41_0 41_1 41_2 42_2 42_3 43_2 63_2 65_2 65_3 76_2 136_3 136_6 138_2 138_3 141_1

myself 1_4 6_0 6_1 6_2 7_2 8_0 10_3 11_1 11_3 12_4 13_0 13_2 13_4 42_1 47_2 63_2 137_2

mystified 35_1 126_2

N

nadir 155_1

nag 106_2 111_2

nagged 91_2 135_2

nags 65_3

name 65_1 65_3 82_0

Napoleon 4_2

narrow 158_3

nation 61_2

nations 132_1

natural 31_2 53_4 118_3 139_3

naturally 58_1 74_0 99_1 109_1 146_3

nature 19_4 21_1 107_1 59_2 68_4 72_1 107_1 115_1 115_2

Nature 12_1

natured 10_1

natures 52_2

ne'er 1_2

near 5_5 8_3 51_1 57_3 107_0 161_1

nearer 106_3

nearest 31_3

nearing 155_1

nearly 2_1 15_1 19_1 104_3 108_1

nearness 75_2

neatly 45_2

necessarily 33_3 101_0 131_2

necessary 27_5 72_2 73_0 79_3 109_0 111_1 142_1 143_0 146_1 155_2 158_2

necessities 140_1

necessity 5_1 14_6 19_4 34_2 68_4 74_2

need 7_4 8_3 16_3 21_0 26_4 29_3 44_3 46_2 50_2 76_3 76_4 87_1 90_2 94_2 97_1 102_1 102_3 111_3 115_1 115_3 116_3 118_2 119_1 119_2 120_1 146_1 148_1 156_3 163_0

needed 12_6 45_0 47_1 47_2 63_1 68_4 98_0 116_3

needless 146_0

needlessly 79_2 82_0 112_0

needs 20_0 49_0 70_2 82_2 90_3 91_1 98_1 131_2 141_1

neglect 97_3 129_3

neglected 97_1 126_1 126_2

neglectful 119_1

negligible 11_2

neighbor 153_0

neither 10_3 43_3 69_2 85_0 135_3

nerve 126_1

nerves 6_1 22_0 39_2

nervous 32_2 35_2

nervousness 37_3 109_1

net 5_1

neurotic 122_3

neutrality 85_0

never 10_1 14_2 17_2 22_3 23_1 25_2 26_3 27_2 27_4 30_3 30_4 31_2 39_2 42_0 46_2 50_1 51_2 53_0 55_0 57_0 64_0 68_3 73_0 73_2 77_2 78_0 83_3 87_1 89_3 90_4 92_2 99_3 102_2 102_3 103_1 105_3 105_4 111_1 111_2 114_1 115_0 120_3 123_3 127_1 133_2 143_2 146_2 158_0 158_4 163_4

nevertheless 5_1 26_1 40_1 48_2 77_1 87_0

new 1_1 12_5 12_5 13_4 13_5 14_0 18_5 27_4 28_2 30_4 41_0 45_2 46_2 50_4 52_1 62_3 63_1 72_1 83_4 84_2 85_0 89_2 95_1 98_3 99_2 100_1 103_1 107_2 115_2 117_1 119_1 119_2 120_1 123_2 124_0 125_0 126_0 128_1 129_0 131_1 131_2 132_0 134_1 134_3 135_1 150_0 151_1 152_4 159_2 160_0 161_0

New 1_1 4_1 9_0 41_1 53_1 131_2

newcomer 100_3 133_2 159_3

newcomers 15_2 72_2 89_2 132_1

news 17_3 47_3 158_5

newspaper 137_0

newspapers 51_2

newsreels 52_2

next 3_1 6_0 6_1 8_3 21_2 41_1 61_1 84_2 87_1 88_3 90_4 104_2 109_1 111_2 112_3 142_3 146_3 160_1

nice 41_1 126_2

nicer 116_3

night 2_1 3_2 4_0 6_1 6_2 8_3 22_0 41_1 46_0 56_2 56_5 81_0 86_1 97_1 100_2 126_1 128_1 134_0 158_3 159_2 159_3

nightclubs 101_3

nightmare 73_2

nil 58_3

nine 78_1 138_2 158_0

nip 43_1

nobody 157_6

nominal 42_2

nonalcoholic 31_1 39_1 44_1

nonchalant 24_3

none 114_2 23_1 25_1 33_2 107_2 156_5

nonexistent 24_1

nonsense 98_1

nonspiritual 34_2

noon 128_1

nor 10_3 19_1 26_4 33_1 33_3 38_3 43_3 69_2 73_3 83_4 85_0 90_4 132_1 133_1 135_3 140_2 143_0 147_0

normal 21_1 22_3 31_0 35_2 38_0 66_2 92_1 113_2 131_1 141_0 150_0 151_1

normally 17_2 33_1 85_0

note 101_4 136_4

nothing 7_0 13_2 18_4 18_5 25_1 25_2 28_3 36_1 36_3 40_0 41_0 49_0 52_4 53_2 54_1 54_2 59_1 75_2 77_2 79_3 89_1 91_3 105_3 117_0 130_1 131_2 132_0 138_2 139_0 141_0 141_1 159_0

nothingness 54_2

noticed 120_3 134_0

notion 33_1 36_1 110_0

novel 12_2 144_0

November 8_3

now 6_1 7_2 8_0 9_5 14_4 16_3 17_2 28_5 37_3 41_2 43_0 47_2 55_5 58_2 59_0 63_2 68_2 71_0 75_2 76_1 76_2 83_1 94_1 96_2 102_2 110_2 116_1 118_3 119_1 123_2 124_2 129_2 133_1 135_3 137_2 141_3 142_2 153_3 154_3 156_2 156_4 157_0 157_6 158_5 159_2 161_0 162_1 163_1

nowadays 48_3 61_2 136_1

nowhere 10_3 32_2 49_0

number 31_2 64_3 79_0 109_0 109_2 110_2 112_3 113_2 140_3 153_4 161_1 162_0

numbers 16_0 33_3 144_3 159_2

numerous 48_2

nurse 95_2 156_3

nurses 156_4

nut 65_2

O

oasis 9_0

oath 31_2

oaths 105_2

obeyed 131_0

obituary 137_0

object 45_2 64_1 90_3 143_0 160_0

objectionable 76_1

obligation 94_1 147_1

obligations 129_1

obligatory 132_0

obliged 37_3 110_1 115_4 125_0 130_3 137_1

oblivion 6_1 19_2 151_2

obscure 24_1

obscured 55_2

observations 20_4 23_1

observe 125_2

observed 5_4 49_2 73_2

observing 111_4

obsession 23_2 30_1 151_1 155_2

obstacle 29_0

obstacles 8_0 72_1 123_1

obstinacy 48_0

obtained 2_1 80_1 87_2

obviously 11_4 18_5 35_0 45_1 99_2 164_2

occasion 35_3 61_1 101_4 102_0 102_1 105_3 109_0 124_2

occasional 87_0

occasionally 34_1 134_0 134_1 139_2

occasions 35_3 109_0

occupations 17_2 19_1

occupied 159_0

occur 24_2 42_0

occurred 39_2

occurrences 27_4

occurring 27_4

October 4_1

off 2_3 4_1 7_3 8_2 20_3 21_1 22_0 23_1 31_1 31_2 33_1 38_1 41_0 41_2 61_1 65_2 66_1 68_4 71_0 77_2 78_1 85_0 94_1 130_2 138_2 145_0 145_1 145_3 153_4 156_4

offended 67_0 94_1

offender 64_3

offense 78_3

offer 23_1 63_2 78_1 87_2 92_2 96_1 143_1 144_0

offered 13_2 43_2 57_1 97_3

office 4_1 65_2 78_1 145_3

officer 138_1

officers 1_1

often 5_1 7_2 10_3 16_0 21_1 23_2 24_3 33_3 48_0 62_2 66_0 70_0 74_0 75_2 81_0 81_1 86_3 96_1 98_1 102_3 107_0 109_1 110_2 113_3 125_2 126_1 128_2 130_3 131_0 133_1 133_2 133_3 134_3 137_3 141_1 147_2 148_1 149_1 158_3 162_2

oil 113_2

old 1_2 4_1 8_4 9_5 10_2 12_1 15_1 24_2 43_0 52_0 52_1 55_2 58_3 80_3 99_2 102_1 107_2 117_1 120_0 123_2 124_3 151_1 152_0 154_3 159_1 161_2

omega 49_1

ominous 1_3

omitted 75_3

omnipotence 133_0

once 3_0 3_3 7_3 17_1 21_1 22_3 22_4 27_4 28_5 32_0 36_1 63_3 64_0 68_1 68_3 84_2 86_1 92_0 94_2 95_1 96_1 97_1 105_0 107_2 109_1 109_2 113_1 113_2 117_1 118_3 120_1 124_1 127_0 129_0 133_0 146_1 147_1 151_1 153_1 156_4 157_6

ones 30_4 105_0 106_5 118_1 123_2 140_3 153_2

only 9_0 12_4 13_4 28_3 29_3 31_2 33_2 37_0 40_2 41_2 42_2 43_1 44_1 47_3 55_1 55_3 55_4 59_3 61_0 61_1 62_0 63_3 64_3 66_0 66_1 70_1 73_0 74_2 78_3 82_2 87_1 89_3 94_0 94_1 95_2 96_3 98_2 101_1 103_3 105_2 107_2 108_1 108_5 109_0 112_0 113_2 117_1 124_0 124_1 124_2 126_3 129_0 132_0 134_1 137_3 138_2 140_1 141_3 155_2 158_3 161_3 163_1 163_2 164_2

open 6_2 46_2 48_0 77_0 78_0

opened 9_1 80_3 116_1 136_5 154_2

openly 9_0

operative 21_0

opinion 20_1 26_3 43_2 73_3 117_3 149_1

opinions 19_4 68_4 139_2

opportunity 5_3 19_2 74_2 77_0 90_1 96_1 133_0 133_3 138_1 138_2 147_2 164_0

opposite 65_1 122_1 129_2

option 3_0

optional 63_3

ordained 74_0

ordeal 125_0

order 14_0 60_1 77_0 79_2 164_2

ordered 36_1 36_2 41_1

ordinary 98_0 101_3 125_1 148_1

organization 139_4 147_2 148_3 149_1

organized 49_2

organizers 137_1

original 44_3

originated 10_3 11_4 49_0

others 13_4 14_5 14_6 15_0 20_0 25_1 45_3 52_3 52_4 59_2 66_0 66_3 67_2 70_0 70_1 70_2 74_1 79_2 80_1 82_3 84_0 84_2 86_1 87_1 89_1 89_2 90_3 96_1 97_1 100_0 102_2 104_2 120_0 122_1 123_1 124_2 125_1 125_2 127_3 132_0 132_1 132_2 135_1 144_3 153_0 153_3 158_5 159_2 161_2 163_3 164_0 164_2

otherwise 113_2

ought 21_2 68_0 79_3 81_1 83_1 83_2 91_3 103_0 112_0 120_0 127_1 130_1 131_2 136_1 148_0 158_1

ounce 36_2 128_3

ours 20_4 28_4 39_1 51_1 67_2 162_0

ourselves 15_1 24_2 24_3 25_2 29_3 37_2 37_3 38_3 45_1 46_0 46_1 47_1 47_2 48_0 49_0 49_1 49_2 50_1 51_2 52_2 54_1 55_1 55_2 59_2 62_0 62_2 63_1 63_2 64_0 64_3 66_0 66_1 67_0 67_3 68_1 70_2 71_0 72_1 72_2 74_2 76_3 77_0 79_1 83_3 84_0 86_1 87_1 87_3 88_0 100_1 106_3 106_4 109_1 110_2 121_1

outburst 105_2

outcome 66_0 80_4

outer 73_1

outgrow 68_3 125_2

outlaw 62_0

outlined 42_2 88_2

outlines 53_3

outlook 21_2 84_0

outset 128_1

outside 1_2 113_2 131_1

outsider 82_1

outsiders 131_1 132_2 160_1

outward 48_3

over 2_2 5_2 7_3 8_0 9_0

Word Index

Subject Index

Order Form:

	Mini	First Edition			Study Edition			
						Hardcover		e-AA
Qty	Edition	Softcover	Hardcover	Index	Softcover	Burgundy Black	Gilding	
1	$2.35	$3.50	$15	$1	$5.75	$15.75		$20
10	$23	$33	$136	$8	$53	$140		
20	$42	$63	$245	$14	$100	$250		
50	$84	$150	$525	$30	$240	$550		
100	$145	$285	$920	$50	$450	$990	$5	$5
500	$450	$1375			$2200			
1000	$800							

Call for pricing on larger quantities

Optional gold gilding adds $5 per book (*in all quantities*). Indicate number of each color with gilding:
Burgundy   Black
Gilding on hardcover only

Indicate quantity in boxes

Anonymous Press
PO Box 1212
Malo WA 99150
Fax (509)779-4339

(800) 800-4398
anonpress.org
secure ordering

Name _____

Address _____

Shipping to USA only. Minimum order $10. Phone or e-mail _____

Choose a shipment method: *Choose a payment method:*

☐ Book Rate (2-4 weeks) **Free!**   ☐ Check, payable to: The Anonymous Press

☐ UPS Ground (3-8days) add 15% ($4.50 minimum) ☐ Visa/MC/Discover ▶ Expiration __/__

☐ Priority Mail (3-7days) add 30% ($6.00 minimum) |_|_|_|_|_|_|_|_|_|_|_|_|_|_|_|_|

Also available from The Anonymous Press:

The Anonymous Press Mini Edition of
Alcoholics Anonymous
- The first 164 pages in pocket size.
- The Anonymous Press Worldwide AA Telephone Directory.
- The least expensive Big Book available.

The Anonymous Press Study Edition of
Alcoholics Anonymous
- Same as this book with the addition of a hardbound leather cover, heavier
  paper and place keeping ribbons.
- Available in burgundy or black leather.
- Gold gilding available.
- 576 full-size pages on fine heavy weight paper.
- Special lay-flat binding for easy study.
- Two ribbons to keep your place.
- The finest edition available anywhere.

First Edition Reprint - Hardcover
Reprint of the first printing of the first edition of *Alcoholics Anonymous*. Only
the name of the publisher and the copyright page have been changed. Includes
a reproduction of the original dustjacket.

First Edition Reprint - Softcover
The only inexpensive reprint of the first edition of *Alcoholics Anonymous*.
Includes an appendix detailing the 79+ differences (in the 1st 164 pages)
between this original text and the modern text. Cover is designed to look like
the original dustjacket.

The Anonymous Press Index
A lite version of the indexes found in this book. Word, subject and dictionary
references are combined and indexed by page only (does not include paragraph
references as found here). Designed to be simple, inexpensive and to fit inside
a standard Big Book.

Electronic Editions
See our website at anonpress.org for electronic editions of *Alcoholics Anonymous*. Both the text and extensive reference material available for almost all
types of computers. Downloads for Windows, Macintosh, Linux, Palm, Pocket
PC, EPOC and more.

Order form on reverse.